First Corinthians
Verse-by-Verse

First Corinthians
Verse-by-Verse

Steve Lewis

Bible Study Companion Series:

First Corinthians Verse-by-Verse

Steve Lewis

Cover image by Harrison Fitts on Unsplash.com

Preface to the Bible Study Companion Series

B ible study is such an important activity because knowing and doing the will of God depends on an accurate understanding of His written Word. The obedient Christian life is based on the assumption that believers know the truth about what they are to obey. God has not been silent, and He has not left us without detailed instructions for living. We have God's complete revelation for us today in the Bible.

The Bible is a collection of writings that God directed and inspired men to write. It was recorded in the common languages that people used to communicate their ideas to each other. We must remember this as we study the Bible. The principles for Bible study follow the same rules we use every day to understand the meaning of any written communication.

As we study the Bible our goal should be to understand the message that the original text was intended to communicate. This means we are not allowed to make the Bible say what we want it to say. We must let the Bible speak for itself. The hard work of Bible study involves carefully examining the written text of Scripture in order to understand exactly what that text was intended to communicate.

Since the biblical authors used normal language, we must use the regular principles of grammar and sentence structure to understand the Bible's message. Scripture was not written in some secret code that requires a hidden formula to decipher. Instead it was written in the common languages of the people who lived during those times (Hebrew, Aramaic, and Greek). For that reason, this Bible Study Companion contains many references to the words, grammar, and sentence structure of the original languages. This is necessary because most of us are not familiar with the ways that ancient writers communicated, and these insights will help us to clearly understand their message.

We must also remember that the biblical writings were recorded at specific times in human history. They were written to specific readers in specific historical, geographical, and cultural situations. In order to understand the purpose and message of the Bible, we must also study the history, geography, and culture of the original writers and readers. The meaning of each biblical expression is influenced and even determined by the context in which it was written. As one scholar has said,

> Just as we may be puzzled by the way people do things in other countries, so we may be puzzled by what we read in the Bible. Therefore it is important to know what the people in the Bible thought, believed, said, did, and made. To the extent we do this we are able to comprehend it better and communicate it more accurately. If we fail to give attention to these matters of culture, then we may be guilty of reading into the Bible our own ideas. [Zuck, 79]

This Bible Study Companion will provide help as you go through the text of the Bible just as it was written, in a verse-by-verse manner. Since the original text was written and read in successive order, this companion guide will include definitions, concepts, and ideas that will help you to understand the meaning of the phrases and sentences in the order in which they unfold. It is our prayer that God will guide and direct your study of His Word so that you will experience the rich blessings that come from studying the Bible.

Reference Abbreviations

Barclay	William Barclay, *The Letters to the Corinthians* (Westminster, 1975).
Barnes	Albert Barnes, *Notes on the Bible* (in e-Sword).
Barrett	Charles K. Barrett, *First Epistle to the Corinthians* (Hendrickson, 1968).
BBC	Willian MacDonald, *Believer's Bible Commentary: 1 Corinthians* (Nelson, 1990).
BKC	John Walvoord and Roy Zuck, *Bible Knowledge Commentary* (Victor, 1983).
Boyer	James L. Boyer, *For a World Like Ours* (BMH Books, 1971).
Chafer	Lewis Sperry Chafer, *He That Is Spiritual* (Zondervan, 1967).
e-Sword	eSword Bible Study Software, https://eSword.net
Expositors	W.R. Nicoll (ed), *Expositor's Bible Commentary* (in e-Sword).
Gill	John Gill, *Exposition of the Bible* (in e-Sword).
Hodge	Charles Hodge, *First Epistle to the Corinthians* (Eerdmans, 1950).
Ironside	H.A. Ironside, *First Epistle to the Corinthians* (Loizeaux, 1938).
ISBE	*International Standard Bible Encyclopedia* (in e-Sword).
JFB	Jamieson, Faucett, Brown, *Commentary on the Bible* (in e-Sword).
Josephus	Flavius Josephus, *Antiquities of the Jews* (in e-Sword).
Kent	Homer Kent, *Jerusalem to Rome* (BMH Books, 1972).
MacArthur	John MacArthur, *First Corinthians* (Moody, 1984).
Massey	Craig Massey, *The War Within You* (Moody, 1977).
McDougall	Donald McDougall, "Cessationism in 1 Cor 13:8-12" *Master's Seminary Journal*, Vol 14:2 (Fall 2003).
Morgan	G. Campbell Morgan, *Corinthian Letters of Paul* (Revell, 1946).
Pentecost	J. Dwight Pentecost, *Designed to be Like Him* (Discovery House, 1994).
RWP	A.T. Robertson, *Word Pictures in the New Testament* (in e-Sword).
Ryrie	Charles C. Ryrie, *Basic Theology* (Moody, 1999).
SRL	Stephen Lewis, "The New Covenant: Enacted or Ratified?" *Chafer Seminary Journal* Vol 8:4 (Oct 2002).
Tenney	Merrill C. Tenney, *New Testament Times* (Eerdmans, 1965).
Thayer	J.H. Thayer, *Thayer's Greek Definitions* (in e-Sword).
Thomas	Robert L. Thomas, *Understanding Spiritual Gifts* (Kregel, 1999).
Unger	Merrill F. Unger, *Baptism and Gifts of the Holy Spirit* (Moody, 1974).
Vine	W.E. Vine, *Dictionary of New Testament Words* (in e-Sword).
VWS	M.R. Vincent, *Word Studies in the New Testament* (in e-Sword).
Wiersbe	Warren Wiersbe, *Bible Exposition Commentary: Vol 1* (Victor, 1989).
ZNBC	Kenneth Barker and John Kohlenberger, *Zondervan NIV Bible Commentary Vol 2: New Testament* (Zondervan, 1994).
Zodhiates	Spiros Zodhiates, *May I Divorce and Remarry?* (AMG, 1994).
Zuck	Roy B. Zuck, *Basic Bible Interpretation* (Victor, 1991).

Contents

Introduction to First Corinthians

The apostle Paul's first letter to the church at Corinth is one of the treasures of the New Testament. Because of this letter, we have more detailed information about the life of this church than about any other church during that time. As we will see in a moment, Paul himself was the one who started the church at Corinth. In order to understand his letter to these Christians, we will begin by looking at the background and culture of Corinth. Then we will review the travels of the apostle Paul which brought him to the point of starting this church and finally writing this detailed letter to the believers there.

The Background of the City of Corinth

Corinth is located on the mountainous peninsula of Greece that juts down into the Mediterranean Sea. The lower portion of this peninsula is almost an island, but it is connected to the mainland by a narrow isthmus which is only four miles wide. The ancient city of Corinth is located near this isthmus.

Corinth was served by two seaports: Lechaeum to the northwest and Cenchrea to the southeast. To avoid the two hundred mile voyage around the dangerous southern tip of Greece, traders often put their ships on rollers and moved them across the isthmus from one port to the other. This difficult four mile portage saved time and avoided the risks of sailing around the southern end of the country. Sailing in those days was dangerous, and the voyage around the southern coast of Greece (Cape Malea) was especially treacherous. The Greek writer Strabo said, "When you round Malea, forget your home!" Another Greek saying was, "Let him who sails round Malea first make his will!" The Greek writer Pindar described Corinth as "The bridge of the seas," so it became an excellent location for commerce and the inhabitants accumulated great wealth. Corinth was also an important military location for

Location of the city of Corinth

the defense of Greece.

Commercial products from Italy and the nations to the west were unloaded at Lechaeum, and merchandise from the islands of the Aegean Sea, Asia Minor, the Phoenicians and the other eastern nations was brought from Cenchrea on the east. "Objects of luxury soon found their way to the markets which were visited by every nation in the civilized world: Arabian balsam, Phoenician dates, Libyan ivory, Babylonian carpets, Cilician goat hair, Lycaonian wool, Phrygian slaves." [Barclay]

The city of Corinth became the commercial crossroads between Asia and Europe. It was said that Corinth "covered the sea with its ships," and it formed a strong navy to protect its commercial interests. The Corinthians built ships with a new design, and this naval force was respected by the surrounding nations. Corinth gained population, wealth, and influence through the influx of foreigners. It became a city that was distinguished by its prosperity, its commercial importance, and its strong naval force. The city of Corinth gained a reputation among all the ancient cities for its riches, its luxury, and its morally decadent lifestyle. Since luxury, pleasure, and self-indulgent immorality grew unchecked, Corinth became known as the most degenerate city of its times

Another factor which contributed to its character of depravity and corruption was its religion. Corinth was dedicated to two Greek deities: Poseidon, the god of the sea (Roman name, Neptune), and Aphrodite, the goddess of sexual love and the protector of sailors (Roman name, Venus). Another of their favorite gods was Apollo, who was the god of music and prophecy. All of these so-called gods required that appropriate sacrifices be offered to them.

> Ancient cities were devoted usually to some particular god or goddess, and were supposed to be under their peculiar protection. Corinth was devoted or dedicated thus to the goddess of love or shameless passion. The temple of Venus was erected on the north side or slope of the Acrocorinthus, a mountain about half a mile in height on the south of the city. It was enjoined by law that 1,000 beautiful females should officiate as courtesans, or public prostitutes, before the altar of the goddess of love. [Barnes]

Some of these women were world famous for their beauty. The income of these female slaves was also a major source of revenue for the city. The degrading practice of prostitution, along with the looseness of morals that often characterized a seaport with a transient population, gave Corinth a reputation for wickedness far beyond the other great cities of the day. In fact, the Greeks invented the verb "Corinthian-ize," to live like a Corinthian in an immoral lifestyle. Corinth was a city that was obsessed with self-indulgent pleasure.

One scholar provided almost a walking tour of the city:

> Entering along the Lechaeum road from the north, one passes first between the fish market and the baths. The fish market originally was surmounted by a large tank in which live fish could be kept until they were purchased. The baths and public latrines were just across the road, where they could utilize the overflow of water from

View of ancient Corinth. Main road through the marketplace. Temple of Apollo column tops visible in the background (right). High acropolis in the distance (center) where the fort and Temple of Aphrodite were located. [Image by Vassilis Terzo on Unsplash.com]

the open pool fed by the spring of Peirene farther up the southern slope. North of the fish market was the Basilica, which was the Roman center for business and legal offices. The sanctuary of Apollo next to the baths probably occupied the site of the meat market in Paul's day, where surplus offerings of the temple were placed on sale. At the public square the road ended in a formal gate, the Propylea, east of which was the spring of Peirene...On the west side of the Propylea was the open square, flanked on north and south by rows of shops with arched roofs, opening into a long colonnade. In almost every shop on the south side was a circular opening in the floor. These were wells that gave access to a flowing underground stream that fed the pools of Peirene, into which pots of perishable foods and wine could be lowered for cooling. [Tenney, 272-273]

When the Romans started to conquer Greece, the city of Corinth led the opposition and it was attacked and destroyed by the Roman general Mummius in 146 BC. Enormous riches were found in the city, at least equal to those of Athens, and this treasure was carried off to Rome. For almost 100 years the city lay in ruins until 44 BC when Julius Caesar sent a colony of retired soldiers to rebuild it and make it the capital of the Roman province of Achaia. Almost immediately it regained its former importance as the richest and most powerful city of Greece. The relative newness of the city also gave it a modern atmosphere.

The impact of all of these factors on the morals of the city was devastating. Corinth became the most morally permissive, self-indulgent, and degenerate city of Greece. When Paul arrived in Corinth it was as immoral as at any previous time in its history. It was due to the grace of God and the power of the gospel that a church was established in that city of luxury and decadence, and it shows that the gospel is able to overcome all kinds of wickedness and to appeal to all classes of people. If a church could be established in the most worldly city of ancient times, then the gospel could have the same effect in any city in the world at any time in history.

Paul in Corinth

Why did Paul travel to Corinth? Several factors may have influenced him. Corinth was the capital of the Roman province of Achaia, and it was an important city for both government and commerce. There was also a large Jewish population in Corinth, and it was always Paul's desire to minister to the Jews first (Rom 1:16). The culture and lifestyle in Corinth promoted all kinds of wickedness, so Paul was very much aware that these people desperately needed salvation through the Lord Jesus Christ.

When Paul arrived in Corinth he stayed with Aquila and Priscilla who were already Christians (Acts 18:1-3). They had recently left Rome because of the decree of Claudius issued in AD 49. The Roman writer Suetonius said, "Because the Jews at Rome caused continuous disturbances at the instigation of Crestus, he expelled them from the city." Suetonius may have been referring to riots in the Jewish community over the preaching of Christ, but he misspelled the name and perhaps assumed that Christ was actually the rebel leader in Rome. This mistake is understandable because Suetonius was not born until AD 69 and he wrote at least 40 years after the event itself.

At first Paul made tents during the week and spoke in the synagogue every Sabbath. When Silas and Timothy came from Macedonia, they brought some funds that freed Paul to devote more time to ministry (2 Cor 11:8-9; Phil 4:15). It was at this same time that Paul wrote the two letters to the church in Thessalonica.

Paul's synagogue ministry was fruitful, and a ruler named Crispus became a Christian. He is one of the few believers that Paul personally baptized (1 Cor 1:14-16). However, Jewish opposition arose and Paul moved next door to the house of Titus Justus (Acts 18:4-8). At this point in his ministry Paul must have needed a dose of encouragement, because the Lord appeared to Paul and encouraged him to continue his work in spite of the opposition. As a result of this encouragement, Paul stayed in Corinth for eighteen months.

The church in Corinth was made up of some Jews, but mostly Gentiles (1 Cor 12:2). Most of the converts were probably from the lower classes of slaves, laborers, and craftsman (1 Cor 1:26). Some of the believers had been living in blatant immorality (1 Cor 6:9-11). At one point in his ministry, the unbelieving Jews of Corinth seized Paul and took him to the Roman court (Acts 18:12-17). Gallio, the proconsul of

Achaia, was the brother of the philosopher Seneca who was Nero's tutor. Paul was accused of activity that was contrary to the law, but Gallio immediately saw through the Jews' charges and threw the entire case out of court. He ruled that this was a difference of religious opinion which would not fall under the jurisdiction of the Roman courts.

If Gallio had taken the case and ruled against Paul, this precedent would have been recognized by the other provincial governors and would have made the spread of Christianity much more difficult. But by the grace of God this did not happen. In effect, Gallio ruled that Paul was free to continue to minister as he pleased. As a side note, neither Gallio nor Paul knew it at the time but they would only have about ten more years to live, and they would both die in the same year by the command of the future emperor Nero.

After the case was dismissed, there was a disturbance in the crowd and a man named Sosthenes, the new leader of the Jewish synagogue, was beaten. There are two possible interpretations of this event from Acts 18:16-17.

1. When the case was dismissed the Jews may not have left immediately, so Gallio may have ordered them to be driven out and the Jewish leader Sosthenes might have been given a beating by officials responsible for courtroom order.

2. Sosthenes may have hinted that he was a Christian sympathizer, and so after the case was dismissed the Jews themselves may have given him a beating in response to Gallio's order that they handle this matter themselves.

Paul continued teaching in Corinth for some time after this event. He probably wanted to take full advantage of Gallio's policy, which was almost an official sanction for his ministry (Acts 18:18). At some point during this time Paul apparently took a Nazarite vow (Num 6:1-21). It must be remembered that this was a period of transition during which Jewish Christians often continued to observe certain rites of dedication as a matter of choice. After the period of the vow, Paul's hair was cut off and the requirement was that it be burned with a sacrifice in Jerusalem.

Paul left for Jerusalem and Aquila and Priscilla went with him. They traveled to the eastern port of Cenchrea, which was the home of Phoebe and the location of another church (see Rom 16:1), and from there they sailed to Ephesus. They were invited to stay in Ephesus (Acts 18:19-21), but Paul was eager to go on to Jerusalem. Aquila and Priscilla did remain in Ephesus, though, and began helping the new Christians there. Paul continued by ship to Caesarea, then went up to Jerusalem and finally journeyed north to Antioch (Acts 18:22). This marked the end of his second missionary journey.

Apollos in Ephesus and Corinth

Some time after Paul had visited Ephesus, Apollos arrived there and ministered in the synagogue. He was a Jew from Alexandria Egypt who was a trained orator and very knowledgeable in the Old Testament scriptures. Apparently Apollos had been tutored by a disciple of John the Baptist and had learned some of the facts of Jesus' life, but he did not understand the finished work of Christ, the coming of the Holy Spirit at Pentecost, or the significance of Christian baptism. He had received the baptism of repentance (John's baptism), and was well prepared for the Messiah. He was probably in the same category as other Old Testament saints who hoped for salvation in the Messiah and had not rejected Him as had the majority of the Jews. The situation of Apollos is probably similar to the case of the twelve men Paul met later in Ephesus (Acts 19:1-7).

Aquila and Priscilla were still attending the synagogue in Ephesus, and it is clear that during this transitional period there was not always a distinct break between the synagogue and the Christian gatherings. They heard Apollos speak in the synagogue and took him aside to instruct him further. Apollos responded well to their teaching, and when he wanted to minister in Achaia the Christians in Ephesus wrote him a letter of recommendation (Acts 18:27). Apollos was trained in the Alexandrian school and probably had a sophisticated style that would appeal to the philosophy-loving Greeks. The people of Corinth would have had the typical Greek attraction to intellectualism, just like those in Athens about whom Paul said, "Now all the Athenians and the strangers visiting there used to spend their time in nothing other than telling or hearing something new." (Acts 17:21)

Paul's Third Missionary Journey into the Province of Asia

After staying in Antioch for a time, Paul traveled to Ephesus through the "upper country," which meant he took the more direct high road instead of the typical trade route that followed the Lycus and Meander River valleys. Paul began his teaching ministry in Ephesus at the synagogue where he spoke for three months before opposition arose. Paul then moved his ministry headquarters to the lecture hall of Tyranus (Acts 19:8-12). During the next two years the Word of God was proclaimed throughout the entire province of Asia, of which Ephesus was the capital. The churches in Colosse, Hierapolis, Laodicea, and the others mentioned in Revelation chapters two and three were probably established during this time period. Paul also wrote several letters to Corinth and he made a brief visit there.

The timing of Paul's Corinthian correspondence:

– While in Ephesus, Paul wrote his "previous letter" to Corinth (see 1 Cor 5:9).
– Afterward news came to Paul in Ephesus of continuing problems, so he wrote First Corinthians and sent Timothy and Erastus to deliver the letter (see Acts 19:2; 1 Cor 4:17; 16:7-11).
– Things continued to grow worse, so Paul made a brief "painful visit" to Corinth (see 2 Cor 2:1; 12:14; 13:1-2).
– His visit did not solve the problems in Corinth, so Paul wrote a "severe letter" (see 2 Cor 2:4; 7:8) and sent Titus to deliver it (see 2 Cor 8:6; 12:18).
– Paul was worried about the response to his "severe letter" and could not wait for Titus to return with news, so he set out to meet Titus (see 2 Cor 2:12-13; 7:5). Somewhere in Macedonia Paul met Titus and learned that all was well (see 2 Cor 7:6-7, 13).

Probably at Philippi Paul wrote Second Corinthians, his letter of reconciliation with the church in Corinth, and he sent Titus to deliver it (see 2 Cor 8:6, 16, 23).

– Paul made one last visit to Corinth after he made his final tour of Macedonia, then he traveled to Jerusalem with the collection for the needy saints there (see Acts 19:21; 1 Cor 16:1-5).

The Occasion for Writing First Corinthians

It is clear that this epistle was written as a reply to a letter that had been addressed to Paul by the church at Corinth: "Now concerning the things about which you wrote" (1 Cor 7:1). That letter had been delivered to Paul by Stephanas, Fortunatus, and Achaicus who had come to consult with him about the problems in the church at Corinth (1 Cor 16:17-18). Paul had also heard other news of specific problems in the church which required his attention and correction. Those issues were reported by some members of the family of Chloe (1 Cor 1:11).

The topics that Paul would deal with included:

– Factions and a divisive spirit within the church.
– Pride in human wisdom and incorrect concepts of the gospel.
– Fleshly behavior and carnality among the Corinthian believers.
– Wrong ideas about the work of ministers.
– Sexual immorality within the church.
– Lawsuits among believers in the church.
– Christian liberty and the life of the body of Christ.
– Advice regarding marriage.
– Christian liberty and meat sacrificed to idols.
– Impropriety in public worship services.
– Improper use of spiritual gifts.
– Denial of the resurrection and its importance in the gospel.
– Collecting funds for needy saints.

Ancient Corinth was a prosperous city, and sometimes prosperity can be a spiritually dangerous thing by distracting Christians from complete devotion to the Lord. As it did in Corinth, however, the grace of God and the power of the gospel message can overcome any obstacle in the lives of those who believe. We should never underestimate the supernatural power of God that can do amazing things in our lives as well as in the lives of those around us.

Just as with the apostle Paul in Corinth, God knows when we most need encouragement and He will provide exactly what we need to keep going and to keep growing in our journey of faith. Each Christian has his own unique style and special gifts from God. Paul and Apollos ministered in very different ways, and Priscilla and Aquila were just an ordinary couple whom God used to minister to others informally in their own home. Each of us today is called and gifted by God with unique abilities and perspectives. We should accept each other and strive to work together to use our gifts for the glory of God.

Beginning with God's Faithfulness

(1 Corinthians 1:1-9)

In the introduction we saw that the apostle Paul was writing in response to news and questions he had received from the church in Corinth. Letter writing was a common practice in New Testament times, and Paul followed the normal format for letters in his day which is slightly different from the format for written letters today.

First, the Signature (1:1)

1 Cor 1:1 Paul, called as an apostle of Jesus Christ by the will of God, and Sosthenes our brother,

In New Testament times the signature, the name of the author, came first. Paul gives his name, and then follows this with a brief description of himself.

Called as an apostle = Literally this says, "a called apostle." Paul was establishing his authority for writing this letter to the church he had started in Corinth.

By the will of God = His apostleship was not of his own choosing, but he was an apostle because God set him apart for this office. Apostleship was an important office that was required during the early years of the church. It involved the work of laying the foundation for the New Testament church (see 1 Cor 3:10; Eph 2:20).

In most of Paul's letters his typical practice was to mention the name of someone who would be familiar to the recipients. In this case Paul associated himself with Sosthenes in the heading of this letter to Corinth, because Sosthenes was probably one of the leaders of their congregation (see Acts 18:17). This does not mean that Sosthenes was the coauthor of the letter, but that he was someone respected by the readers and was with Paul at the time he wrote the letter. This would have given his approval to the sending of a letter like this to the church at Corinth. Paul is an apostle, while Sosthenes is simply a brother.

Next, the Address (1:2)

1 Cor 1:2 To the church of God which is at Corinth, to those who have been sanctified in Christ Jesus, saints by calling, with all who in every place call on the name of our Lord Jesus Christ, their Lord and ours.

In New Testament times the second part of a letter listed the names of those to whom the letter was written. Paul identifies those he is addressing in three ways:

He addressed the organized church in Corinth as an entire congregation: "to God's assembly which meets in Corinth." This would certainly call attention to the official body or assembly of the members of the church. The Corinthian church is God's assembly. It does not belong to any man or leader. This will be significant as the first chapter of this letter continues.

This letter is also addressed to the individual people who make up the church body: "to those who have been sanctified in Christ Jesus." Notice the change in number, from the one church to the many individual members.

Sanctified (hagiazo) = The perfect passive tense shows the present condition of believers which was the result of the past action of being sanctified by God. The word means to be set apart for the service of God or declared as belonging to God. All those who have placed their faith in the Lord Jesus Christ are sanctified at the moment they believe, and God's act of sanctification will have results that continue throughout the Christian's life.

Saints by calling = Literally this says, "a called saint." The word saint comes from the same root word as "sanctified" and means "separated ones." We are saints by divine calling and by God's work, not by our own effort to maintain a state of holiness of life. The status of being a saint was the present condition of the Corinthian believers, even though they had severe problems which prompted Paul to write this letter. One does not need to be perfect in order to be a saint. Sanctification is a work of God on our behalf that sets us apart as belonging to Him. These people were not an elite group or the recipients of some special blessing which made them sinless. The call of God on a believer's life separates the believer as having a special relationship with God. This is what true sainthood means.

The letter is also addressed to "all who in every place call on the name of our Lord Jesus Christ, their Lord and ours." Here Paul broadens the address to include believers in other places besides Corinth. Paul seems to be aware that he was not simply writing a letter that would be read by a single congregation, but one which would have lasting significance for believers at other times and places. Those whom God calls are then able to call upon God. To "call upon the name of our Lord Jesus Christ" is used in other places as a euphemism for believing in the Lord and expressing saving faith (see Acts 9:14, 21; Rom 10:13). It can probably be broadened to include prayer and worship that is directed to the Lord, since these activities typically characterize Christian believers.

Next, the Salutation (1:3)

1 Cor 1:3 Grace to you and peace from God our Father and the Lord Jesus Christ.

This was the third part of the heading of a letter in New Testament times. Today we might write, "Dear Sir." In Paul's day the salutation was usually expressed using a form of the word "to rejoice" (**chairein**), which was intended to mean "May you be glad" or "I wish you well" or simply "Greetings." Among the Jews the customary greeting included the Hebrew word "peace" (**shalom**). Paul combined these two salutations in most of his letters. He used the Greek word **charis** (a form of the word **chairein**) because of its Christian connotation of the grace of God, and then he added the Greek word for the Hebrew idea of peace, putting it in the form of a wish or prayer: "May grace and peace be yours." The source and provider of these blessings is "God our Father and the Lord Jesus Christ." In all of his letters Paul always gave the Father and the Son equal status regarding their deity.

Then, the Ascription of Appreciation (1:4-9)

The final part in the heading of letters during New Testament times was a declaration of appreciation or thanksgiving, and it was often addressed to a pagan deity. Here the writer of the letter would tell something about the recipient for which he is grateful. It is especially interesting to see what Paul finds to be thankful for in the lives of the Corinthian believers.

His thankfulness for God's blessings to them in the past (1:4-6)

1 Cor 1:4 I thank my God always concerning you for the grace of God which was given you in Christ Jesus,

The verb is in the past tense (Greek aorist). Paul is referring to their initial salvation experience when he first shared the gospel with them and they received the saving grace of God. This was a past blessing.

1 Cor 1:5 that in everything you were enriched in Him, in all speech and all knowledge,

Paul is thankful for their past spiritual enrichment, especially in the area of spiritual gifts: "You were enriched." The gifts named here are the gifts of speaking and knowledge, which were the outward public gifts that seemed to characterize the Corinthian church. They were very proud of them, but the misuse of these gifts was causing much of the trouble in the church. Normally knowledge should come before speech, but here Paul reversed the order. Speech is given the emphasis, and this fact may point to the Corinthians' speaking before thinking.

1 Cor 1:6 even as the testimony concerning Christ was confirmed in you,

Paul is thankful for the past confirmation they had experienced regarding the truth of the gospel and their salvation. When Paul first preached the gospel to them, its truth was confirmed by the powerful activity of the Holy Spirit (see 1 Cor 2:4).

His thankfulness for their hope of future blessings (1:7-9)

1 Cor 1:7 so that you are not lacking in any gift, awaiting eagerly the revelation of our Lord Jesus Christ,

They had hope as they eagerly waited for the future return of the Lord Jesus Christ. "Eagerly awaiting" (**apekdechomai**) means intensified expectation, and it indicates the attitude they should have about this future event. Here the "revelation" (**apokalupsis**) means the unveiling or manifestation of Christ, which points to the future time when He will return from heaven to receive His own at the resurrection of church-age saints. In another place Paul described this event as the "blessed hope" of the church (see Tit 2:13).

1 Cor 1:8 who will also confirm you to the end, blameless in the day of our Lord Jesus Christ.

Paul is thankful that God will confirm them to the end. "To the end" **(telos)** may suggest the degree (to the fullest extent possible) or the time (until the time of the revelation of Christ). Either one would make sense, because the result will be that they will stand blameless (degree) before the Lord at His coming (time). "Blameless" **(anegkletos)** means that they cannot be accused of any wrong doing in a court of law. It does not mean that they are sinless, but that there is no charge that can be brought against them successfully. This is the condition of all people who have placed their faith in Christ and received salvation through His work on their behalf. There are no charges against them, and this will continue to be true as they look forward to the "day of our Lord Jesus Christ," the day when the saints will stand before Him.

1 Cor 1:9 God is faithful, through whom you were called into fellowship with His Son, Jesus Christ our Lord.

Paul is thankful that God is faithful, and it is the faithfulness of God that will continue to keep their calling sure to the end. Paul's confidence does not rest on the faithfulness of the Corinthians in their present shameful condition. His confidence rests on the faithfulness of God who called them in the past and will make their calling sure until the end. God will do what He has promised to do!

> God is true and constant, and will adhere to his promises. He will not deceive. He will not promise and then fail to perform; he will not commence anything which he will not perfect and finish. The object of Paul in introducing the idea of the faithfulness of God here is to show the reason for believing that the Christians at Corinth would be kept into everlasting life. The evidence that they will persevere depends on the fidelity of God; and the argument of the apostle is that as they had been called by Him into the fellowship of his Son, his faithfulness of character would render it certain that they would be kept to eternal life. [Barnes]

Notice that Paul gave thanks for their past and for their future, but he did not give thanks for the present condition of the Corinthians. "The fact that he can find cause to give thanks to God only for their past and their future brings a serious implication of failure in their present spiritual condition." [Boyer]

The heading of Paul's letter to the Corinthian church has now come to an end. Starting in verse ten Paul will begin the content of his letter, sharing the message that he wants to communicate to the believers in Corinth. The Lordship of Christ is mentioned several times in these opening verses, and this will become important as the apostle Paul deals with the problems within the Corinthian church. The problems they have can all be solved by submitting to the Lordship of Christ.

God is the central focus of Paul's introduction to this letter. God called Paul as an apostle. God established the church in Corinth and it belongs to God alone. God is the source of the grace and peace that believers have. God is the One we must thank and praise for all that we have. God is the One who enriches us with all kinds of gifts, and He is the One who will confirm and establish us until the Lord's return. God is the One who is completely faithful, and it is God's faithfulness alone that we can rely on for everything past, present, and future.

Just as those believers in Corinth were called and sanctified, we too should understand what our sanctification means. Just as they were enriched by God, God has also given us so many riches and privileges. Just as they were eagerly awaiting the return of the Lord, we too should have the eager expectation and hope of His coming. In view of all that God has done for us, how should we respond? How should we live our lives as a result?

Divisions Within the Church

(1 Corinthians 1:10-17)

Disagreements and quarrels seem to be a frequent part of life. Even little children bicker and fight when they cannot get their own way. From birth to death this kind of self-centeredness is the natural inclination of every person. And even believers are continually tempted to fall back into lives of self-centeredness. Christians are still influenced by the pull of the flesh even though they have been justified before God, and quarrels and conflict are inevitable when sin is allowed to have its way in our lives.

Paul's Exhortation (1:10)

1 Cor 1:10 Now I exhort you, brethren, by the name of our Lord Jesus Christ, that you all agree and that there be no divisions among you, but that you be made complete in the same mind and in the same judgment.

Now = This begins the body of Paul's letter. Paul addresses the first issue that God has put on his mind.

I exhort you, brothers = To exhort (**parakaleo**) means to come alongside to help. This is the language of affectionate exhortation rather than of stern rebuke, and Paul addressed them as his brothers and members of the same family. Paul appeals to them on the basis of his relationship with them as brothers and on the basis of the Lordship of Jesus Christ. One Bible scholar shared some reasons why Paul appealed to Christ's name and authority here.

> The whole family in heaven and earth should be named after him (Eph 3:15), and should not be named after inferior and subordinate teachers. The reference to the name of Christ here stands opposed to the various human names under which they were so ready to enlist themselves. Christ should be regarded as the Supreme Head and Leader of all his church. It was improper, therefore, that the church should be divided into portions and its different parts enlisted under different banners. The prime and leading thing which Christ had commanded his church was union and mutual love (John 13:34; 15:17), and for this he had most earnestly prayed in his memorable prayer (John 17:21-23). It was well for Paul thus to appeal to the name of Christ, the sole Head and Lord of his church, and thus to rebuke the divisions and strifes which had arisen at Corinth. [Barnes]

Paul's exhortation included three things:

1. **That you all speak the same thing** = As opposed to speaking different things (see 1 Cor 1:12), Paul wanted them to "keep on speaking" the same thing (present active subjunctive).
2. **That there be no divisions among you** = Again Paul used the present active subjunctive to say that divisions should not continue to exist. Divisions

(schismata) is from the Greek word **schizo**, which means to split, tear, or rip apart (Matt 9:16; Mark 2:21).

3. **That you be perfectly joined together (katartizo)** = This word means to restore, mend, or repair that which is torn or out of order (Matt 4:21; Mark 1:19). The word was used for mending broken bones or for the realignment of a dislocated joint. Paul also wanted them to be of **"the same mind."** This was not just the intellect itself but what is in the mind, the thoughts, counsels, and plans. They should be of a mind to treat each other with kindness and live in harmony. He also desired that they use **"the same judgment."** This word means knowledge, opinion, attitude, and sometimes the purpose of the mind or the will. They should have a brotherly attitude and be sympathetic toward each other.

"Union of feeling is possible even where people differ much in their views of things. They may love each other much, even where they do not see eye-to-eye. They may give each other credit for honesty and sincerity, and may be willing to suppose that others may be right and are honest even where their own views differ." [Barnes]

What Is the Problem? (1:11)

1 Cor 1:11 For I have been informed concerning you, my brethren, by Chloe's people, that there are quarrels among you.

I have been informed = It had been made clear to Paul; it was clearly communicated.

By Chloe's people = We do not know whether these were the servants, the children, or other members of Chloe's household. It is uncertain whether Chloe lived in Corinth or Ephesus. It is clear, however, that the Corinthian believers knew exactly who she was. The problem Paul was dealing with was not something that was spread by gossip. These people were willing to be identified and Paul gives specific details of the situation. "He mentions this family by name to show that he had not taken up an idle tale and received reports from anybody, nor from a single person only, but from a family of repute among them." [Gill]

There are quarrels = This word means contention, conflict, or dissent. It is listed in the works of the flesh as "strife" (Gal 5:20).

The Details of the Problem (1:12)

1 Cor 1:12 Now I mean this, that each one of you is saying, "I am of Paul," and "I of Apollos," and "I of Cephas," and "I of Christ."

Now I mean this = Paul is saying, "This is exactly what I mean by quarrels."

Each one of you = This tells us who was at fault. All of the individuals within the church were involved in taking sides and participating in different divisions or factions. Every person was somehow involved in the problem.

I am so-and-so's follower = This tells us what were they claiming. They were saying "I belong to this group!" These were not the forerunners of modern denominations. They were individual preferences and opinions about particular church teachers, and their preferential attitudes were causing bickering and rivalries among the members. This was a reflection of the typical Greek mindset, its love of philosophical speculation, and its enthusiasm for following the intellectual trends and fads of the day. Who were the leaders?

Paul had founded the Corinthian church, and all of the original members would have been his converts. Paul had always emphasized Christian liberty and the end of the Mosaic Law, so this group may have been attempting to take Christian liberty to an extreme, using their freedom to do whatever they pleased, and trying to justify it by saying they were following Paul.

Apollos came after Paul and had the polished, cultured style of the Alexandrian school which would have been very attractive to the philosophy-loving Greeks. The Alexandrians were the ones who intellectualized Christianity, so this group may have consisted of intellectual believers who wanted to view Christianity as a new school of philosophy.

Cephas was the Aramaic name for Peter. He was considered to be the apostle of the circumcision (Gal 2:7), and he was probably being claimed by the Jewish element in the congregation. This group may have been legalists who were emphasizing the Mosaic Law and opposing Christian liberty.

Christ was probably being claimed by those in the congregation who assumed an attitude of superiority and rejected all human leadership. The way it is listed here with the other names of leaders indicates that it was being claimed in a divisive spirit. "Their real fault was not in saying they belonged to Christ, but in acting as if Christ belonged to them." [Barclay] They may have had the right name, but they did not have the right attitude.

Paul's Argument Against Their Divisive Spirit (1:13-17)

1 Cor 1:13 Has Christ been divided? Paul was not crucified for you, was he? Or were you baptized in the name of Paul?

Paul does not ask any of these questions because he is expecting an answer. He is simply forcing the Corinthians (and us) to think about their implications for the divisions within the church. Paul shudders to think that anyone would say, "I am Paul's man and I belong to Paul."

Has Christ been divided? The Greek word for divided (**merizo**) means to cut something into pieces and to distribute the parts to various people. This is almost like saying, "Was Christ dismembered or cut into pieces and given to different factions?" Paul's graphic imagery emphasized his amazement at the divisive spirit in Corinth. Here Paul appeals to the person of Christ. "His human body was not to be divided; a bone of him was not to be broken (John 19:36); the seamless garment he wore was not to be rent asunder (John 19:23); nor is his body, the church, to be torn in pieces by schisms and divisions." [Gill]

Was Paul crucified for you? Paul showed his tact by using himself as the illustration, rather than Apollos or Cephas. Here he refers to redemption by appealing to the cross of Christ. In the Greek, the phrasing of the question demands a strong negative answer: "Surely it was not Paul that was crucified for you, was it?" In the previous question the majesty of Christ made it impossible for Him to be divided. In this question the insignificance of Paul makes it impossible for him to be crucified for them and to be the source of redemption. "If there is anything that will recall Christians of different names and of contending sects from the heat of strife, it is the recollection of the fact that they have been purchased by the same blood and that the same Saviour died to redeem them all." [Barnes]

Were you baptized into the name of Paul? It was through the ordinance of Christian baptism that they declared their personal identification with the death, burial, and resurrection of Christ on their behalf. In comparing this question with the last, one commentator has written: "The cross claims us for Christ as being redeemed by Him; baptism as being completely dedicated to Him." [JFB] Here Paul appeals to their identification with Christ, and in this question he makes it clear how silly it is that he could be put on par with Christ. He knows what Jesus said in Matt 28:19, and it is completely ridiculous that Paul could be regarded as equal with Christ. "He numbers himself first as having no claims to be regarded as a religious leader among them or the founder of a sect. Even he, the founder of the church and their spiritual father, had never desired or intended that they should call themselves by his name." [Barnes]

1 Cor 1:14-15 I thank God that I baptized none of you except Crispus and Gaius, so that no one would say you were baptized in my name.

The rest of the verses in this passage deal with Paul's actual practice of baptizing those who believed. He gives thanks for God's providential protection from being accused of baptizing converts into his own sect. "To him it was a subject of grateful reflection that he had not done this. He had not given any occasion for the suspicion that he intended to set himself up as a leader of a sect or party." [Barnes] Paul's point is that the human agent in baptism is really unimportant. What is important is that through the act of baptism the believer expresses his complete identification with Christ and his complete dedication to the Lord.

Paul did not personally baptize very many believers. He mentioned Crispus and Gaius here, who were probably Paul's first converts in Corinth. As he looked back on the situation Paul recognized that the Lord kept him from a practice that might have led to future misunderstandings. Very few people could say they were baptized by Paul, and no one could say they were baptized into the name of Paul.

1 Cor 1:16 Now I did baptize also the household of Stephanas; beyond that, I do not know whether I baptized any other.

As he was composing this letter, Paul also remembered that there were a few more people in Corinth that he had baptized. Stephanas himself was probably there when Paul was dictating this letter (see 1 Cor 16:17), and he may even have been the one to remind Paul that he had baptized him.

If Paul almost forgot that he had baptized Stephanas then he realized he might not have remembered others too, so he included the possibility that he might have baptized others also. This incident does not argue against the inspiration of Scripture. Inspiration did not interfere with the personal style and characteristics of the writers of Scripture. Inspiration did not somehow make the apostle Paul omniscient. Inspiration guaranteed that what was written was exactly what the Lord wanted written. Here the Holy Spirit inspired Paul to record his own forgetfulness in order to create the impression which He wanted, that the human agent in baptism is not significant. What is important in baptism is not the one who does the baptizing, but the One into whom the believer is baptized.

1 Cor 1:17 For Christ did not send me to baptize, but to preach the gospel, not in cleverness of speech, so that the cross of Christ would not be made void.

Christ did not send me to baptize = Literally this says, "to be a baptizer." Here Paul reminds us of his function in the New Testament church. He was given the office of apostleship which involved preaching the gospel and establishing churches. He sometimes baptized the first few converts until the church was organized, and then the function of baptizing was given to the officers of the local church.

Cleverness of speech = Literally this says, "wisdom of words" (**sophia**), and it means philosophical reasoning that is presented with theatrical language and sophisticated logic. This kind of wisdom would have been highly valued by the Greeks. "Preaching was Paul's calling, but it was not as a pretentious philosopher or a professional man of rhetoric that Paul appeared before the Corinthians (1 Cor 2:1-5). Some who followed Apollos may have been guilty of a desire for external show, though Apollos was not a mere performer and juggler with words. But the Alexandrian method did have a tendency toward lavish rhetoric." [RWP]

Paul's concern was that the simple truth of Christ's work on the cross, which purchased the salvation of mankind, might be emptied of its power "by men thinking more of the human reasoning and eloquence in which the Gospel was set forth than of the Gospel itself." [JFB] Another man wrote, "The focus of the apostolic preaching was on one simple fact: Christ crucified. To preach it as a philosophic system would be to empty it of its saving power, a truth which finds abundant and lamentable illustration in the history of the church." [VWS]

Here Paul hinted at the main cause for the divisions in the Corinthian church. These divisions had been caused by the influence of philosophy and the ambition for honor and the exhibition of philosophical eloquence among the Corinthian believers.

> To have adorned the gospel with the charms of Grecian rhetoric would have obscured its wisdom and efficacy, just as the gilding of a diamond would destroy its brilliance. The design of Paul here cannot be to condemn true eloquence and just reasoning, but to rebuke the vain parade and the glittering ornaments and dazzling rhetoric which were objects of so much esteem in Greece. [Barnes]

The Corinthian believers were causing quarrels within the church by taking sides with different Christian leaders. This was not just something that was common to that time, because this has continued to happen in our own day. We, too, need to be on our guard against being so devoted to specific people that we cause conflict within our local churches. Even when we do not see eye-to-eye with fellow believers, we must give each other credit for honesty and sincerity, and we should be willing to continue to love each other despite differences of opinion.

Believers must focus on the important truths of the faith. Unity on doctrinal matters, coupled with a humble willingness to love others, will minimize divisions within the church. There were no doctrinal differences between Paul, Apollos, and Peter even though there were differences in their gifts, callings, and emphases. We must clearly evaluate whether our own disagreements are about the fundamental truths of the faith, or whether they concern matters of style. When we hear ourselves saying, "I am a follower of so-and-so on this particular issue," we should immediately check our motives and our attitudes. Even claiming to belong to Christ Himself can be done with a wrong attitude.

The Gospel Appears Foolish to the Philosopher

(1 Corinthians 1:18-2:5)

In the last chapter we talked about Paul's transition into the cause for the divisions within the Corinthian church. In 1 Cor 1:17 Paul hinted that the problem of divisions in the Corinthian church was due to the influence of philosophy. The word "philosophy" is made up of two Greek words: **philos** (love) and **sophia** (wisdom). A philosopher is one who loves wisdom in the form of sophisticated intellectual reasoning.

> The transition verse which introduces this section uses the expression, 'with wisdom of words.' To the Greek mind it would suggest their love of intellectualism and their schools of philosophy. Evidently, these divisions in the church were following the pattern of the Greek philosophers, with each following the leader he preferred and accepting his system. [Boyer]

Paul will now explain that there were two main causes of their factions. First they had a wrong conception of the nature of the gospel (1 Cor 1:18-3:4). Second, they had a wrong conception of the role of ministers (1 Cor 3:5-4:21).

In this section the apostle Paul explains that the gospel seems like foolishness to those who are caught up in intellectualism, philosophy, and the preeminence of human reasoning. Paul begins discussing how the gospel might appear to be foolish, and later he will discuss how it really is wisdom. Here he addresses three issues:

1. The apparent foolishness of its content (1 Cor 1:18-25)
2. The apparent foolishness of its recipients (1 Cor 1:26-31)
3. The apparent foolishness of its preachers (1 Cor 2:1-5)

The Foolishness of Its Content (1:18-25)

Paul begins by discussing the apparent foolishness of the gospel message itself. Notice that the subjects of the sentences are in the third person ("They/Them").

1 Cor 1:18 For the word of the cross is foolishness to those who are perishing, but to us who are being saved it is the power of God.

For = This transition word tells us Paul will give some additional explanation for saying that the wisdom of words might empty the cross of Christ of its power.

The word of the cross = Literally this could be translated "the word, the one concerning the cross." This clearly connects what Paul is saying here with what he had said in 1 Cor 1:17. "Not in wisdom of words, so that the cross of Christ would not be made void." Paul wants to answer the question, "How could the wisdom of words empty the cross of its power?"

The "word of the cross" refers to the simple message that Christ died on the cross as our substitute to pay the penalty for our sins. Paul says that this message concerning the cross is considered to be foolishness by a specific group of people, those who are perishing. "Perishing" means bringing something to ruin, but it does not mean total annihilation. The present tense and middle voice tell us that the action is ongoing. They are on the road to ruin and are in the process of destroying themselves.

The terms foolish or foolishness are used ten times in the first four chapters of First Corinthians. They are from the Greek words **moros/moria** and mean absurd, stupid, and by implication irreligious or ungodly. Our English terms moron and moronic come from this root word.

But = By contrast with "those who are perishing," those who are being saved view the simple gospel message as containing the power of God for the salvation of those who believe.

Being saved = This present passive participle contrasts with the middle voice previously used for the word "perishing." Our salvation has three tenses. We were saved (Rom 8:24, past); We are being saved (present); We will be saved (Rom 5:9, future). It is reassuring that God takes care of our past, present, and future!

Power of God = The Greek word for power (**dunamis**) means inherent strength or ability. The gospel is the channel through which God exerts his power in the salvation of sinners. The power of God is what saves us from the power of sin. The best aspect of the gospel is not its wisdom (that it makes sense to us), but its power (that it is what God works through). In the next three verses Paul will describe God's attitude toward human wisdom.

1 Cor 1:19 For it is written. "I WILL DESTROY THE WISDOM OF THE WISE, AND THE CLEVERNESS OF THE CLEVER I WILL SET ASIDE."

First Paul quoted Isaiah 29:14 which was Isaiah's prophecy against the arrogance of God's people when they faced the Assyrian invasion by Sennacherib. Paul applies this Old Testament example of the failure of worldly wisdom to the Corinthian philosophers' opinion of the gospel in his day. As one commentator said,

> The meaning of the passage as used by Isaiah is that such was the iniquity and stupidity of Jerusalem that God would so execute his judgments as to confound their wise men and overwhelm those who boasted of their understanding. But it expresses a general principle of divine administration, that the coming forth of God is often such as to confound human prudence in a manner which human wisdom would not have devised. This sentiment is applicable to the gospel and expresses just the idea which the apostle wished to convey, that the wisdom of the wise should be confounded by the plan of God. [Barnes]

1 Cor 1:20 Where is the wise man? Where is the scribe? Where is the debater of this age? Has not God made foolish the wisdom of the world?

Here Paul used language similar to Isaiah 33:18, again alluding to the defeat of the Assyrian forces by the miraculous intervention of God when the Jews' human wisdom had failed.

A man familiar with the Bible will naturally often make use of Scriptural expressions in conveying his ideas. In Isaiah, the passage refers to the deliverance of the people from the threatened invasion of Sennacherib. The 18th verse represents the people as meditating on the threatened terror of the invasion, and then in the language of exultation and thanksgiving at their deliverance saying, 'Where is the wise man that laid the plan of destroying the nation? Where is the Inspector General employed in arranging the forces? Where is the weigher or paymaster of the forces? Where is the man that counted the towers of Jerusalem, and calculated on their speedy overthrow? They are all baffled and defeated; and their schemes have all come to nothing.' So the apostle uses the same language in regard to the boasted wisdom of the world in reference to salvation. It is all baffled and is all shown to be of no value. [Barnes]

There are three Greek words used in this passage. Probably wise man (**sophos**) refers to the Greek philosopher, scribe (**grammateus**) to the Jewish leader, and debaters (**sunzetetes**, questioners together) applies to both the Greek and Jewish disputers.

Did not God make foolish = In the original language, this is a strong negative form. It means that God actively negated the wisdom of the world. Paul might have patterned this phrase after the wording of Isaiah 44:25, which says that God was "making fools out of diviners, causing wise men to draw back, and turning their knowledge into foolishness."

1 Cor 1:21 For since in the wisdom of God the world through its wisdom did not come to know God, God was well-pleased through the foolishness of the message preached to save those who believe.

For = This introductory word tells us that Paul is about to give further explanation for what he has just said in his allusions to verses from the Book of Isaiah. **Since** = Literally this could be translated, "seeing that." It is plain for all to see.

In the wisdom of God = It was God's plan that the world would not come to know Him by means of its own human wisdom. The **world** refers to the people of the world, and especially to the worldly philosophers. One commentator said this was the "solemn dirge of doom on both Greek philosophy and Jewish theology that failed to know God." [RWP]

God was pleased = God thought it best that this was how people would be saved. Here Paul may be alluding to Jesus' words: "You have hidden these things from the wise and prudent, and have revealed them unto babes." (Luke 10:21)

Through the foolishness of the proclamation = This does not refer to the act of preaching, but to the content or ideas that are being preached. Paul is not saying that public speaking is foolish, but that the message of the cross is regarded as foolish and absurd by the people of this world.

This is the heart of God's plan of redemption, the proclamation of salvation for all those who trust Jesus Christ on the basis of his death for sin on the Cross. The mystery religions all offered salvation by initiation and ritual as the Pharisees did by ceremonialism. Christianity reaches the heart directly by trust in Christ as the Saviour. It is God's wisdom. [RWP]

1 Cor 1:22-23 For indeed Jews ask for signs and Greeks search for wisdom; but we preach Christ crucified, to Jews a stumbling block and to Gentiles foolishness,

For indeed = Literally this says, "and seeing that" which continues the thought from verse twenty-one. Again, these things are plain for all to see.

Jews ask for signs = It was the common practice of the Jews to demand supernatural signs from anyone claiming to speak for God. At the time Paul was writing this letter to Corinth there were several false messiahs who promised miraculous signs.

In AD 45 a man called Theudas had persuaded thousands of people to abandon their homes and follow him out to the Jordan by promising that, at his word of command, the Jordan would divide and he would lead them dry-shod across. In AD 54 a man from Egypt arrived in Jerusalem claiming to be the Prophet. He persuaded thirty thousand people to follow him out to the Mount of Olives by promising that at his word of command the walls of Jerusalem would fall down. That was the kind of thing that the Jews were looking for. [Barclay]

As another scholar explained, "They expected a Messiah that would come with the exhibition of some stupendous signs and wonders from heaven; they looked for the displays of amazing power in his coming, and they anticipated that he would deliver them from their enemies by mere power; and they, therefore, were greatly offended by the simple doctrine of a crucified Messiah." [Barnes]

Greeks search for wisdom = The people of the Greek culture were constantly searching for systems of philosophy based on sophisticated human reasoning. "It is almost impossible to exaggerate the almost fantastic mastery that the silver-tongued rhetorician held in Greece. Plutarch says, 'They made their voices sweet with musical cadences and modulations of tone and echoed resonances.' The Greeks were intoxicated with fine words, and to them the Christian preacher with his blunt message seemed a crude and uncultured figure to be laughed at and ridiculed rather than to be listened to and respected." [Barclay] The Greek philosophers also emphasized the absolute transcendence of God. The philosopher Celsus wrote that if God descends to the level of men it involves change for him, and specifically a change from good to bad, from beautiful to ugly, from happiness to unhappiness, from what is best to what is worst. A God who suffers was something inconceivable to the Greeks. Plutarch declared that it was an insult to God to involve him in human affairs. The very idea of the incarnation, of God becoming a man, was revolting to the Greek mind.

We preach Christ crucified = Preaching is not the same as giving a sign or providing reasoned arguments. The gospel consists of proclaiming the historical facts concerning a crucified Messiah.

Stumbling block = This is the word **skandalon** which means a trap or snare; something that causes one to fall; or an offense. The gospel was a snare that tripped the Jews who wanted a conquering Messiah rather than a condemned and crucified one. They could point to their own Law which said, "Cursed is anyone who is hanged on a tree" (Deut 21:23). The crucifixion of Christ served as proof to the Jews that Jesus was not the Messiah. To the Jews a crucified Messiah is an offense, and it represents the Messiah's defeat rather than His victory. A crucified Messiah was a sign of weakness rather than of power.

Foolishness = To the Greeks who wanted wisdom and rational philosophy, the cross did not make sense. It was like trying to convince a group of intellectuals that an executed criminal is really the savior of the world.

1 Cor 1:24 but to those who are the called, both Jews and Greeks, Christ the power of God and the wisdom of God.

But = Here Paul provides a stark contrast from the unsaved Jews and Greeks who are perishing.

To those who are called = This identifies a specific group of people, those that God has called to salvation (see 1 Cor 1:2, 9). God's calling crosses racial and cultural boundaries, and it includes those who were formerly Jews and Greeks.

Power and Wisdom = The Jews saw Christ crucified as a sign of weakness, and the Greeks saw it as stupidity. But the ones that God calls see the power and wisdom in God's plan of a crucified Messiah. "They see the plan as wise. They see it to be suited to procure pardon and sanctification and eternal life." [Barnes]

1 Cor 1:25 Because the foolishness of God is wiser than men, and the weakness of God is stronger than men.

Foolishness of God = Literally this could be translated, "the foolish act of God." Paul is not saying that God could ever commit a foolish act. This presents the Greek perspective about a preacher who declares that a crucified criminal is the savior of the world. "This is especially true of the plan of salvation, a plan apparently foolish to the mass of people, yet accomplishing more for the renewing of people and for their purity and happiness than all the schemes of human contrivance." [Barnes]

Wiser than men = This verse uses a Greek comparison that is very forceful. It sets aside all the wisdom of men as if it were nothing compared to the wisdom of God.

Weakness of God = Literally this says, "the weak act of God." Again, Paul is not saying that there is any weakness in God's actions. It presents the Jewish perspective concerning the crucifixion of the Savior of the world.

Stronger than men = This Greek comparison is also very strong. It sets aside all the strength of men as if it were nothing compared to that of God.

The Foolishness of Its Recipients (1:26-31)

In this section Paul explains that the gospel also could be viewed as foolishness because of the types of people who receive it. Notice that the main subject of the sentences switch to the second person ("you/your").

1 Cor 1:26 For consider your calling, brethren, that there were not many wise according to the flesh, not many mighty, not many noble;

For = This transition word tells us that Paul will begin giving additional evidence for his argument. He appeals directly to the Corinthians and uses their own actual experience as an illustration to make his point.

> The design of the apostle here is to show that the gospel did not depend for its success on human wisdom. His argument is that in fact those who were blessed by it had not been of the elevated ranks of life mainly, but that God had shown his power by choosing those who were ignorant, and vicious, and abandoned, and by reforming and purifying their lives. [Barnes]

Not many wise = There were not many believers from the group who were ranked as philosophers.

According to the flesh (sarx) = This word typically denotes man in his fallen human nature. "According to the standards of the flesh and to be used not only with **sophoi** (wise, philosophers), but also **dunatoi** (men of dignity and power), **eugeneis** (noble, high birth), the three claims to aristocracy (culture, power, birth)." [RWP]

Not many mighty = There were not many believers from the group who exercised power within the city. The word may refer to those who hold power of any kind, whether derived from office, class, or wealth.

Not many noble = Literally this could be translated, "well born." There were not many believers who came from noble families. There were a few people of high rank and wealth at Corinth who became Christians. For example, Crispus and Sosthenes were rulers of the synagogue there (Acts 18:8, 17); Gaius was a wealthy believer who was Paul's host (Rom 16:23); and Erastus was the administrator of public works for the city of Corinth (Rom 16:23). But these men were the exception rather than the rule. There were not many philosophers, rulers, or aristocrats within the church. Celsus was an anti-Christian writer of the second century who belittled believers when he said, "Let no cultured person draw near, none wise, none sensible; for all that kind of thing we count evil; but if any man is ignorant, if any is wanting in sense and culture, if any is a fool let him come boldly." He said that Christians were "like a swarm of bats, or ants creeping out of their nests, or frogs holding a symposium round a swamp, or worms in convention in a corner of mud. We see them in their houses, wool dressers, cobblers and fullers, the most uneducated and vulgar persons." This was the attitude of the cultured Greeks to those who became believers.

1 Cor 1:27-28 but God has chosen the foolish things of the world to shame the wise, and God has chosen the weak things of the world to shame the things which are strong, and the base things of the world and the despised God has chosen, the things that are not, so that He may nullify the things that are,

But = This word introduces a direct contrast with the wise, mighty, and noble. God delights in using things that appear foolish and weak in order to put human wisdom to shame.

God chose = The Greek word for "chose" (**eklegomai**) means to personally select, or to pick something out so it can belong to you. It is used three times to emphasize the sovereign action of God Himself.

To shame = The word for shame (**kataischuno**) literally means "to shame down." This means to make people ashamed or to humble them.

The contrast in these verses is very clear: the foolish vs. the wise, the weak vs. the strong; that which is considered to be nothing or worthless or as having no existence vs. that which is considered to be something or valuable or as having worthwhile existence. When a Greek philosopher would speak of lower-class people he would refer to them as "those who are not."

To nullify = This word means to render something useless; to prove that human wisdom is useless and powerless. "By bestowing his favors on the humble and the poor, by choosing his people from the ranks which they despised and bestowing on them the exalted privilege of being called the sons of God, he had poured dishonor on the rich and the great and overwhelmed them and their schemes of wisdom with shame." [Barnes]

1 Cor 1:29 so that no man may boast before God.

So that = This phrase introduces God's intention or purpose in doing this.

Not could boast = The Greek grammar brings out clearly that not a single boast can be made. The aorist tense is used to indicate specific or definite cases of boasting. The middle voice is used to show that they were boasting in or for themselves.

All/any flesh = This points to anything made of flesh and blood. God's action eliminated all boasting about human effort and ability.

1 Cor 1:30 But by His doing you are in Christ Jesus, who became to us wisdom from God, and righteousness and sanctification, and redemption,

But by His doing = Literally this could be translated "out of Him." It clearly communicates that salvation is not through human wisdom or strength or status (1 Cor 1:28).

Became to us wisdom = True wisdom from God was contained in His plan of salvation through the substitutionary death of Christ on the cross.

> Philosophers had attempted to become wise by their own investigations and inquiries. But Christians had become wise by the work of Christ; that is, it had been by his instructions that they became acquainted with the true character of God, with his law, with their own condition, and with the great truth that there was a glorious immortality beyond the grave. None of these truths had been obtained by the investigations of philosophers, but by the instructions of Christ. [Barnes]

This wise plan of salvation included the things described by the final three terms in this verse:

Righteousness (dikaiosune) = To be declared righteous or to be justified before God.

Sanctification (hagiasmos) = To be set apart as belonging to God and for His service.

Redemption (apolutrosis) = To give freedom to a ransomed slave. It is put last for emphasis, even though it is the foundation for the previous two. Christ paid the price for each of us, to set us free from the bondage of sin and death.

"The leading idea of the apostle, which should never be lost sight of, is that the Greeks by their philosophy did not become truly wise, righteous, sanctified, and redeemed; but this was accomplished through Jesus Christ." [Barnes]

1 Cor 1:31 so that, just as it is written, "LET HIM WHO BOASTS, BOAST IN THE LORD."

So that = This verse is connected to 1 Cor 1:29 where the topic was human boasting. Here Paul summarized the idea of Jeremiah 9:23-24. If a man is going to do any boasting, he should boast in what the Lord has accomplished on his behalf rather than in his own wisdom or strength or power. He should boast only in Christ and His wisdom, righteousness, sanctification, and redemption.

The Foolishness of Its Preachers (2:1-5)

The gospel also has no claim to wisdom on the basis of the quality or eloquence of the ones who do the preaching. Paul used himself as the illustration of this truth. Notice that the main subjects of the sentences switch to the first person ("I").

1 Cor 2:1 And when I came to you, brethren, I did not come with superiority of speech or of wisdom, proclaiming to you the testimony of God.

When I came to you = When Paul first arrived in Corinth he had just come from Athens, the headquarters of Greek philosophy. There he had spoken to the philosophers at the Areopagus, which in earlier days was a court. This was where Socrates had been tried and sentenced to death for introducing strange gods. In Paul's case it was a hearing rather than a trial (Acts 17:17-21). In his presentation to the philosophers, Paul did not specifically discuss the cross of Christ. Even so, one member of the court was converted (Acts 17:34).

> It was at Athens that, for the one time in his life as far as we know, he had attempted to reduce Christianity to philosophic terms. There on Mars Hill he had met the philosophers and had tried to speak in their own language. But it would almost seem that he had said to himself, Never again! From now on I will tell the story of Jesus in utter simplicity. I will know nothing but Jesus Christ, and him upon his cross. [Barclay]

Superiority of speech = This describes a manner of speaking that rises above what is normal. This was one of the main characteristics of the philosophers of that day.

Testimony of God = This phrase is equivalent to the "word of the cross" from 1 Cor 1:18. The conclusion from this verse is that Paul's manner of speaking was very ordinary.

1 Cor 2:2 For I determined to know nothing among you except Jesus Christ, and Him crucified.

For = This word tells us that Paul will begin giving additional explanation for what he just said.

To know nothing = Literally this could be translated, "not did I choose to know anything" except specific truths concerning Jesus Christ and His crucifixion. "He resolved not only to make the Messiah the grand object of his knowledge and attention there, but even a crucified Messiah; to maintain the doctrine that the Messiah was to be crucified for the sins of the world, and that he who had been crucified was in fact the Messiah." [Barnes] The conclusion from this verse is that Paul's range of subject matter was very limited.

1 Cor 2:3 I was with you in weakness and in fear and in much trembling,

I was with you = Literally this says, "I became toward you."

Weakness = This word means frailty or lack of strength. Paul was not trusting in his own strength.

Fear and trembling = This phrase means anxious concern for carrying out one's responsibilities. Paul knew that he had many opponents and he understood his own personal shortcomings as a public speaker. He also knew how much the Greeks valued elegant rhetoric, so he proclaimed his message with some anxiety and concern as to how it would be received. The conclusion from this verse is that Paul demonstrated his own personal limitations and sense of inadequacy.

1 Cor 2:4 and my message and my preaching were not in persuasive words of wisdom, but in demonstration of the Spirit and of power,

Message and preaching = These are the Greek terms for words (**logos**) and proclamation (**kerygma**). Throughout this section Paul had used both of these terms to describe his message, so he included both of them here in his summary.

Persuasive words of wisdom = This is a restatement of 1 Cor 1:17, meaning that he did not use the wisdom of words. This time Paul added the descriptive adjective "persuasive" which further clarified what he meant when he used the phrase "wisdom of words." He was pointing to the philosophers' methods of rhetoric and oratory which were intended to appeal to the mind and emotions of the listeners.

Demonstration = This term refers to a clear proof that is drawn from facts or documents, rather than from theoretical speculation. It was not human persuasiveness that converted the Corinthians, but the manifestation of the power of the Holy Spirit. It was God's effort rather than man's effort. The conclusion from this verse is that Paul's method of presentation did not involve persuasive speaking.

1 Cor 2:5 so that your faith would not rest on the wisdom of men, but on the power of God.

So that = This phrase introduces Paul's reason for using a simple approach.

Your faith would not be in the wisdom of men = Paul did not want their faith to be the result of or exist on the basis of human philosophy or persuasion.

Wisdom of men vs. **Power of God** = This contrast links to the previous verse (1 Cor 2:4). True faith is the result of God's powerful working in and for people. The skillfulness of a persuasive preacher is never an adequate foundation for faith. Paul desired that their "faith in Christ and in the doctrines of his Gospel might not be attributed to the force of human eloquence and oratory; or stand upon so sandy a foundation as that which might be puffed away by a superior flow and force of words, but that it might be ascribed to almighty power, stand in it, be supported by it, and at last be finished and fulfilled with it." [Gill]

Our own age is also filled with humanism, intellectualism, and an emphasis on man's reasoning. When we share the simple message of Christ's substitutionary death on the cross, we too need to realize that it will probably appear foolish to those who are perishing. Those people whom God has called out from the world will believe our words. They will see, like we do, that the simple gospel message is really the power of God which is working in and for us.

Just as in Paul's day, in our time God delights in humbling the arrogance of man. A person does not need to be a trained orator or philosophical thinker in order to be used by God to share the simple message of salvation through Christ. This is very reassuring, because very few of us have all of the qualifications and credentials that the world desires. Each of us can say, "God can use even me!"

The True Wisdom of the Gospel

(1 Corinthians 2:6-16)

P aul had discussed the problem of divisions within the church at Corinth, with individuals claiming allegiance to different teachers. He then explained how the gospel message appears to be foolish or stupid to those who are perishing. It seems foolish because of the message itself, because of those who tend to receive it, and because of those who proclaim the message of the gospel. But several times Paul reminded us that even though the gospel may appear foolish from a worldly perspective, it is really the power and wisdom of God.

1 Cor 1:18 = To those who are being saved it is the power of God.

1 Cor 1:21 = It was God's wise plan that the world would not come to know Him by means of the so-called wisdom of their own human reasoning.

1 Cor 1:24 = To those who are called, Christ crucified is the power and wisdom of God.

1 Cor 1:30 = It is by God's doing that we are in Christ, who is the wisdom of God.

In this section of Scripture Paul goes on to affirm that God's plan for saving mankind represents true wisdom in the greatest sense of the word.

Evidently, they were thinking of the gospel as another of the philosophical movements of the day and were comparing it and its advocates with others as a type of rival philosophy. Paul has made clear that the gospel is far from being another philosophy; it is wisdom, but an entirely different kind of wisdom. He goes on to show in what sense the gospel is wisdom. [Boyer]

There has always been and always will be a distinction between God's wisdom and man's wisdom. The infinite Creator has wisdom which is incomprehensible to those He has created. Man's finite and limited wisdom cannot even be compared to God's wisdom (see Isa 55:8-9; Rom 11:33). God is not just like us, only bigger somehow! "Who has put wisdom in the innermost being or given understanding to the mind? Who can count the clouds by wisdom or tip the water jars of the heavens" (Job 38:36-37).

It is True Wisdom to a Specific Group of People (2:6a)

Paul had just said that God delights in nullifying human wisdom so our faith would not rest upon the so-called wisdom of men, but on the powerful working of God in and through us (1 Cor 2:5). We have seen previously that the true wisdom of the gospel is not obvious to everyone. Paul had already explained that to unbelieving Jews and Greeks it appeared to be weakness and foolishness.

1 Cor 2:6a Yet we do speak wisdom among those who are mature;

Yet = With this introductory word Paul sets up a clear contrast. Although the gospel was viewed as foolishness from a worldly perspective, here he declares "We DO speak wisdom!" The verb is in the present tense and the word "wisdom" is in the emphatic position at the beginning of the sentence. It could literally be translated, "Wisdom we are speaking." One commentator described Paul's thought process by saying,

> Though the wise philosophers among the Gentiles accounted the Gospel as foolishness; and though the apostle, by an ironical concession, had called the ministry of it the foolishness of preaching and the foolishness of God, and had thought best for wise reasons to deliver it in a plain and simple manner without the embellishments of human wisdom; yet he vindicates it from the charge of folly: it was not folly, but wisdom which he and his fellow ministers preached. [Gill]

Those who are mature = The Greek word **teleios** means finished, brought to fulfillment, lacking nothing for completeness. Only people who are characterized by this quality are able to see the true wisdom of the gospel. Who are the mature?

> There are two answers to this question. Some say they were the advanced or mature Christians as distinguished from the babes in Christ. Others say they were believers as opposed to unbelievers. In favor of the latter view it may be argued that 1) those who regarded Paul's doctrine as foolishness were not the babes in Christ but the unbelieving wise men of the world, so those to whom it was wisdom were simply believers; 2) if the mature here means advanced Christians as distinguished from babes in Christ, then the wisdom which Paul preached was not the gospel but some other more advanced doctrines. But this cannot be because it is the doctrine of the cross, of Christ crucified, which he declares to be the wisdom of God. The contrast is between the wisdom of the world and the wisdom of God, not between the rudimentary vs. advanced doctrine of the gospel. [Hodge]

What is it that has been finished or completed in the lives of believers? This alludes to the finished work of Christ on our behalf, and especially of the final application of that work in each of our lives at the moment we put our trust in Christ as our Savior. At that moment our salvation is complete and assured. Those "who are being saved" (1 Cor 1:18), and especially those Christians who are growing to Christian maturity, are able to see the wisdom of God's plan for the salvation of mankind.

This does not mean that these believers are perfect, completely mature, or in a state of sinless perfection. In this life even the most mature Christians are still growing and have room for improvement. Christianity is not like the mystery religions where only those at the highest levels of the initiation process are allowed to know the deep truths of their cult. Here we should see that those who are chosen, called, and saved by God are the ones who are able to see the wisdom of His plan.

It is True Wisdom Because of Its Unique Source (2:6b-9)

1 Cor 2:6b a wisdom, however, not of this age nor of the rulers of this age, who are passing away;

As he so often does, Paul begins by discussing the negative side of the issue. This wisdom does NOT have its origin in this age or in the rulers of this age who are passing away.

This age = As in 1 Cor 1:20, this wisdom does not belong to the passing age of temporal things which is focused so often on human wisdom and independent thought.

The rulers of this age = This refers to those who are considered to be of the highest rank in the society of men. Paul will elaborate on this later in 1 Cor 2:8.

Who are passing away = The Greek word **katargeo** means to be rendered useless or to be nullified, and it was the same word used in 1 Cor 1:28. The present passive participle represents a process of being brought to nothing. Their so-called wisdom is transient and will not last beyond this present age.

1 Cor 2:7 but we speak God's wisdom in a mystery, the hidden wisdom which God predestined before the ages to our glory;

Now Paul turns to the positive side of the issue. This wisdom has its origin in God Himself, rather than being concocted by men.

Wisdom in a mystery = Mystery refers to something that was not previously revealed by God but which is now being made known (see Rom 16:23; Col 1:26; Eph 3:5). "The word refers not to something which is mysterious or hard to understand, but rather to something which is known only by revelation. A mystery is something you cannot know until you are told. You cannot figure it out; it must be revealed to you." [Boyer] Paul will say more about this in 1 Cor 2:10 when he talks about God's revelation.

God predestined before the ages = God exists outside of time, and in that sense God's plan of salvation could be said to be "predestined before the ages," before the ages of created time or history began. His plan was not a recent invention or something that He created in order to deal with new developments in human history. In His eternal counsel, God determined that this was how He would take action for the salvation of His creatures.

> The Egyptians and Grecians boasted much of the earliness of their wisdom, but neither of them are to be mentioned with the Gospel for the antiquity of it. It is the birth of God's counsels of old, which he purposed in Christ before the world was; a scheme of things he drew in his eternal mind which was from everlasting. [Gill]

To our glory = This phrase means, "in order to accomplish our ultimate glorification." It is amazing to think that God ever had you and me in mind when He predestined this wise plan.

1 Cor 2:8 the wisdom which none of the rulers of this age has understood; for if they had understood it they would not have crucified the Lord of glory;

Which = This word is parallel to "which" in the previous verse, and what follows will add to the description of God's wise plan.

For if = The Greek language has several types of conditional clauses. In the first class conditional clause the statement is assumed to be true, and in the second class conditional clause the statement is assumed to be false. The third class conditional clause is proposed as a remote possibility. Here in this verse we have a second class conditional clause, which expresses something as being false or unfulfilled. God knows all of the future, both what will happen and what could possibly happen. This verse describes one of those possibilities which God knows could never happen. It was God's wise plan that Christ would be put to death on the cross at the hands of His own creatures, the very ones for whose sin He was dying in order to pay the penalty. Could a little understanding on man's part have foiled the wise plan of God? No! This phrase gives the impression that if mankind had only known about God's plan then they would not have participated in fulfilling it, but the Greek grammar tells that this is not the case. Even if mankind had known all about God's wise plan, they would have done exactly as they did! Such is the depraved nature of fallen humanity.

Lord of glory = The person who was crucified was definitely a divine person! It was out of ignorance, envy, and selfishness that those rulers engineered the crucifixion of Christ (see Acts 3:17). "The fact that the princes of this world were so blind as not to see that Christ was the Lord of glory, Paul cites as proof of their ignorance of the wisdom of God." [Hodge]

1 Cor 2:9 but just as it is written, "THINGS WHICH EYE HAS NOT SEEN AND EAR HAS NOT HEARD, AND which HAVE NOT ENTERED THE HEART OF MAN, ALL THAT GOD HAS PREPARED FOR THOSE WHO LOVE HIM."

Just as it is written = Paul is giving the general idea of Isaiah 64:4, although not quoting it specifically.

> Some consider the apostle to be using scriptural language without intending to give the sense of the original. This we often do, and it is not infrequently done in the New Testament (Rom 10:18). 'As it is written' is not, in this case, the form of a quotation, but is rather equivalent to saying, 'To use the language of Scripture.' The apostle may not intend to quote any one passage of scripture, but to appeal to its authority for a clearly revealed truth. [Hodge]

Isaiah 64:3 says God does things that we do not expect, and in Isaiah 64:6 he says that all of our so-called righteous deeds are like filthy rags. In Isaiah 64:8 he proclaims, "But now, O LORD, You are our Father, We are the clay, and You our potter; And all of us are the work of Your hand." The original context of Paul's reference clearly highlights the distinction between the Creator and the creature. This emphasizes that none of His creatures can completely understand the ways of God.

Eye has not seen, Ear has not heard, heart has not understood = The eyes, ears, and heart of man represent his ability to gather information and understand himself and the world. Here Paul says that it is impossible for fallen human beings to comprehend the ways of God. One commentator said,

> Neither externally nor internally, objectively nor subjectively, can man discover God. His external searching is empirical, experimental—represented by seeing and hearing. God's truth is not observable by the eye or the ear, no matter how many sophisticated instruments we may use. We are just as helpless in trying to discover His truth subjectively, through our minds. Rationalism cannot reason out God's truth. Man's two greatest human resources, empiricism and rationalism, his observation and his reason, are equally useless in discovering divine truth. Ultimately they lead men to crucify Christ. [MacArthur]

This is why we so desperately need what Paul is going to talk about in the next few verses!

It is True Wisdom Because of How it is Communicated (2:10-16)

Receiving True Wisdom by Revelation (2:10-11)

1 Cor 2:10 For to us God revealed them through the Spirit; for the Spirit searches all things, even the depths of God.

For = Now Paul will give additional explanation for saying, "We speak God's wisdom in a mystery, the hidden wisdom of God" (1 Cor 2:7).

To us = We must clearly understand from this verse who were the recipients of God's revelation. God was revealing His wisdom to the apostles and prophets during the period before the entire New Testament was completed. "To us" means, "unto those to whom this revelation was made, namely the holy apostles and prophets (Eph 3:5)." [Hodge]

God revealed = This verb means to make known what was previously unknown.

Through the Spirit = This phrase tells us about the instrument God used to reveal His truth. Here we see that the Holy Spirit is the agent of God's revelation.

The Spirit searches = This word means to search accurately and diligently, so as to have thorough knowledge. "Here it means that the Holy Spirit has an intimate knowledge of all things. It is not to be supposed that he searches or inquires as people do who are ignorant, but that he has an intimate and profound knowledge such as is usually the result of a close and accurate search...And he uses a word more emphatic than simple knowledge because he designs to indicate that his knowledge is profound, entire, and thorough." [Barnes] This describes the omniscience of the Holy Spirit. He understands all of the profound plans and counsels of God.

1 Cor 2:11 For who among men knows the thoughts of a man except the spirit of the man which is in him? Even so the thoughts of God no one knows except the Spirit of God.

One commentator explained the two points that Paul makes in this verse: "First, as no one knows the thoughts of a man but the man himself, so no one knows the thoughts of God but God himself. Second, as every man does know his own thoughts, so the Spirit of God knows the thoughts of God. The point to be illustrated here is the knowledge of the Spirit." [Hodge] This tells us that the Holy Spirit is thoroughly qualified to deliver the revelation that Paul is discussing.

Transmitting True Wisdom by Inspiration (2:12-13)

1 Cor 2:12 Now we have received, not the spirit of the world, but the Spirit who is from God, so that we may know the things freely given to us by God,

Now we OURSELVES = In the original language there is an extra pronoun included to emphasize that it was the apostles and prophets who were the recipients of God's New Testament revelation. "Here the whole connection shows that the apostle is speaking of revelation and inspiration; and therefore 'we' must mean we apostles, and not we Christians generally." [Hodge]

Not the spirit of the world = Here Paul identified the spirit that the apostles and prophets received. It was not the world's spirit, the one which operates in and controls the fallen world system and the one that the "rulers of this age" had received.

So that = This purpose clause could be translated, "in order that; for the purpose that." God took action so that men might know of His wise plan. There was not only an eternal purpose in the mind of God (1 Cor 2:7), but a revelation of those truths to the apostles and prophets so that others might also know of God's plan.

The process of the inspiration of Scripture is briefly described in 2 Pet 1:21. One commentator explained this process in the following words:

> Though spoken through the instrumentality of men, it is a Divine word by virtue of the fact that these men spoke 'as borne by the Holy Spirit.' The Biblical writers do not conceive of the Scriptures as a human product breathed into by the Divine Spirit, and thus heightened in its qualities or endowed with new qualities; but as a Divine product produced through the instrumentality of men. [ISBE]

The things freely given = Often this verse is applied to what all believers can know about the blessings they have been given in Christ. But we must be careful to let the passage speak for itself. The meaning of every passage is limited by its context. "This clause does not refer to inward spiritual blessings now enjoyed by believers, nor to the future blessedness of the saints, except so far as these are included in the general subject of Paul's preaching. The connection is with verse 10. 'What human reason could not discover, God has revealed to us apostles, in order that we might know what he has thus graciously communicated.' The subject is the wisdom of God (the gospel), as distinguished from the wisdom of the world." [Hodge] Unless you claim to be one of the inspired writers of the New Testament and that God is giving you new revelation today, then this passage is not referring to you. It does tell us about the process God used to deliver New Testament revelation to the apostles and prophets so that they could record it for all to see.

1 Cor 2:13 which things we also speak, not in words taught by human wisdom, but in those taught by the Spirit, combining spiritual thoughts with spiritual words.

Which things we also speak = Paul is saying that the apostles and prophets not only were given God's truth, but they also communicated those things which God had given them. They did not keep those words to themselves.

Not taught by human wisdom = This was not done in words which man's wisdom would have chosen. "This is verbal inspiration or the doctrine that the writers of the Scriptures were controlled by the Spirit of God in the choice of the words which they employed in communicating divine truth." [Hodge]

Combining spiritual thoughts with spiritual words = The term "combining" (**sungkrino**) means not only to mentally combine or compare, but also to explain. So, joining spiritual things to spiritual words means explaining the things of the Spirit in the words of the Spirit.

> The apostle had said that the truths which he taught were revealed by the Spirit, and that the words which he used were taught by the Spirit, which he sums up by saying that he explained spiritual things in spiritual words. The other interpretation, comparing spiritual things with spiritual, whether it means comparing the Old Testament with the New, as some say, or as others understand it, comparing one portion of the Spirit's teaching with another, is inconsistent with the context. [Hodge]

The context makes it clear that Paul is explaining how the inspiration of the Holy Spirit operated in the lives of those to whom God had chosen to give New Testament revelation. As one scholar explained, "Clearly Paul means that the help of the Holy Spirit in the utterance of the revelation extends to the words. No theory of inspiration is here stated, but it is not mere human wisdom. Paul's own Epistles bear eloquent witness to the lofty claim here made. They remain today after nearly nineteen centuries throbbing with the power of the Spirit of God, dynamic with life for the problems of today as when Paul wrote them for the needs of the believers in his time, the greatest epistles of all time, charged with the energy of God." [RWP]

Understanding True Wisdom by Illumination (2:14-16)

In the next two verses Paul contrasts two categories of men: the **Natural** vs. the **Spiritual**. All men fall into one of these two categories.

1 Cor 2:14 But a natural man does not accept the things of the Spirit of God, for they are foolishness to him; and he cannot understand them, because they are spiritually appraised.

A Natural Man (psuchikos) = This term could be translated soul-ish.

This word was used by the Greek writers to distinguish the noblest of men from the dissolute and pleasure-loving man who lives on the level of the brute beast. The natural man is the man commended by philosophy, who is actuated by the higher thoughts and aims of the natural life, not the sensual animal man who is ruled by the passions of his body. This term therefore was chosen by the Apostle Paul to describe to the Corinthians the unregenerate man at his very best, but a man who is limited to the realm of the soul. His spirit, that part of him which is capable of communion with God, is dead and unresponsive. [Boyer]

The natural man is under the influence of his own nature, and although the things of the Spirit are clearly revealed and have been communicated in words given through the Spirit, the natural man cannot accept them. "By natural man, therefore, we must understand the unrenewed man; the man under the influence of human nature, as distinguished from those who are under the influence of the Holy Spirit. The natural or unrenewed man does not receive the things of the Spirit." [Hodge]

Does not accept = We could paraphrase this to say that the truths of the Spirit bounce right off of the natural man. Without God's help, the natural man tends to reject God's truth every time. "Certainly the initiative comes from God whose Holy Spirit makes it possible for us to accept the things of the Spirit of God." [RWP]

He cannot understand them (ginosko) = This word means to gain an intimate, personal knowledge of something, especially in the sense of loving or approving of those truths. The natural man needs God's help in order to understand and accept God's truth. "What the apostle here affirms of the natural or unrenewed man is that he cannot discern the truth, excellence, or beauty of divine things. It is not simply that he does not do it; or that he will not do it; but he cannot do it. His inward state must be changed by the influence of the Spirit before he can apprehend the truth and excellence of the gospel." [Hodge]

They are spiritually discerned (anakrino) = This word means to spiritually examine or investigate. It was used of examining the Scriptures with the idea of coming to an accurate conclusion (Acts 17:11). The basic meaning of the word is examining, inquiring into, or following up a set of particulars in order to distinguish truth from error. As one commentator said, the truths of God "are perceived by the aid of the Holy Spirit enlightening the mind and influencing the heart." [Barnes]

The illumination of Scripture is the special ministry of the Holy Spirit which helps the believer to understand the truths of the Bible. This requires the indwelling presence of the Spirit in the believer, which means an unbeliever cannot experience this special aid for understanding God's truth.

The experience of illumination is not by direct revelation. The canon of Scripture is closed. The Spirit illumines the meaning of that closed canon, and He does so through study and meditation. Study employs all the proper tools for ascertaining the meaning of the text. Meditation thinks about the true facts of the text, putting them together into a harmonious whole and applying them to one's own life. Illumination is not concerned merely with understanding facts but with using those facts to promote Christlikeness. [Ryrie]

1 Cor 2:15 But he who is spiritual appraises all things, yet he himself is appraised by no one.

The Spiritual Man (pneumatikos) = This term refers to someone who is filled with and governed by the Spirit of God. This person meets the requirements for the ministry of illumination by the Holy Spirit.

> Here a spiritual man means every man that is born of the Spirit; seeing what is born of the Spirit is Spirit or spiritual; the regenerate man is denominated spiritually, he is such a one that is quickened by the Spirit of God, and lives spiritually by faith in Christ. He is one that is renewed by the Holy Spirit in the spirit of his mind, has a new heart, and a new spirit put within him; and is become a new creature in Christ; he has the good work of grace wrought in his soul; and in him grace is the reigning principle; in him the Spirit of God himself dwells, and he is led by him out of himself to Christ, and into all truth. [Gill]

All things = The spiritual man is qualified to sift, to examine, to decide rightly, because he has his heart illuminated by the Holy Spirit. What are ALL things? Does this mean that a Christian can be omniscient? On the contrary, it only indicates that believers have access to all of the truths of God which were revealed to the apostles and prophets. "The all things here spoken of are limited by the context to the things of the Spirit." [Hodge] Another commentator explained it this way.

> Unlike God's revelation and inspiration, which were given to the biblical writers, His illumination is for all Christians. We all can rightly appraise the Word when we rely on the Giver of the Word. The doctrine of illumination does not mean we can know and understand everything (Deut 29:29), that we do not need human teachers (Eph 4:11-12), or that study is not hard work (2 Tim 2:15). It does mean that Scripture can be understood by every Christian who is diligent and obedient. [MacArthur]

Yet he himself is appraised by no one = This tells us that the spiritual man will not be appreciated by the man who does not have the Spirit. That should not bother the spiritual man because he was once only a natural man himself. "The contrast is obvious. The one who is not spiritual, by implication, is not even equipped to examine the evidence, let alone to pass judgment on a spiritual man." [Boyer]

1 Cor 2:16 For WHO HAS KNOWN THE MIND OF THE LORD, THAT HE WILL INSTRUCT HIM? But we have the mind of Christ.

For = Paul is providing additional explanation for his previous statement that the natural man is not qualified to judge the spiritual man. Paul quoted Isaiah 40:13 which is a passage describing the majesty and infinity of the Creator, as distinguished from His creatures. This clearly points to the Creator-creature distinction.

But we OURSELVES have the mind of Christ = The emphatic pronoun here in this verse again identifies the apostles and prophets (see 1 Cor 2:12). The mind refers to the wisdom of God given by revelation through the Holy Spirit. As one Bible scholar points out, the mind is "the understanding of the Lord. The divine counsels or purposes which are the results of the divine thought." [VWS]

> For any man to pronounce spiritual doctrines false, and to judge those who held them, supposes he is able to teach the Lord. As no one can do this, no one can judge those who have the mind of Christ, that is, those whom Christ by his Spirit has taught the truth. The philosophers of Greece and the scribes among the Jews had sat in judgment upon Paul and pronounced his preaching foolishness. He tells them they are not competent judges. The natural man cannot discern the things of the Spirit, and is incompetent to judge those whom the Spirit has taught. As what we teach is the mind of the Lord, to condemn our doctrine or to judge us as its teachers, is to condemn the Lord. [Hodge]

From eternity past God predestined His wise plan of salvation, but now that He has revealed it to us this plan is not meant to be kept hidden. It is not to be kept secret like the knowledge of the mystery religions. God intends that those of us who now know about His wise plan should share it with anyone we meet. Every believer has access to the illumination of the Holy Spirit, but in order to experience this special ministry we must be actively reading and studying the Word of God. We should not complacently do nothing and then expect the Holy Spirit to give us scriptural illumination. As someone once said about riding a bicycle, it is very difficult to steer the bicycle unless it is already moving forward. In the same way, we must be actively moving forward in reading, studying, and meditating on the Word of God so the Holy Spirit can guide us and give special insights into His revealed truth.

Believers Acting Like Unbelievers

(1 Corinthians 3:1-4)

Paul had just established the contrast between two categories of men, the Natural and the Spiritual. Now he will focus on one of these two categories to explain it still further. Here Paul will describe the current condition of the Corinthians, which was what required him to write as he did in this letter. In this section he will refer all the way back to 1 Cor 1:11 to the divisions they were experiencing within the church, so he is still discussing that issue throughout this section.

The Facts of Their Immaturity (3:1-2)

1 Cor 3:1 And I, brethren, could not speak to you as to spiritual men, but as to men of flesh, as to infants in Christ.

Here Paul literally says, "And I, brothers, **NOT was I given power to speak.**" This refers to the truths of the wisdom of God that Paul received from the Holy Spirit and desired to share with them (see 1 Cor 2:12-13). But he was not able to speak to them as he wanted to because of their condition.

Brethren = Paul established immediately that he was speaking to brothers in Christ. These people belonged to the group of **Spiritual** people. "Spiritual truth can only be discovered and acquired by a spiritual nature. It takes an entirely new capacity to receive divine truth. Apart from that new capacity, the natural mind perceives divine truth as foolishness and nonsense." [Pentecost]

Notice the comparative word "as" in each of Paul's three comparisons below. Paul was forced to speak:

NOT as to Spiritual = He was not able to speak to them as being spiritual, which is the category to which they belonged!

BUT as to fleshly (sarkinos) = This word means made of flesh, consisting of the material of flesh. Paul is saying that he must speak to them like he might speak to ones who were completely made of flesh (the Natural man). In 1 Cor 3:3 he will say they are fleshly, but Paul used a different word there (**sarkikos**) which has a slightly different meaning. **Flesh (sarx)** means the outlook oriented toward selfishness, which pursues its own ends in self-sufficient independence from God. The flesh has a worldly identity and a desire to do what the world does.

As to infants (nepios) in Christ = Literally this word means "not speaking," like very young children. This clearly implied that the Corinthians had experienced the new birth in Christ and belonged to the category of spiritual men, but they were acting like spiritual newborns.

The normal progression is from the natural man, through conversion, to being a babe in Christ followed by a normal growth toward spiritual maturity. There is no fault in starting the Christian life as a spiritual infant. However, Paul is not saying

Progress of the Christian Life

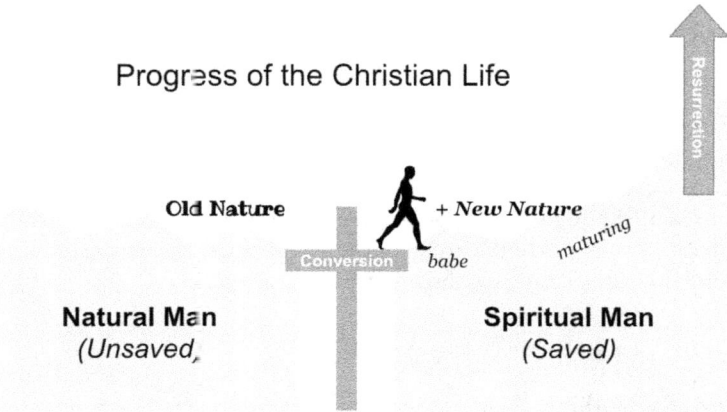

Old Nature   + New Nature

Conversion   babe   maturing

Resurrection

Natural Man   **Spiritual Man**
(Unsaved)   *(Saved)*

they were babes because they were newly born into the family of God, but because they were inexcusably immature.

At the time when a person becomes a believer in Christ, we can picture a new nature being poured in with the old and a hostile coexistence begins.

> Don't be deceived into thinking that your old mind has been changed because you have been born into the family of God. The mind we have read about in Scripture is the mind we receive by physical birth. We possess within ourselves the same capacity for carnality, vanity, fleshly defilement, corruption, enmity, and attention to earthly, material things that characterized us before we were born into God's family. And if that old mind is allowed to exercise itself, that mind will produce words and actions that are in keeping with the corruption, defilement, blindness, and deadness God says characterizes the mind of the unsaved. However, it is biblical to understand that in the area of mind, the Christian has two capacities—the capacity for divine things through the new mind, and the capacity for carnal, fleshly, sinful, dead things through the old mind. And there is a constant, ceaseless, incessant, unrelenting opposition from the old mind to the new mind as it seeks to glorify God. [Pentecost]

The chart on the next page shows the contrast between the capabilities of the Natural Man and the Spiritual Man. Even after a believer begins to grow, he can sometimes look back on the shadowy reflection of what he once was as an unbeliever. It is possible for a Christian to behave like an unbeliever. As one writer has said, "The old nature is older than the new nature, and the old nature continues to grow, even though the Christian's new nature may be progressing, for the old nature's contact with the world constantly teaches him new things. With every new thing the old nature learns, there are more conflicts with the new nature." [Massey] The natural man is at home in the world, but the spiritual man is currently living in a familiar world that is out of sync with his new spiritual nature. He is a citizen of

Natural Man	Spiritual Man
One nature (old, fleshly, fallen nature)	Two natures (old nature + new spiritual nature)
Unsaved	Saved
At home in this world	An alien in this world
Independence from God	Submission to God

heaven who must continue to live in an environment hostile to his spiritual growth. One commentator vividly described this inner spiritual conflict in the following words:

> Suppose a person is forty-seven years old. Not only is that the age of his body, it is also the age of his old nature. Suppose he met Christ when he was seventeen. That was his second birthday, the birthday of his new nature. His new nature is thus thirty years old. The old man is obviously older and has had more experience than the new man...It is not the new nature that responds to temptation; it is the old nature. It is not the new nature that doubts; it is the old nature. It is not the new nature that experiences fear and depression; it is the old nature. It is not the new nature that clashes with people in a power struggle; it is the old nature. The new nature does not use profanity, but the old nature does. The new nature does not think of evil or incite evil, but the old nature does. It is not the new but the old nature that envies, covets, lies, steals, and shows indifference. It is not the new nature that loses its temper or is bitter, malicious, angry, or arrogant; it is the old nature. Many sincere Christians have encountered periods of time when it seemed impossible to cope with life. The key is not so much in escaping the loneliness, depression, guilt, discouragement, or self-pity as it is in accepting it as the activity of the old nature. With this understanding of the hostility of the old nature, the new nature can, by calling on the Lord for support, prevent it from overwhelming his outlook. [Massey]

Just because a person has put his trust in Jesus Christ for salvation does not mean that his old nature is immediately eradicated or neutralized. The old nature still exerts a powerful pull toward the old habit patterns that have been developed through the years. Those old habits and behavior patterns can only be changed through the work of the new nature as it submits to the Lord and obeys the Word of God. However, there will always be a possibility for the old nature to rear its ugly head as we walk through the rest of the days that God gives us here in this world.

Sometimes the term "carnal" is applied to Christians who, even though they are saved, are behaving like unsaved men. "They are carnal because the flesh is dominating them. The carnal Christian is characterized by a walk that is on the same plane as that of the natural man The objectives and affections are centered in the same unspiritual sphere as that of the natural man." [Chafer] The old nature wants to resist the new nature's desires and decisions to follow God's Word and to do His will. When you see cases of believers falling into immorality, you can identify in them the battles that the old nature has won over the new nature. It is important for Christians to understand that there is a war going on between these two natures.

> A Christian is not characterized by sin; it no longer represents his basic nature. But he is still able to sin, and his sin is just as sinful as the sin of an unbeliever. Sin is sin. When a Christian sins, he is being practically unspiritual, living on the same practical level as an unbeliever. Consequently Paul is compelled to speak to the Corinthian believers much as if they were unbelievers. [MacArthur]

With this background in mind we must understand, however, that Paul expected more from the Corinthian believers at this stage in their spiritual growth. They should have grown up in ways that would allow them to control themselves and act in more godly and spiritual ways than they were acting. The proof of their prolonged infancy can be seen in their diet of milk rather than solid food.

1 Cor 3:2 I gave you milk to drink, not solid food; for you were not yet able to receive it. Indeed, even now you are not yet able,

I gave you milk = This phrase is parallel to the phrase "I speak" in the previous verse. When Paul speaks what God has revealed to him, this is what constitutes the process of feeding others with the nourishment that the spiritual nature requires in order to grow and develop. This food must be something that is appropriate to a believer's developmental level in order to be effective in causing growth. We should focus on feeding the new nature, not the old, and we must feed it the most appropriate food for its health and growth. "When Paul first preached to the Corinthians he taught the more easily digestible elementary truths of doctrine, the milk. But now, some five years later, they still needed to be fed milk. They could not yet spiritually digest solid food. Like many Christians today, the Corinthians seemed quite content to stay on a milk diet." [MacArthur]

There is an old poem about the struggle of the Christian life and the key to controlling the flesh:

Two natures beat within my breast: One is foul, the other blest;
The one I love, the one I hate; The one I feed will dominate.

One commentator aptly described this struggle as a process of starving the old nature.

> The believer should understand that there are moments when his old nature will dominate and defeat him, but he will know the situation is temporary and that victory will ultimately be his. The believer must be aware that the old nature is present and eager to take over. We must be vigilant. Then the believer should understand how his old nature operates. Under the guidance of the Holy Spirit, he can set up a program for starving the old nature. [Massey]

In the Christian life the new nature is at somewhat of a disadvantage because the old nature is at home in the world and finds plenty of carnality to feed on, and this was as true in the city of Corinth as it is in modern times. Because the new nature has no natural food source in this world, believers must make time for Bible study, sound Bible teaching, fellowship, worship, and prayer in order to feed and sustain their spiritual growth. Unless the new nature is fed with healthy spiritual food, the sin of the old nature may lead to costly defeat in the Christian life.

The Proof of Their Immaturity (3:3-4)

1 Cor 3:3 for you are still fleshly. For since there is jealousy and strife among you, are you not fleshly, and are you not walking like mere men?

Fleshly (sarkikos) = This word means flesh-like, related to flesh, or controlled by the flesh. Here Paul is directly addressing the Corinthians and he says they are flesh-like. They were acting like people who were living only in the flesh. Notice, however, that Paul never classified them as natural men.

Jealousy and strife = These words are listed in the works of the flesh in Gal 5:20. **Jealousy (zelos)** means contentious rivalry; passion in pursuing or defending something. **Strife (eris)** means contention, wrangling, quarreling (see 1 Cor 1:11). These two problems represent many other aspects of fleshly attitudes and behavior. "Carnality is a general evil that has many manifestations. It will corrupt the morals, weaken personal relationships, produce doubt about God and His Word, destroy one's prayer life, and provide fertile ground for heresy. It will attack right doctrine and right living, right belief and right practice." [MacArthur]

Walking like mere men = This phrase means they were behaving according to human motives or feelings, and acting like the Natural unsaved man would behave.

1 Cor 3:4 For when one says, "I am of Paul," and another, "I am of Apollos," are you not mere men?

Now Paul reminds them of the sinful, worldly behavior in their church that had been identified in the first chapter of the letter (1 Cor 1:11-12). Here he is saying that the factions and so-called political parties in the Corinthian church were direct evidence that they were letting the old nature defeat them. This is Paul's proof that the Corinthians were acting no differently than unsaved men.

As we conclude this section we should remember the ideas that Paul has presented here. Believers must understand that they now have both an old fleshly nature as well as a new spiritual nature struggling within them. Spiritual growth and maturity can only come as believers learn how to starve the old nature while nourishing the new nature. This internal battle between the flesh and the spirit is one that will only end when the believer receives his resurrection body. No matter how hard they try, believers cannot eradicate their old nature. As one commentator put it, "We must remember that God gave up on the old nature and killed it!" [Massey] The flesh is not something we can repair or reform. It must be controlled and ultimately destroyed. At the time of a believer's glorification, it will be completely replaced by the one spiritual nature in the new resurrection body.

The struggle for Christian maturity will continue throughout our earthly lifetime. Some believers may seem more mature than others, and even some elderly believers may not act their age. One writer explained the situation in these words:

> That word maturity seems to hold the key to the concept of spirituality, for Christian maturity is the growth which the Holy Spirit produces over a period of time in the believer. To be sure, the same amount of time is not required for each individual, but some time is necessary for all. It is not the time itself which produces maturity. Rate multiplied by time equals distance, so that the distance to maturity may be covered in a shorter time if the rate of growth is accelerated. And it will be accelerated if none of the control which ought to be given to the Holy Spirit is retained by self. [Ryrie]

Paul has given us some important insights into the situation of the believers in the Corinthian church. For the most part, they were being defeated as they allowed their old fleshly nature to dominate the spiritual nature. "The tragedy of these Corinthians is that they have allowed the spirit to be overcome in their lives by the flesh, and are therefore living like natural, unsaved men. This is a tremendous challenge from the apostle Paul to all Christians that their lives should be different." [Boyer]

Ministers Are Merely God's Servants

(1 Corinthians 3:5-23)

P aul had just finished his section discussing their wrong conception of the gospel, and he had reminded them of the proof of their worldliness, which were the divisions and factions in the church. Now Paul will discuss the next cause of their divisions, which was a wrong conception of the role of ministers in the church.

1 Cor 3:5 What then is Apollos? And what is Paul? Servants through whom you believed, even as the Lord gave opportunity to each one.

The Corinthians were claiming a special relationship and loyalty to specific leaders, so Paul used himself and Apollos to stand as representatives for all ministers. He asked an important question about himself and his fellow worker.

What is Apollos? What is Paul? = The Corinthians were claiming to belong to specific factions, and to raise Apollos or Paul to an exalted position of leadership and authority over others. So Paul clarified what he and Apollos really were. In essence he is implying that they have no intrinsic honor or worth in themselves. "Why should a party be formed which should be named after Paul? What has he done or taught that should lead to this? What eminence does he have that should induce anyone to call himself by his name? All of them are but ministers or servants and have no claim to the honor of giving names to sects and parties." [Barnes]

Servants (diakonos) = This word identifies a lowly serving man; one who executes the commands of another; one who runs errands, waits on tables, or does menial tasks.

> The original word **diakonoi** denotes properly servants in distinction from masters, and denotes those who are in an inferior rank of life. They did not have command or authority, but were subject to the command of others. It is applied to the preachers of the gospel because they are employed in the service of God, because they go at his command and are subject to his control and direction. They did not have original authority, nor are they the source of influence or power. The idea here is that they were the mere instruments or servants by whom God conveyed all blessings to the Corinthians; that they as ministers were on the same level, were engaged in the same work, and that therefore it was improper for them to form parties that should be called by their names. [Barnes]

Through whom = This phrase tells us that ministers are merely the agents or instruments God uses to accomplish His purposes.

The Lord gave/granted = God is the source and director of the activity of salvation. Paul immediately makes it clear that the men they thought of as exalted leaders of factions were in reality merely delivery boys in God's program for the salvation of mankind. No minister like Apollos or Paul has any basis for pride or conceit, and others should not make them into leaders of rival factions. No one builds a movement around a waiter or bus boy. The Lord uses servants to deliver the food to your table, but He is the one who provides the food. We should glorify the One who provided the food that was delivered.

> The world honors and tries to immortalize great men because men are the highest thing it knows. The world cannot see beyond itself. But Christians know God—the Creator, the Sustainer, the Savior, the Lord of the universe, and the Source of all things. He alone is worthy of honor. We are but His servants, His instruments. If an artist is to be honored, you do not make a statue of his brush or his palette. It makes no more sense for Christians to glorify men, even a Paul or an Apollos, who are only brushes or palettes in the Master's hands. They are to be esteemed and loved for their work (1 Thess 5:12-13), but not worshipped or set against each other as leaders of rival sects. [MacArthur]

Paul has introduced his main point and now he will illustrate this point by using pictures from both agriculture and architecture.

An Illustration from Agriculture (3:6-9)

1 Cor 3:6-7 I planted, Apollos watered, but God was causing the growth. So then neither the one who plants nor the one who waters is anything, but God who causes the growth.

I planted, Apollos watered = Both of these verbs are in the past (aorist) tense, indicating definite acts that took place. "The planting of souls in Christ and the implanting of grace in them are things purely divine and peculiar to God; but his meaning is that he was the first that preached the Gospel to them at Corinth; and was an instrument of the conversion of many souls, and of laying the foundation, and of raising and forming a Gospel church." [Gill] Planting might be considered the first work for producing a crop but there is also seed production, site selection, and soil preparation. Once the seed is planted, it requires water, nutrients, sunshine, and protection from harm. The Creator and Sustainer of the Universe is the only One ultimately who can ensure growth. It takes a sovereign, omnipotent, omniscient, omnipresent God to coordinate all of these activities. Conclusion #1: Different workers serve different functions.

God was causing the growth (auxano) = This word means to cause growth; to generate an increase; to cause to become greater. The verb is in the imperfect active indicative and it implies that God was continuously involved in the work both of Paul and Apollos.

> It would be vain for the farmer to sow his seed unless God would give it life. There is no life in the seed, nor is there any inherent power in the earth to make it grow. Only God, the Giver of all life, can quicken the seed and make it live. So it would be in vain for the farmer to water his plant unless God would bless it. There is no living principle in the water; no inherent power in the rains of heaven to make the plant grow. The seed would not germinate if it was not planted, nor grow if it was

not watered; but the life is still from God. [Barnes]

Neither the one who plants nor the one who waters is anything = This tells us that each of the workers is not anything in terms of actually causing the growth. Because of this we might say that all workers are equal in terms of their ultimate function. Their job is to serve as instruments in the hands of God. This does not mean that God does not use men to accomplish His purposes, or that men are unimportant. It simply indicates that they all sink into insignificance in comparison to God. Conclusion #2: Different workers are of equal value in the hands of God.

1 Cor 3:8-9 Now he who plants and he who waters are one; but each will receive his own reward according to his own labor. For we are God's fellow workers; you are God's field, God's building.

He who plants and he who waters are one = Paul used the singular number to show how the planter and the waterer work together. If no one planted, the watering would be useless. If no one watered, the planting would come to nothing. They must literally function as a single unit. They are doing different work, but they are one regarding the goal to be accomplished. The one is as necessary as the other to accomplishing the task. Ministers are not in competition, but they complement, balance, or supplement each other in doing God's work. The sower and the waterer are working together to ensure that a crop is able to grow. They have one goal and one purpose, so they are not rivals or competitors. Conclusion #3: Different workers are not rivals, they are a single team.

Each will receive his own reward according to his labor = The word "reward" (**misthos**) means payment for work done; wages that result from effort. This is not a reward in the sense of an undeserved gift. The reward will be based on the amount of **effort (karpon)** expended, especially through pressure and suffering. Conclusion #4: Workers are distinct in their responsibilities as well as in their rewards.

We are God's fellow-workers = Literally this could be translated, "It is of God that we are the fellow workers." Ministers are simply field hands in God's garden. They are fellow laborers employed by God and are under His direction.

You are God's field = The Corinthians, those being ministered to, are the field and God is at work to cause growth in their lives. He often uses the efforts of ministers to accomplish His purposes.

God's building = This phrase serves as a transition to the next illustration.

An Illustration from Architecture (3:10-17)

This illustration draws on the idea of constructing a building. It discusses the foundation, the builders, the structure, the building materials, the quality testing, and the outcome.

1 Cor 3:10-11 According to the grace of God which was given to me, like a wise master builder I laid a foundation, and another is building on it. But each man must be careful how he builds on it. For no man can lay a foundation other than the one which is laid, which is Jesus Christ.

According to the grace of God = Everything Paul accomplished was due to the empowerment of God in his life. Paul was merely the instrument in God's hand. God's grace was what made Paul a wise master builder.

A wise master builder (architekton) = This word means a chief technician, rather than the actual Master Architect. This suggests Paul's own responsibility for what was happening in Corinth. "Architekton occurs in the papyri and inscriptions sometimes of the chief engineers. Here Paul claims primary responsibility for the first work in the church at Corinth. 'All the workmen (tektones, carpenters) work under the direction of the architect' (Plato, Statesman, 259). Much depends on the wisdom of the chief technician in laying the foundation." [RWP]

Laid a foundation, another is building on it = Paul's foundation was solid. Subsequent teachers did not need to remove it and lay another foundation. They only needed to continue building on that original foundation according to the original work of the first engineer.

But each man must be careful how he builds = Literally the word "be careful" (blepo) means to see or perceive; then metaphorically, to see with the mind's eye, to consider or contemplate. The technician must watch carefully and pay attention. Applying this to the church one scholar said, "Let him be careful what instructions he shall give to a church that has been founded by apostolic hands, and that is established on the only true foundation. This is designed to guard against false instruction and the instructions of false teachers." [Barnes]

A foundation other than the one which was laid = Here Paul tells exactly what foundation he laid, and it consisted of the truths concerning the person and work of the Lord Jesus Christ. This foundation is the only adequate foundation for the church, and no other foundation needed to be laid by subsequent ministers in the church. Paul had done his original work very well.

1 Cor 3:12-13 Now if any man builds on the foundation with gold, silver, precious stones, wood, hay, straw, each man's work will become evident; for the day will show it because it is to be revealed with fire, and the fire itself will test the quality of each man's work.

Gold, silver, precious stones vs. wood, hay, straw = These materials represent things that are extremely valuable and are not easily destroyed by fire compared to those things that are relatively inexpensive and are completely consumed by fire. Wood, hay, and straw can be obtained quickly and cheaply, and they can be built into a large structure almost overnight. However, gold, silver, and precious stones are more costly and rare. They take time to acquire and to build into a structure.

Gold/Silver/Stones = These represent the serious, significant, and valuable truths of the faith.

Wood/Hay/Straw = These do not represent false teaching or heretical doctrine, because those things would not be compatible with the original foundation of truth. Instead they represent meaningless, trivial, or useless things. This is referring to teaching that may not be harmful, but only mediocre or of minimal value. "If any man builds upon this foundation, let him look to whether he teaches the substantial, vital truths of Christianity or propagates vain subtleties and conceits which, although they do not entirely destroy the foundation, disgrace it as a squalid edifice would do to a grand and extensive foundation laid with great pomp and solemnity." [Barnes] Unfortunately many of the pulpits of churches today emphasize this second category of teaching, which consist of the trivial things that tickle the ears and entertain those who come to listen. There is much wood, hay, and straw preached from today's pulpits that is intended to meet the fleshly felt needs of worldly believers.

Each man's work will become evident (phaneros) = This means something that shines and can be clearly and publicly seen.

The day will show it (deloo) = This means to declare the quality. The true light of day will allow the work to be seen for what it is. This could simply refer to daylight, but the definite article ("the day") points to a specific day or event. Which day is this? It probably refers to the future day when ministers' works will be evaluated by the Lord. This will occur at the judgment seat of Christ in heaven after the resurrection of church-age saints (see 2 Cor 5:10).

It is to be revealed (apokalupto, uncovered) with fire; fire will test (dokimazo) the quality = Here Paul uses an illustration from the field of metallurgy, which is the process of refining building materials. The word **dokimazo** was used of heating metals to test whether they were genuine or not. Here the test of quality is being applied to the efforts of ministers. It is a test of works, but not a test of individuals.

1 Cor 3:14-15 If any man's work which he has built on it remains, he will receive a reward. If any man's work is burned up, he will suffer loss; but he himself will be saved, yet so as through fire.

Work remains—reward = The only work that can remain after such a test is the work that is analogous to the gold, silver, and precious stones (the valuable materials). If ministers do valuable work, then they will receive their just reward (**misthos** = payment for services rendered).

Burned up—suffer loss = If ministers do work that is frivolous or worthless (analogous to the perishable materials), then they will not receive whatever wages they thought they were due. This is what constitutes loss. They must have a previous expectation of gain which will be withheld from them. What they produced was not worthy of wages. "The man's work is burned up—sermons, lectures, books, teaching, all dry as dust." [RWP]

He himself will be saved = Paul makes it very clear here that this is not an evaluation of the person, but of the quality of work that a minister has produced. If he had not included this phrase, then we might have been left to wonder whether the minister could lose his salvation.

As through fire = This means that the final verdict will come after the work is evaluated by testing. The idea here is that whatever is valuable in a minister's work will be rewarded, and the man himself will be saved; but whatever is not valuable in a minister's work will burn up, and the man himself will still be saved. Remember that the context is discussing the work of ministers, not the lives of believers in general.

> It is the tragedy of a fruitless life, of a minister who built so poorly on the true foundation that his work went up in smoke. His sermons were empty froth or windy words without edifying or building power. They left no mark in the lives of the hearers. It is the picture of a wasted life. The one who enters heaven by grace, as we all do who are saved, yet who brings no sheaves with him. There is no garnered grain the result of his labours in the harvest field. There are no souls in heaven as the result of his toil for Christ, no enrichment of character, no growth in grace. [RWP]

1 Cor 3:16-17 Do you not know that you are a temple of God and that the Spirit of God dwells in you? If any man destroys the temple of God, God will destroy him, for the temple of God is holy, and that is what you are.

You are God's temple (naos) = In 1 Cor 3:9 Paul had said, "You are God's field, God's building." Here he concludes his illustration from architecture by telling them specifically what kind of building they are; they are God's "holy place." There were many temples in the city of Corinth, so this illustration would ring true for the Corinthians.

> Among the pagans, temples were regarded as sacred. They were supposed to be inhabited by the divinity to whom they were dedicated. They were regarded as inviolable. Those who took refuge there were safe. So the apostle says of the Christian community that they were regarded as his temple—God dwelt among them and they should regard themselves as holy, and as consecrated to his service. [Barnes]

The Spirit of God dwells in you = God makes His home in the believer. Every believer is indwelt by the Holy Spirit.

Destroys the temple of God, God will destroy (phtheiro) him = This word means to shrivel, wither, waste, spoil, or ruin. "The sense is, 'If any man by his doctrines or precepts shall pursue such a course as tends to destroy the church, God shall severely punish him.'" [Barnes] This warns us that God will repay in kind. The fleshly actions of the Corinthians will result in definite consequences. "It is a gross sin to be a church-wrecker. There are actually a few preachers who leave behind them ruin like a tornado in their path. There is warning enough here to make every pastor pause before he tears a church to pieces." [RWP]

Holy, and that is what you are = Here Paul reminds the Corinthians of their status of belonging to God and being set apart for His use.

> The Corinthians themselves in their angry disputes had forgotten their holy heritage and calling, though this failing was no excuse for the ringleaders who had led them on. Paul reminds the Corinthians that they are the temple of the Holy Spirit, which fact they had forgotten in their immoralities. [RWP]

The Conclusion From These Illustrations (3:18-23)

To the Corinthian ringleaders promoting factions (3:18-20)

1 Cor 3:18 Let no man deceive himself. If any man among you thinks that he is wise in this age, he must become foolish, so that he may become wise.

Let no man deceive himself = This implies that some of the Corinthians were actually deceiving themselves. Self-deception is a very common and dangerous problem among believers, and particularly among ministers. The context specifies that this self-deception involves believing that you are wise according to the world's standards of wisdom. This describes a minister who has "vain notions of serving God and of doing the churches good by his carnal and worldly wisdom." [Gill]

Thinks he is wise in this age = The deception Paul is talking about involves thinking one is wise in the sense in which the people of this world are considered wise. It is a dangerous thing for a believer to pride himself on his reputation for worldly wisdom.

> Much division in the church would be eliminated if individuals were not so impressed with their own wisdom. If a church had ten men with doctorates who were only nominal in their commitment to the Lord and to His Word, and ten other men who had only finished high school but were completely committed to the Lord and steeped in His Word, it should not be hard to decide which ten were most qualified to lead the church. [MacArthur]

He must become foolish so that he may become wise = Here Paul is saying that a Christian should be willing to be regarded as a fool by the world's standards in order to be wise by God's standards. Paul had already explained that God's wisdom appears foolish to the intellectual philosopher. He now says that by renouncing worldly wisdom and fame, a believer becomes truly wise when he embraces what the world calls foolishness.

> Not that, properly speaking, folly is the way to wisdom; but that the man who would be wise in a spiritual sense must first learn to know himself and acknowledge his own folly, embrace the Gospel of Christ, which is esteemed foolishness by the world; submit to the ordinances of Christ, which are despised by men; take up the cross of Christ, and follow him, bearing reproach and persecution for his sake.

Nothing is more ridiculous to carnal men than this: he must deny his worldly wisdom, his carnal self-righteousness, and wholly rely on Christ and his righteousness for eternal life and happiness, and so will he become truly wise unto salvation. [Gill]

1 Cor 3:19-20 For the wisdom of this world is foolishness before God. For it is written, "He is THE ONE WHO CATCHES THE WISE IN THEIR CRAFTINESS"; and again, "THE LORD KNOWS THE REASONINGS of the wise, THAT THEY ARE USELESS."

The wisdom of this world is foolishness before God = Paul is quoting Eliphaz' description of the wise politicians of the world, whose schemes are thwarted and the snares they laid for others are what they are captured in themselves (Job 5:13). This proves how foolish the world's wisdom is, since God uses their own wisdom to trap the ones who think themselves so wise.

> However crafty, or cunning, or skillful they may be; however self-confident, yet they cannot deceive or impose upon God. He can thwart their plans, overthrow their schemes, defeat their counsels, and foil them in their enterprises. He does it by their own cunning or craftiness. He allows them to involve themselves in difficulties or to entangle each other. He makes use of even their own craft and cunning to defeat their counsels. He allows the plans of one wise man to come in conflict with those of another, and thus to destroy one another. [Barnes]

Paul then quoted Psalm 94:11, adding the testimony of David to that of Eliphaz. The Lord knows the finite, limited thought processes of man fall far short of His true wisdom. In that sense, they are foolish, empty, and useless.

To the Corinthians participating in these factions (3:21-23)

1 Cor 3:21-23 So then let no one boast in men. For all things belong to you, whether Paul or Apollos or Cephas or the world or life or death or things present or things to come; all things belong to you, and you belong to Christ; and Christ belongs to God.

Let no one boast in men = This takes us back to 1 Cor 1:12, 29, 31; 3:4. It summarizes what the Corinthians were doing when they emphasized the different parties or factions within the church. "It was common among the Jews to align themselves under different leaders, such as Hillel and Shammai; and for the Greeks also to boast of being followers of Pythagoras, Zeno, or Plato. The same thing began to be manifest in the Christian church; and Paul here again rebukes and opposes it." [Barnes]

For all things belong to you = Paul gives another reason why they should not align themselves in parties or factions under different leaders. Since they shared in the common benefits of the labors of all of their ministers, and since their ministers belonged to Christ and everything belonged to God, it was improper to be split up into factions as if they had received these benefits from any one person. It is as if

Paul were saying, "For you to glory thus in men is lowering yourselves from your high position as heirs of all things. All men (including your teachers) belong to Christ, and therefore to you by your union with Him; He makes them and all things work together for your good." [JFB] If the Corinthians had focused on understanding and following what their leaders taught, rather than on how they looked or spoke, the church might have been united rather than divided. "The wealth of the Christian includes all things, all leaders, past, present, future, Christ, and God. There is no room for partisan wrangling here." [RWP]

You belong to Christ = Paul reminds them that they belong to Christ and could be considered His property. How dare they act as if they belong to someone else? "You are bound therefore, not to devote yourselves to a man, whoever he may be, but to Christ and to the service of that one true God in whose service even Christ was employed. And as Christ sought to promote the glory of his Father, so should you in all things." [Barnes]

Christian workers can till the soil, plant the seed, and tend the garden, but without God there will be no growth. Church leaders should provide the best possible spiritual nourishment for the body of Christ, rather than catering to the worldly desires of some members. A Bible that is not studied carefully or taught clearly cannot be followed accurately, and where God's Word is not followed there will be divisions in the church. We need to praise and honor God who is the source of life and the cause of all growth, and let us always remember that "We belong to Christ!" (1 Cor 3:23)

Ministers Are Stewards of God's Truth

(1 Corinthians 4:1-21)

In 1 Cor 3:5 Paul said that ministers are simply servants of God. He illustrated their role in the church as being like field hands in God's field, or as builders in God's construction project. Now Paul shares a third illustration of the role of ministers, and then he ends with a personal appeal to the Corinthians to end their divisive spirit.

An Illustration from Household Life (4:1-5)

1 Cor 4:1 Let a man regard us in this manner, as servants of Christ and stewards of the mysteries of God.

In this verse Paul gives two ways to properly regard any minister.

As servants of Christ (huperetes) = Literally this word means "under rowers." It originally referred to the men below decks who were rowing on a galley ship of that time period. It became a general term for any subordinate or worker who was obligated to carry out his master's wishes. The use of this term emphasizes the personal responsibility that each worker had to Christ alone.

As stewards of the mysteries of God = Literally the word steward (**oikonomos**) means "house ruler." This described the servant who was put in charge of the affairs of the household, and it also emphasizes the personal responsibility of that steward to the owner of the house. This steward was typically responsible for the property of the master, and in this case Paul says ministers are stewards of the **mysteries of God**. A mystery is something that can only be known through revelation. It cannot be figured out by human wisdom alone, but instead it must be revealed by God. Christ's servants have been entrusted with the treasures of God's truth, which were not previously known but were being revealed at that time to the apostles and prophets of the early church. It was their responsibility to be stewards or managers of those truths according to the instructions and desires of the Master. Ministers are called by God to be good stewards of His truth and good managers of His church. "Though they are not to be looked upon as masters of the household that have power to dispose of things in the family at their own pleasure; yet they are to be regarded as stewards, the highest officers in the house of God; to whose care are committed the secret and hidden things of God." [Gill]

1 Cor 4:2 In this case, moreover, it is required of stewards that one be found trustworthy.

Since ministers are stewards of God's treasured revelation, the primary qualification they must have is faithfulness to their Master. The first job requirement for a steward is trustworthiness. If you were going to turn over the management of all your finances to someone, you would need to have absolute trust in that individual.

You would probably also want to implement some guarantees of accountability, so that you would have a solid basis for your trust in that person.

> The apostles acted from a higher principle than a desire to please man or to be regarded as at the head of a party, and they ought to esteem them like all stewards as bound to be faithful to the master whom they served. In other offices other virtues may be particularly required, but here fidelity is demanded. This is required particularly because it is an office of trust; because the master's goods are at his disposal; because there is so much opportunity for the steward to appropriate those goods to his own use, so that his master cannot detect it. [Barnes]

1 Cor 4:3-4 But to me it is a very small thing that I may be examined by you, or by any human court; in fact, I do not even examine myself. For I am conscious of nothing against myself, yet I am not by this acquitted; but the one who examines me is the Lord.

Since human leaders are God's workmen doing whatever work He assigns them, they are responsible to God alone and human judgment is not the final authority for their actions The members of the divisions and factions in Corinth were evidently evaluating their leaders on the basis of their own preferences and choosing between them based on their own standards. This itself demonstrates that they had a wrong conception of the role of ministers.

Examined (anakrino) = This term means to investigate or conduct a preliminary examination, but not to pass the final judgment upon something.

By you = Here Paul may be saying, "As dear as you are to me, my main goal is not to have your esteem or to avoid your displeasure, but to obey my Master."

Any human court = The word "court" **(hemera)** literally means "day" (see 1 Cor 3:13), as in having your day in court. Paul's statement "might seem to look like arrogance, or appear as if he looked upon them with contempt. In order to avoid this construction of his language, he here says that it was not because he despised them, or regarded their opinion as of less value than that of others, but that he had the same feelings in regard to all people." [Barnes]

The one who examines me is the Lord = As God's steward, Paul (and every minister) is aware of the fact that he must please God alone. In effect he says here, "It is unimportant what you Corinthians think of me; it is not important what men in general think of me; it isn't even important what I think of myself!" Regarding this last point Paul says, "I do not know of anything against myself, but that does not mean I am innocent. I might be wrong, biased, deceived, or simply ignorant." He concludes by saying that the only One whose judgment counts is the Lord! "He may see evil where I see none. I would not, therefore, be self-confident; but would, with humility, refer the whole case to him. Perhaps there is here a gentle and tender reproof of the Corinthians who were so confident in their own integrity; and a gentle admonition to them to be more cautious, as it was possible that the Lord would detect faults in them where they perceived none." [Barnes]

1 Cor 4:5 Therefore do not go on passing judgment before the time, but wait until the Lord comes who will both bring to light the things hidden in the darkness and disclose the motives of men's hearts; and then each man's praise will come to him from God.

Do not go on passing judgment = Paul gives them a clear command: "Stop passing judgment, stop criticizing as they were doing. The censorious habit was ruining the Corinthian church." [RWP] They are "not to pass a harsh opinion on the conduct of any man, since there are so many things that go to make up his character which we cannot know; and so many secret failings and motives which are all concealed from us." [Barnes]

Before the time = It is as if Paul is saying, "Do not get ahead of the Lord's day of judgment (**krisis**) by your preliminary investigation (**anakrisis**) which will certainly be useless and incomplete."

The motives of men's hearts = This phrase refers to the purposes, plans, and intentions of men. All of our hidden thoughts will be made known on that Day, so no one can conceal his purposes under the scrutiny of the Lord.

Each man's praise (epainos) = This word indicates that which is due to a person as a result of his actions, after having been evaluated in light of the person's actual motives. Every person will receive justice on that day, and each one will finally be treated as he deserves to be treated.

Paul's Personal Example (4:6-21)

1 Cor 4:6 Now these things, brethren, I have figuratively applied to myself and Apollos for your sakes, so that in us you may learn not to exceed what is written, so that no one of you will become arrogant in behalf of one against the other.

Paul's argument was that the divisive spirit in Corinth was partly caused by a wrong concept of ministers, and he was one of those ministers. Here he closes his argument with a personal appeal to them to have the right attitude toward him and all of their other leaders.

Figuratively applied to myself and Apollos = Here Paul states that he used himself and Apollos to stand for all the ministers or leaders which the Corinthians were holding in high regard.

Learn not to exceed what is written = Paul wants the Corinthians to learn something from his previous discussion. When faced with dilemmas like this, Paul's standard approach is to ask, "What does the Bible say? Do not go beyond what is written in the Scriptures." Sometimes there is not a specific Bible passage that provides exactly the solution one needs, but in these cases we need to learn that we cannot always be dogmatic about the Lord's will in every situation. As one writer said, "Revere the silence of Holy Writ as much as its declarations: so you will not dogmatize on what is not expressly revealed." [JFB] We must let the Bible say what it says—

no more and no less.

Become arrogant in behalf of one against the other = This refers to their divisive spirit. When one said, "I am of Paul" they were also saying, "I am against all the others!" They were saying, "Up (**huper**) with Paul," and this Greek word means over, above, or beyond. At the same time they were implying, "Down (**kata**) with everyone else!" They were taking pride in being "for and against" something. Paul will defeat their pride by asking three pointed questions in the next verse.

1 Cor 4:7 For who regards you as superior? What do you have that you did not receive? And if you did receive it, why do you boast as if you had not received it?

Who regards you as superior? = Literally this means, "Who distinguishes you above another?" The Greek word **diakrino** means to distinguish, sift through, or separate things. Who has separated you from others, making you superior to others? Pride rests on the idea of superiority in terms of human effort or ability. So, in the next question, Paul addressed those supposed superior abilities.

What do you have that you did not receive? = What abilities or gifts do you have that do not come from God? However you obtained it, it was ultimately the gift of God. No one can say that his so-called superior abilities are really his own. He should not take credit for something that was really a gift which was given to him.

Why do you boast as if you did not receive it? = Why do you boast as if it were the result of your own effort or skill?

> A man who makes the most painful and faithful effort to obtain anything good, will trace his success to God. And he will be grateful that he was enabled to make the effort; not vain, or proud, or boastful that he was successful. This passage states a general doctrine, that the reason why one man differs from another is to be traced to God; and that this fact should repress all boasting and glorying, and produce true humility in the minds of Christians. [Barnes]

1 Cor 4:8 You are already filled, you have already become rich, you have become kings without us; and indeed, I wish that you had become kings so that we also might reign with you.

The Corinthians were acting like the masters of the house, rather than like members of the house to whom the stewards or household managers were ministering. Here Paul used sarcasm to set up a dramatic contrast between their so-called exalted position and his own lowly position as an apostle. "It is generally agreed that this is spoken in irony, and that it is an indignant sarcasm uttered against the false and self-confident teachers in Corinth. The whole passage is an instance of the most pungent and cutting sarcasm, and shows that there may be occasions when irony may be proper, though it should be rare." [Barnes]

You are already filled (korennumi) = This word occurs only here and in Acts 27:38, "And when they had eaten enough." It is usually applied to a feast, and pictures those who have stuffed themselves.

Have already become rich (plouteo) = This term means to be richly supplied or affluent in resources.

Have become kings without us (basileuo) = This phrase assumes that their coronation had already taken place.

The emphasis in these three word pictures is on the terms "already" and "without us." The implication is that the Corinthians thought they had somehow attained all they can spiritually.

> The first metaphor is taken from persons filled with food; the second from those who are so rich that they do not feel their lack of more; the third from those who are raised to a throne, the highest elevation, where there was nothing further to be reached or desired. And the phrase means that they had been fully satisfied with their condition and attainments, with their knowledge and power, that they lived like rich men and princes—reveling, as it were, in spiritual enjoyments, and disdaining all foreign influence, and instruction, and control. [Barnes]

It is as if Paul is saying, "You did not feel the need for our involvement, and you did not regard our authority. You supposed you could get along as well without us as with us."

I wish you had become kings = The implication is, "I wish it were so, but it is not!" They were so puffed up and satisfied with their own favorite teachers and their own spiritual attainments, that they feel like those filled full at a feast, or as a rich man priding himself in his riches. "Paul here drops the irony and addresses them in a sober, earnest manner. It is the expression of a wish that they were as truly happy and blessed as they thought themselves to be." [Barnes]

1 Cor 4:9 For, I think, God has exhibited us apostles last of all, as men condemned to death; because we have become a spectacle to the world, both to angels and to men.

This introduces a direct contrast: "You have become kings, but the case is very different with us."

Last of all = Paul seems to be saying, "Apparently God has put us apostles at the end of your victory procession, like those under a sentence of death, to show us off as spectacles of shame to the world and to angels and to men." [Boyer]

Condemned to death = This probably refers to the practice of placing condemned criminals in the amphitheater to fight with wild beasts or with one another as gladiators. "The gladiators, on entering the arena, saluted the presiding officer with the words, 'We who are to die greet you.' The vast range of an amphitheater under the open sky well represents the magnificent vision of all created things, from men up to angels, gazing on the dreadful death struggle; and then the contrast of the selfish Corinthians sitting by unconcerned and unmoved by the awful spectacle." [VWS]

Become a spectacle (theatron) = Literally this means, "a theatrical spectacle." This illustration is from the Roman amphitheaters where exhibitions were put on display for the pleasure of the spectators. "Criminals condemned to die in Paul's time were exhibited as a gazing-stock to amuse the populace in the amphitheater. They were 'set forth last' in the show to fight with wild beasts." [JFB]

1 Cor 4:10 We are fools for Christ's sake, but you are prudent in Christ; we are weak, but you are strong; you are distinguished, but we are without honor.

These three contrasts are in the areas of knowledge, ability, and worldly position:

– **We are fools, you are prudent (phronimos)** = This word means sagacious, clever, enlightened.
– **We are weak (asthenes), you are strong (ischuros)** = These words mean without strength or impotent vs. forceful and mighty.
– **You are distinguished (endoxos), we are without honor (atimos)** = These terms mean 'in glory,' held in esteem vs. without value/worth/dignity, despised, looked down upon.

One commentator described the situation in the following words:

The whole design of this irony is to show the folly of their boasted wisdom. That they should be wise and prudent, and the apostles fools, was in the highest degree absurd; and he puts this absurdity in a strong light by his irony. The very reverse was probably true. Paul was bold, daring, fearless in declaring the truth, whatever opposition it might encounter; and probably many of them were timid and time-serving, and endeavoring to avoid persecution, and to accommodate themselves to the prejudices and opinions of those who were wise in their own sight; the prejudices and opinions of the world. [Barnes]

1 Cor 4:11-13 To this present hour we are both hungry and thirsty, and are poorly clothed, and are roughly treated, and are homeless; and we toil, working with our own hands; when we are reviled, we bless; when we are persecuted, we endure; when we are slandered, we try to conciliate; we have become as the scum of the world, the dregs of all things, even until now.

Here Paul drops the irony and begins a serious description of his actual sufferings and trials. These hardships were still continuing and they were to be regarded as a normal part of the life of an apostle.

Scum of the world (perikatharmata) = This term means to cleanse all around, or that which is thrown off by cleansing, like refuse or trash. It indicates something that is collected by sweeping a house, or that is cast away after purifying or cleansing anything. "It would not be possible to employ stronger expressions to denote the contempt and scorn with which they were regarded." [Barnes]

Dregs of all things (peripsema) = Literally this word means "scraping around." It denotes garbage or dirt that is rubbed off of something.

1 Cor 4:14-16 I do not write these things to shame you, but to admonish you as my beloved children. For if you were to have countless tutors in Christ, yet you would not have many fathers, for in Christ Jesus I became your father through the gospel. Therefore I exhort you, be imitators of me.

Paul follows harsh words with tenderness and encouragement so the Corinthians will follow his fatherly example.

I do not write = Paul is saying that it was not his intention to put them to shame by showing how little they suffered in comparison with him. He did not desire to ridicule them or to mock them. His purpose was much higher and nobler.

> I speak as a father to his children, and I say these things for your good. No father would desire to make his children ashamed. In his counsels, entreaties, and admonitions, he would have a higher object than that. No man, no minister, ought to reprove another merely to overwhelm him with shame, but the object should always be to make a brother better. [Barnes]

To shame you (entrepo) = Literally, to turn in upon oneself in shame.

To admonish you (noutheteo) = This word means to put something into the mind, with the purpose of gently correcting the person.

Countless tutors, but one father = All the subsequent teachers in Corinth should be considered as merely tutors or instructors, because only Paul could be considered their spiritual father. He was the one who was used by God initially to bring them to Christ. He was the instrument of their conversion.

Be imitators of me (mimetes) = This phrase literally means to keep on becoming imitators (present middle imperative). "Probably Paul had particularly in his eye their tendency to form parties; and here admonishes them that he had no disposition to form sects, and entreats them in this to imitate his example. A minister should always so live as that he can, without pride or ostentation, point to his own example and entreat his people to imitate him." [Barnes]

1 Cor 4:17 For this reason I have sent to you Timothy, who is my beloved and faithful child in the Lord, and he will remind you of my ways which are in Christ, just as I teach everywhere in every church.

For this reason = Paul's purpose was that they might be better imitators of him and more obedient to his instructions.

Timothy = Timothy was very dear to Paul as a companion and co-worker. Timothy was also a Christian minister proven to be trustworthy over his years of service with Paul.

Remind you of my ways = To remind means to bring up before the mind. "Way" (**hodos**) meant a well-traveled road, and also by implication a habitual course of conduct; a way of thinking, feeling, and deciding.

As I teach everywhere in every church = Timothy (as Paul's spokesman) will remind the Corinthians of Paul's teachings, the doctrines or truths of the faith which Paul shared everywhere he went. A large part of the work of a minister is teaching the Word of God, because people cannot come to believe and practice truths that they do not know. "This was designed probably to show them that he taught them no new or special doctrines; he wished them simply to conform to the common rules of the churches, and to be like their Christian brethren everywhere." [Barnes]

1 Cor 4:18-19 Now some have become arrogant, as though I were not coming to you. But I will come to you soon, if the Lord wills, and I shall find out, not the words of those who are arrogant but their power.

Paul now warns of his coming with discipline and rebuke. Some of the Corinthians might think that he is sending Timothy because he does not want to face them himself. Arrogance is a key result of having a divisive spirit within the church. Where there is arrogance, there is a real problem.

> Probably he had been detained by the demand on his services in other places, and by various providential hindrances from going there, until they supposed that he stayed away from fear. And possibly he might apprehend that they would think he had sent Timothy because he was afraid to come himself. Their conduct was an instance of the haughtiness and arrogance which people will assume when they suppose they are in no danger of reproof or punishment. [Barnes]

But I will come = Paul promises that he will visit them as soon as the Lord allows.

I will know (ginosko) = This phrase means, "I will fully understand and (by implication) I will put to the test."

Not the words = Paul was not concerned about their high-sounding speech or their philosophical rhetoric. Talk is cheap, but the question is whether they will be able to stand up to the exercise of God's apostolic authority wielded by the apostle Paul.

But their power (dunamis) = This word means the inherent power in something by virtue of its basic nature; the quality of the soul and the reach of its influence. "Faith that does not result in right living may have many words to support it, but it will have no power. A person's true spiritual character is not determined by the impressiveness of his words but by the power of his life." [MacArthur]

1 Cor 4:20-21 For the kingdom of God does not consist in words but in power. What do you desire? Shall I come to you with a rod, or with love and a spirit of gentleness?

Kingdom of God (basilea) = This seems to be presented as a contrast with 1 Cor 4:8 where Paul had said the Corinthians had become kings (**basileuo**), that they had assumed the throne. Here he contrasted that with the true kingdom (**basileia**). God's kingdom will not consist of empty speeches, but the demonstrated power of the Holy Spirit. It is the powerful rule or reign of God, and God's power or authority was to be exercised in the government and discipline of the church.

What do you desire? = Whether Paul responds in tenderness or strictness is totally up to them. He will come, either as a stern disciplinarian or as their loving father in the Lord. "If you do not heed my exhortations or the labors of Timothy, if you still continue your contentions and do not remove the occasions of offense, I shall come with severity and the language of rebuke." [Barnes] When a Christian slips into wrong behavior or wrong doctrine, he needs to be corrected. He needs to be told in love, but with firmness, that his Christian life is not what it should be or that he is not acting on the principles he has already learned. Such confrontations are never easy, but they are sometimes necessary.

Ministers should be faithful. We should regard ministers as the servants of Jesus Christ, honor them for their Master's sake, and respect them for their faithfulness in their work. What the world thinks is of little importance. It is a good thing for ministers to have a unblemished reputation (Prov 22:1), but it should not be their main focus. As desirable as it is to have a good name, the opinion of the world is not to be valued too highly. Even the admiration of friends should not be the focus of our efforts. It is not nearly as valuable as the approval of God.

All that we have (beauty, health, wealth, honor, grace) has been given to us by God. We should constantly remember this fact and express our gratefulness to Him. We should certainly not be proud of what we have, as if we received it by our own efforts. We have nothing to boast about in ourselves.

Irony and sarcasm are sometimes necessary tools for expression (1Cor 4:8-10), but they are not as safe for us to use as they were for the apostle Paul under the inspiration of the Holy Spirit. Very few people can use sarcasm properly, and so very few people should allow themselves to indulge in it. Sarcasm is rarely used in the Bible, and it is hardly ever used in real life where it does not do some kind of harm. "The cause of truth can be usually sustained by sound argument, and that which cannot be thus defended is not worth defense." [Barnes]

In this passage we have seen a wonderful example of the way that ministers can endure reproach, contempt, and scorn (1Cor 4:12-13). The apostles imitated the example of their Master and followed His precepts. They prayed for their enemies, and there is nothing but true spirituality that can produce this kind of response.

Failure to Deal with Sin in the Church

(1 Corinthians 5:1-13)

The first consideration for studying this chapter is to determine how this new subject is connected with the previous comments that Paul has made. There are several key words and concepts that appear in both sections. Specifically, the subjects of arrogance and boasting are continued in chapter five. In first Corinthians chapter four, Paul had just described the arrogance of the Corinthians which was a major component of their divisive spirit (1 Cor 4:6, 18, 19). Here Paul provides a specific instance of their arrogant attitude, in this case regarding the sin of one of their members. Also in 1 Cor 1:29, 31; 3:21; and 4:7 Paul spoke about their boasting, first in their own human achievements and then in the supposed superiority of their teachers or leaders. Now in this new chapter Paul will continue to discuss their boastful arrogance as it applied to their tolerance of one member who was living in gross immorality.

The Sin of One Believer (5:1)

1 Cor 5:1 It is actually reported that there is immorality among you, and immorality of such a kind as does not exist even among the Gentiles, that someone has his father's wife.

The fact that this sin was being tolerated in Corinth might point to the influence of an "antinomian" group within one of the Corinthian sects or parties. They may have claimed Paul as their leader because he might be considered the best advocate for Christian liberty. But Paul would never have approved of taking Christian liberty to the extreme of justifying known sin because a believer is "free in Christ." See Gal 5:13 for Paul's early comments on liberty vs. license. Salvation brings freedom from sin, but not freedom to sin.

The term "antinomian" comes from **anti** (against) and **nomos** (the law). It is the idea that since a Christian is saved by grace rather than by works, then he is free from all moral obligations and principles. It says that a believer can live any way he chooses because he has been forgiven by God. But this is contrary to the New Testament admonitions to "live holy lives" (see 1 Pet 1:16), and it is exactly the type of antinomianism that Paul rejects here as well as in Galatians and Romans. This antinomian attitude was practiced by many different philosophical sects. They believed there was a broad gulf between the physical and the spiritual, that physical matter was corrupt and irrelevant, so sensual desires could be freely indulged. In fact many sects encouraged this so that the spiritual would shine brighter by comparison. One pagan Gnostic leader said: "Give to the flesh the things of the flesh, and to the spirit the things of the spirit." You can just imagine the apostle Paul's reaction against such a statement!

In this verse Paul described the specific situation that existed in the Corinthian church. Literally he says, "It is generally or everywhere heard." The whole community (and possibly the whole region) would have heard that this situation existed within the Corinthian church, so the reputation of the church at large was being affected.

There is immorality (porneia) among you = This is a general term for forbidden sexual intercourse of several kinds. At the end of the verse Paul gives some additional details when he says that someone among the believers **"has his father's wife."** Literally he said, "For one to go on having a wife of his father." The present tense indicates this was not a single incident, but an ongoing relationship. The phrase "father's wife" indicates that it was not his own mother. There is some debate about the actual situation implied by this description, but whatever the case the Corinthians knew exactly what Paul was referring to. It could be that the believer's father had died or divorced his wife (who was probably the believer's step-mother), and afterward the son and the step-mother either were married or living together.

Does not exist even among the Gentiles = This type of sexual relationship was forbidden in the Old Testament Scriptures (Lev 18:7-8), and it was also a violation of the standards of the pagan community.

> This greatly aggravated the offense, that in a Christian church a crime should be tolerated among its members which even gross pagans would regard with abhorrence. That this offense was regarded with abhorrence by even the pagans has been abundantly proved by quotations from classic writers. Cicero says expressly that 'it was an incredible and unheard of crime.' When Paul says that it was not 'so much as named among the Gentiles,' he doubtless uses the word (**onomazetai**) in the sense of 'named with approbation, tolerated, or allowed.' The crime was known in a few instances, but chiefly of those who were princes and rulers; but it was nowhere regarded with approbation, but was always treated as abominable wickedness. [Barnes]

It is likely that the man's step-mother was not a believer, because the apostle Paul only addressed the sin of the Christian man who was involved. This described the specific sin of the individual believer, but now Paul goes on to discuss the sin of the church.

The Sin of the Church (5:2)

1 Cor 5:2 You have become arrogant and have not mourned instead, so that the one who had done this deed would be removed from your midst.

Instead of mourning over this sin and excluding the brother from church fellowship until he repented, the Corinthians were puffed up. This toleration for an obvious sin was another example of their arrogant and boastful attitude, and it was probably directly related to the divisive spirit within the church. Even if an antinomian sect within the church was not actually boasting of its toleration of this sin, at the very least the church was continuing to be puffed up in spite of an obvious sin in their midst. "The Corinthians were proud and boastful of their wisdom, their knowledge, their spiritual gifts, and even this terrible situation had not punctured their pride." [Boyer]

The spiritually mature response to this situation would have been to grieve over this shameful immoral situation. They should have mourned as over the dead, but they did not do this nor had they taken any action to remove the sinner from their midst. In their prideful state, they saw nothing worthy of grief or correction.

Correcting the Sinning Believer (5:3-5)

1 Cor 5:3 For I, on my part, though absent in body but present in spirit, have already judged him who has so committed this, as though I were present.

This is a direct contrast with the previous verse. "You may be puffed up, but I take a completely different view." Paul is absent from them physically, but all his spiritual and mental energy is presently focused on them and their problems. "Neither Paul's capacity nor his authority to judge, nor his power to execute his judgment depended on his bodily presence. He was present in spirit." [Hodge]

Have already judged (krino) = This term means to pronounce an opinion concerning right and wrong; to give a verdict in court. Is this a contradiction with what Paul said in 1 Cor 4:5? In that context Paul was dealing with the Corinthians' passing judgment on the leaders of the different divisions within the church, not regarding any sin but in regard to their own personal opinions of their giftedness for leadership. There Paul stated that God alone is qualified to judge and reward a minister's internal motives and his faithfulness to his assigned tasks. But here the context makes it clear that the leaders of the church have the right and the authority to make judgments in cases of obvious sin in members of the church. The situations are very different in these two contexts. Paul's words could be paraphrased as, "I have made up my mind; have decided, and do decide. That is, he had determined what ought to be done in the case. It was a case in which the course which ought to be pursued was plain, and on this point his mind was settled." [Barnes]

1 Cor 5:4-5 In the name of our Lord Jesus, when you are assembled, and I with you in spirit, with the power of our Lord Jesus, I have decided to deliver such a one to Satan for the destruction of his flesh, so that his spirit may be saved in the day of the Lord Jesus.

By the authority vested in him as an apostle, Paul pronounced his judgment regarding the sin of this believer, and he went on to ask the church to enforce this judgment at their next meeting. Paul's first concern is for the salvation of the erring member, as well as for the purity of the church.

Deliver such a one to Satan = This is an unusually strong phrase if it was intended as a synonym for putting him out of the church fellowship. There are two possible interpretations:

1. It simply means excommunication from church fellowship. Since Satan rules in the sphere outside the church (see 1 John 5:19), then to be delivered to Satan is to be put out of the church into the realm where Satan rules.

2. It involves the additional visitation of physical sickness or even death. Physical afflictions are sometimes attributed to Satan, and the spiritual benefits of such afflictions are sometimes described in Scripture. Simple excommunication would not seem to have the effect of destroying the flesh, so something more may be intended by this expression.

For the destruction of his flesh (sarx) = This typically means the fallen human nature, but from Paul's earlier reference this will not happen until the time when each believer receives an incorruptible resurrection body. The flesh will not be destroyed in this life, indicating that Paul may be referring to the affliction of the physical body or the death of this individual. "If a man was handed over to Satan it was not that Satan might have his way with him, but with a view to his ultimate salvation. Satan in fact was being used as a tool in the interests of Christ and the church. Satan's power, though limited, was real. He would destroy the offender's flesh. Suffering at least is meant, probably death. This dreadful process is intended to lead to the salvation of the man's spirit." [Hodge] In 1 Cor 11:30 Paul also mentions a case of discipline which leads to death, with the ultimate goal being the salvation of the individual there as well.

So that = The purpose for this punishment was the ultimate salvation of his spirit. It is implied that Paul was also hoping for his repentance and restoration to fellowship.

Correcting the Sinning Church (5:6-8)

1 Cor 5:6 Your boasting is not good. Do you not know that a little leaven leavens the whole lump of dough?

Boasting (kauchema) = This term does not refer to the act of boasting, but to the subject or content of their boastful words. They were boasting in their so-called exalted status as a church, their achievements and those of their favorite teachers, but there was a major blemish on their character and reputation.

A little leaven leavens the whole lump = In Gal 5:9 Paul had quoted this as a proverb that was commonly known. But in the following verses, Paul builds an extensive illustration which draws pictures from the Old Testament Jewish ritual of the Passover and the Feast of Unleavened Bread that was celebrated immediately after the Passover. We must realize that this is merely an illustration Paul used to make his point. In no way is Paul saying that Christians should continue to observe these Jewish rituals. Instead, he used this well-known Old Testament practice as an analogy to illustrate his point about the pervasiveness of sin. Even a little bit of yeast will permeate the entire lump of dough, just as a small virus can infect the entire body. Church discipline of sinning believers should be based on the same principle.

1 Cor 5:7 Clean out the old leaven so that you may be a new lump, just as you are in fact unleavened. For Christ our Passover also has been sacrificed.

Here Paul saw the Passover lamb as a picture of Christ's sacrifice to accomplish our deliverance from sin. He draws a lesson from the Feast of Unleavened Bread, when for seven days the Jews ate nothing but bread made without yeast. Their law required that they remove all leavening or fermenting agents from the entire household (see Deut 16:3-4). Jewish sources describe the meticulous search which was made to guarantee that no leaven was present in the house. Leaven represents the overt sin which Paul had just described within the Corinthian church. So, based on the illustration of the Jewish practice of cleansing the household, Paul commands the Corinthian church to remove the old leaven (the sinning believer) from their midst. **A new lump** = They are to make a fresh start as a community with the contamination removed.

They are unleavened = The command (imperative) in this verse is based on a statement of fact (indicative). The Lord had freed them from bondage to sin through His death, burial, and resurrection. Because this is an established fact, they should avoid sin and strive to live in a way which will please their Lord. In position, they were unleavened; now they should make their practice correspond to their position. They should strive to be what they already are. The imperative is impossible without the indicative. The command could not be accomplished if it were not based on the facts concerning what Christ had already accomplished on their behalf.

Christ our Passover has been sacrificed = Jesus already accomplished His work, so it is possible for us to obey His commands. Paul is also saying that the Lamb was already slain (Passover), but they have not yet removed the leaven that was a prerequisite for Passover!

1 Cor 5:8 Therefore let us celebrate the feast, not with old leaven, nor with the leaven of malice and wickedness, but with the unleavened bread of sincerity and truth.

Here Paul concludes his illustration by urging the church to "celebrate the feast," that is, they should live the Christian life in light of Christ's finished work. As the Jews would only celebrate their feast after accomplishing all the required preparations, in the same way the church should take the required action to remove the sinning believer from their fellowship.

Let us keep on keeping the feast = This present active subjunctive implies a perpetual feast, as well as an admonition to continue keeping the leaven out.

Not with old leaven = Not under the influence of the feelings of the corrupt and unrenewed human nature. The word leaven is very descriptive of our old condition, and it refers to the corrupt and self-seeking passions of our old nature.

Malice (kakias, evil in general) and wickedness (porneia) = These two words represent all evil, and especially the specific case of the sexual sin of the Corinthian believer.

Illustration	Application
A little leaven leavens the whole lump	Leaven = sin (especially the specific case of immorality Paul mentioned). One sin contaminates the church: 1) the reputation of the whole church is damaged; 2) sin that is tolerated can be imitated by other believers.
Clean out the old leaven	Remove the sinning believer from fellowship with the church.
You may be a new lump	Restore your reputation as an uncontaminated church.
Just as you are in fact unleavened	Positionally, God already sees them as holy.
Christ our Passover has been sacrificed	Jesus has already accomplished everything that was required to make it possible for the church to obey His commands and pursue holiness.
Therefore let us celebrate the feast	Let the church live the Christian life in light of Christ's finished work.
Not with old leaven	Not under the influence of the old nature; not continuing to indulge the passions of the flesh (specifically malice and wickedness).
But with the unleavened things	With holiness of life that when held up to the light is found to be pure.

Sincerity and truth = In contrast to evil, they should exhibit sincere purity based on doctrinal truth, discipline, and holy living. The Greek word for "sincerity" literally means a thing which, when examined by the sun's light, is found to be pure and unadulterated. "Paul's purpose in using this paschal imagery is clear: the sacrifice has been offered, potentially Christians are participating in a feast which involves perfect purity of character and conduct, and they must make every effort to realize this potentiality." [Barrett] The chart on the next page summarizes the truths taught in this illustration.

Paul Clarifies His Previous Instructions (5:9-13)

1 Cor 5:9 I wrote you in my letter not to associate with immoral people.

Here we learn that Paul had written at least one previous letter to the church at Corinth. The only thing we know about the content of that letter is that Paul instructed them not to associate with immoral people. "The discipline God commands

His church to take against the unrepentant is to be of a certain kind and should be exercised within certain bounds." [MacArthur]

Not to associate (sunanamignumi) = Literally this means, "to mingle together up and down among." It means not only close association, but continual or habitual contact. This was the same instruction Paul had earlier given to the Thessalonian church for dealing with a few insubordinate or unruly believers there (2 Th 3:14).

Immoral people (poneros) = This means those who indulge in forbidden sexual intercourse. This phrase could mean not to associate with immoral people in any social interaction or specifically in the context of fellowship among believers within the church. Paul will now clarify which of these two options he intended when he wrote to them previously, because they had obviously misunderstood him. This tells us that the reader of Scripture cannot determine his own meaning for the text of the Bible. Paul had a specific meaning in mind when he wrote to the Corinthians, and he will take great pains to clear up their misunderstanding. Scripture should be carefully interpreted in order to ensure we give the text the meaning it was intended to have.

1 Cor 5:10 I did not at all mean with the immoral people of this world, or with the covetous and swindlers, or with idolaters, for then you would have to go out of the world.

Here Paul clarifies his previous instructions. **Negatively**, Paul did not mean they should avoid any immoral person in the entire world. He used the same word **(poneros)** to indicate those engaging in forbidden sexual intercourse. Then he added several other categories of sinful behavior to show that his prohibition was not limited to the sexually immoral. He included the covetous (one who is greedy for gain, especially that which belongs to others), swindlers (extortioners, robbers, hijackers, or con artists), idolaters (one who worships or sacrifices to false gods—as strange as it seems, it is possible for a professing Christian to engage in idolatry—see 1 John 5:21). Paul could have named many more sins!

Here Paul is saying that a Christian would need to leave this world in order to avoid any association with sinful people. "The attempt to get out of the world, in violation of God's will that believers should remain in it but keep themselves from its evil, led to monasticism and its consequent evils." [JFB] Evidently some of the Corinthians had taken Paul's instruction "not to associate with immoral people" to mean that they should have no association with any immoral or wicked person inside the church or outside in the world. Since they thought this was an impossible assignment they simply ignored it and considered Paul's teaching to be ridiculous.

1 Cor 5:11 But actually, I wrote to you not to associate with any so-called brother if he is an immoral person, or covetous, or an idolater, or a reviler, or a drunkard, or a swindler--not even to eat with such a one.

Positively, Paul had intended to communicate that they should not associate with any fellow believer who was engaging in any of these sinful practices.

If any man that is named a brother = This includes any person who is being named as a believer, that is a professing Christian within the church fellowship. The Greek sentence is a third class conditional clause, which indicates there is a possibility of it being true. It is neither definitely true or false, but it is possible that this situation could occur. A believer could possibly engage in the kinds of sinful activities that are mentioned in this verse.

Paul repeats **immoral (poneros)**, **covetous**, **swindler**, and **idolater**. He also adds **reviler** (one who is a railer or is verbally abusive) and **drunkard** (one addicted to alcoholic drink).

Not even to eat with such a one = This says they were not to take food in company with (**sunesthio**) someone like this.

> The instructions are hardly explicit enough to become the basis of a legalistic procedure. The principle, however, is clear. The tense used indicates a continuing relationship. They were not to continue in social fellowship with the offender. But the treatment is to be severe and absolute, even to the point of refusing to continue eating with him. If an offending Christian brother should be subjected to this treatment, so cut off from all ordinary social fellowship with his Christian brothers even to the extent that they refuse to eat with him, that would exert tremendous pressure on him to amend his ways. [Boyer]

Paul's instructions clearly differentiate between the believers' contact with the unsaved in the world vs. their contact with those in the church fellowship who are acting like unbelievers. It is clear that the unsaved have only the old, sinful, fallen nature. But believers have the new, spiritual nature that exists alongside their old nature. They have the potential to live in such a way as to please their Lord, even though they sometimes do not do this. Paul's instructions imply that a believer who lives like an unbeliever is a contradiction, that there is something wrong in that situation, and it should be dealt with accordingly. If a believer acts like a non-Christian, he should no longer be treated as a Christian.

This may seem like we are to treat sinning believers more harshly than we are to treat the sinners out in the world. But that is because a believer who lives in habitual sin is a contradiction, and this contradiction must be dealt with differently. A true believer cannot go back through the "turnstile" on the cross; he cannot give back his new nature. He must be admonished to live in keeping with his new nature, rather than his old nature. Paul will now explain that the church has a responsibility to help fellow believers to realize this fact.

1 Cor 5:12-13 For what have I to do with judging outsiders? Do you not judge those who are within the church? But those who are outside, God judges. REMOVE THE WICKED MAN FROM AMONG YOURSELVES.

Judging outsiders (krino) = This word means to pass a sentence of judgment. The leaders of the church have no jurisdiction over the sinners of the world. They are not meant to sit in judgment on the unsaved in this world. All of the rules of the church apply only to those who are within the church.

Do you not judge those within? = The Christians' jurisdiction is over those who are within the church and are professing to be members of the body of Christ. He will have more to say about this later. "Paul here gives an anticipatory censure of their going to law with saints before heathen tribunals, instead of judging such causes among themselves within." [JFB]

God judges those outside = It is clear that the unsaved are going to be judged, but it is not the role of the church to accomplish that judgment in this present age. It is God who will judge the world.

> Those who are unconnected with the church are under the direct and special government of God. They are indeed sinners, and they deserve punishment for their crimes. But it is not ours to pronounce sentence upon them or to inflict punishment. God will do that. Our province is in regard to the church. We are to judge these and these alone. All others we are to leave entirely in the hands of God. [Barnes]

Remove the wicked man from among yourselves = The word remove (**exairo**) means to put out away from. This command seems to echo several Old Testament commands to "purge the evil from your midst" (Deut 17:7; 19:19; 22:21,24; 24:7).

This section of Paul's letter to the Corinthians shows the proper method and attitude for church discipline of a sinning believer. It should not be done with harshness, bitterness, revenge, or persecution. Rather, it should be done with tenderness toward the offender, with deep grief that the reputation of the church has been affected, and with such an awareness of the impact of sin that it leads to prompt action. The responsibility to discipline a sinning believer belongs to the church alone. The church at Corinth was to deal with the matter in its regular meetings. But it was not to act simply as an exercise of raw power. It was to act in humility and compassion, which would hopefully lead to the repentance of the member.

> Faithful believers are not to keep close company with any fellow believers who persistently practice serious sins such as those mentioned here. If the offenders will not listen to the counsel and warning of two or three other believers and not even to the whole church, they are to be put out of the fellowship. They should not be allowed to participate in any activities of the church. If he is a true believer he will not lose his salvation because of the sin, but he is to lose contact with fellow believers, in order not to corrupt them with his wickedness and to suffer the consequences of his sin. The pain of such isolation may drive the person to repentance. No church is healthy enough to resist contamination from persistent sin in its midst, any more than the healthiest and most nutritious bushel of apples can withstand contamination from a single rotten one. The only solution in both cases is separation. [MacArthur]

In this chapter we also learned how believers are to respond to those outside the church. This is a difficult issue, and Christians often feel they are in danger of being contaminated by the world. In reaction, they often want to withdraw almost entirely from the world. Believers often ask, "Where do we draw the line?" Here Paul tells us that we are not to withdraw from contact with the people of this world. We are to live in the world, but we are not to be worldly. We should act righteously toward every person, no matter what his status, character, or beliefs. We are not to be conformed to the world, though. We are not to do anything that would give the impression we belong to the world. And we are not to do anything that gives an unfavorable impression of the church, the gospel, or the Savior.

This chapter also tells us that God will be the final judge the world. Those who are outside the domain of church will ultimately give an account to God. They are constantly moving toward His courtroom, and He will pronounce their doom. This should motivate us to share the gospel with them as if we are throwing them a life preserver while they are traveling toward the edge of a powerful waterfall.

Lawsuits? And What About Sexual Purity?

(1 Corinthians 6:1-20)

As we did with the last section, it is important to determine how this new chapter is connected with the previous comments that Paul has made in First Corinthians. Again, there is no specific transition or connecting word as Paul begins this section. He seems to abruptly start talking about believers engaging in lawsuits with one another in the secular courts. Here the connection is based on the subject of judging which Paul dealt with specifically in chapter five. He spoke about the responsibility of the church to judge sinning believers (1 Cor 5:3, 12), but to leave the judgment of unbelievers to God (1 Cor 5:13). In chapter six Paul will explain another failure of the church to deal with the differences and disputes within the Corinthian congregation.

The location of this instruction is important. It occurs within the larger section which discusses immoral behavior within the church. Since there is no break in the context throughout these opening chapters of First Corinthians, the sin Paul talks about here should be considered right alongside those discussed beforehand and afterwards. Paul had included covetousness in his list of sins in the church (1 Cor 5:10-11; 6:9-10), and that may be the cause for believers bringing their disputes into the secular courts. In any case, what Paul addressed here was another symptom of the divisive spirit within the Corinthian church. The church was quickly losing its testimony in the city of Corinth. Not only did the unsaved know about the specific sin of the sexually immoral believer, but they were also aware of the lawsuits involving members of the church.

Lawsuits Among Believers Within the Church (6:1)

Here Paul discusses the Corinthians' practice of settling their non-criminal property cases before the Roman law courts.

1 Cor 6:1 Does any one of you, when he has a case against his neighbor, dare to go to law before the unrighteous and not before the saints?

Has a case against his neighbor = Paul does not give any specifics of the cases that were brought by believers against each other, but because of the close connection with chapter five it is possible that a lawsuit could have arisen over the events surrounding the believer who had his father's wife (1 Cor 5:1). There were obviously other kinds of lawsuits between believers, too. "The Greeks were known for their involvement in the courts. The Greek playwright Aristophanes has one of his characters look at a map and ask where Greece is located. When it is pointed out to him, he replies that there must be some mistake because he cannot see any lawsuits going on!" [Wiersbe]

Dare to go to law = To dare (**tolmao**) meant to bear oneself boldly. They were showing a bold arrogance by taking their disputes before the secular courts. The fact that they were doing this tells us about the severity of the contention and strife within the church. It was of the type that usually calls for arbitration by a third party.

Before the unrighteous and not before the saints = The word unrighteous means the ungodly, unsaved, or non-Christians. The saints are those consecrated and set apart as belonging to God, believers, or Christians. By using the word unrighteous Paul does not mean that the Roman courts were unjust, because he himself had benefited from them. But believers are in a sad state when they think they are more likely to get justice from unbelievers than from their own brothers.

> In speaking of Christians taking other Christians to court, Paul does not specify any criminal cases, for he teaches elsewhere that these, along with any punitive penalties, must be handled by the state (Rom 13:1-7). The legal cases referred to here, therefore, include different kinds of property cases. In this way, he allows for the possibility that under some circumstances Christians might take cases to the secular courts. Paul himself, who had received his Roman citizenship according to Roman law, appealed to the courts—to the Roman commander (Acts 22:25-29), to the governor (Acts 23:27; 24:20-21), and to the emperor (Acts 25:4-12)—to establish his right to a proper trial and proper treatment as a Roman citizen (Acts 16:37-39). In modern life this biblical principle allows for church cases to be brought into civil courts to determine the extent of the rights of the congregation, as for example their right to own and retain their own church property. What concerned Paul was that the Corinthians were failing to exercise their prerogative in settling non-criminal cases themselves. [ZNBC]

It seems that some of the members of the church were acting viciously in trying to get their own way, and they were using the Roman court system to do this.

Believers are qualified to arbitrate their own disputes (6:2-11)

1 Cor 6:2 Or do you not know that the saints will judge the world? If the world is judged by you, are you not competent to constitute the smallest law courts?

Do you not know = This phrase appears six times in this chapter (1 Cor 6:2, 3, 9, 15, 16, 19), and the implication is that the Corinthians should have known all of these truths that Paul is going to share, and that this would have helped to prevent the problems they were now experiencing. Paul had probably taught these truths during the course of his ministry in Corinth, since he states them as undeniable facts.

Saints will judge the world = The fact that believers will have a role in the government of the millennial kingdom had been implied in the Old Testament (see Dan 7:22) as well as in the New Testament (see Matt 19:28; 2 Tim 2:12; Rev 2:26-27; 20:4). In 1 Cor 5:12 Paul had stated that the church was not to judge the world during the church age. That was a task which God Himself would accomplish. But that statement appeared in the context of judgment during this present age. Here Paul states that believers will have a part in the future judgment of the world. This seems to refer to the role of believers during the millennial kingdom.

Are you not competent to constitute the smallest law courts? = Paul's implication is that you who will judge the world in the future should be capable of deciding relatively trivial cases among yourselves now

1 Cor 6:3 Do you not know that we will judge angels? How much more matters of this life?

We will judge angels = We know from Jude 1:6 and 2 Peter 2:4, 9 that angels will be judged, but here we learn that believers somehow will be involved in that process. This was a truth that the Corinthians already knew, but which may be new to the readers of this letter today. "We probably should understand that the apostle Paul had taught this truth when he was with them." [Boyer]

Matters of this life (biotikos) = Literally this means "things of this life" or matters pertaining to one's livelihood. In the Egyptian papyri discovered by archaeologists this word refers to business matters. This important word tells us exactly what kind of lawsuits the believers were bringing against each other. They were not spiritual or religious in nature, but they had to do with money and property. This helps us understand why Paul had included covetousness in his lists of sins. Paul argues from the greater to the lesser when he says that the saints ought to be able to judge these smaller matters.

1 Cor 6:4 So if you have law courts dealing with matters of this life, do you appoint them as judges who are of no account in the church?

Appoint them as judges (kathizo) = The form of this verb can be either a statement (indicative) or a command (imperative). The NIV translates it as a command, while the NASB translates it as a statement in the form of a question. If it is a command, then "those of no account" would refer to men in the church who are not regarded as being very wise. But this seems to be contrary to what Paul states in verse five, that it does require a wise man to arbitrate between believers.

If it is a question, then "those of no account" would refer to men who are not accounted as members of the church (the "unrighteous" of verse 1, the "unbelievers" of verse 6). This seems to be the best way to translate the phrase. As one commentator explained, "Paul does not belittle the secular courts here. There is not one word of criticism or disrespect for the courts of the land. On other occasions Paul himself had appeared before these courts, and on several occasions was benefited by them. What he is condemning here is the practice of Christians taking Christians before secular or outside courts." [Boyer]

1 Cor 6:5-6 I say this to your shame. Is it so, that there is not among you one wise man who will be able to decide between his brethren, but brother goes to law with brother, and that before unbelievers?

I say this to your shame = It is a shameful thing that believers were taking their minor disputes before the secular courts. Is it possible that in a church which boasted of its great wisdom they could not find one of their own members to help settle their disputes?

Decide between (diakrino) = This word means to arbitrate a dispute. Instead of referring the matter to the arbitration of another believer, they were taking their cases into the secular courts. If their disputes needed arbitration, they should find a Christian wise enough to handle them rather than opposing each other in secular litigation. "That there should be disputes about **biotika** is bad; that Christian should go to law with Christian is worse; that Christians should do this before unbelievers is worst of all." [RWP]

1 Cor 6:7 Actually, then, it is already a defeat for you, that you have lawsuits with one another. Why not rather be wronged? Why not rather be defrauded?

Already a defeat (ettema) = This word indicated a judicial defeat in court, which is pictured here as a moral defeat in God's eyes.

Wronged = This word meant to be treated unjustly.

Defrauded = This term means to be robbed or deprived of something.

The Corinthians may have said, "Paul, you don't understand! Brother so-and-so cheated me in business dealings." Paul's answer was, "Why not be wronged or treated unjustly rather than damage the reputation of the church and the name of Christ?" It is much better to receive a wrong than to commit one. Because their greed dishonored God, Paul stated that they have lost even before their case was tried. Here he means that earthly loss was preferable to the spiritual loss which lawsuits produced.

> The meaning is: You have already lost your case before you even get to court. Even if you win the decision you are still a loser because you have lost your brother's fellowship and respect. You have lost your testimony before that brother and others who know of the situation. Rather than go before heathen courts, rather than even set up Christian courts to handle the matter, they ought to have submitted to injustice, to have yielded their personal rights. [Boyer]

This implies that, under the specific circumstances the Corinthian believers were experiencing, it was wrong to go to court even to protect themselves from personal loss. The specifics of their cases were not sufficient to justify formal legal action.

1 Cor 6:8 On the contrary, you yourselves wrong and defraud. You do this even to your brethren.

The Greek text emphasizes the word "You." It is as if Paul is pointing his finger at them when he tells them that they are wronging and robbing their brothers in Christ. "By going to court, the Corinthians were actually trying to wrong and to rob the ones they claimed were trying to rob them. They were recompensing evil for evil (Rom 12:17)." [Boyer]

1 Cor 6:9-10 Or do you not know that the unrighteous will not inherit the kingdom of God? Do not be deceived; neither fornicators, nor idolaters, nor adulterers, nor effeminate, nor homosexuals, nor thieves, nor the covetous, nor drunkards, nor revilers, nor swindlers, will inherit the kingdom of God.

Unrighteous men will not inherit the kingdom of God = This refers to the unbelievers, the unsaved who are not heirs of the kingdom through a personal relationship with Jesus Christ. The kingdom of God refers to that future millennial kingdom. We know that at His second coming Jesus Christ will exclude all unbelievers from the millennial kingdom (Matt 25:31-46).

Do not be deceived = The deception is that a person can actually be a believer and yet continually or habitually live an immoral lifestyle. If one who calls himself a believer is constantly engaging in immorality, like those things mentioned here, then he has a basis for questioning his relationship to Christ.

Neither fornicators nor adulterers (moichos) = Adulterers refers to married individuals who commit sexual immorality.

Nor effeminate, nor homosexuals = These two terms specify the passive and the active perpetrators of this act. "Homosexuality and male prostitution were especially characteristic of Greco-Roman society. Plato lauded homosexual love in 'The Symposium.' At the time Paul wrote this letter, Nero was about to marry a young boy. It is likely that 14 of the first 15 Roman emperors practiced homosexuality." [BKC]

Thieves = This word means those who steal by stealth, in contrast to robbers who steal by force.

> This illustrated the gap which existed between the Corinthians' future position and their present practice. The wicked would have no share in God's future kingdom because they were not related to Christ. The wicked would one day be judged by the saints, yet the saints were acting no differently. Their future role should have radically affected their practice in the present. If they thought otherwise, Paul warned, they were deceived. [BKC]

Paul reminded the Corinthians that if they act wickedly, then they are no better than those who will not inherit heaven. "The application to believers is clear. 'Why then,' Paul asks, 'do you keep living like the unsaved? Why do you keep falling into the ways of your old life, the life from which Christ saved you? Why are you following the old standards, and having the old selfish, ungodly motives?'" [MacArthur]

1 Cor 6:11 Such were some of you; but you were washed, but you were sanctified, but you were justified in the name of the Lord Jesus Christ and in the Spirit of our God.

Some of the Corinthian believers would have directly identified with one or more of the sins on Paul's list. Some individuals who were now believers once participated in some of these unrighteous activities. But they were now forgiven and had experienced the new birth in Christ, and they were able to forsake their old lifestyles.

But (alla) = This word emphasizes the strong contrast between their former state and their present position in Christ.

Washed = This word implies an overall purification (see Titus 3:5).

Sanctified = This means being set apart as belonging to God and devoted to the service of God.

Justified = This was a legal term meaning "declared righteous in the sight of God and His law."

When a person has been washed, sanctified, and justified he should not continually live in immorality.

A Proper View of Christian Liberty and Sexual Purity (6:12-20)

1 Cor 6:12 All things are lawful for me, but not all things are profitable. All things are lawful for me, but I will not be mastered by anything.

Here Paul continues his discussion from the idea that believers are now washed, sanctified, and justified. They are saved by grace, and nothing can condemn them any longer.

All things are lawful for me = This was apparently a specific quote from some of the believers in Corinth. They were probably using this statement in order to justify their immorality. The problem with this assertion is that it is not true unless some limitations are placed on it. Christian liberty must always be restricted by the principle of Christian love. Liberty that was detrimental to someone was not loving and was to be avoided. "The introduction of the subject of Christian liberty at this point suggests that the Corinthian Christians were defending their tolerance of the gross immoralities in their midst by appealing to that doctrine." [Boyer]

Not all things are profitable (sumphero) = This term means to bring together or contribute; to be expedient or worthwhile. "Many things, harmless in themselves in the abstract, do harm to others in the concrete. We live in a world of social relations that circumscribe personal rights and liberties." [RWP]

I will not be mastered by anything = To be mastered means to be brought under the power of something; to be enslaved by something. Many activities of the flesh can be addictive, and the principle Paul stressed was that a Christian should not be enslaved by the things of the flesh. If so-called Christian liberty leads to slavery, then it is not liberty at all.

1 Cor 6:13 Food is for the stomach and the stomach is for food, but God will do away with both of them. Yet the body is not for immorality, but for the Lord, and the Lord is for the body.

Food for the stomach and the stomach for food = This was apparently another direct quote from some of the believers in Corinth who were seeking to justify their lifestyle. They were saying that since food is required to sustain the body, and since eating is also pleasurable, then there is nothing wrong with indulging in the pleasures of eating in order to satisfy the natural urges of the stomach. In the same way, they were arguing that sex was pleasurable and necessary. When their flesh signaled the desire for sex, they were justified in giving in to those urges.

> Undoubtedly there were some Christians in Corinth who claimed that it was permissible for them to do anything they desired. In making such claims to unrestricted freedom, they evidently argued that since the physical activity of eating food did not have any bearing on Christian morals and one's inner spiritual life, other activities such as promiscuous sex did not touch on morals or spiritual life. [ZNBC]

The body is not for immorality, but for the Lord = The stomach is simply a digestive organ in the body, but Paul here refers to the body as being more than just its organs and parts. "Even the natural body is matter informed by soul; and if there is a natural body there is also a spiritual body, matter informed by the spirit. The belly is a material organ which I use for a short time; the body is myself." [Barrett] Believers should not live as though the most important thing in life is to satisfy their appetites. The body of a believer is not meant to be used as a tool for the fulfillment of the selfish desires of the flesh. It is meant for service to the Lord in this life, and it will be destroyed at death to be resurrected as an incorruptible body.

The Lord is for the body = The body is intended for the Lord's service, and the Lord has given himself for the body. "Not only is the body for the Lord, but the Lord is for the body. This means that the Lord is interested in our bodies, their welfare, and their proper use. God wants our bodies to be presented to Him as a living sacrifice, holy, acceptable (Rom 12:1)." [BBC]

1 Cor 6:14 Now God has not only raised the Lord, but will also raise us up through His power.

Here Paul tells us that in the future the body will be glorified, just as was the body of the Lord Jesus Christ. This presents another good reason why we should avoid using the body for sinful, self-indulgent purposes here in this life.

> This verse is parallel to the second clause of 1 Cor 6:13. Of the stomach and meats it is said, God will destroy both it and them; of the Lord and the body it is said, as he raised up the one he will also raise up the other. The cases, therefore, are widely different. The relation between our organs of digestion and food is temporary; the re-

lation between Christ and the body is permanent. What concerns the former relation is a matter of indifference; what concerns the other touches the groundwork of our nature and the design for which we were created. [Hodge]

1 Cor 6:15-16 Do you not know that your bodies are members of Christ? Shall I then take away the members of Christ and make them members of a prostitute? May it never be! Or do you not know that the one who joins himself to a prostitute is one body with her? For He says, "THE TWO SHALL BECOME ONE FLESH."

The Corinthians might not think that having relations with a prostitute was a wrong use of the body, even though Paul clearly explained that believers' body parts have become Christ's by virtue of their redemption. These people should have known better since the Scriptures prove otherwise. "The union of two people involves more than physical contact. It is also a union of personalities which alters both of them." [BKC] Yet some of the believers saw no harm in visiting the temple prostitutes in Corinth and committing this kind of immorality. "If our bodies are members of Christ's body, then for us to use those bodies for fornication is equivalent to putting Christ in bed with a prostitute, an utterly abhorrent idea." [Boyer]

Paul is not saying that normal sexual intimacy in the context of marriage is wrong. Paul argues that sex outside of marriage is a wicked perversion and a violation of the divinely established marriage union.

> Sex outside of marriage is like a man robbing a bank: he gets something, but it is not his and he will one day pay for it. Sex within marriage can be like a person putting money into a bank: there is safety, security, and he will collect dividends. Sex within marriage can build a relationship that brings joy in the future; but sex apart from marriage has a way of weakening future relationships. [Wiersbe]

1 Cor 6:17 But the one who joins himself to the Lord is one spirit with Him.

Here Paul extends his previous idea that union with someone creates a binding relationship. The same principle applies to our relationship with Christ as we yield our body in service to Him. How can believers be joined to Christ and joined to sin at the same time? It is impossible to indulge in sinful pleasures and expect this will not impact our relationship with the Lord.

> Body is a neutral term that represents the human self at the place of decision. It may be the servant of sin, or the servant of righteousness. If one places his body at the disposal of a harlot, and so becomes one body with her, the body has taken a wrong turn and becomes flesh, which for Paul signifies human nature perverted. The body is also capable, however, not in its own strength but by the operation of the Holy Spirit, of turning in the right direction. If this happens it moves into the realm not of flesh but of spirit—not because it has ceased to be material but because it is controlled by the Spirit of God. [Barrett]

1 Cor 6:18 Flee immorality. Every other sin that a man commits is outside the body, but the immoral man sins against his own body.

Flee immorality = This is the only proper response to the temptations of the flesh: RUN AWAY!

Every sin a man commits is outside the body = This may be another slogan used by those Corinthian believers who were seeking to justify their immorality. But Paul directly contradicts this statement. He calls it a lie by saying that the immoral man DOES sin against his own body!

1 Cor 6:19-20 Or do you not know that your body is a temple of the Holy Spirit who is in you, whom you have from God, and that you are not your own? For you have been bought with a price: therefore glorify God in your body.

Temple (naos) = There are several Greek words for "temple" but this word means the inner sanctuary where God dwells, the Holy of Holies in the Jewish temple. In the temples at Corinth, the pagan deity was thought to dwell inside. In the case of believers, God the Holy Spirit actually does dwell within our bodies.

Here Paul explains how Christians should view the body. They should remember that the body is the dwelling place of the Holy Spirit. Christians have received the Spirit from God to help them overcome sin and the flesh. Christians have no right to pervert and misuse the body because they are not their own master. God gave a high price to purchase them and they belong to Him rather than to themselves.

Paul's conclusion is that Christians must **glorify God** in the use of the body. Onlookers should be able to see how glorious God truly is when they look at how believers use their bodies.

In this chapter we saw the tragedy of lawsuits and disputes between Christians. "The contention and strife; the time lost and the money wasted; the hard feelings and bitterness caused; the ruffled tempers and the lasting animosities, always injure the cause of Christ." [Barnes] Believers should be willing to suffer injustice at the hands of their fellow believers, rather than take their non-criminal cases before the secular courts. "How much better that my purse should be empty of glittering dust, even by the injustice of others, than that a single gem should be taken from His crown! Can silver, can gold, can diamonds be compared in value to the honor of Christ and of his cause?" [Barnes]

It is sometimes good for Christians to reflect on their life before salvation, just as Paul prompted the Corinthians to do. We would still be in that wretched condition except for the mercy of God. We need to remember that we are not our own, but we belong to Christ. In deciding about the holy use of our bodies, believers should ask themselves several questions: Is this activity beneficial to me or to others? Will this activity overpower or dominate me, and will the result affect others? Will this activity demonstrate that God owns my body and He intends for it to be used to bring glory to Him?

Sexual Purity and Marriage

(1 Corinthians 7:1-16)

Paul had just discussed the issue of sexual immorality (1 Cor 5:1-13; 6:9-20), and it appears that the Corinthians also had misconceptions about sexual relations even within marriage. So in this new chapter Paul will continue to deal with the subject of sexual purity, and he addresses the subject of marriage as well. From the opening words of this verse is it clear that Paul is answering some questions the Corinthians asked in a letter they wrote to him. Unfortunately we do not have their original letter so we cannot see exactly what Paul was responding to here. We only have the answers that Paul gave, and it is almost like listening to one side of a conversation. We must infer the questions based on Paul's answers. In the first sixteen verses Paul addressed at least four groups of people, and for each of these groups he discussed a specific topic of importance.

Married believers are the first group being addressed, and Paul discusses the subject of sexual purity within marriage (7:1-7). The second group addressed is the unmarried or widowed believers, and Paul discusses the possibility of their marriage in the future (7:8-9). Married believers are again addressed, this time with the possibility of divorce or remarriage (7:10-11). Finally Paul will talk to those in mixed marriages or inter-faith marriages, and he will discuss the possibility of separation or divorce (7:12-16).

1 Cor 7:1 Now concerning the things about which you wrote, it is good for a man not to touch a woman.

Here Paul begins to answer the specific questions asked by the Corinthians in their letter. It is possible that this letter was delivered by the members of Chloe's household (1 Cor 1:11), or more likely by Stephanas and Fortunatus and Achaicus(1 Cor 16:17) who were probably the official representatives of the Corinthian church.

It is good for a man not to touch a woman = In order to understand this phrase, we need to determine in what sense a man is not to touch a woman. The word "touch" (**haptomai**) can be taken at least three ways:

1. To have any physical contact.
2. To "kindle or inflame" in the sense of having sexual relations.
3. To touch in the sense of clinging or attaching to a woman in marriage.

This is a case where the context of the passage determines the intended meaning. Here it occurs in the context of abstaining from sexual immorality (1 Cor 5:1-5; 1 Cor 6:9-20; 1 Cor 7:2, 1 Cor 7:9), and that is the sense in which a man is not to touch a woman. Paul is continuing to discuss the issue of sexual immorality, and this will lead him into a discussion of marriage because marriage is the God-ordained institution which provides a legitimate outlet for sexual passions.

While one group of Corinthians believed they were free to indulge in sexual immorality, it appears that another group believed that there should be total sexual abstinence even in marriage. It is possible that Paul is quoting some of the Corinthians' own words when he includes this phrase. We have seen him do this before. "All things are lawful for me" (1 Cor 6:12); "Food for the stomach and the stomach for food" (1 Cor 6:13); "Every sin a man commits is outside the body" (1 Cor 6:18). So, here, he may be quoting a Corinthian teacher who was saying that, "It is good for a man not to touch a woman." If this is the case, then it gives us some insight into what was going on in the church. It is quite possible one of their teachers was saying that sex was unspiritual, and that celibacy was the only way to maintain spiritual purity.

This attitude certainly was expressed by some of the Greek philosophers who abstained from marriage. They were probably among the false teachers that Paul condemned in 1 Timothy 4:3. In direct contrast with these false teachers, Paul was not against marriage. As we will see later in 1 Cor 7:25-40 Paul thought there were certain practical advantages of remaining single, but in no way could Paul be accused of forbidding or demeaning marriage. In the Corinthian church there was a distinct contrast between the traditional Jewish view that marriage was mandatory, and a Greek philosophical teaching that celibacy was required. In this section of his letter, Paul will help the church to resolve this conflict.

To Christians who are Married (7:2-7)

1 Cor 7:2 But because of immoralities, each man is to have his own wife, and each woman is to have her own husband.

But = This verse begins with a strong contrast word. Paul was saying, "But in contrast to the idea that it is good for a man not to touch a woman, each man is to have his own wife." The reason Paul gives for each man having his own wife, and each woman having her own husband, is **because of immoralities (porneia)**, which means any kind of forbidden sexual intercourse. This is the same word that was used in 1 Cor 5:1; 6:13; and 6:18 when Paul discussed sexual immorality, so we can see that Paul is continuing that same discussion here.

Paul acknowledges that believers may experience sexual temptations while living in a fallen world, and he is reminding Christians that God provided a sanctioned way for their sexual desires to be satisfied. "Men and women have sexual urges, and if they are expressed within the institution that God Himself has appointed they are less likely to be expressed in ways that God has forbidden." [Barrett] Paul is not saying here that the only thing marriage is good for is as a place to satisfy sexual desires. Marriage has many noble purposes, and Paul does discuss them elsewhere. But here in the context of his discussion on sexual immorality Paul emphasized one of the many purposes for marriage, and that is to provide for sexual purity.

1 Cor 7:3 The husband must fulfill his duty to his wife, and likewise also the wife to her husband.

In this verse Paul tells us that both the husband and the wife have a mutual obligation to each other regarding their normal sexual desires. The words Paul used are also used of the obligation to repay a debt that is owed.

> There is a great deal of delicacy used here by Paul, and his expression is removed as far as possible from the grossness of pagan writers. His meaning is plain, but instead of using a word to express it which would be indelicate and offensive, he uses one which is not indelicate in the slightest degree. By the word which he uses, he reminds them of the sacredness of their vow, and of the fact that in person, property, and in every respect they belong to each other. [Barnes]

One important aspect of this verse is the mutual and equal obligation of the man and the woman to each other. This is not a one-sided duty, but it is something that both partners must do equally for each other. Physical relations within marriage are not simply a privilege and a pleasure but a responsibility.

> That celibacy is wrong for those who are married should be an obvious truth, but it was not obvious to some of the Corinthian believers. Because of their erroneous belief in the spiritual superiority of total sexual abstinence, some members in the church practiced it even within marriage. Some overzealous husbands apparently had decided to set themselves apart wholly for God. In doing so, however, they neglected or even denied their responsibilities to their wives, especially in the area of sexual relations. Some wives had done the same thing. The practice of deprivation probably was most common when the spouse was not a believer. But Paul applies his command to all marriages, as is clear from vv. 10-17. Married believers are not to sexually deprive their spouses, whether or not the spouse is a Christian. [MacArthur]

1 Cor 7:4 The wife does not have authority over her own body, but the husband does; and likewise also the husband does not have authority over his own body, but the wife does.

In the previous verse Paul made it clear that the husband and wife should fulfill their duty to each other in an active sense. Now in this verse Paul addresses the other side of the issue, which is the idea of passive submission or relinquishing control of one's own body for the benefit of the marriage partner. Paul is saying here that when the man and woman enter into the marriage covenant, an exclusive transfer of authority takes place. They assign to each other, and only to each other, the right and responsibility for the proper sexual use of each other's bodies. It is not just the woman who does this, but the man also assigns this authority to his wife.

An important point in this verse is that the proper sexual use of one's body is assigned for the exclusive use of the marriage partner. As one commentator said, it would be wrong to "abuse one's body by self-pollution, fornication, adultery, sodomy, or any acts of uncleanness. The wife, and she only, has power over it and a right to it. This power over each other's bodies is not such as that they may consent to lie with another." [Gill]

1 Cor 7:5 Stop depriving one another, except by agreement for a time, so that you may devote yourselves to prayer, and come together again so that Satan will not tempt you because of your lack of self-control.

Here Paul hints at what was happening in some of the Christian marriages within the Corinthian church. Some couples were practicing celibacy within their marriage relationship. Paul refers to that practice as **depriving one another** and he tells them to stop doing this. Only one exception is allowed to the rule regarding the duty of husbands and wives to each other, and this exception is carefully restricted:

 – Abstinence must be by the mutual agreement of both partners.
 – It must be for a limited time period.
 – It must be for a religious purpose.
 – It must be only temporary.

Normal marital relations should be continued afterward. The reason Paul gives for this is that Satan is able to tempt believers to feed their fleshly impulses, and he may tempt the unsatisfied marriage partner to engage in sexual immorality. The basic problem in the life of the believer which Satan is able to take advantage of is a lack of self-control in the area of sexuality. We need to realize that the desires of the flesh are powerful, and it takes a great deal of self-control to master these fleshly desires. Fortunately, self-control is a fruit of the indwelling Spirit (Gal 5:22-23).

1 Cor 7:6 But this I say by way of concession, not of command.

The meaning of this verse depends upon what the word "this" refers to. There are at least two possibilities

1. Married couples are allowed to abstain, but not commanded to abstain. The nearest antecedent for "this" is the exception clause that Paul was just discussing (1 Cor 7:5). It is as if Paul is saying, "You should not rob one another of your rights, but I will make this concession to the ascetics among you: If husband and wife both agree, they may abstain from normal relations for a short time in order to give themselves to prayer without distraction. But this is a concession, not a command, and if you do practice abstinence it must be for a limited time, and with a view to returning to each other." [Barrett] God did not give a commandment that said, "Thou shalt abstain from marital relations periodically to enhance your prayer life." But married believers are permitted to do so if they follow the guidelines Paul just gave them.

2. Marriage is not commanded for believers. Singleness and marriage are both permitted. With this possible interpretation Paul might be referring to the idea first stated in 1 Cor 7:2 that marriage is God's sanctioned outlet for sexual desires. In this case Paul may be saying, "I am aware of the benefits of being single and celibate, and I am also aware of the privileges and respon-

sibilities of being married. But I am not commanding that every believer should be married. If you are single that is good, and if you are married, then stay married and maintain normal marital relations. Your spirituality is not determined by your marital status." [MacArthur] To remain single or to get married is not a matter of right and wrong, or of duty and commandment. Either state is permitted. God did not give a commandment that said, "Thou shalt get married." It is a matter of individual choice according to the gifts that God has given. This is what Paul elaborates on in the next verse, so the context seems to support this second possibility for the meaning of the verse.

1 Cor 7:7 Yet I wish that all men were even as I myself am. However, each man has his own gift from God, one in this manner, and another in that.

Yet I wish = This expresses Paul's wish or desire. It is what he would personally prefer, especially under the present circumstances (see 1 Cor 7:26).

All men were even as I myself am = This implies that at that time Paul was not married, which is confirmed by 1 Cor 9:5. We do not know whether Paul was a widower or whether he had never been married, but the very next verse gives the impression that he was in one of those two categories. What Paul is specifically referring to here, however, is that he is currently in the category of "single and celibate." He holds himself up as an example of a person who is able to control his sexual desires through exercising self-control as well as appropriating the special gift that God has provided for him to remain single and celibate.

> When he wishes that all people were like himself, he evidently does not intend that all should be unmarried, for this would be against the divine institution and against his own precepts elsewhere. But he would be glad if all people had control over their passions and propensities as he had, and could abstain from marriage when circumstances would make it proper. We may add that when Paul wishes to exhort to anything that is difficult, he usually adduces his own example to show that it may be done. [Barnes]

Each man has his own gift from God = This tells us that God can provide a believer with the ability to live in a state of singleness and celibacy, and to be content and productive in that lifestyle. It reminds us of Jesus' own teaching on the topic of marriage and divorce in Matthew 19:1-12. There the Pharisees were trying to cleverly trick Jesus, and in light of His strict reply regarding the permanence of marriage His own disciples said, "If the relationship of the man with his wife is like this, it is better not to marry." Jesus then said, "Not all men can accept this statement, but only those to whom it has been given. For there are eunuchs who were born that way from their mother's womb; and there are eunuchs who were made eunuchs by men; and there are also eunuchs who made themselves eunuchs for the sake of the kingdom of heaven." (Matt 19:11-12) Jesus said that there were several types of people who were content to live in a state of singleness and celibacy, but that not everyone was able to do likewise.

One man expressed it this way: "Some have the gift of foregoing the blessings of married life for the sake of the kingdom. Others have the gift of being married and establishing a home, serving God in that way. The decision as to whether a person should get married or not should be made in the light of the gift which God has given him." [Boyer]

To Unmarried and Widowed Believers (7:8-9)

1 Cor 7:8 But I say to the unmarried and to widows that it is good for them if they remain even as I.

Paul now directly addressed the unmarried and those who had been married but whose spouse had died. They were currently in a state of singleness and (hopefully) celibacy just as Paul was, so Paul discussed the possibility of marriage in their future. He restates his preference from verse seven that all believers could follow his own example of controlling their fleshly passions and remaining content with their current state of singleness. Notice he said it would be good but he did not say that it would be the best or the only state that would please God. He specifically said it would be good if they are able to remain as he is. One scholar wrote,

> If they have to stay as widows, God will give them the necessary strength to live a moral life and not to constantly burn with the desire that they should be married. If they decide to stay in a state of singleness, there is nothing wrong with it as long as they exercise continence. The apostle Paul is not demanding that they should remain single, but if they decide to remain single as he also had done, it is perfectly all right. [Zodhiates]

If a person decides to remain unmarried, he should follow Paul's example and keep his sexual desires under control. But what if he finds it impossible to do this? That is what Paul deals with in the next verse.

1 Cor 7:9 But if they do not have self-control, let them marry; for it is better to marry than to burn with passion.

If single believers are not able to exercise sexual self-restraint, if they find themselves constantly inflamed with sexual urges, then they should marry. Single believers may find life and service for the Lord to be difficult if they continually burn with sexual passions, even if their passions never give way to immorality. "A state of constant desire for sexual fulfillment can be devastating to a person's spiritual life. The single person, therefore, must be on the alert in avoiding scenes and situations whereby the sexual instinct is aroused. It is foolish to pretend such desires do not exist or to think oneself fireproof in its presence. The only alternative to this state is marriage." [Zodhiates] It is very important for single believers to control these passions and not to engage in sexual sin.

Self-control is something that every believer should exercise as enabled by God's indwelling Holy Spirit. It is never an excuse for a believer to say he fell into sexual sin because God did not give him the necessary self-control.

> Paul was not single because he had no struggle with his sexual urges, nor did he remain single because of the simplicity of the single life. He remained single because he knew that in his case it was the best way for him to accomplish God's calling in his life. It was within his power to marry, and apparently there was no reason why he could not marry. But as long as he could control his sexual desires and have victory and joy in the accomplishment of God's purpose for his live, he remained single. [Zodhiates]

It is obvious that a lack of sexual self-control is not the only reason to get married. God may have given you the desire and even the gift of being married, being a life-long helper and partner to someone, as well as raising a family to the glory of God. Here is what one man wrote about this type of desire:

> It is never God's will for Christians to marry unbelievers (2 Cor 6:14), but neither is it right just to marry the first believer who will say yes. Though we may want very much to be married, we should be careful. Strong feelings of any sort tend to dull the judgment and make one vulnerable and careless. There are several things that Christians in this dilemma ought to do. First, they should not simply seek to be married, but should seek a person they can love, trust, and respect, letting marriage come as a response to that commitment of love. People who simply want to get married for the sake of getting married run a great risk of marrying the wrong person. Second, it is fine to be on the lookout for the right person, but the best way to find the right person is to be the right person. If believers are right with God and it is His will for them to be married, He will send the right person – and never too late. Third, until the right person is found, our energy should be redirected in ways that will be the most helpful in keeping our minds off the temptation. Two of the best ways are spiritual service and physical activity. We should avoid listening to, looking at, or being around anything that strengthens the temptation. We should program our minds to focus only on that which is good and helpful. We should take special care to follow Paul's instruction in Philippians 4:8. Fourth, we should realize that, until God gives us the right person, He will provide strength to resist temptation (1 Cor 10:13). Finally, we should give thanks to the Lord for our situation and be content in it. [MacArthur]

To Married Believers (7:10-11)

1 Cor 7:10 But to the married I give instructions, not I, but the Lord, that the wife should not leave her husband;

Now Paul directly addressed married Christians, and he discusses the issue of divorce and remarriage.

I give instructions, not I, but the Lord = Here Paul is reminding the believers of the direct teaching of Jesus on the subject of divorce and remarriage. He used the same Greek word he had previously used in his Thessalonian letter for a direct command (**parangello**). So what Paul says here is not a matter of preference, but a matter of following the commandment of the Lord Jesus Christ.

> Paul had no commands from Jesus to the unmarried men or women, but Jesus had spoken to the married (Matt 19:3-12; Mark 10:9-12; Luke 16:18). The Master had spoken plain words about divorce. Paul reinforces his own inspired command by the command of Jesus: What therefore God has joined together let no man separate. [RWP]

The wife should not leave her husband = The word "leave" (**chorizo**) means to separate from, put away, or depart. This is the same word used by Jesus when He said, "What therefore God has joined together, let no man separate." (Matt 19:6) It refers to the wife seeking a divorce from her husband. We do not know exactly why some believers were seeking to divorce each other, but it could be that they thought they could live holier lives if they returned to a single and celibate state. It seems that Paul was primarily addressing the issue of divorce for supposedly spiritual reasons.

1 Cor 7:11 (but if she does leave, she must remain unmarried, or else be reconciled to her husband), and that the husband should not divorce his wife.

Taking the last part of this verse first, Paul commands the **husband not to divorce his wife** either. Paul used a different word (**aphiemi**) which is translated "divorce." It means to send away, to leave or depart from. This is the same word Paul will use in 1 Cor 7:13 when he says the wife must not send her husband away either. Again, Paul is reminding believers of the words of the Lord Jesus Christ who taught that marriage should be life-long and that divorce is wrong. The first part of this verse provides a parenthetical comment. Although Jesus' command forbids divorce between Christian marriage partners, Paul recognized that some Christian marriages might break up. Here he gives some guidelines for how to handle this situation.

If = This is a Greek third class conditional clause, which indicates there is a future possibility that this situation might happen. If believers do leave their partner, here are their only options:

1. Remain unmarried, or
2. Be reconciled to their original partner.

One commentator said:

> Since this verse really applies to both husband and wife, whoever decides to separate from the other, it is primarily the one who separates who must make the effort to reconcile with the spouse. This reconciliation, however, could not take effect if the departing spouse decided to remarry. This is why Paul's admonition is to remain unmarried and to make every effort toward reconciliation. The apostle Paul implies that in any separation, there should be no hurry to remarry or even to consider re-

marriage. There are, of course, cases where such reconciliation is impossible, but in these cases then it is the duty of the one who left to stay unmarried. [Zodhiates]

This being said, there may be situations when an innocent partner should separate from a spouse who is engaging in sinful or criminal behavior.

It is possible for an innocent spouse to depart when it comes to saving one's life or one's children from cruelty by the deserted partner. The picture then is that of an innocent partner waiting for the guilty spouse to repent so that a reunion may be effected. But that is not the situation envisioned by Paul in this verse. It is the situation of an unjustifiable desertion. It is what we would call today incompatibility. If a marital partner deserts the spouse because they just cannot get along, that classifies the deserting partner as guilty and consequently one who should return and be reconciled to the other partner. [Zodhiates]

To the Rest / Mixed Marriages (7:12-16)

1 Cor 7:12-13 But to the rest I say, not the Lord, that if any brother has a wife who is an unbeliever, and she consents to live with him, he must not divorce her. And a woman who has an unbelieving husband, and he consents to live with her, she must not send her husband away.

To the rest = Some of the people in Corinth had come to faith in Christ after they were already married, and some of their marriage partners had not trusted Christ at that time. This created a situation where there were mixed marriages, a believer being married to an unbeliever. Some of these believers may have thought it would be wrong for them to remain married to an unbeliever, and that the marriage covenant they entered into as unbelievers became void after they put their faith in Christ. In a mixed marriage like this the spiritual partner might come to the conclusion that the spouse does not share the same spirituality or the same calling for service to God, and that separating from such an unspiritual partner would please the Lord. But Paul says, "No." He says that a husband and wife who were married as unbelievers cannot claim that their new faith nullifies their marriage.

I say, not the Lord = Earlier Paul had restated the direct teaching of the Lord Jesus concerning divorce, but Christ had not given any instructions about mixed marriages. So here he is saying that since Jesus had not given any teaching on this subject, God was using Paul to address it now. One commentator set the stage this way:

> What were Christians to do who were already married to unbelievers, possibly even to immoral and idolatrous pagans? Were they free to divorce the one to whom they were unequally yoked and then free to live singly or marry a believer? Those were honest questions. In light of Paul's teaching that their bodies were members of Christ and were temples of the Holy Spirit (1 Cor 6:15-20), the Corinthian Christians were justifiably concerned about whether or not to maintain marital union with an unbeliever. Some may have thought that such a union joined Christ to Satan, defiling the believer and dishonoring the Lord. [MacArthur]

95

The first point we can see in this verse is that the original marriage is still valid even after one of the partners becomes a Christian. The believer must not initiate any action that would break up the marriage or cause the unbelieving spouse to leave. The second point in this verse is that the condition for continuing the marriage can only be decided by the unbelieving spouse: **"if she/he consents to live with him/her."** There is no question that the believing partner is obligated to stay with the unbelieving spouse if the unbeliever is willing to do so.

1 Cor 7:14 For the unbelieving husband is sanctified through his wife, and the unbelieving wife is sanctified through her believing husband; for otherwise your children are unclean, but now they are holy.

Normally when Paul speaks about sanctification and holiness they are the distinguishing mark of a Christian, but here he says unbelievers are sanctified or made holy in some way. To understand this we must remember that Paul began this section by dealing with the sexual relationship within marriage. Some believers in Corinth may have wanted to separate from their unbelieving partners thinking that they would be defiled by the non-Christian, and the children of such a union would somehow be unclean. Paul answers this concern by saying that quite the opposite is true.

Instead of the unbeliever defiling the relationship, the believer has the effect of sanctifying the marriage partner in the sense of setting him apart for special and direct spiritual influence. Calvin commented that "the godliness of the one does more to sanctify the marriage than the ungodliness of the other does to make it unclean." [Barrett] Another man said, "Clearly he means that the marriage is sanctified so that there is no need of a divorce. If either husband or wife is a believer and the other agrees to remain, the marriage is holy and should not be set aside." [RWP]

> Christians married to unbelievers were not to worry that they themselves, their marriage, or their children would be defiled by the unbelieving spouse. On the contrary, the very opposite was the case. Both the children and the unbelieving spouse would be sanctified through the believing wife or husband. Such a home is not Christian in the full sense, but it is immeasurably superior to one that is totally unbelieving. One Christian in a home graces the entire home. God's indwelling that believer and all the blessings and graces that flow into the believer's life from heaven will spill over to enrich all who are near. In addition, although the believer's faith cannot suffice for the salvation of anyone but himself, he is often the means of other family members coming to the Lord by the power of his testimony. [MacArthur]

1 Cor 7:15 Yet if the unbelieving one leaves, let him leave; the brother or the sister is not under bondage in such cases, but God has called us to peace.

If the unbeliever leaves, let him leave = Paul had dealt with the case of a mixed marriage in which the unbeliever was willing to stay, so now he deals with the other alternative. If the unbeliever leaves, then the believer should allow him to leave.

Not under bondage = If the unbeliever agrees to remain, then the believer is bound to the marriage; but if the unbeliever leaves, then the believer is not bound. "The sense of the expression 'is not bound' is that if they forcibly depart, the one that is left is not bound by the marriage tie to make provision for the one that departed. He is at liberty to live separately." [Barnes] Another commentator explained,

> The believer is free from the obligation to preserve the marriage. Probably there is little he can do anyway for the unbeliever would hardly share his scruples against divorce. This word of the apostle would free the believer from any self-imposed stigma or blame for the separation which he could do nothing about. But the initiative for the separation must come from the unbeliever, never from the believer. [Boyer]

God has called us to peace = This phrase applies to the previous part of the verse, so Paul was saying that if the unbeliever departs he is to be allowed to do so peaceably rather than to have contention and strife, for God has called us to a life of peace. Another man wrote,

> To be deserted by one's husband or wife is a very traumatic experience. But no matter how traumatic it is, it is possible for that one's peace to be preserved. The believer's peace is not primarily derived from or dependent upon the husband or wife but upon Jesus Christ Himself. Although we may be deserted by even our spouse, this cannot destroy the peace that we have received because we are in Christ. [Zodhiates]

Does this free the deserted believer to remarry? Some say that "desertion is a breach of the marriage contract, and a dissolution of the bond, and the deserted person may lawfully marry again." [Gill] But notice that in this passage the apostle Paul does not address the issue of remarriage after separation from an unbelieving partner. He does say that after separation from a believing spouse, a believer should remain unmarried (1 Cor 7:11). We do not have any specific instructions here about remarriage in cases when the unbelieving former spouse is still living. The only time remarriage is specifically permitted is if one's spouse has died (1 Cor 7:39). What if the unbelieving spouse left and then immediately remarried, does that mean the first marriage is officially dissolved and the deserted believer is then free to remarry? Again, Paul does not address that specific case here. But it seems that throughout this entire context Paul has been working to ensure that marriages remain intact. He has been encouraging believers to keep their marriages together, rather than to break them up and start over again in another marriage. If a believer's marriage partner is still living, then this passage does not specifically give the believer permission to remarry.

1 Cor 7:16 For how do you know, O wife, whether you will save your husband? Or how do you know, O husband, whether you will save your wife?

Whether you will save = Obviously only God can save any person, so this is salvation in the sense of the witness of a Christian partner in marriage. Paul had already said that the unbelieving partner lives under the direct influence of the believing partner, so there is good reason to hope that the unbeliever might eventually become a Christian as well. But even if the unbelieving spouse leaves, it is still possible for him to be converted. One man expressed it this way:

> You don't know whether your example in Christ shall eventually save your unbelieving husband in spite of and possibly even through this separation. Therefore, let not his departure destroy your peace in Christ. God can still save him, even away from you. Don't blame yourself for something that you cannot help and that you cannot effectively bring about. [Zodhiates]

In this section of chapter seven, the apostle Paul provided several important truths that we can apply to our lives today. The overall message is that no matter what our circumstances, Christians need to maintain sexual purity. God has provided the marriage relationship as the institution for expressing our legitimate sexual desires, and the biblical pattern for Christian marriage is: One man plus One woman —for life.

Paul also gave a great deal of comfort for believers who are married to unbelievers, perhaps because they were saved after they were already married. Even though this type of marriage relationship may be more difficult than when both partners are believers, God can show Himself strong in that relationship and there is an amazing possibility to see His miracle-working power at work to transform lives.

The Principle of Peace and Contentment

(1 Corinthians 7:17-28)

C an you think of a time in your life when you were willing to accept some difficult circumstance because you personally knew and completely trusted the one who put you into that situation? In explaining the principle that God has called believers to live in peace (1 Cor 7:15), Paul showed that Christians should live contentedly in any situation of life in which God has placed them.

> They should live obediently to God with full confidence in his sovereign purpose whether married or unmarried, Jew or Gentile, slave or free. He wants individual Christians to realize and accept God's sovereign purpose in saving and keeping them regardless of the level of society they are in...God's people can and must live as Christians, whatever social, economic, and religious level of society they are in. Their conditions do not affect their relationship and service to Jesus Christ. [ZNBC]

The Sovereignty of God in the Life of Believers (7:17)

1 Cor 7:17 Only, as the Lord has assigned to each one, as God has called each, in this manner let him walk. And so I direct in all the churches.

Here Paul expands his thoughts about the believer's call to peace by including other areas besides that of marital status.

Assigned = This word elaborates on God's "gifting" to each individual believer (1 Cor 7:7) as well as His "calling" upon each individual believer (1 Cor 7:15). This expresses the sovereignty and providence of God in the life of every Christian.

> Paul had discussed the question whether a husband and wife ought to be separated on account of a difference in religion. He now says that this general principle ought to rule everywhere; that people who become Christians ought not to seek to change their condition or calling in life, but to remain in that situation in which they were when they became Christians, and show the excellence of their faith in that particular calling. The object of Paul, therefore, is to preserve order, industry, and faithfulness in the relations of life, and to show that Christianity does not seek to break up social and domestic relations. [Barnes]

Paul is saying that believers should view their current circumstances as a calling from God. As one writer said, "Our circumstances are not the products of chance, but the products of providence." [Zodhiates]

Paul wants to emphasize that believers should be content with the situations in which God has placed them. If they are able to grow, improve, or change their circumstances, then they should continue to demonstrate their trust in God through those new situations. "This was designed to counteract the notion that embracing a new religion dissolved the relations of life which existed before. Paul's object is to show that the gospel, instead of dissolving those relations, only strengthened them and enabled those who were converted to better discharge the duties which grow out of them." [Barnes]

So I direct in all the churches = This is not some special rule just for the Corinthians, but this was the general principle that Paul taught in all churches. Paul then proceeded to illustrate this principle in two areas: circumcision and servitude.

An Illustration from Circumcision (7:18-20)

1 Cor 7:18 Was any man called when he was already circumcised? He is not to become uncircumcised. Has anyone been called in uncircumcision? He is not to be circumcised.

In the New Testament, circumcision and uncircumcision are frequently used as synonyms for the Jews and the Gentiles. The typical word for circumcision is **peritemno** (to cut around) and for uncircumcision it is **akrobustia** (having the foreskin).

Become uncircumcised (epispaomai) = Here Paul used a different word which meant to put on the foreskin. This is the only time this word is used in the New Testament. Some Jews did this at the time of Antiochus (1 Maccab 1:14-15).

> Menelaus and the sons of Tobias were distressed, and retired to Antiochus, and informed him that they were desirous to leave the laws of their country and the Jewish way of living, and to follow the king's laws and the Grecian way of living. Wherefore they desired his permission to build them a Gymnasium at Jerusalem. And when he had given them leave, they also hid the circumcision of their genitals, that even when they were naked they might appear to be Greeks. Accordingly, they left off all the customs that belonged to their own country, and imitated the practices of the other nations. [Josephus]

Paul is saying that those who had been circumcised and had now become Christians were not to change their mark of circumcision. The point is that a Jew is to keep the marks of his Jewishness, and a Gentile is to remain a Gentile. The two groups are on an equal basis in the church. This freedom in the area of circumcision illustrates the freedom in the area of mixed marriages.

1 Cor 7:19 Circumcision is nothing, and uncircumcision is nothing, but what matters is the keeping of the commandments of God.

Circumcision is nothing / Uncircumcision is nothing = This term means the two things are not anything of significance or importance.

Keeping the commandments of God = Circumcision was formerly a commandment of God to Abraham and his natural descendants, but it is no longer what God requires. This external ritual is now of no consequence one way or the other.

It was a distinguishing mark of the people of the Jews, until the Messiah came: but now it is nothing, being with the rest of the ceremonies abolished by Christ; it gives no preference to the Jew above the Gentile. He that has this mark in his flesh is not a whit the better for it, and he that is without it is not at all the worse; and this is the reason why both the one and the other should be easy and not attempt any alteration in themselves with regard to this, or think the better or worse of themselves on account of it. This is said in direct opposition to the sentiments of the Jews, who extol circumcision to the skies. [Gill]

In Galatians 5:6 Paul explained what it now means to keep the commandments of God. It involves faith in Christ which expresses itself through love of others. "Circumcision was a commandment of God: but not forever." [JFB]

1 Cor 7:20 Each man must remain in that condition in which he was called.

Each man must remain in that condition in which he was called = Here Paul restated the general principle, and obviously it is not to be taken in an absolute sense, meaning that no change is ever permitted. "It does not design to teach that a man is never to seek a change in his profession when he becomes a Christian. But it shows that Christianity encouraged social order." [Barnes]

One of the challenges of the Christian life is learning how to use discernment in applying the commandments of the Lord to specific situations in life.

We must discern the circumstances in which they apply as, for instance, in Corinth in the case of a believer and an unbelieving spouse and also between two believing spouses. It is our duty to discern which general commandment of God applies to a specific situation, and we are then responsible for the guarding of the commandment that is applicable there. The admonition to continue in the state that one finds himself when he is saved is not without exception. We must know the commandments of God that apply to each situation. [Zodhiates]

It is clear from the very next verse that Paul's instructions here were not intended to prevent any change in a believer's circumstances. There were some situations where a change after conversion would have been good and proper. Barnes provides three examples of this:

1. When a person was a slave and could obtain his freedom (1 Cor 7:21).
2. When a person was pursuing a wicked occupation when he was converted, even if it is lucrative, he should abandon it as speedily as possible. Thus, if a man is engaged, as John Newton was, in the slave-trade, he should at once abandon it. Nothing can make a business which is evil into one that is proper or right.
3. Where a man can increase his usefulness by choosing a new profession. Thus, the usefulness of many a man is greatly promoted by his leaving an agricultural, or mechanical employment; or by his leaving the bar or the mercantile profession, and becoming a minister of the gospel. In such situations, religion not only permits a man to change his profession, but it demands it.

[Barnes]

Another writer said it this way: "A prostitute who is saved cannot continue in her prostitution. A drug trafficker cannot continue in that vocation after he is saved." [Zodhiates]

An Illustration from Servitude (7:21-24)

Paul continued explaining this principle using an illustration from slavery or servitude. Servitude was very common in New Testament times. At one point, for example, the population of Athens consisted of ninety-five percent slaves. There were probably many slaves in Corinth who had become Christians since the gospel had first been preached there. So they may rightly have been concerned about the implications of Christ's work of redemption for their earthly freedom.

1 Cor 7:21 Were you called while a slave? Do not worry about it; but if you are able also to become free, rather do that.

Paul is saying, "If you were called while in servitude, do not let it cause you concern or give you care." Slavery was usually a permanent condition, but even a slave could be a good servant of Christ. "In that time churches were often established on a household basis, and the membership of these churches included both masters and servants. A perfect example of this is found in Paul's letter to Philemon. The fact is that household slavery, which Paul is referring to here and which is the only kind referred to in the entire New Testament, was generally governed by a feeling of good will and affection." [Zodhiates]

But if you are able to become free = It seems Paul is setting up a contrast between serving Christ while in slavery vs. becoming a free man and continuing to serve Christ.

Rather do that = Literally this could be translated, "But make use." The word "that" is not in the Greek text. What were they to make use of, then? Paul could mean they were to use their bondage or use their freedom. He may be saying "Remain in slavery" or he may be saying "Take advantage of an offer of freedom." The context could support either option, but most modern English translations choose the second option. However, it must be understood that in no way is Paul encouraging slave revolts. Paul is encouraging peace and contentment.

In those days there was a legitimate way for a slave to earn his freedom. One man described the process this way:

> In the ancient world it was possible for a slave to purchase his freedom. In the little spare time he had, he took odd jobs and earned some money. His master had the right to claim commission even on these poor earnings. But the slave would deposit everything he earned in the temple of some god. When he had his complete purchase price laid up in the temple, he would take his master there, the priest would hand over the money, and then symbolically the slave became the property of the god, and therefore free of all men. [Barclay]

It was as if a transfer of slave ownership would take place from one master to another. But after that transfer, the human master no longer had any claim on the slave. He was free of that master, but technically he was obligated to his new owner.

1 Cor 7:22 For he who was called in the Lord while a slave, is the Lord's freedman; likewise he who was called while free, is Christ's slave.

This is equivalent to saying in the previous illustration that "Circumcision is nothing, and uncircumcision is nothing." Here Paul says, "Slavery is nothing, and un-slavery is nothing." He declares that a Christian slave is Christ's freeman and a Christian freeman is Christ's slave.

> The sense is this. You were formerly a slave to sin, but now you are liberated. Your spirit is free; while those who are not slaves, and perhaps your own masters, are even now under a more severe and odious bondage than yours. You should rejoice, therefore, in deliverance from the greater evil, and be glad that in the eye of God you are regarded as his freeman, and endowed by him with more valuable freedom than it would be to be delivered from the bondage under which you are now placed. [Barnes]

1 Cor 7:23 You were bought with a price; do not become slaves of men.

You were bought with a price = The price was the blood of Christ which was of infinite worth, and by this purchase the Lord has become the owner of every individual believer. This is the same phrase used in 1 Cor 6:20, but there they were to glorify God with their bodies while here they are not to become enslaved to men.

Slaves of men = It is very interesting that in 1 Cor 1:12 Paul had said the Corinthians were becoming "slaves of men" as they divided into rival factions with different leaders. Here he is reminding them that they should obey God's Word and follow Christ, rather than letting questionable teachers tell them how they should behave.

> Paul's reason for bringing this subject into the general marriage discussion is to emphasize that no one has the right to dictate to the believer what his marital status should be. It is a personal matter between each child of God and his Lord. A common danger in Christianity has always been for one Christian to assume such leadership as to tell others exactly how to behave and what to do. Christians are not under the law of another, but they are under the law of Christ unto themselves. [Zodhiates]

1 Cor 7:24 Brethren, each one is to remain with God in that condition in which he was called.

Again, Paul is restating the principle of contentment.

Each one is to remain with God in that condition in which he was called = Now Paul adds the important phrase "**with God**." There is great comfort in this phrase. Even a slave can endure difficult circumstances with God at his side. Also this verse provides a qualification or limitation to Paul's principle that each individual should remain in whatever situation he was in when God called him. "If a man's calling be not favorable to his abiding with God (retaining holy fellowship with Him), he may use lawful means to change it." [JFB] So if a believer was involved in an occupation that is not honoring to God, he should cease doing that work and find work that is more productive for the Lord.

How does this discussion of contentment in the life of a slave apply to the situation of married believers?

> As in the same household a newly converted marital partner may be considering whether he should continue to live with a nonbeliever, so in the same household there may be a slave who has become a believer who must consider his attitude toward a master to whom he is bound. Even as a Christian spouse should endeavor to preserve the marriage relationship with a non-Christian spouse, so must a slave who has become a Christian continue in his relationship with his master. The first and immediate responsibility after salvation, is that slaves please God by their faithful service (Eph 6:5-8; Col 3:22). So by application to the marriage situation, we could say Paul implies here that a new believer should not attempt to break his bonds of marriage with his unbelieving spouse. God is able to give grace to face each situation which may arise as a result of someone being saved and being in a position which he has no power to change and from which God does not provide release. [Zodhiates]

Applying This Principle to the Unmarried (7:25-28)

1 Cor 7:25 Now concerning virgins I have no command of the Lord, but I give an opinion as one who by the mercy of the Lord is trustworthy.

Paul went on to apply the principle of peace and contentment to the unmarried believers in the Corinthian church. Evidently the Corinthians specifically asked a question about whether unmarried believers should seek to get married at all. Here is where Paul answers their question in light of the principle he just explained.

Concerning virgins = This term (**parthenos**) referred to virgin young women of marriageable age. Even though Paul used a term that specifies unmarried young women, the following verses show that he is discussing both the men and the women who might want to marry. For example, "For a man to remain as he is" (1 Cor 7:26); "Bound to a wife...but if you marry you have not sinned" (1 Cor 7:27-28). The fact that the Corinthians asked Paul to comment on this issue implies that it was related to the issue of celibacy, and that some false teachers in Corinth were probably saying sex was unspiritual and that celibacy was the only way to maintain spiritual purity. The Corinthians were asking whether unmarried believers should remain single and celibate, or whether they could marry if they had that desire.

No command of the Lord, but I give an opinion = Paul could not point to any previous teaching of Jesus on the subject of unmarried young women and their desire for marriage. He is saying, "There is no existing Word from the Lord regarding this issue, but I give my judgment under the inspiration of the Holy Spirit."

Trustworthy = Paul had proven himself to be a trustworthy advisor and he shared his opinion, in the words of one commentator, "as one who would not give advice for any selfish or worldly consideration; as one known to act from a desire to honor God and to seek the best interests of the church, even though there is no explicit command from Jesus." [Barnes]

Some critics of Christianity cite this verse to refute the doctrine of the inspiration of Scripture, saying that the Bible simply contains the opinions of men. But, "far from being a disclaimer of inspiration, this language is an express claim to the help of the Lord in forming this duly considered judgment, which is in no sense a command, but an inspired opinion." [RWP] Paul could be paraphrased as saying, "The Lord inspires me in this case to give you a recommendation which you are free to adopt or reject; it is not a positive command." [JFB]

1 Cor 7:26 I think then that this is good in view of the present distress, that it is good for a man to remain as he is.

I think then = Here Paul states the opinion mentioned in the previous verse, which he does not call a command but simply his advice.

Good (kalos) = This word means that which is well adapted to the circumstances; something that is beneficial.

In view of the present distress (ananke) = This term identifies impending circumstances with the added implication of stress, need, or necessity in those circumstances. It is not clear exactly what these impending stressful circumstances were, but we do know that the Roman emperor Nero came to power in AD 54 and began persecuting Christians in AD 64.

To remain as he is = Notice that this is different from Paul's previous command to "remain even as I am" (1 Cor 7:8). Here Paul refers to a man's current marital status, and he addresses the group of believers who are presently unmarried. He might have said, "In the present circumstances it is probably good for a man to remain unmarried, but I am not giving a strict rule which every believer must obey."

1 Cor 7:27 Are you bound to a wife? Do not seek to be released. Are you released from a wife? Do not seek a wife.

Bound to a wife (deo) = This term means bound by law (as in 1 Cor 7:39 and Rom 7:2).

Released from a wife = This word means loosed or not in bondage. Paul used this expression by way of contrast with "bound" (married). Here he simply means unmarried, and it could have been translated "Are you single?" It does not imply that the person formerly had been married. This is a clear application of the principle

Paul previously shared. If you are married, stay married; if you are unmarried, stay unmarried. Neither the married nor the unmarried are required to change their situation as a result of becoming a Christian.

1 Cor 7:28 But if you marry, you have not sinned; and if a virgin marries, she has not sinned. Yet such will have trouble in this life, and I am trying to spare you.

But if you marry = Here Paul is referring to unmarried male believers who were seeking his advice, and to which he had just said it was his opinion that they should remain as they are. Now Paul tells them that if they do get married, they are not sinning. His advice was simply his opinion in light of the impending circumstances, but if they decided to marry they were not committing a sin.

And if a virgin marries = Paul includes this phrase to show that what he is talking about applies both to male and female unmarried believers.

Paul's instructions emphasize the principle of individual responsibility, which is a balancing truth to God's sovereignty that was presented in the previous section. Each believer is to obey God's leading in whatever circumstances he has been assigned by God, and this involves making personal choices from among several possible options. This does not always involve a choice between something that is sin and something that is not sin. A believer should always avoid sin, but sometimes his choices are between several options that are not sinful. One option may be good and another option better, but the choice is left to the individual.

Such will have trouble (thlipsis) = This word includes pressure, tribulation, affliction, and stress. It provides a picture of what might characterize the "present distress" that Paul mentioned in 1 Cor 7:26. Even as Paul was writing this letter to the Corinthians, he himself was experiencing intense pressure in Ephesus (1 Cor 4:11-13; 15:32). "Such young men and virgins who choose to marry and who generally expect a great deal of pleasure, shall meet with a great deal of trouble, even when they expect the most satisfaction and delight." [Gill] Another writer described the situation this way:

> Persecution is difficult enough for a single person, but the problems and pain are multiplied for one who is married. If Paul had been married, his suffering would have been magnified by his worry about his family and knowledge of their worry about him. They would have suffered every time he was beaten or stoned or imprisoned and would have been constantly fearful for his life. Who would have taken care of them in his absence? Who would have taught his children and comforted his wife? His suffering and his practical problems would have increased and the effectiveness of his ministry decreased. Married believers who go through social turmoil and persecution cannot escape carrying a much heavier load than those who are single. [MacArthur]

I am trying to spare you = It was Paul's intention to help them avoid unnecessary care and tribulation. He believed that the time was coming for them when having a Christian spouse and possibly young children to care for would bring increased worry, distress, and anxiety which would not be the case for a single believer in similar times. This thought leads directly into Paul's counsel to married believers in the next section of his letter.

We must remember that God is sovereign over each of our lives. Nothing can touch us that God does not permit. We must also remember that God will always be with us as we walk through the circumstances He has ordained in our lives. Remember that you were bought with a price and you are not your own. It is as if a transfer of ownership has taken place and you now belong to God.

There is an old saying: "Bloom where you are planted!" This is a good way for us to remember that we can show forth the glory of God in any circumstance or situation of life where God has called us to be His. If we have an opportunity to make ourselves more useful to God then we should consider doing that, but in general we should always remember to "Bloom where we are planted!"

Marriage During Difficult Times

(1 Corinthians 7:29-40)

In the previous section, Paul's intention was to help the Corinthian believers avoid unnecessary care and tribulation. He believed that the time was coming for unmarried believers when having a Christian spouse to care for would bring increased worry, distress, and anxiety, and that this would not be the same for a single believer. In this section Paul will describe married life during difficult times.

Advice About Marriage in Difficult Times (7:29-35)

In this section Paul will give two principles to help the Corinthians decide whether to marry or to remain single:

1. The opportunity to serve the Lord is short in this life.
2. The way things are as we now know them is changing. This world system is passing away. One way to summarize this would be to say that every believer should live his life with eternity in view.

1 Cor 7:29 But this I say, brethren, the time has been shortened, so that from now on those who have wives should be as though they had none;

The time has been shortened (sustello) = This means the opportunity for action was being drawn together, compacted, and made short. It is a term that is used only here and in Acts 5:6 where it described binding up a corpse. The same word was used in classical Greek for furling sails, packing luggage, and reducing expenses. "Perhaps there was a reference here to the fact that the time was contracted or made short by their impending persecutions and trials." [Barnes] Paul then begins to list five situations which should not distract us from our devotion to God. All of these circumstances are intended to help illustrate what Paul was teaching about marriage.

#1 If a believer is married, he should not put his spouse before the Lord.

Those who have wives should be as though they had none = This cannot mean that Christian couples are to live celibate lives or to separate from each other in order to be more spiritual, because Paul had already dealt with that issue when he affirmed that married believers are to remain married and fulfill all of their duties toward their partner. Here Paul is saying that believers should not allow their attachment to their loved ones to interfere with their duty to God. The Corinthians lived in a world of pressure and they were about to experience additional anxiety. But as Christians they were obligated to live their lives in devotion to God, and they were not to allow their love for a spouse to alienate their affections from God. Married believers ought to be just as faithful to God as if they were unmarried. They should not allow their marital status to determine their level of spirituality.

#2 Sorrowful circumstances should not keep us from glorifying God.

1 Cor 7:30 and those who weep, as though they did not weep;

Those who weep (present active participle) = This could be translated "the weeping ones," referring to those whose lives are characterized by weeping. Obviously there are circumstances in life when weeping is appropriate, but even in those circumstances we should remember that God is in control, that "this too shall pass." We should not let sorrow completely consume us, but we should focus on God especially during difficult times.

#3 The joys of life should not distract us from fulfilling God's purpose.

...and those who rejoice, as though they did not rejoice;

Those who rejoice (present active participle) = This could be translated "the rejoicing ones," referring to those whose lives are characterized by circumstances that bring joy or happiness Obviously Christians should rejoice (Philippians 3:1; 4:4), but we should not allow the joys of this present earthly life to distract us from focusing on our devotion to God and our ultimate joy in His presence for eternity. "Paul is concerned that our rejoicing on this earth may not in any way diminish our full utilization of the ministry opportunities entrusted to us by the Lord for a short while." [Zodhiates]

#4 Commercial gain should not hinder us from gaining true spiritual riches.

...and those who buy, as though they did not possess;

Those who buy (present active participle) = This could be translated "the buying ones," referring to those whose lives are characterized by a focus on commercial and career success. Our involvement in business should never be allowed to get in the way of our complete devotion to God. We should never allow the getting and keeping of material possessions to be the focus of our lives.

#5 Believers should not indulge in everything the world has to offer.

1 Cor 7:31a and those who use the world, as though they did not make full use of it;

Those who use the world (present deponent/middle participle) = This refers to those whose lives are characterized by fully using the resources of this earthly world system, to the point of overusing or abusing them. Obviously it is right to use the resources of this world in appropriate ways so that we can provide food, clothing, shelter, protection, and the necessities of life for ourselves and our loved ones. Here Paul is condemning someone who goes to extremes and uses worldly resources to excess, centering his life around worldly pleasure and material comfort, or taking full advantage of the world system by surrounding himself with everything he desires from the world. "Whatever this world of ours has to offer, let us use it but never abuse it so that Christ and His kingdom suffer in any way. We are here to work for that which is permanent and eternal." [Zodhiates]

> None of the five areas about which Paul warns is inherently bad. Marriage, sorrow, rejoicing, possessions, and pleasure all have a proper place in the Christian life. In fact, each is a part of God's provision for life here. Asceticism not only is not taught in Scripture, it is forbidden (Col 2:18, 23; 1 Tim 4:3). But human relationships, emotions, possessions, and pleasures become sinful when they dominate thought and behavior, and especially when they distract us from the Lord's work. [MacArthur]

1 Cor 7:31b ... for the form of this world is passing away.

For = This word tells us that Paul will give additional evidence or explanation for the statements he had just made. This phrase also helps us to understand what Paul meant when he said that the time has been shortened. The form **(schema)** of this earthly world system is passing **(parago** = to lead along) . This world system is like the scenery for a stage play, and its time for use will soon come to an end. By way of application to marriage, believers should understand that the divine institution of marriage also belongs to an age that is passing away.

> Although it is God-ordained and blessed, marriage is not an eternal relationship. Speaking of the angels in heaven, Jesus said that 'they neither marry nor are given in marriage' (Matt 22:30). Marriage will disappear with this world, because it is designed only for this world, not the next. Cults that teach about marriage in heaven contradict one of the Lord's clearest and most specific teachings: Marriage will pass away. [MacArthur]

Maintaining undistracted devotion to God (7:32-35)

1 Cor 7:32 But I want you to be free from concern. One who is unmarried is concerned about the things of the Lord, how he may please the Lord;

For believers who are completely wrapped up in the affairs of this world, including marriage or commerce, for example, it will be almost impossible for them to be free from anxiety or care. But it is God's desire for all believers that they be "without anxiety; not troubled by cares." This is possible for a Christian who understands that God is in control and that the world as we know it is passing away, that there is more to life than what we see here.

Concerned (merimnao) = This word means seeking to promote or care for, looking out for, focusing the effort and energy.

Please (aresko) = This term means to be agreeable; to accommodate oneself to the opinions desires and interests of others.

Unmarried = Paul now contrasts what an unmarried vs. a married person is concerned about. The unmarried believer is able to focus more undivided attention on serving the Lord, accommodating himself primarily to the Lord's desires and interests. "His attention is not distracted by the cares of this life, his time is not engrossed and his affections are not alienated by the concerns of a family, and especially by concerns for them in times of trial and persecution. He can give his main attention to the service of God. Paul's own example showed that this was the course which he preferred." [Barnes]

1 Cor 7:33 but one who is married is concerned about the things of the world, how he may please his wife,

The one who is married = In some ways a married believer cannot help being concerned about some of the things of this world and about pleasing his wife. The same will be said of the wife in the very next verse, so what is said here applies equally to both male and female believers. Barnes provides four examples of the distractions that married life may cause:

> The apostle here plainly intimates that there is a danger that the man would be so anxious to gratify his wife as to interfere with his direct religious duties. This may be done in many ways:
>
> 1. The affections may be taken off the Lord and bestowed upon the wife. She may become the object of an improper attachment by taking the place of God in his affections.
> 2. The time may be taken up in devotion to her, which should be given to prayer and to the duties of religion. She may demand his attention when he ought to be engaged in doing good to others, and endeavoring to advance the kingdom of Christ.
> 3. She may be frivolous and fashionable, and may lead him into improper expenses, into a style of living that may be unsuitable for a Christian, and into society where his piety will be injured and his devotion to God lessened; or,
> 4. She may have wrong ideas on the doctrines and duties of religion; and a desire to please her may lead him to modify his views, or to pursue a more lax course of life in his religious duties. [Barnes]

1 Cor 7:34 and his interests are divided. The woman who is unmarried, and the virgin, is concerned about the things of the Lord, that she may be holy both in body and spirit; but one who is married is concerned about the things of the world, how she may please her husband.

His interests are divided (merizo) = This word means to separate into distinct pieces and to distribute or scatter those parts in different places. This is the main problem that Paul wants to guard against in the life of a believer, whether married or single. Our devotion to God should not be divided or parceled out between the things of this world and the things of God.

The woman = Here Paul addressed Christian women and makes the same point as before.

Holy in both body and spirit = This implies that the outward appearance of spirituality, without internal holiness, will be of little value. Both outward and inward holiness are the goal for a Christian woman.

How she may please her husband = The married woman may be in danger of losing her zeal for the Lord by focusing her attention primarily on her husband, and by exerting constant effort to please her husband. Barnes again gives several examples of how this might happen:

1. As in the former case with the husband (1 Cor 7:33), the Christian wife's affections might be transferred from God to the partner of her life. Her time and energy would be taken up by attention to him and to his will; and there would be danger that that attention would be allowed to interfere with her communion with God.

2. Much of her time will be taken up with the cares of a family, and the time which she before gave to the Lord's work might now be given to please her husband and children. Before her marriage she may have been active in several efforts to do good; but afterward she may need to set aside this work and withdraw from these ministries.

3. Her purity may be compromised by wrong ideas of what she should do to please her husband. If he is a worldly man, she may be asked to please him in questionable activities. Instead of cultivating a "gentle and quiet spirit," she may try to make herself attractive by adorning her body more than her mind and spirit.

4. If her husband is opposed to religion, or if he has lax opinions on the subject, or if he is skeptical and worldly, she will be in danger of compromising her beliefs in regard to the doctrines of the faith, and of conforming more to his attitudes and beliefs.

5. To please her husband she may attend frivolous activities and will forget that she has devoted herself to God. She may be in danger of forsaking godly friends who may have encouraged her in her spiritual walk, since her relationship with her husband takes priority over relationships with former friends. As a result of all this, she may become more worldly and carnal in her outlook, and less and less like Christ. [Barnes]

Here in this passage Paul describes the difficulties of Christian marriage. One can only imagine how those difficulties would be magnified in a mixed marriage. The point Paul is making here is that, whether married or single, a believer must try to maintain a single-minded devotion to the Lord.

1 Cor 7:35 This I say for your own benefit; not to put a restraint upon you, but to promote what is appropriate and to secure undistracted devotion to the Lord.

It is obvious from this verse that Paul's motive is only for their good. He does not intend his advice about marriage to put a restraint upon them. Remember, he has not given the unmarried a command, but simply a considered opinion in view of the impending circumstances. He leaves the ultimate choice completely up to them as individuals, and either choice is acceptable. Their marital status is not a matter of holiness vs. sin. Paul's main goal is to promote **undistracted devotion to the Lord**, regardless of a believer's marital status. This same word was used in Luke 10:40 of Martha being so distracted by all the food preparations that she failed to enjoy the presence of the Lord. Whether married or single, if a believer is distracted from his devotion to the Lord then something is wrong.

1 Cor 7:36 But if any man thinks that he is acting unbecomingly toward his virgin daughter, if she is past her youth, and if it must be so, let him do what he wishes, he does not sin; let her marry.

If any man = Here Paul addresses a man who is responsible for a virgin under his care. In order to correctly identify this man, it may be best to begin with the verb in verse 38 (**gamizo** = to give in marriage, to permit to marry). The subject of this verb cannot be the groom, but the one who is giving away the bride. It seems best, then, to identify this man as the Christian father or guardian of a young unmarried woman who is also a believer.

Thinks he is acting unbecomingly toward his virgin daughter = What would lead a Christian father to think he may be acting unfairly toward his virgin daughter? This may have been a father who wanted to keep is daughter at home in view of the benefit and service she was contributing to the household. There may have been any of several selfish reasons for doing this, but this is not what a loving father should do. The welfare and the future of the daughter should come before his own.

> In light of the extant teaching about the advantages of singleness, some of the fathers in Corinth apparently had dedicated their young daughters to the Lord as permanent virgins. But when the daughters became of marriageable age, many of them no doubt wanted to be married, and their fathers were in a quandary. Should they break the vow they made for the girl? It is likely that many of the girls did not have the gift of singleness and were struggling with their desire to get married and their desire to please their fathers and the Lord. This problem was among those mentioned in the church's letter to Paul. [MacArthur]

Two characteristics of the virgin daughter are given:

1. She is **past her youth** = This word means ripe, and perhaps over-ripe, implying she is of marriageable age or even older than the typical age for marriage.
2. **If it must be so** = This term indicates that there is a present necessity. In other words, the time has come to consider it seriously. This implies that a potential groom has come into view.

This presents a picture of a father realizing that he has kept his virgin daughter at home beyond the age at which she might have married, and he is questioning his decision. He now realizes that it may be improper for him to do this, especially when she may have a suitable prospect of marriage. Paul's decision in this case is that the father should **do what he wishes, he does not sin**. Just as Paul did not put any restraint on unmarried believers in his earlier instruction (1 Cor 7:35), here he does not put any restraint on a Christian father to keep his daughter in a state of singleness.

Let them marry = The word "them" also indicates that there is already a groom in view. The plural here refers to the daughter and the man she wants to marry. Evidently the turning point in the father's thinking has occurred because a suitable husband has appeared on the scene.

1 Cor 7:37 But he who stands firm in his heart, being under no constraint, but has authority over his own will, and has decided this in his own heart, to keep his own virgin daughter, he will do well.

But = Here Paul presents the contrasting point where the father believes he has not treated his daughter unfairly by keeping her unmarried and at home.

Stands firm in his heart = The father does not believe he should allow his Christian daughter to marry. He still thinks he is doing the right thing in keeping his daughter unmarried, and that she can serve the Lord better by remaining single than by being married.

> The father here realizes that not giving his daughter into marriage is within his own jurisdiction, but in this instance it is a conclusion that he has come to after having considered all circumstances including the natural inclination of his daughter. It is quite possible that such a situation is one of a father who has a daughter so dedicated that she would prefer to serve the Lord on some mission field alone rather than to be married and stay home with one who does not share her burden for the lost. When a woman is to decide between Christ or a husband, Christ must take the preeminence. Not, of course, that she cannot serve Christ being married, but if the choice must be made between Christ and a husband, it is better to fulfill the call that she has received from God and give up the idea of getting married. [Zodhiates]

Keep (tereo) = This word means to guard, watch over, keep safe, and protect from harm.

He will do well (kalos) = In the first case (which is the opposite of this), Paul showed that it is not a sin for the father to let the couple get married. In this case where the father keeps his daughter unmarried and under his protection, Paul says the father is doing a good thing. "When one considers the customs of that day, because it was considered a great shame for a girl to remain unmarried, many were forced into an unsatisfactory marriage. We can see the concern Paul is showing towards these women. He is saying that the father has the right to keep his daughter at home and protect her from an unsatisfactory marriage. It is not a bad decision for parents to keep their daughter at home and not to give her to marriage, if God's life-long goals for the daughter, the circumstances, and the will of the daughter are taken into account." [Zodhiates]

1 Cor 7:38 So then both he who gives his own virgin daughter in marriage does well, and he who does not give her in marriage will do better.

Paul concludes by reviewing both situations:

1. The father who gives his virgin daughter in marriage does well, and
2. The father who does not give her in marriage will do better.

Paul is expressing his inspired opinion in view of impending events that remaining unmarried may be better under the circumstances. But it is not a matter of one decision being a sin while the other decision is the right choice. Both decisions may be right or perfectly acceptable given a prayerful evaluation of the circumstances in each specific case.

Instruction about the Permanence of Marriage (7:39-40)

1 Cor 7:39 A wife is bound as long as her husband lives; but if her husband is dead, she is free to be married to whom she wishes, only in the Lord.

Bound as long as her husband lives (deo, perfect tense) = The perfect tense emphasizes the continuing state or condition that results from the past event of marriage. This says that the partners are bound by law for the entire span of time (**chronos**) that the partner is alive. It clearly implies that the bond of marriage can only be broken by the death of one of the marriage partners. Nothing is said here about the possibility of divorce and remarriage for believers whose spouse is still living, and no exception clause is given in this passage. If a believer wanted to justify divorcing his wife in order to remarry, this Scripture passage would not support that option.

If her husband is dead, she is free to marry = This addresses the issue of remarriage for a Christian widow. She is no longer bound to her former marriage relationship but is free to remarry. However, she must marry another believer (**"only in the Lord"**). This is one passage that teaches against the idea of a believer deliberately entering into a mixed or inter-faith marriage. Paul is discussing the permanence of the Christian marriage relationship, but this has implications for the unmarried believers he has been addressing in this chapter. Although unmarried believers are free to get married, they should keep in mind that they are bound to that relationship for the rest of their lives!

1 Cor 7:40 But in my opinion she is happier if she remains as she is; and I think that I also have the Spirit of God

Paul again shares his inspired opinion regarding whether believers who are currently unmarried should enter into the marriage relationship.

Happier (makarios) = This word describes the inner peace that is experienced by a believer despite the outward circumstances. In view of the impending circumstances, Paul advocates remaining single. However, in 1 Tim 5:11 Paul implies that younger Christian widows should remarry if they are unable to control their passions (also 1 Cor 7:8-9). So, again, Paul leaves the choice up to the individual believer whether or not to get married.

I also have the Spirit of God = This may contain a hint of sarcasm, that he too had access to the Spirit of God. Apparently the false teachers in Corinth were claiming to teach truth from the Spirit of God.

Paul was under the influence of the infallible Spirit, and that his advice was such as accorded with the will of God. Perhaps he alludes to the fact that the teachers at Corinth deemed themselves to be under the influence of inspiration, and Paul said that he judged also of himself that he was divinely guided and directed in what he said. [Barnes]

In this section dealing with the question of whether to marry Paul had said that it depends on the situation, and he allowed freedom for both options. Marriage is a wonderful institution sanctioned by God, but it is not without its spiritual distractions. Christian men and women should encourage each other's spiritual growth even if it means sacrificing their own needs, desires, or expectations. They should help each other to put God first in their lives, as individuals and as a couple. For this reason, it is very important to choose carefully when selecting a marriage partner. It is important to select someone "in the Lord" (a believer), but it is also very important to select a Christian who holds very similar doctrinal and spiritual beliefs. Spiritual compatibility may be more important than compatibility in other areas.

As Christians we should remember that our time in this world is short, and we should always live with eternity in view. We should remember not to get too wrapped up in the things of this world, but to hold them in an open hand. We should focus on undistracted devotion to the Lord in whatever circumstance of life He has placed us. We should also remember that God's plan for marriage is that it should be a life-long commitment between one Christian man and one Christian woman. Each of us, whether we are married or single, should uphold this important truth. We can pray that God would use us to glorify Him by encouraging others to live according to this truth.

Abusing Christian Liberty: Pagan Temple Feasts

(1 Corinthians 8:1-13)

In the last chapter Paul addressed the subject of marriage, and he left room for personal choice in light of individual circumstances. He emphasized that there may be several choices, none of which were sinful. Here in chapter eight Paul will address another issue that was not sinful in itself, but it was a case in which personal choice or Christian liberty was being abused. We have seen in our previous studies that pride and arrogance were problems among the believers in Corinth, and their abuse of their Christian liberty was yet another example of this arrogant attitude.

As we previously discussed in 1 Cor 1:10-17, it is possible that those who claimed to be followers of Paul may have had antinomian tendencies. This is the idea that since a Christian is saved by grace rather than by works, then he is free from all moral obligations and principles. It says that a believer can live any way he chooses because he has been forgiven by God. An antinomian attitude of moral license was practiced by many Greek philosophical sects. They believed there was a clear division between the physical and the spiritual, so that sensual desires could be freely indulged without affecting one's spirituality. In fact many sects encouraged this so that the spiritual would shine brighter by contrast.

Paul had always emphasized Christian liberty, so this faction in Corinth may have been attempting to take Christian liberty to an extreme by using their freedom to do whatever they pleased and trying to justify it by saying they were following Paul. We saw a possible instance of this kind of behavior in the life of the Christian who was living in known sin with his father's wife (1 Cor 5:1-13). We also saw how Paul described the relationship between the physical body and the spiritual life in 1 Cor 6:12-20, where he said that the body was not for immorality but for the Lord, and he commanded Christians to flee from immorality. Even in 1 Cor 7:34 Paul connected our spirituality with our behavior when he stated that Christians should be holy in both body and spirit.

What was the specific problem?

Here in chapter eight Paul will discuss a specific area where the Corinthian Christians came into contact with the pagan culture in which they lived. Specifically, this involved the believer's relationship to things used in the rituals of idolatry and paganism in the city of Corinth. From our background study we know that Corinth was filled with pagan temples, each practicing its own rituals of sacrifice to its god. We can imagine how much of the produce of the city passed through the pagan temples on its way to the market, and that a budget-conscious homemaker could often get otherwise good meat at bargain prices after it had been offered in one of the temples. This practice of eating meat that had been sacrificed to idols became a point of controversy between the factions in the Corinthian church, and this was another issue that aggravated their divisive spirit.

There were several ways that Christians in Corinth might come into contact with meat that had been sacrificed to idols:

1. Buying meat in the marketplace. Even meat that was not specifically taken to the temple priests was often consecrated by the merchant as a token offering to an idol. So when a Christian went grocery shopping there was always a possibility that the meat had been offered to an idol (see 1 Cor 10:25).

2. Eating dinner at the home of friends and neighbors. When Christians were invited to eat dinner with unsaved neighbors there was no guarantee that the meat they were served had not been sacrificed to an idol (see 1 Cor 10:27).

3. Eating at the pagan temple feasts themselves. Some of the pagan temples would often be used as public meeting halls which could accommodate a large gathering for public affairs or community social functions. The subject of these meetings had nothing to do with the religious purpose of the meeting place, but there were often community banquets held in these halls which Christians might attend. The meat at these banquets would probably have been offered to the temple god.

Two different viewpoints arose in the church at Corinth about how a believer should handle this situation. One group considered the food to be defiled, polluted, or tainted by its association with the pagan idol. This group refused to eat such food, and they were offended by other believers who did partake of this food. The other group claimed that the food itself was not defiled in any way, and that it could be eaten without any adverse affect on a believer or his testimony. They ate such food, and they may have looked down on other believers who held stricter beliefs.

As we begin looking at this passage we may not understand why this was such a controversy in Corinth, but in our own culture today we also have areas where Christians are forced into contact with the unbelieving world system. Some of the controversies Christians face today include whether a believer should drink alcoholic beverages, smoke cigarettes, play cards, wear makeup, go dancing, listen to particular styles of music, play the lottery, or go to the theater. The principles Paul shared in this passage can be applied in our day to many areas of our own lives that are analogous to the issue of eating meat offered to idols in Corinth.

Identifying the root cause of the dispute (8:1-3)

1 Cor 8:1 Now concerning things sacrificed to idols, we know that we all have knowledge. Knowledge makes arrogant, but love edifies.

Now concerning = This marks Paul's answer to another question asked by the Corinthians. There was a strong difference of opinion on this issue among the Corinthian Christians. There was a group that saw themselves as more enlightened, and they acted on the basis of their so-called superior knowledge about the fact that the gods represented by these idols did not really exist; they were not real deities.

Things sacrificed to idols = The priests were entitled to a part of the meat that was offered in the temple, and often they would put it up for sale in the market. In Corinth it was commonly referred to using the Greek words **hierothuton**, a temple sacrifice, or **theothuton**, a sacrifice to a god. But here Paul used the Greek word **eidolothuton**, a sacrifice to an idol. In Corinth there was a close connection between idolatry and immorality, which Paul told the Corinthians to avoid (1 Cor 6:12-20).

We all have knowledge (gnosis) = This phrase connects with the issue Paul began addressing in 1 Cor 1:5 (also see 1:21; 2:8,14). Paul is probably quoting the words of the Corinthians themselves, perhaps from the letter they sent to him. They were saying that they knew the truth about the emptiness of idol worship, but Paul is probably quoting their words sarcastically because in verse seven he will plainly declare that all of the Corinthian believers do not have this knowledge. Here Paul goes right to the heart of the issue and pinpoints the root cause of the problem. Paul says that even if all Christians did have this knowledge, the dispute cannot be solved by knowledge because of the limitations of human knowledge.

Knowledge makes arrogant, but love edifies = This connects us back to what Paul previously said concerning the arrogance of the factions in Corinth (1 Cor 4:6,18-19; 5:2). It was one of the characteristics of the Corinthian believers to be puffed up. Being puffed up means selfishly focusing on pleasing oneself, while edifying (1 Cor 3:9) implies a focus on pleasing others. As we saw in 1 Cor 6:12, Knowledge only says, "All things are lawful for me," but Love adds, "All things are not profitable." The Corinthians were claiming to act on their knowledge of Christian liberty. Paul agreed that they had knowledge in general, but he insisted that knowledge alone was not a sufficient basis for Christian behavior. Knowledge is essential, but it is not enough. A believer should always use the formula: Knowledge + Love = Responsible Action. Love should set the limits on Christian liberty.

> Love as well as knowledge should be allowed to come in as a guide in such cases, and together they will be a safer guide for action than mere knowledge. Knowledge combined with right feelings, with pure principles, with a heart filled with love to God and human beings, may be trusted: but not mere intellectual attainments; mere abstract science; the mere cultivation of the intellect. Unless the heart is cultivated with that, the effect of knowledge is to fill a man with vain ideas of his own importance and thus to lead him into error and to sin. [Barnes]

One argument for abstaining from food that had been sacrificed to idols was that eating it might somehow lend support or approval to pagan idolatry. In fact this may have been one of the reasons why the first church council at Jerusalem advised the Gentile believers to abstain from eating meat offered to idols (Acts 15:29). Here Paul does not refer to that earlier decree of the Jerusalem Council, but instead he explains the foundational principle upon which that decree was based. The true intent of that decree was to outline a course of action for Gentile believers that would express true Christian love for Jewish believers, to whom eating such meat would have been an abomination. In that case it was a way for Jewish and Gentile believers to continue to have table fellowship. Limiting one's liberty for the sake of other believers has always been the most loving thing to do.

1 Cor 8:2 If anyone supposes that he knows anything, he has not yet known as he ought to know;

If anyone supposes that he knows anything = The first step to knowledge is to know the limitations of our own knowledge. We are finite, fallen creatures with limited knowledge. God is the infinite, omniscient Creator, so only He has absolute and trustworthy knowledge.

Has not yet known as he ought to know = The believer that is confident in his knowledge is probably in danger of the same pride and arrogance demonstrated by the Corinthians. Knowledge that is not accompanied by love is not true knowledge.

> This is designed to condemn that vain conceit of knowledge or self-confidence which would lead us to despise others or to disregard their interests. If anyone is conceited of his knowledge, is so vain, and proud, and self-confident, that he is led to despise others and to disregard their true interests, he has not yet learned the very first elements of true knowledge as he ought to learn them. [Barnes]

1 Cor 8:3 but if anyone loves God, he is known by Him.

In verse one Paul set up the contrast between knowledge and love, and in verse two he focused on the inadequacy of knowledge by itself. Here in verse three he says something more about love, and especially a believer's love of God. Essentially he says, "If anyone loves God, it is a sign that God took the initiative to establish the relationship with him."

Is known by Him (ginosko) = This word for knowledge indicates that a personal relationship exists between the knower and the thing that is known. This implies a strong influence of what is known on the person who has this knowledge.

> There is no true and real knowledge which is not connected with the love of God. This will prompt a man also to love his brethren, and will lead him to promote their happiness. A man's course, therefore, is not to be regulated by mere knowledge, but the grand principle is love to God and love to man. Your conclusion on this question should not be formed from mere abstract knowledge, but you should ask what Christian love would demand. If the love of others would permit you to partake of this food, then it might be done; but if not, if it would injure them, then whatever your knowledge might dictate, you should not do this. The doctrine is that the love of God and of each other is a better guide in determining what to do than mere knowledge. [Barnes]

The truth about false gods (8:4-6)

Paul now will explain what this knowledge was that some of the believers were boasting about. In simple terms, they knew that an idol is nothing and there is only one true God (1 Cor 8:4). Paul will go on to prove this by acknowledging that there were many so-called gods, but that they are gods in name only and not by nature (1 Cor 8:5). He will then restate the common doctrine of Christians, that there is only one God (1 Cor 8:6).

1 Cor 8:4 Therefore concerning the eating of things sacrificed to idols, we know that there is no such thing as an idol in the world, and that there is no God but one.

No such thing as a idol = Here Paul seems to say that an idol does not have any real existence. As in Hab 2:18, "What profit is the idol when its maker has carved it, Or an image, a teacher of falsehood? For its maker trusts in his own handiwork when he fashions speechless idols." Some of their gods were complete fakes, but Paul also knew that others represented real demonic beings. These demonic beings do have real existence, but none of them are truly gods. They have a certain type of reality, but they do not have deity. As one commentator said:

> We are not so stupid as to suppose that the block of wood or the carved image or the chiseled marble is a real intelligence and is conscious and capable of receiving worship, or benefiting its votaries. There is no doubt that the more intelligent pagan had this knowledge; and doubtless nearly all Christians possessed it, though a few who had been educated in the grosser views of paganism might still have regarded the idol with a superstitious reverence. [Barnes]

There is no God but one = What Paul means here is that neither the statue nor the demonic being it represents is what a Christian means when he talks about the one true God. There is only one true God, so an idol is a false or imaginary god which is of no significance when compared with the infinite Creator.

1 Cor 8:5 For even if there are so-called gods whether in heaven or on earth, as indeed there are many gods and many lords,

For = Here Paul provides further explanation for what he means by so-called gods in comparison with the one true God. Literally he says **"called gods,"** that they are reputed to be gods. Paul is really denying the deity of these so-called gods. Later in this letter, however, he will explain that those who worship idols are really worshiping demons, evil spirits, and agents of Satan (1 Cor 10:19-21).

Whether in heaven = Some of the gods were supposed to reside in heaven. He may be referring to the pagan celestial deities represented by the sun, moon, and planets (Jupiter, Mercury, Venus, etc.)

Or in earth = Some of the gods were supposed to reigned over parts of the earth or sea (Neptune, etc.) The pagans worshiped some gods that were supposed to dwell in heaven; others that were supposed to reside on earth, and others that presided over the remote parts of the universe.

There are many gods = Paul is saying that there are many things that the pagans regard as gods which they believe to have some influence over the things they care about. However, when the pagans use the word god, they were not talking about the God of the Bible.

There are many lords = This term identifies the things that rule over them or things they submit to and whose laws they obey. The title "lord" was often given to their idols or false gods.

> This cannot be an admission by Paul that they were truly gods and ought to he worshiped; but it is a declaration that the pagans esteemed them to be such, or that a large number of imaginary beings were thus adored. The emphasis should be placed on the word many, and the intention is to show that the number of these that were worshiped was not a few but was immense; and that they were in fact worshiped as gods and allowed to have the kind of influence over their minds and lives which they would have had if they were real. [Barnes]

1 Cor 8:6 yet for us there is but one God, the Father, from whom are all things and we exist for Him; and one Lord, Jesus Christ, by whom are all things, and we exist through Him.

Yet for us = Christians know the truth about these so-called gods as well as about the one true God. "The drive of his argument is towards the assertion that, whatever other spiritual or demonic beings there may be, for us there is only one whom we recognize as God, who created the universe and all that is in it." [Barrett] Paul describes **God** as **the Father** who is the **Creator** of all things. The best starting point for talking about the one true God is to emphasize the Creator-creature distinction. There is an infinite distance between the Creator and what He has created. Idols of wood or stone are made of material things, and even demonic spirits are merely creatures who are not on the same plane as their Creator.

Paul then described our relationship to this one true God. We exist **for Him**, and not the other way around. In contrast to the many lords in the previous verse, Paul here explained that there is only ONE **Lord Jesus Christ**, and He is the One through whom all things were created, including we ourselves. Christ was the agent of our creation, just as He was the agent of our redemption.

The difference between believers' consciences (8:7-8)

Not all believers have an adequate knowledge about these things, and their consciences may be weak so they become defiled by eating such food through the example of others (1 Cor 8:7). Paul realized that this fact should be discussed next.

1 Cor 8:7 However not all men have this knowledge; but some, being accustomed to the idol until now, eat food as if it were sacrificed to an idol; and their conscience being weak is defiled.

Not all men have this knowledge = This directly contradicts the claim of the enlightened Corinthians which Paul was probably quoting in 1 Cor 8:1. If all of the believers recognized the essential unreality of idols, then there would be no problem. But not all of the believers had this knowledge.

Being accustomed to the idol until now (sunetheia) = This term means to be intimate or to have habitual contact with something . "It is the force of habit that still grips them when they eat such meat. They eat it as an idol sacrifice, though they no longer believe in idols. The idol-taint clings in their minds to this meat." [RWP]

> Some in the Corinthian church did not have this clear-cut knowledge of the non-existence or unreality of idols. They had been converted from paganism. The idol had been a very real thing to them before, and even now it represents to them a very real memory of their old life and the things they had put behind them. When they ate meat which had been offered to idols, they did so with a very real conscience or consciousness of that fact. It reminded them vividly of their former practices, and in revulsion they said, 'We ought not to be doing this.' [Boyer]

Their conscience being weak is defiled = The conscience is that part of every person which tells him he should do what he believes to be right, and that he should not do what he believes to be wrong. It does not actually teach us what is right and wrong, but it urges us to do what we have been taught. We must realize that the conscience is part of our human nature, and as such it was damaged by the Fall. It is possible for our conscience to urge us to do something which is really a sin, based on the fact that we have been taught something and therefore believe something that is false. Paul described these believers as being **weak in conscience** because they believed they must avoid something that actually was not a sin. In that case, their conscientiousness was based on a false belief. This passage shows that it is possible for the conscience of a believer to operate on the basis of error. The conscience is not an infallible guide even for the believer.

> Even though the act in itself is not morally or spiritually wrong, it becomes wrong when it is committed against conscience. A defiled conscience is one that has been ignored and violated. Such a conscience brings confusion, resentment, and feelings of guilt. A person who violates his conscience willingly does what he thinks to be wrong. In his own mind he has committed sin; and until he fully understands that the act is not sin in God's eyes, he should have no part in it. [MacArthur]

These Corinthians believed that something was a sin even though it was not really a sin. But at their point of understanding and maturity, they believed that this activity was sinful and should not be done. Notice Paul never says they should go against their conscience, even though it was operating on a false assumption. The conscience is something that should not be crossed. Paul says this **defiles** the conscience and causes it to operate incorrectly. Instead, believers should be taught what is true so that the conscience will operate on the basis of the truth.

1 Cor 8:8 But food will not commend us to God; we are neither the worse if we do not eat, nor the better if we do eat.

In this verse Paul teaches these believers the truth about eating food sacrificed to idols. We see that idols have absolutely no effect on the meat itself. If idols are nothing, then they can do nothing to the meat. Holding some meat in front of a piece of wood or stone does not change the nutritional value of the meat, and it does not defile the meat in any way. Therefore, the meat could certainly be eaten by a Christian without having any adverse affect on his physical body.

Food will not commend us to God = If you do something that God has not forbidden, then you have not affected your relationship with God. Dietary habits do not earn any favor with God. "God does not regard this as a matter of importance. He does not make his favor depend on unimportant circumstances like this." [Barnes]

We are neither the worse if we do not eat, nor the better if we do eat = This issue has absolutely no significance in God's eyes, as far as gaining His commendation or earning His praise.

There is a common misconception about freedom in general, and especially about Christian liberty. People think that if they are free to do something, then they must do that thing. In other words, they must participate in something in order to prove they are really free to do it. But this makes the Christian a slave to his own freedom! In this verse Paul had just said that exercising our freedom does not commend us to God in any way, and that refraining from exercising our freedom does not hurt us in any way. So it is just as much an exercise of Christian liberty not to eat the meat as it is to eat the meat.

If Paul had stopped his line of reasoning here, then the Christian liberty faction in Corinth could have claimed the victory in their dispute with those who were more strict in their beliefs. But Paul continued in the next few verses by putting limits on the principle of Christian liberty.

The mature Christian response to the issue (8:9-13)

Paul already stated that eating food sacrificed to idols did not make believers better or worse in God's estimation (1 Cor 8:8), but here Paul explains that exercising one's Christian liberty could cause harm to others. It can be a stumbling block to the weak (1 Cor 8:9) and it might cause them to injure their weak consciences by doing something they believe to be sinful (1 Cor 8:10). The harm this can cause is very serious (1 Cor 8:11), and being the cause of such sin means sinning against Christ Himself (1 Cor 8:12). Paul tells them that, rather than cause a more immature brother to sin, it was better for them to forfeit their Christian liberty in these cases (1 Cor 8:13). Those who have the greater knowledge and spiritual maturity are the ones who should accommodate to the less mature or weaker believers by abstaining from activities that might harm the faith and life of those who are less mature.

1 Cor 8:9 But take care that this liberty of yours does not somehow become a stumbling block to the weak.

Take care (blepo) = Literally this means to see, look out, or be aware. Notice this is addressed to the mature believers, and not to the immature Christians. There is no command from God here for the immature believers to "grow up!" The command is to the mature believers, that they should exercise self-control in order not to cause the less mature to fall into sin. In effect, Paul is saying, "Do not look at your own freedom. Instead, look at the needs of the less mature Christians around you. If you love them as God commands you to do, then you will not exercise your Christian liberty in any way that will weaken their faith."

Liberty (exousia) = This word means authority, power, privilege, or right. In this context it means the authority or right to eat any kind of food. "Personal liberty becomes a battle cry to those who wish to indulge their own whims and appetites regardless of the effect upon others." [RWP]

A stumbling block to the weak (proskomma) = This term describes an obstacle that is put in the path which could cause people to stumble if they strike their foot against it. We do not live alone, and the things we leave in our wake will have an effect on others around us.

> The voice of a Christian's conscience is the instrument of the Holy Spirit. If a believer's conscience is weak it is because he is spiritually weak and immature, not because the leading of his conscience is weak. Conscience is God's doorkeeper to keep us out of places where we could be harmed. As we mature, conscience allows us to go more places and to do more things because we will have more spiritual strength and better spiritual judgment. As they grow in knowledge and maturity the limits of the conscience are expanded. We should never expand our actions and habits before our conscience permits it, and we should never encourage anyone else to do that. If an immature brother sees us doing something that bothers his conscience, his spiritual life is harmed. We should never influence a fellow Christian to do anything that the Holy Spirit, through that person's conscience, is protecting him from. It is never right to cause another believer to violate his conscience. [MacArthur]

Knowledge alone says, "Go ahead and eat." Knowledge + Love says, "How will this affect other believers?"

The danger to the weaker believer (8:10-11)

1 Cor 8:10 For if someone sees you, who have knowledge, dining in an idol's temple, will not his conscience, if he is weak, be strengthened to eat things sacrificed to idols?

For if = Paul now shares a concrete example for what he has just said. In the Greek, this is a third class conditional clause indicating something that is a possible case, something that could potentially happen. A more mature believer might decide to exercise his Christian liberty by eating at one of the local banquets which may be held in a public meeting hall in one of the temple buildings. A less mature believer may see this and decide to go against what his own conscience is telling him. But what actual impact does this have on the immature believer? Paul answers that question in the next verse.

1 Cor 8:11 For through your knowledge he who is weak is ruined, the brother for whose sake Christ died.

Through your knowledge = The knowledge and actions of the more mature believer could set an example which the less mature believer may choose to imitate, even though his conscience tells him not to.

He is ruined (apollumi) = This is a very strong term that means to be ruined or corrupted. It indicates the severity of the impact of the mature believer's behavior on the immature believer.

For whose sake Christ died = Christ died for this immature believer, but the so-called mature believer does not seem willing to give up part of his supper for the sake of this brother in Christ. If Jesus died for this weaker Christian, then surely the stronger Christian can forfeit a single meal for his sake!

The danger to the stronger believer (8:12)

1 Cor 8:12 And so, by sinning against the brethren and wounding their conscience when it is weak, you sin against Christ.

Sinning against the brethren = The unrestrained exercise of Christian liberty by engaging in non-sinful behavior could become a sin against another believer if it wounds his conscience. The unloving exercise of Christian liberty can actually be sinful. There is a serious danger to the spiritual life of the mature believer as well.

Wounding their conscience (tupto) = This word means to beat or strike a blow. This is what the mature believer is doing to the immature believer. He is striking a blow at the other person's conscience.

You sin against Christ = Not only is the mature believer sinning against his brother, he is said to sin against Christ Himself. Sinning against one member of the body is a sin against the entire body, including the Head.

The example of Paul (8:13)

1 Cor 8:13 Therefore, if food causes my brother to stumble, I will never eat meat again, so that I will not cause my brother to stumble.

Notice that Paul does not command the more mature believer not to eat meat if it will cause others to fall into sin. Paul simply presents his own personal example or conviction, and he expects them to learn from it. He says, "I will never eat meat again if it causes my brother to stumble." Paul is willing to limit his own personal liberty so he does not injure the spiritual life of other believers. Paul closes this chapter by again holding himself up as an example. He shares his own principle of conduct in such situations, which other believers can imitate.

How should a Christian decide whether or not to engage in a certain activity?

You can ask yourself several questions:

- Is this activity really necessary, or is it something that is not really essential in my life?
- Is this activity really helpful or profitable, or is it something that I would do just for fun?
- Is this activity something Jesus would do if He were in my place right now?
- Does this activity promote what is good, right, or true according to God's standards?
- Is this activity something that would set a good example for other Christians to imitate?
- If my unsaved friends saw me doing this activity, would it lead them closer to trusting Christ or would it show that Christ does not really make a difference in my life?
- Will this activity help me and others around me to become more mature spiritually?
- Will my participation in this activity bring glory and praise to God?
- If I engage in this activity, can I be sure that other believers will not be harmed by following my example?

Our choices and our behavior should be motivated and characterized by self-sacrificing love for those around us, rather than by knowledge alone. A Christian is much more likely to behave correctly if he is acting from unselfish love, rather than from self-assured knowledge. Love produces an outlook that is humble, kind, accepting of others, and aware of one's own weaknesses. This leads a Christian to do what is right. "The people that have been most eminent in knowledge have also been distinguished for humility; but the heart was right; and they saw the folly of depending on mere knowledge." [Barnes]

We should understand that knowledge by itself tends to produce pride and arrogance. We should not be self-confident in our wisdom, but should clearly understand the limits of our own finite knowledge. This does not mean that knowledge is unimportant, because loving behavior can only come from a correct understanding of God's truth. But knowledge must be united with love. This passage points out that even godly believers can believe things that are not true. This fact leads us to see the importance of continually teaching the truths of God's Word to others, so that we may all grow to maturity in our faith.

One of the main messages of this chapter is that Christians should be careful how they behave. Otherwise their conduct, even in things that are not forbidden by God, might lead other believers to violate their own consciences and fall into sin. "Christians very often pursue a course of conduct which may not be in itself unlawful, but which may lead others who have not their intelligence or strength of principle, into error. One man may be safe where another man is in danger. They should so live that it would be safe and right for all to imitate their example." [Barnes] We are each accountable to God to set a good example, and this should include self-denial and abstinence from certain things for the sake of others.

Paul's Example of Yielding His Rights

(1 Corinthians 9:1-27)

This chapter is really a continuation of Paul's discussion on Christian liberty. We saw in the last verse of chapter eight that Paul used his own example as a model for the Corinthians to imitate regarding giving up one's Christian liberty for the benefit of less mature Christians. Here in chapter nine Paul gives specific examples in several areas of his life that illustrate the principle he shared in chapter eight. He begins with a series of rhetorical questions which establishes his apostolic authority, and he lists some of the rights that he was free to exercise as an apostle.

Paul establishes his apostolic rights (9:1-6)

1 Cor 9:1 Am I not free? Am I not an apostle? Have I not seen Jesus our Lord? Are you not my work in the Lord?

Am I not free = It is as if Paul is saying, "Do you suppose that because I limit my freedom out of love that my freedom does not exist?" As we saw in the previous section, some people think that if you do not use your freedom, then you really are not free. But this is a fallacy. Freedom does not cease to exist simply because you choose not to exercise it in every possible situation.

Am I not an apostle = Here Paul is stating, "If any Christian can claim to be free then I certainly can, because I am an apostle!" Logic would dictate that an apostle of Christ would have more freedom than the average Christian. But somehow the Corinthians were not being very logical, so Paul goes on in the next few verses to prove that he is an appointed apostle of Christ who does have great freedom.

Have I not seen Jesus = Here Paul gives the basis for his apostolic office. An apostle was required to have seen the resurrected Christ (Acts 1:21-22). It is the appearance of the resurrected Lord, and Christ's official appointment of Paul to apostleship, that is the basis for his apostolic office.

Are you not my work = In addition to a person having seen the risen Christ, an apostle could be identified from his work. This rhetorical question is part of Paul's proof that he is an apostle. The very existence of the church in Corinth authenticated Paul's apostolic ministry. Paul will elaborate on this in the next verse.

1 Cor 9:2 If to others I am not an apostle, at least I am to you; for you are the seal of my apostleship in the Lord.

At least I am an apostle to you = Here Paul appeals directly to their own personal experience of his apostleship.

You are the seal of my apostleship = A seal (**sphragis**) is a visible proof, confirmation, or authentication of something that already exists. In Paul's day a seal was used to indicate the authenticity and genuineness of something, or to officially declare the authority of the person responsible for the accomplishment. So the founding of the church at Corinth did not make Paul an apostle, and his apostleship did not depend on that work. The founding of the church was simply evidence of Paul's genuine apostolic activity. It was proof of his apostleship.

1 Cor 9:3-4 My defense to those who examine me is this: Do we not have a right to eat and drink?

My defense (apologia) = This word was used of a defense in court.

To those who examine me (ankrino) = This term meant cross-examining someone during a court proceeding. It shows that some members of the church in Corinth were questioning Paul's apostolic authority. This must have been an on-going problem, because his second letter to the Corinthians provides an even stronger defense of his apostolic authority.

A right to eat and drink = This refers to the legitimate right of an apostle to "eat and drink" at the expense of the church. The official leaders had the right to receive support from the churches they served.

> Paul was willing to impose a serious limitation on his Christian liberty. He had, it seems, good reason to suspect that this attitude would not only provoke opposition among the Christians at Corinth whose watchword was spiritual liberty, but also lead to questioning of his own authority. 'If this man were a true apostle, and enjoyed the apostle's authority, he would not allow himself to be restricted in this way.' It is to this sort of complaint that Paul immediately proceeds to reply in chapter 9. Paul would hardly have spent so long on the question of apostolic rights if his own apostolic status had not been questioned in Corinth. [Barrett]

1 Cor 9:5 Do we not have a right to take along a believing wife, even as the rest of the apostles and the brothers of the Lord and Cephas?

A right to take along a believing wife = This shows that apostles, just like any other Christians, have the right to be married if they wish. But this also implies that as apostles labor among the churches, they have the right to the support of the church for their entire family, including their wife and children. One commentator explained Paul's case by saying, "Though he chose the status of singleness, he had every right in the Lord to be married. He also had the right, as did the other apostles, to take his wife with him as he ministered and to have her supported along with him." [MacArthur] Paul will now provide several examples of this practice among the apostolic community.

As the rest of the apostles, and the brothers of the Lord, and Cephas = This implies that the majority of the other apostles were married and took their wives with them as they ministered among the churches. Paul includes the best known apostles, the Lord's brothers, and Peter (Cephas), as those who were following this common practice.

1 Cor 9:6 Or do only Barnabas and I not have a right to refrain from working?

Do only Barnabas and I not have this right = The fact that Paul and Barnabas did not take advantage of their right to the support of the churches could have been misunderstood by the Corinthians to mean that they were not really apostles, or maybe that they were second-class apostles. So next Paul defends his apostolic right to support from the churches by giving a series of arguments that prove he has the same rights as any other apostle.

The Right of Ministers to Support from the Churches (9:7-14)

Argument #1: The analogy from everyday occupations (9:7)

1 Cor 9:7 Who at any time serves as a soldier at his own expense? Who plants a vineyard and does not eat the fruit of it? Or who tends a flock and does not use the milk of the flock?

The soldier, the farmer, and the shepherd all enjoy the rewards of their labors. This shows that it was the common practice to pay workers who diligently labor in their calling. Soldiers do not fight during the day and then work at civilian jobs all night to support themselves and their families. Farmers do not freely labor all day in the fields and then afterward do some other work in order to make a living. Shepherds do not tend the flocks without expecting some of the milk in payment for their time. Payment for labor has always been the expected, right, and customary thing in every society. Therefore, Christian workers should expect nothing less.

Argument #2: Scriptural testimony for supporting ministers (9:8-11)

1 Cor 9:8 I am not speaking these things according to human judgment, am I? Or does not the Law also say these things?

According to human judgment = The customs of human societies are not the only proof. Even God's Law addressed this topic and can be applied to the issue of supporting Christian ministers.

1 Cor 9:9 For it is written in the Law of Moses, "YOU SHALL NOT MUZZLE THE OX WHILE HE IS THRESHING." God is not concerned about oxen, is He?

Here Paul quoted Deut 25:4, not to show God's concern for the humane treatment of animals, but His concern that a person who serves the Lord in the harvest field should share in the results of the harvest. This should be expressed in some physical way that is analogous to the work of an ox who is allowed to eat some of the physical grain. It does not mean that God does not care about animals, because He is concerned about a sparrow that falls to the ground (Matt 10:29). But if God cares this much for the animals, how much more does He care about the support and livelihood of Christian workers? What is true for animals in this analogy is true for human beings to a much greater extent.

1 Cor 9:10 Or is He speaking altogether for our sake? Yes, for our sake it was written, because the plowman ought to plow in hope, and the thresher to thresh in hope of sharing the crops.

For our sake it was written = The context of Deuteronomy 25 has to do with social and economic relationships, and verse four used the practice of not muzzling the ox to teach that human workers should be paid for their work. "The LAW was not made for irrational beings, but for those that have mind and reason. Paul means that the command was given in order to support the true principle that the workman should reap some reward for his labor." [Barrett]

1 Cor 9:11 If we sowed spiritual things in you, is it too much if we reap material things from you?

If we sowed spiritual things = This Greek phrase is a first class conditional clause which is assumed to be true. It is as if Paul were saying, "Since we sowed spiritual things." A genuine spiritual ministry actually did take place, and it is not too much to ask that support be given to genuine godly ministers who bring spiritual growth. This verse implies that there is a condition which must be met before the church supports Christian workers. The ministers must sow spiritual things, rather than just claiming the authority of ministers without actually producing any valuable result among God's people. "Obviously we should give our money only to ministers that are biblically sound and responsible. Every appeal made in the Lord's name does not deserve the support of the Lord's people. Being wise in our giving is part of our stewardship." [MacArthur]

Argument #3: They were giving support to other ministers (9:12)

1 Cor 9:12 If others share the right over you, do we not more? Nevertheless, we did not use this right, but we endure all things so that we will cause no hindrance to the gospel of Christ.

If others share the right over you = Apparently the Corinthians were already giving support to some of their other ministers, and this proved that they understood this principle. As an apostle and as the founding pastor of the church in Corinth, Paul had even more of a claim to their support than the others did.

Nevertheless, we did not use this right = Here Paul strongly restated his own example of yielding the right of support.

We endure all things (stego) = This word means to bear; to cover over with silence; to silently forbear.

So that we will cause no hindrance to the gospel = This purpose clause explains why Paul chose not to exercise his right to support. He was constantly asking himself how it would look to the unsaved, and he did not want to hinder the gospel in any way.

Potential converts might think twice about accepting the Gospel if they saw that it would lead to financial commitments on behalf of the missionaries. The Gospel, which turned upon the love and self-sacrifice of Jesus, could not fitly be presented by preachers who insisted on their rights, delighted in the exercise of authority, and made what profit they could out of the work of evangelism. [Barrett]

We must understand that Paul was not against the practice of paying Christian ministers. He was very concerned that the church should recognize the genuine right of Christian ministers to their support. But in his own ministry, Paul was determined not to use his legitimate right to support because of the possibility of hindering the gospel. See Acts 20:33 and 2 Thess 3:8.

Argument #4: This was the common practice in both pagan and Jewish temples (9:13)

1 Cor 9:13 Do you not know that those who perform sacred services eat the food of the temple, and those who attend regularly to the altar have their share from the altar?

Do you not know = This is Paul's way of saying, "Of course you already know." It was common knowledge that those who ministered in the temples received their support from the proceeds of the temple. This was true in the Jewish temple as well as in the pagan temples of Corinth.

Argument #5: Jesus Himself supported the practice (9:14)

1 Cor 9:14 So also the Lord directed those who proclaim the gospel to get their living from the gospel.

Probably this is a reference to the words of the Lord Jesus: "The laborer is worthy of his hire" (Matt 10:10; Luke 10:7). Even Jesus Christ declared that this arrangement was the proper method for supporting Christian workers (see also Galatians 6:6). Notice that the Lord commanded they should **"get their living."** This does not mean that they should get rich from Christian service. As one man wrote,

They should be made comfortable; not rich. They should receive so much as to keep their minds from being harassed with cares and their families from want, not so much as to lead them to forget their dependence on God or on the people. Probably the true rule is that they should be able to live like the majority of the people among whom they labor. [Barnes]

Why Paul practiced the principle of self-denial (9:15-27)

So far Paul had argued very convincingly for the right of the Christian worker to expect financial support for his spiritual service. But even though Paul could have done this, he did not take advantage of his rights. He certainly did not question the right of any other minister to receive support from the church, but here in this next section Paul explains that he was motivated by a higher principle which prompted him to give up his rights. Paul was motivated by a higher reward than the benefits of material support in this earthly life. Notice that the subjects of these next few sentences shift to the first person ("I"), which indicates that Paul was sharing his own personal example.

Reason #1: Because of his call to preach the gospel without charge (9:15-18)

1 Cor 9:15 But I have used none of these things. And I am not writing these things so that it will be done so in my case; for it would be better for me to die than have any man make my boast an empty one.

I have used none of these = One of the reasons Paul could say this relates to some of the things he said in chapter seven.

> Paul's special gift of continency which enabled him to abstain from marriage, and his ability to meet his needs without seriously interrupting his ministry, made something expedient to him which is ordinarily inexpedient; namely, that he went without the support of the church. What to Paul was a duty would be the opposite to someone, for instance, to whom God had given a family, without any other means of support. [JFB]

Better for me to die = Paul was not writing so that they would begin supporting him. He would rather die of hunger than have someone deprive him of the privilege of preaching the Gospel without charge and therefore without hindrance to anyone. This was what Paul could glory in (**kauchema**), a word that did not mean some kind of proud boasting, but legitimate rejoicing or glorying in what God had called him to do (see Gal 6:4).

1 Cor 9:16 For if I preach the gospel, I have nothing to boast of, for I am under compulsion; for woe is me if I do not preach the gospel.

Paul is saying that preaching the gospel gives him no extra credit, because he has no choice in the matter. He cannot do anything else BUT preach the gospel! He can claim no special reward for doing what he was commissioned to do. He simply received God's revelation and was carrying out his duty to tell others what God had said. It would be disobedient for Paul to do anything but preach the gospel, and this explains why Paul would say, "Woe is me if I do not preach the gospel."

1 Cor 9:17 For if I do this voluntarily, I have a reward; but if against my will, I have a stewardship entrusted to me

If I do this voluntarily = This is a Greek third class conditional phrase, which is a supposition for the sake of argument. Paul was saying, "Let's suppose for the sake of argument that I am simply exercising my own human choice in deciding to preach the gospel. If so, then I might expect a special reward of some kind. But for the sake of argument suppose I am under compulsion to preach the gospel, despite my own choice or desire. In this second case then I am merely functioning as a steward who has been entrusted with a task, and there is no special reward. I would simply be doing my duty." Paul belongs to this second case in his argument. He is a commissioned apostle with a stewardship entrusted to him by God Himself. Paul cannot help but carry out this task (see 1 Cor 4:1-2). He is not a volunteer or an independent contractor who is doing a job for God, but who could terminate his employment at will. Instead he is a bondservant whom God has purchased and assigned to do some work as He sees fit. This means that Paul is in no position to claim pay or reward, and the question naturally follows: "What then is my reward?"

1 Cor 9:18 What then is my reward? That, when I preach the gospel, I may offer the gospel without charge, so as not to make full use of my right in the gospel.

Reward (misthos) = This word connects with what Paul had previously said regarding Christian ministers (see 1 Cor 3:8, 14). The verses that follow continue Paul's discussion of the work of Christian ministers, especially apostles, and specifically Paul's own example or practice in his ministry work.

I may offer the gospel without charge = It was with great satisfaction that Paul refused to take advantage of his legitimate right to support, and he did this in order to make a contribution of his own to the work of spreading the gospel.

> Paul does not mean that his practice of taking no pay from men will lead to his being rewarded by God; the preaching without charge is itself the reward, because it means that he is putting no stumbling block in the way of the gospel and thus has a better chance of seeing the gospel flourish than would otherwise be possible. It is consistent with the role of an apostle that he should renounce his rights than that he should claim them. It is not his own advantage or even his desires and inclinations, but those of his hearers that should govern his actions. [Barrett]

Make full use of my right = This shows that Paul did indeed have every right to support from the church. "He possesses as much right as anyone to enjoy apostolic privileges." [Barrett] But he did not even want to allow the possibility of over-using or abusing (**katachraomai** = to use excessively or consume by use) his right to support in his ministry.

> His sense of responsibility toward the gospel was too strong to allow thinking of it as a way of making a living. Instead it was a stewardship laid on him which earned no credit and deserved no pay. He saw himself as a slave doing his duty (Luke 17:7-10). There was one thing Paul could do to please his Master and gain a basis for pride in his work. He could voluntarily renounce his right to support, support himself, and make the gospel without cost to those he served! [Boyer]

Reason #2: For the sake of winning souls (9:19-23)

This is Paul's second reason for practicing the principle of self-denial by limiting his own Christian liberty.

1 Cor 9:19 For though I am free from all men, I have made myself a slave to all, so that I may win more.

Though I am free from all men, I have made myself a slave to all = Paul was a free man and a Roman citizen, which was a rare status in the society of his day. But because of his love for God and his commission to share the gospel with all men, he figuratively became a slave to all men. He limited his freedom for their sake.

> He would modify his habits, his preferences, his entire lifestyle if any of those things caused someone to stumble, to be offended, or to be hindered from faith in the Lord. Paul, as all believers, was free to do as his conscience allowed. But love would not let him do anything that the consciences of weaker believers would not allow. Love would not even allow him to do things that would be offensive to unbelievers to whom he witnessed. He would put every questionable thing in his life under the control of love. [MacArthur]

So that I may win more = Why did Paul do this? To win more people to Christ. What Paul did by limiting his freedom was not part of the gospel message, but it helped many people listen to the gospel and be more open to receiving it.

1 Cor 9:20-22 **To the Jews I became as a Jew, so that I might win Jews; to those who are under the Law, as under the Law though not being myself under the Law, so that I might win those who are under the Law; to those who are without law, as without law, though not being without the law of God but under the law of Christ, so that I might win those who are without law. To the weak I became weak, that I might win the weak; I have become all things to all men, so that I may by all means save some.**

Became as a Jew = Paul was a Jew, so how could he become as a Jew? "He could become a Jew only if, having been a Jew, he had ceased to be one and become something else. In Jesus Christ, Judaism had been fulfilled and the law brought to its intended goal. To be a Jew is to be under the law and thereby related to God in legal terms. Paul is no longer related to God in this way; at the most he may pretend to be so related. He is not under the law, but he may behave as if he were under the law." [Barrett] In other words, Paul would be as Jewish as necessary when he was working with unbelieving Jews. He could follow the ceremonial regulations, observe a special day, or avoid eating certain foods if doing those things would help him win those who are under the Law. However, Paul did not teach that following the Mosaic Law would provide any spiritual benefit whatsoever. It was only a way for him to open the door to minister among the unbelieving Jews of his day.

To those who are without law, as without law = Here Paul was willing to live like a Gentile when he was working among Gentiles. "Paul identified as closely as possible with Gentile customs. He ate what they ate, went where they went, and dressed as they dressed. The purpose again was to win the Gentiles to Christ." [MacArthur] The Gentiles are described as people who believe themselves to be outside of God's jurisdiction, and they do not acknowledge His Law in any way.

Though not being without the law but under the law of Christ = Paul adds this phrase to clarify that, even though he is able to live like the Gentiles in order to win some of them, he fully understands that he is not like they are in terms of being "without law" and refusing to acknowledge God's jurisdiction. In the previous verse Paul clearly stated that he is not under the Mosaic Law, but here he explains that this does not mean he has no moral obligation whatsoever. One man explained it this way:

> He is not free of legal obligation to God, but under legal obligation to Christ. He is not related to God by legal observance, but by grace and faith, and in Christ only— but precisely in this non-legal relationship he is Christ's slave, who owes absolute obedience not to a code but to Christ as a person, and to the absolute principle of universal love which Christ both taught and exemplified. This discussion has now made clear the difficulty in which Paul found himself. He must direct the Corinthians' obedience in the way of Christ, but he must do this without permitting Christianity to become a new law. [Barrett]

To the weak I became weak = The term "weak" connects with what Paul had previously said regarding Christians who were weak in conscience (1 Cor 8:7). "Paul was willing to identify with those, whether Jew or Gentile, who did not have the power of understanding to grasp the implications of the gospel. He stooped to the level of their weakness of comprehension." [MacArthur] But if the "weak" are Christians, then how can Paul speak of "winning" them? It seems that Paul is applying the general principle of adapting his lifestyle to provide a basis for a winning relationship with unbelievers as well as with weak believers. He means "winning them from paganism to Christianity" as well as "winning them from an inadequate understanding of Christianity."

I have become all things to all men = This was a general principle that applied to Paul's relationships with anyone he might encounter. He would identify with them in order to help them put their complete trust in what Christ did by purchasing their salvation. Notice that Paul himself would adapt to the circumstances, but he would not adapt the truth of the gospel to any circumstance.

> He did not compromise the gospel. He would not change the least truth in the least way in order to satisfy anyone. He would never set aside a truth of the gospel, but he would gladly restrict his liberty in the gospel. He would not offend Jew, Gentile, or those weak in understanding. If a person is offended by God's Word, that is his problem. If he is offended by biblical doctrine, standards, or church discipline, that is his problem. That person is offended by God. But if he is offended by our unnecessary behavior or practices—no matter how good and acceptable those may be in themselves—his problem becomes our problem. Paul's life centered in living out the gospel and in preaching and teaching the gospel. Nothing else was of any concern to him, therefore he set aside anything that would hinder its power and effectiveness. [MacArthur]

1 Cor 9:23 I do all things for the sake of the gospel, so that I may become a fellow partaker of it.

Here we catch a glimpse of the passion of Paul's life for the work that God had commissioned him to do.

> These verses bring us to the very heart of the motivating force which drove Paul to this and every other act of self-denial, his love for lost souls. Though he was free, yet he deliberately made himself a slave to all that he might win the more. To win the Jews, he was willing to forego his liberty and subject himself to the burdens of the law. To win the Gentiles who were without law, he was willing to forego his personal preference for the higher Jewish standards. To those weak ones who were having trouble with the meats offered to idols, Paul was willing to put himself in their place in order that he might win them. All this he is willing to do for the sake of the gospel in order that he might, along with them, share in its blessings. [Boyer]

Reason #3: For the sake of a minister's reward (9:24-27)

Here is the third reason Paul gave for practicing the principle of self-denial in limiting his own Christian liberty.

1 Cor 9:24 Do you not know that those who run in a race all run, but only one receives the prize? Run in such a way that you may win.

Do you not know = Here Paul asked a direct question of the Corinthian Christians, and he used the illustration of the Isthmian Games where athletes would compete in sporting events near Corinth in order to be acknowledged as winners. Very strict training was required of all the athletes who participated.

> Contestants in the games had to prove they had rigorously trained for ten months. The last month was spent at Corinth, with supervised daily workouts in the gymnasium and on the athletic fields. If an athlete expected to excel, he voluntarily and often severely restricted his liberty. His sleep, his diet, and his activities were not determined by his rights or by his feelings, but by the requirements of his training... Most people, including many Christians, are slaves to their bodies. Their bodies tell their minds what to do. Their bodies decide when to eat, when to sleep and get up, and so on. An athlete cannot allow that. He follows the training rules, rather than what his body is telling him to do. He runs when he would rather be resting, he eats a balanced meal when he would rather indulge himself, he goes to bed when he would rather stay up, and he gets up early to train when he would rather stay in bed. An athlete leads his body; he does not follow it. It is his slave, and not the other way around. [MacArthur]

Run in such a way that you may win = Paul ends this verse with a command (imperative). He is saying, "Run your race in the right way so that you will win." You will not win if you do not carefully train and adapt yourself to the conditions of the track. The terms **prize** and **win** are connected to the idea of **reward** for the Christian worker (1 Cor 3:8, 14; 9:17-18).

A great difference between those races and the Christian race is that every Christian who will pay the price of careful training can win. We do not compete against each other but against the practical, physical, and spiritual obstacles that would hinder us. In a sense, every Christian runs his own race, enabling each one of us to be a winner in winning souls to Christ. Holding tightly to liberties and rights is a sure way to lose the race of soul-winning. Many of the Corinthian Christians seriously limited their testimony because they would not limit their liberty. [MacArthur]

1 Cor 9:25 Everyone who competes in the games exercises self-control in all things. They then do it to receive a perishable wreath, but we an imperishable.

As was mentioned in the last verse, all of the athletes in the games would train themselves by exercising self-control in every area of their lives in order that they could do their best during the race. By way of analogy, Paul says that Christian liberty cannot be yielded or limited without exercising that same kind of self-control. In Paul's analogy the worldly athlete is motivated by a perishable earthly prize, but the Christian should be motivated by a much more valuable prize: a reward that will last into eternity. The **imperishable wreath** is analogous to the reward for a Christian worker which is given at the Judgment Seat of Christ (see 1 Cor 3:14; 2 Cor 5:10). Therefore, the Christian should exercise self-control much more diligently. One writer applied this truth to modern believers in this way: "The athlete's disciplined self-control is a rebuke of half-hearted, out-of-shape Christians who do almost nothing to prepare themselves for ministry." [MacArthur]

1 Cor 9:26-27 Therefore I run in such a way, as not without aim; I box in such a way, as not beating the air; but I discipline my body and make it my slave, so that, after I have preached to others, I myself will not be disqualified.

Paul had a definite purpose or aim in running his race as a Christian. His goal was to win as many people as possible to faith and maturity in the Lord Jesus Christ. In this final section, Paul switches his illustration to another of the sports in the athletic games, that of boxing. He says he does not box as if he is only "beating the air." He is not training himself to shadow box or merely pretend to fight. He trains himself for real spiritual battle.

It is clear from 1 Cor 9:27 that a major part of this battle is against our own flesh, and that our training should involve disciplining the body as a whole, physically, mentally, emotionally, and volitionally. The word **discipline (hupopiazo)** literally means "to hit under the eye." Paul would figuratively give himself a black eye, or knock it out if necessary, in order to put it into subjection to God's purposes. "Here Paul recognizes the need to beat his body out of its all too ready obedience to sin, in order that it may be brought into the service of God. The body is not evil, but it must be made to serve the right master, not the wrong one." [Barrett]

This is the kind of discipline that is required by Christians in order to yield our Christian liberty so we do not cause people to reject the gospel or to destroy the faith of less mature believers. The term **disqualified** relates to the potential reward for service in ministry, and we know from Paul's previous statements in this letter that it is possible for a minister to lose the reward that he could have received in his service to the Lord (see 1 Cor 3:15). As Paul ends this chapter with the description of his life of self-discipline, we can see that a God-honoring life involves the limitation of Christian liberty as often as the enjoyment of our freedom in Christ.

Warnings About Abusing Liberty

(1 Corinthians 10:1-13)

I n First Corinthians chapter nine the apostle Paul illustrated the principle of yielding personal rights by giving his own example of yielding his apostolic rights for support from the churches. To Paul, it was more important to set aside his legitimate Christian liberty for the good of others. Now in First Corinthians chapter ten the apostle Paul continues to illustrate this same principle by describing some events from the history of his people Israel.

> He had illustrated in his own case his rights as an apostle, and the right he had to be maintained as a minister of the gospel...He had been dealing with the tremendous privilege of his apostleship, the rights for which he was prepared to fight...The apostle now took an illustration from the history of Israel. Of course he was writing to Christians, to Greeks, to Gentiles, but he uses illustrations from his own life and the history of his own nation in writing to them. [Morgan]

An Old Testament Example of Freedom (10:1-5)

The Privileges of the Israelites (10:1-4)

From the life of his own people, the Jews, Paul gave the perfect biblical example of true freedom under God.

1 Cor 10:1 For I do not want you to be unaware, brethren, that our fathers were all under the cloud and all passed through the sea;

For = This word connects this new section with what Paul had just said about the possibility of being disqualified for a minister's reward. Here Paul is giving additional explanations and illustrations of the principles he previously shared. "The opening word of this chapter, the word 'for,' connects it with what he had just written as to the possibility of becoming rejected. There is the closest link between that very solemn word in verse 27, in which he showed the possibility of being a preacher to others and of being rejected...and here with the illustration of that fact from the history of Israel." [Morgan]

Our fathers = In a general sense this means those who have gone before us. In this case it identified the fathers of the Jewish nation of which Paul was a descendant and whose story is recorded in the Old Testament.

Were all under the cloud (Exodus 13:21) = This describes the Divine guidance with which the Israelites were blessed.

Passed through the sea (Exodus 14:19-22) = This points to the Divine deliverance that the Israelites experienced. The Exodus from Egypt saved Israel from their oppressors, but it did not necessarily mean that all of the Israelites were true believers. They had been chosen by God to be a unique nation under His direction, and by way of analogy that was the "race" they were to run. One commentator expressed the situation in the following words:

> The Exodus did not represent the spiritual salvation of God's people. Men have always been spiritually saved only by personal faith in God. The Exodus was God's calling His chosen people, believing and unbelieving, out of their bondage in Egypt and His deliverance of them into His own land that He had promised to them through Abraham (Gen 12:7). They were to be His witnessing community to the world. That was the race that Israel as a nation was called by God to run (1 Cor 9:24). [MacArthur]

1 Cor 10:2 and all were baptized into Moses in the cloud and in the sea.

Just as baptism is an outward sign of union or identification with something or someone, this phrase expresses a sense of unity as a community or nation under Moses who was their divinely appointed leader. "They were all unified under the leadership of Moses, all constituting an assembly. They were baptized to him in the cloud and the sea as they followed the guidance of the cloud; as they passed through, the waters were divided for them, and they became more than a wandering mob. They became a nation and a community." [Morgan]

1 Cor 10:3 and all ate the same spiritual food;

This points to their Divine sustenance (Exodus 16:15).

1 Cor 10:4 and all drank the same spiritual drink, for they were drinking from a spiritual rock which followed them; and the rock was Christ.

Drank the same spiritual drink (Exodus 17:6) = This also illustrates Divine sustenance. "Paul is speaking of the source, not the type, of sustenance. God provided physical food and drink through miraculous means for all of Israel, believers and unbelievers alike. In this sense they were all spiritually sustained, that is, given provisions from a divine source rather than a natural one." [MacArthur]

A spiritual rock which followed them; and that rock was Christ = The word Paul used for rock was not **petros** which is a stone or boulder, but **petra** which is a massive rock cliff. Twice God used a large stone to provide water for Israel (Exodus 17:6 and Num 20:11), but that is not what Paul is referring to here. The spiritual rock that accompanied them through the wilderness was not like those physical rocks, but it represents the Lord Jesus Christ. Christ was in a figurative sense a massive supernatural rock that protected the Israelites and sustained them. How amazing to know that at that time in Israel's history their Messiah was providing for them.

Notice that the word 'all' is repeated five times in these verses. This points to the nation as a whole, every Israelite living during that time, as having experienced the blessing and privileges of God. With these kinds of advantages and privileges, one would assume that their success was guaranteed.

Paul was reminding them how that nation passed out of bondage into liberty and freedom. God provided the cloud, the deliverance, freedom, the meat and the drink, the privileges that were theirs. Everything was of God, and nothing of themselves. Everything was supernatural, the doings of God. Paul now asked these Corinthians to take that as an illustration of a certain great principle. The first feeling may be that a people so privileged cannot fail. If indeed God undertook for them in this way to guide, to deliver, to constitute them a community on a new basis, and supplied their needs physically and spiritually and supernaturally, what a wondrous liberty it was into which they were brought by God! [Morgan]

The Failure of Most of Them (10:5)

1 Cor 10:5 Nevertheless, with most of them God was not well-pleased; for they were laid low in the wilderness.

Nevertheless = Now notice the direct contrast and the word 'most' rather than 'all.' In spite of all their advantages and privileges, they failed to please God.

God was not well-pleased = In the original language, the word "not" is placed toward the front of the sentence for emphasis. It could literally be translated like this: "Not (as one might have expected) with the major part of them was God pleased."

They were laid low in the wilderness = The Old Testament itself gives the historical consequences of the rebellion of the Israelites (Numbers 14:29-30). Despite the great privileges given to them by God, the Israelites did not please Him. In the next section we will see exactly how they did not please God, but here we need to understand that great privilege or blessing does not guarantee holiness of life. Only humble obedience, submission, and dependence upon God will please Him.

All Israel had been graciously blessed, liberated, and sustained by the Lord in the wilderness, but in that so-called 'race' (that test of obedience and service) most of them were 'disqualified' (to use Paul's terminology from 1 Cor 9:24, 27). They misused and abused their freedom and their blessings. In self-centeredness and self-will they tried to live on the edge of their liberty, and they fell into temptation and then into sin. [MacArthur]

The Destructive Use of Liberty (10:6-10)

1 Cor 10:6 Now these things happened as examples for us, so that we would not crave evil things as they also craved.

These things happened as examples for us = In the context of this verse, the word "example" means a cautionary example or a pattern of warning, given so that others do not follow the example that was set. "They are to be held up as furnishing an admonition to us, or a warning that we do not sin in the same way. The same God directs our affairs that ordered theirs; and if we sin as they did, we also must expect to be punished." [Barnes]

That we ourselves would not be cravers of evil things = The word "cravers" means to lust after, to covet, to long for things that are forbidden or have not been given by God.

Lust = They craved something that was not provided for them by God. "So Paul infers that the Corinthian Christians should not lust after or desire the meat offered in sacrifice to idols, lest it should lead them also to sin and ruin." [Barnes] Several biblical examples of the lust of the Israelites are recorded in Numbers 11:4-34 and Psalm 78:27-31; 105:14-15.

Lust is mentioned first in this list probably because it led to the very first sin in the Garden of Eden. It was Eve's desire for something outside of what God had provided that led to the Fall. In a similar way, the chosen people of God were given so many blessings, and yet they too craved more than what God had supplied for them.

Ancient Israel provided Paul with sobering illustrations of the pitfalls of overconfident living. Many of the Corinthian believers thought, and perhaps had said in the letter to Paul (7:1), that they felt perfectly secure in their Christian lives, that they had arrived. Paul surely had that attitude in mind in the sarcastic rebuke of 1 Cor 4:8-14. They thought they were strong enough to freely associate with pagans in their ceremonies and social activities and not be affected morally or spiritually, as long as they did not participate in outright idolatry or immorality. Abusing their liberty not only harmed weaker believers whose consciences were offended but also endangered their own spiritual lives. They could not live long on the far edge of freedom without falling into temptation and then into sin. The mature, loving Christian does not try to stretch his liberty to the extreme, to see how close to evil he can come without being harmed. [MacArthur]

1 Cor 10:7 Do not be idolaters, as some of them were; as it is written, "THE PEOPLE SAT DOWN TO EAT AND DRINK, AND STOOD UP TO PLAY."

Idolatry (Exodus 32:1-6) = In this incident, the Israelites partook of a feast in honor of the golden calf. "The liberated people of God, failing to fulfill their responsibility, turned aside, contrary to the distinct command of God, to make something to represent Him, which misrepresented Him." [Morgan] It was a common practice in Corinth to celebrate a community feast that was held to honor an idol, so this incident in the life of Israel was especially appropriate for cautioning the Corinthians against the danger of participating in the feasts celebrated in the pagan temples. "Those who follow a man-made god may claim they worship the God of Scripture, just as the Israelites claimed their calf worship was to the Lord. But no false god has anything in common with the God of the Bible." [MacArthur]

Idols were very common in the everyday life of Corinth. One might go so far as to say that their entire society revolved around idols.

No religious, social, political, or business function was conducted without some involvement with idol worship or recognition. Many of the Corinthian Christians, overconfident in their own moral and spiritual strength, had become careless about their participation in activities where false gods were worshiped, consulted, or appealed to. They believed they could be associated with such pagan activities without being spiritually harmed. Some of the believers, or professed believers, in Corinth had slipped back into actual idolatry (5:11). Others were in danger of doing the same thing. [MacArthur]

1 Cor 10:8 Nor let us act immorally, as some of them did, and twenty-three thousand fell in one day.

Immorality (Numbers 25:1-9) = Twenty-four thousand of the Israelites actually died because of this incident, but here Paul points out that twenty-three thousand of them fell dead in a single day! It seems that idol worship and sexual immorality almost always accompany each other.

Idolatry and sexual immorality were closely associated in virtually all ancient religions. They were especially associated in Corinth, whose temple to Aphrodite had a thousand ritual prostitutes. It is clear from Paul's warning that the self-confident Corinthian believers were no more immune to immorality than idolatry. Thinking they could live carelessly around corruption without being corrupted, they first were tempted and then gave in to temptation. As the apostle had already told them in this letter (6:18), and probably had told them many times when he was with them in person, immorality is to be fled, not flirted with. Christ gives us freedom so that we may serve him more effectively in righteousness, not so we can see how close we can come to unrighteousness. [MacArthur]

After acknowledging the close relationship between idolatry and sexual immorality, one commentator asked, "How could the Corinthians escape this evil if they allowed themselves to attend the sacrificial feasts within her temple under the pretense that an idol is nothing?" [Hodge]

1 Cor 10:9 Nor let us try the Lord, as some of them did, and were destroyed by the serpents.

Faithlessness (Numbers 21:4; Psalm 78:18) = To try the Lord is to test God's patience by seeing how far you can step over the line that He has drawn. God places boundaries around our lives for own protection.

They had no concern for pleasing God, only for pleasing themselves. They did not use their new freedom to serve Him better but to demand that He serve them better. Christians sometimes use their freedom to push God to the limit, trying to see how much they can get out of Him and how much they can get by with before Him. Many of the Corinthians were pushing their liberty to the limits, to see how much of the flesh they could indulge and how much of the world they could enjoy. They were trying God and risking severe discipline. [MacArthur]

1 Cor 10:10 Nor grumble, as some of them did, and were destroyed by the destroyer.

Discontent (Numbers 14:2, 11-12; 16:41, 49; 17:6) = Grumbling is the manifestation of discontent, and it is a direct attack on the character of God. "When God's people question or complain, they are challenging His wisdom, His grace, His goodness, His love, and His righteousness." [MacArthur] Elsewhere in First Corinthians the apostle Paul referred to Satan as an agent of destruction (1 Cor 5:5), as well as to how abusing the Lord's Supper had led to physical affliction (1 Cor 11:30). So the consequences of this warning already had been experienced to some extent in the life of the Corinthian church.

The Application of This Illustration (10:11-13)

In the first part of this chapter, Paul outlined the great privileges given to the nation of Israel by God. Then he proceeded to give detailed examples of how the Israelites abused their freedom and failed to please God. "His theme is that it is possible to abuse liberty, and his intention throughout is to show that privilege is no insurance against ultimate failure. There is a terrible danger of trusting in our privileges, and in the fact that we are privileged people, forgetting that privilege always entails responsibility." [Morgan] Now Paul is going to tie these illustrations together and apply the Israelites' example to the Corinthians.

Drawing the Analogy (10:11)

1 Cor 10:11 Now these things happened to them as an example, and they were written for our instruction, upon whom the ends of the ages have come.

Now these things happened to them as an example = In 1 Cor 10:6 Paul literally said, "Now these things examples for us became." Here he literally says, "Now these things as examples transpired to them." Because of his emphasis on the word 'them,' Paul added another phrase to show the purpose for these events being recorded in the Scriptures.

They were written for our instruction (nouthesia) = This word means to admonish, exhort, or give a warning, just as the previous word 'example' indicated a negative example or warning. "They were intended as historical pictures, so that we might be admonished to avoid the sins which brought such judgments upon them." [Hodge] Paul is showing them how not to live their lives. They should look at Israel's example and heed the warning.

Upon whom the ends of the ages have come = Here Paul indicates that the time in which he was living, which also has continued down to our own time, is bringing to completion the last days of human history before the Messiah comes to establish His kingdom. "The plural seems to point out how one stage succeeds another in the drama of human history." [RWP] In this verse Paul is indicating that he wants to use the lessons seen in the life of his people, the Israelites, and to apply them to the believers in Corinth.

148

We are living in a greatly different age from that of the Hebrews in the wilderness under Moses, but we can learn a valuable lesson from their experience. Like them we can forfeit our blessing, reward, and effectiveness in the Lord's service if, in overconfidence and presumption, we take our liberties too far and fall into disobedience and sin. We will not lose our salvation, but we can easily lose our virtue and usefulness, and become disqualified in the race of the Christian life. [MacArthur]

The Truth to be Applied (10:12)

1 Cor 10:12 Therefore let him who thinks he stands take heed that he does not fall.

Here is the major lesson that Paul wants us to learn from what he has just said regarding the Israelites and their failure despite the great blessings given to them: "Therefore, let him who thinks he stands take heed that he does not fall!" The same thing that happened to the Israelites was happening to the Corinthians.

> They had let down their guard. They had become victim to sins which were not expected from those with such high spiritual privilege. Arguments about Christian freedom, the right to do some questionable thing, are seldom a mere matter of freedom. There is frequently a real danger of falling. Such has been in the mind of Paul ever since he began his discussion of the subject of eating meats offered to idols, and these strong Christians who felt so sure that they knew the nothingness of idols, were actually skating on thin ice. Paul warns them: Beware. Look what happened to the Israelites. [Boyer]

What does it mean to "**Think you stand**?" This is a good way of describing what we might call over-confidence and self-sufficiency. Freedom and privilege in themselves are no guarantee against failure. There are drastic consequences for abusing liberty.

> No degree of progress we may have already made, no amount of privileges which we may have enjoyed, can justify the lack of caution. False security as to our power to resist temptation rests on an overweening self-confidence in our own strength. None are so liable to fall as they who, thinking themselves strong, heedlessly run into temptation. This probably is the kind of false security against which the apostle warns the Corinthians, as he exhorts them immediately after this to avoid temptation. [Hodge]

As over-confidence increases, so does carelessness in living the Christian life. And as carelessness increases, so does the risk of moving in the direction of sin. It is a tragic thing to have increasing knowledge and confidence, but at the same time to have a decreasing awareness of and resistance to sin. "Confidence in our own security is no guarantee that we are safe. Such a confidence may be one of the strongest evidences that we are in danger. Those are most safe who feel that they are weak and feeble, and who feel their need of divine aid and strength. They will then rely on the true source of strength; and they will be secure." [Barnes]

1 Cor 10:13 No temptation has overtaken you but such as is common to man; and God is faithful, who will not allow you to be tempted beyond what you are able, but with the temptation will provide the way of escape also, so that you will be able to endure it.

Temptation (peirasmos) = This refers to testing or proving. In the original language, this word did not have a negative connotation, so it was not necessarily a bad thing. Our personal response to the situation is what determines whether it is positive or negative, whether it shows our dependence upon God resulting in righteous behavior, or whether it shows our dependence upon ourselves resulting in unrighteous behavior or attitudes. "If we resist something in God's power, it is a test that proves our faithfulness. If we do not stand firm, it becomes a solicitation to sin. The Bible uses the term in both ways, and I believe Paul has both meanings in mind here." [MacArthur]

Such as is common to man (anthropinos) = This word means something that is characteristic of mankind. Temptations are normal human experiences that are common to all of mankind. It is as if Paul is saying, "You have been subjected to no superhuman or extra-ordinary temptations. Your trials have been accommodated to what men are able to bear." [Hodge]

God is faithful = Paul began this letter by proclaiming the absolute faithfulness of God (1 Cor 1:9). Here Paul encourages the believers at Corinth to trust in the faithfulness of God, and to depend or rely on His strength to do what is right.

Who will not allow you to be tempted beyond what you are able = God is sovereign over all the circumstances of our lives. Just as we can trust in His faithfulness, we can trust in His control over our circumstances, and we can rely on His power to use His resources for handling whatever comes our way.

Will provide the way of escape (ekbasis) = This term identified a specific way out or exit. There is a definite way out, which tells us that believers are not trapped in a dead end of temptation. There is always a definite way of escape provided by God.

You will be able to endure it = This word means to bear up under something. When believers rely on the strength and resources of God, they will be able to bear up under the circumstances of life and behave in righteous ways. And even when they fail to do so, believers can still rely on the strength of God to handle their failure the right way, and on the faithfulness of God to forgive and restore.

Verse thirteen is put in as a gracious encouragement to both strong and weak in the face of this ever-present danger. It is an unqualified promise from God, based upon His own faithfulness, that you need not fall. He knows how strong and how weak you are, and He promises never to allow temptation to come against you which is too hard for you. He promises that with every temptation He does permit to come, He sends along with it the necessary way out of it. If Christians once learn the meaning of 1 Corinthians 10:13 they never again will say, 'I couldn't help it.' [Boyer]

Paul ends this section with this wonderful promise for the Christian life because the Corinthians seemed to be practicing exactly the opposite of his advice. It is as if Paul was saying, "You Corinthians should not run toward temptation!" This seems to be exactly what some of them were doing by associating themselves with the feasts in pagan temples. "We all have our trials. We shall find the lure of lower things seduce us from loyalty, and that will destroy liberty." [Morgan] God's faithfulness is wonderful, but we should not become overconfident as a result of all the blessings and privileges we have received, thinking that we are immune from falling into sin.

Abusing our Christian liberty will lead us directly into sin, and it will harm more than just our own Christian walk. We are hurting ourselves and other believers when we abuse our Christian liberty. We are also affecting our witness before the unsaved world, and we are damaging the reputation of God by our actions. Let us walk in humility, relying on His wisdom and strength as we face each circumstance that He allows into our lives. What are some of the great privileges and blessings that God has given to you? Are you pleasing God today by your humble obedience, submission, and dependence upon Him for the things He has brought into your life?

Guidelines about Idolatry

(1 Corinthians 10:14 - 11:1)

Throughout the first letter to the Corinthians, the apostle Paul had given warnings about falling into various sins or causing fellow-Christians to stumble. In chapter eight he showed us that meat sacrificed to idols was not tainted, that an idol has no deity, and that there is no God but one. The bigger issue in that case was not to offend a weaker brother, but to yield our Christian liberty out of love for others. In chapter nine Paul had illustrated this principle from his own life, using his legitimate right of support from the churches, which he yielded in order not to hinder the spread of the gospel. In the first part of chapter ten, Paul provided additional examples from the life of his own people, the nation of Israel. They were given wonderful privileges and blessings, but that was no guarantee of safety from temptation and sin. The Israelites had abused their great freedom and had suffered defeat as a result. In this section of chapter ten, the apostle Paul will give specific instructions for using or yielding Christian liberty. It begins by protecting ourselves from activities that are known to be sin, and it continues by applying the principle of yielding our rights in circumstances that would harm a fellow believer.

The Command (10:14)

1 Cor 10:14 Therefore, my beloved, flee from idolatry.

Therefore = This important transition word means in view of what Paul has just said. The near context is the statement in 1 Cor 10:13 about temptation, and in this case their way of escape is to flee from the temptation of idolatry. Verse fourteen also occurs in the larger context about the Israelite privileges and their fall into sin. Paul will now apply the example of the Israelites to the situation of the Corinthians regarding their participation in the feasts given in honor of an idol. Paul had first discussed this subject in 1 Cor 8:1-13. Here he is going to prove how dangerous this practice would be to the Corinthian believers.

His command is to **flee (pheugo)**, which means to seek safety by flight, to escape safely away from danger. Their response to idolatry must be what the Israelites should have done but did not do: they should flee. Paul had used this same word in 1 Cor 6:18 when he commanded the Corinthians to flee immorality, and in 1 Timothy 6:11 Paul would use this same word when he commanded Timothy to flee from the love of money. As it means in those cases, here it also means to turn in the opposite direction and run away as fast as you can.

> The apostle's meaning is not only that they would not worship idols or commit plain downright acts of idolatry; but that they would stand at the greatest distance from idols, not so much as go into an idol's temple, and there sit down and eat; which if not a real act of idolatry, had at least the show of one; and his sense is, that they should abstain from all appearance of idolatry, from every occasion of it, and

whatsoever led unto it. [Gill]

The Reasoning Behind the Command (10:15-22)

1 Cor 10:15 I speak as to wise men; you judge what I say.

To wise men (phrorimos) = This word means ones who use the mind. This may be a somewhat sarcastic reference to the Corinthians who boasted of their wisdom (1 Cor 4:10; 2 Cor 11:19). He might be saying, "Now here is an opportunity to exercise your so-called wisdom by judging what I say." All sarcasm aside, Paul really did want them to make proper use of their minds to think through what he was about to tell them concerning their association with idolatry.

You yourselves judge = Paul asks them to sit in the judge's seat. "He appeals to the Corinthians, as men of wisdom and understanding in these things, and makes they themselves judges thereof." [Gill]

Communion from the Lord's Supper celebration (10:16-17)

Communion is a word that describes a close fellowship or common union with something, becoming a partaker of something, or establishing a close attachment to something. This is the result of participating in any of several activities. Here Paul will use three different activities to show that there is a close association or communion developed as a result of participating in them.

1 Cor 10:16 Is not the cup of blessing which we bless a sharing in the blood of Christ? Is not the bread which we break a sharing in the body of Christ?

The cup of blessing which we bless & The bread which we break = This identifies Paul's first example as the Lord's Supper, one of the two ordinances to be practiced within the local church. He used a rather Jewish phrase (the cup of blessing) because it represented the cup over which thanks were offered during the Passover meal, and it was during the last Passover meal with His disciples that Christ instituted this part of the Lord's Supper.

A sharing in the blood of Christ & A sharing in the body of Christ = Sharing (koinonia) means fellowship, association, community, communion, joint participation, or intimacy. In the case of the Lord's Supper, believers have close communion and fellowship with the Lord Jesus Christ as members of His body. "The design of this verse seems to be to prove that Christians, by partaking of the Lord's Supper, are solemnly set apart to the service of the Lord Jesus; that they acknowledge Him as their Lord, and dedicate themselves to him." [Barnes] By participating in the ceremony of the Lord's Supper, believers identify themselves with His saving act on the cross and they are dedicating themselves to serving Him as Lord and Master. Paul will soon apply this fact to show that partaking of the table of demons will bring them into communion with demons.

1 Cor 10:17 Since there is one bread, we who are many are one body; for we all partake of the one bread.

We who are many are one body = Being a Christian is not like being dues paying members of some club or organization, so that we could withdraw from the group or miss a meeting or two. Believers are part of something organic, a body of which they form a vital part. Believers are many in terms of their diversity, but they are united together just as the various parts of the body are united to form a single organism. There is a unity among the members, even though they are quite different. Just like a loaf of bread is made up of many different ingredients, the finished outcome is a single loaf of bread.

We all partake of the one bread = The word partake (**metecho**) means to share in or to belong to something. We show publicly that we are united and belong to the same loaf, or the same body, which is the body of Christ. "Paul is deducing the mutual communion of believers from the fact of their communion with their common Lord. By each and all receiving a piece of the one loaf, which represents Christ's body, they signify that they are all bound in one spiritual body, united to Christ and therefore to each other." [VWS]

Communion from the Jewish Temple Ceremony (10:18)

1 Cor 10:18 Look at the nation Israel; are not those who eat the sacrifices sharers in the altar?

Look at the nation Israel = Now Paul steps away from the example of Christian communion and begins to illustrate this principle from the life of his own people, the Nation of Israel.

Are not those who eat the sacrifices sharers in the altar = Among the Jews, those who participated in the temple rituals and sacrifices were regarded as being one people who worship one God. The Israelites who participated in the sacrificial services united themselves with the altar of God. The emphasis in this example is on the word sharers (**koinonos**), which indicates intimate communion.

> With the Jews, as with other nations, only a portion of most sacrifices was consumed upon the altar; the residue was divided between the priest and the offerer (Lev 7:15; 8:31; Deut 12:18). To eat of the sacrifices in the way prescribed in the Law of Moses was to take part in the whole sacrificial service. Therefore the apostle says that those who eat of the sacrifices are partakers of the altar; that is, they are in communion with it. They become worshipers of the God to whom the altar is dedicated...To partake of a Jewish sacrifice in a holy place, was an act of Jewish worship. By parity of reasoning, to partake of a heathen sacrifice in a holy place, was of necessity an act of heathen worship. [Hodge]

Communion from the Pagan temple feasts (10:19-20)

1 Cor 10:19 What do I mean then? That a thing sacrificed to idols is anything, or that an idol is anything?

What do I mean then? = Literally this could be translated, "What then am I declaring?" In other words, "What is my meaning? What follows from all of these illustrations?"

That a thing sacrificed to idols is anything, or that an idol is anything? = It was possible that one of Paul's audience might think he was saying idols are on the same level as the God of both New Testament and Old Testament believers. After all, both the Lord's Supper and the Jewish sacrificial system were associated with the one true God. "The inference might be drawn from the analogies of the Lord's Supper and Jewish sacrifices, that an idol is really what the heathen thought it to be, a god, and that in eating idol-meats they had fellowship with the god. This verse guards against such an inference." [JFB]

In 1 Cor 8:4 Paul told us that the Corinthians knew there was no such thing as an idol and that there is only one true God. The repetition of this phrase should take us back to that point in Paul's argument. As we said regarding that earlier passage, some of their so-called gods were outright fakes, but Paul also knew that some of them were manifestations of real demonic beings. These demonic beings do have real existence, but none of them are truly gods. They have a certain type of reality, but they certainly do not have deity. In that earlier passage Paul denied the deity of their so-called gods, but here in this passage Paul gives additional explanation about the reality of their so-called gods.

1 Cor 10:20 No, but I say that the things which the Gentiles sacrifice, they sacrifice to demons and not to God; and I do not want you to become sharers in demons.

No = Is a thing sacrificed to idols anything or is an idol anything? No! See chapter eight for the explanation.

But... the things which the Gentiles sacrifice, they sacrifice to demons = While it is true that the block of wood or stone is just a representation that has no life of its own, the underlying fact is that demons in the spiritual realm are intimately connected with such false worship. Satan and his demons are in fact the powers worshiped by the heathen, whether or not they are aware of it. It is as if Paul declared, "I am not saying that an idol is anything, but you had better beware of it just the same." If Paul were only concerned with the eating of meat then he could say that neither spiritual harm nor benefit happens as a result of the process of physical eating. But Paul wants them to know that the issue has another more important aspect. The fact is that the pagans were dedicating this meat to demons, and not to God. "He was convinced that the image used in idolatrous worship was a block of wood or stone and nothing more; it was not anything in the world. At the same time he believed in the reality of an unseen spirit-world, and that idolatry was not merely meaningless but a positively evil thing." [Barrett]

I do not want you to become sharers in demons = The word for sharers **(koinonos)** is the same term Paul used for partaking in the Lord's Supper and in the Jewish temple rituals. There is an intimate sharing or association that is part of this type of activity. In effect, he is saying that there was no way to eat the sacrificial meat in the pagan temple feasts without having some kind of association or fellowship with demons. This was not because the eating process was defiling, but because of the place and the circumstances in which they were eating.

Several scholars have described the meals that took place in the pagan temples. For example, one writer said, "The whole service had a religious character; all the provisions, the wine as well as the meat, were blessed in the name of the idol, and thereby consecrated to him in a manner analogous to that in which the bread and the wine on the Lord's table were consecrated to Him...What the apostle means to say is that there is not merely an incongruity and inconsistency in a man's being the guest and friend of Christ and the guest and friend of evil spirits, but that the thing is impossible." [Hodge] Another commentator put it this way: "The effect of the sacrifice lies not in the eating, but in personal relations and in the consequences that flow from them...It is not the eating of sacrificial food (which Paul permits) but direct participation in idolatry that will separate the Christian from fellowship with Christ, and no more will he escape than did the Israelites." [Barrett]

The incompatibility of mixing these activities (10:21)

1 Cor 10:21 You cannot drink the cup of the Lord and the cup of demons; you cannot partake of the table of the Lord and the table of demons.

This is very similar to Paul's teaching in 1 Cor 6:15-20 where he emphasized that our union with Christ should prevent us from being united with something that would damage our relationship with Him. Paul had said, "Do you not know that your bodies are members of Christ? Shall I then take away the members of Christ and make them members of a prostitute? May it never be!" Some of the same truths Paul shared in chapter six certainly can be applied here as well. "The parallel between 1 Cor 6:18 and 10:14 is not fortuitous. Fornication and idolatry are both impossible for a Christian because of his exclusive relationship with Christ." [Barrett]

What Paul is telling the Corinthians is that being a Christian and attending the pagan temple feasts are completely incompatible activities. "The cup of the Lord is that cup which brings us into communion with the Lord; the cup of devils is that cup which brings us into communion with devils." [Hodge] Paul used several illustrations to show that intimate communion is the result of participating in these activities, and once a person is dedicated to the Lord, he cannot also be associated with demons. "As the partaking of the Lord's Supper involves a partaking of the Lord Himself, and the partaking of the Jewish sacrificial meats involved a partaking of the altar of God, and as the heathens sacrifice to devils, to partake of an idol feast is to have fellowship with devils." [JFB] Essentially, Paul is telling the Corinthian believers to avoid attending the meals held at the pagan temples. To do so would mean the Christian is participating in a blatant environment of idolatry, and this is something that a believer should not do under any circumstances.

The Lord's perspective on becoming partakers in demonically inspired things (10:22)

1 Cor 10:22 Or do we provoke the Lord to jealousy? We are not stronger than He, are we?

Provoke the Lord to jealousy = In the last verse we saw that it is impossible to be dedicated to God and participate with demons at the same time. In this verse, we are told why. It is because the Lord Himself will not allow it! One man wrote, "God is a jealous God, and to provoke His jealousy by playing around with idolatry is the utmost in foolishness; unless, of course, you are greater than He is!" [Boyer] Another commentator said, "The Corinthians ought not to attend these feasts unless they intended to excite against themselves in the highest measure the displeasure of the Lord...Eating of the sacrifices offered to idols under circumstances which gave a religious character to the act, was idolatry." [Hodge] The context of the pagan temple and its rituals is what makes this a serious offense for a Christian.

Using our Christian Liberty for God's Glory (10:23-30)

Restating the Guiding Principles (10:23-24)

Here Paul restates a proper view of Christian liberty, since he had already given some of these truths earlier in chapter six.

1 Cor 10:23 All things are lawful, but not all things are profitable. All things are lawful, but not all things edify.

All things are lawful for me = As in 1 Cor 6:12, this was apparently a specific quote from some of the believers in Corinth which they used in order to justify their immorality. This statement was not true unless it was restricted by each clause which follows. Christian liberty is always limited by the principle of Christian love. Liberty that is detrimental to someone is not loving and should be avoided.

Not all things are profitable (sumphero) = This word means to bring together or contribute; to be expedient or worthwhile. This is a word-for-word restatement of his earlier teaching. "A man who acts on the principle that he is free to do anything he likes is in danger of losing his freedom through becoming enslaved to the practices for which he feels himself to be free." [Barrett]

Not all things edify (oikodomeo) = This is a compound word in the original language which means house building; to construct a house; and figuratively, to build something as though you were building a house. This is the term that is used for building up others within the body of Christ toward maturity in their faith. Here Paul adds the fact that others are to be considered in the decision-making process. "Paul acted for the welfare of the church. His object was to save souls. Anything that would promote that object was proper; anything which would hinder it, though in itself it might not be strictly unlawful, was in his view improper. This is a simple rule and might be easily applied by all." [Barnes]

1 Cor 10:24 Let no one seek his own good, but that of his neighbor.

Here Paul makes explicit what he only implied in the previous statement that not all things edify. It is crucial that we take into consideration the good of others before participating in some activities. There may be times when we need to restrict or yield our freedoms in order to ensure that others are edified or built up in their faith. As Christians we should not focus on self-gratification or doing things that selfishly give us as much pleasure as possible in this life. We should focus on serving others and looking out for the needs of others. "It is not a Christian duty to seek out things that a man may be permitted to do; it is a Christian duty to build up the church." [Barrett]

This does not mean that a Christian should never look out for his own welfare or take care of his own needs. What it does mean is that in cases like the ones Paul is discussing, believers must consider the good of others when deciding whether to participate in certain activities. "When there is no positive law against an activity, and when a man's example would have a great influence on others, he should be guided in his conduct not by a reference to his own ease, comfort or gratification, but by a reference to the purity and salvation of others." [Barnes]

In the context of this specific chapter, it obviously meant that the Corinthian Christians should not eat meat associated with idols if it would damage another believer's faith. "Originally it meant, 'Let no man, in regard to the question about partaking of the meat offered in sacrifice to idols, consult his own pleasure, happiness, or convenience; but let him, as the leading rule on the subject, ask what will be for the welfare of others.'" [Barnes]

Specific Instructions for Household Shopping (10:25-26)

1 Cor 10:25 Eat anything that is sold in the meat market without asking questions for conscience' sake;

Eat anything that is sold in the meat market = Meat is simply meat, and it does not matter which market you buy it from. In the grocery store the meat is completely isolated from any context of idol worship and should be treated like any other product on the shelves. Paul is saying that, "Meat, when exposed for public sale in the market, lost its character as a sacrifice, and might be eaten." [Hodge] In the previous verse Paul had stated a very important principle to guide our behavior, that we should consider the good of others. Our influence on others should be a very important factor in determining our activities, but that principle is not meant to be the rule for everything we do. In the case of buying food in the market for our own household use, Paul says in effect, "If it does not bother your own conscience then buy it and eat it."

Christian freedom is a privilege that should be forfeited only when it clearly would be offensive to another person.

> If we refrain from doing certain questionable things, we do not do so from a sense of legalistic compulsion but from the voluntary restriction of our liberty in order to help build up someone else. When we restrict our liberty for the sake of a weaker brother, we should also try to help him grow in the understanding of his own Christian freedom. In other words, we should help his conscience grow stronger, in order that he can come to enjoy his full liberty in Christ and not be restricted in the enjoyment of his privileges. [MacArthur]

Without asking questions for conscience sake = We are not required to make a detailed investigation into the source of everything that we purchase or eat. We do not need to be over-scrupulous or over-principled when it comes to things that are not morally wrong in themselves. This was quite different from how the apostle Paul was raised and lived his life as a Pharisaical Jew. One writer put it this way, "He makes a clean break with Judaism, where conscience demanded of the devout Jew the most searching inquiry before he might eat. Paul had in fact ceased to be a practicing Jew." [Barrett]

1 Cor 10:26 FOR THE EARTH IS THE LORD'S, AND ALL IT CONTAINS.

For the earth = This is a quote from Psalm 24:1, and Paul used this to justify why it was permitted to eat the meat purchased in the marketplace. It all belongs to the Lord! Even though it had been waved in front of a statue of wood or stone, it does not belong to that statue. It belongs to the Lord and it should be eaten with gratitude to God. "Nothing, therefore, can in itself be polluting if used in obedience to the design of its creation. And as the animals offered in sacrifice were intended to be food for man, they cannot defile those who use them for that purpose." [Hodge]

Specific Instructions for Dining with Unbelievers (10:27-30)

1 Cor 10:27 If one of the unbelievers invites you and you want to go, eat anything that is set before you without asking questions for conscience' sake.

If one of the unbelievers = This implies that the social contacts between believers and unbelievers can continue after becoming a Christian. In fact, Jesus accepted such invitations during His earthly ministry (see Luke 5:29-30; 19:7).

You want to go = This leaves the decision up to the individual believer regarding whether to go. "The apostle does not lay any commands upon them to go or not go, but leaves them to their own will, inclination, and discretion; for it might be either proper or improper to listen to an invitation from such a quarter; but if they were inclined and thought it appropriate to go, then they might without sinning." [Gill]

Eat anything that is set before you = As in the situation where you are eating meat in your own home, you may eat meat in another person's home without requiring a detailed investigation into the origin of the food or how it had been prepared (see 1 Cor 10:25). "As the sacrifices lost their religious character when sold in the market, so also at any private table they were to be regarded not as sacrifices but as ordinary food, and might be eaten without scruple." [Hodge]

1 Cor 10:28 But if anyone says to you, "This is meat sacrificed to idols," do not eat it, for the sake of the one who informed you, and for conscience' sake;

But if anyone says to you = With this contrast word Paul now introduces an exception to his rule about eating without asking questions for conscience' sake. When you are eating in the home of others, then the principle of "the good of others" must also be considered (1 Cor 10:24). "There is a difference between taking part in a meal with others and the individualist activity of shopping for a meal at home. At a meal, one's table-companions also must be considered." [Barrett]

This is meat sacrificed to idols = The word Paul had used up to this point for food sacrificed to idols is a term that the Jews and Christians used in a derogatory way to describe "idol food" (**eidolothuton**). Someone who did not want to use this derogatory meaning would use a different word (**hierothuton** = consecrated to deity). This second word is the one Paul used in this verse, possibly because the person speaking was someone who approved of or participated in the worship of idols, or possibly because the speaker did not want to offend such a person. Who is this person that Paul is discussing? He might be the host or a fellow guest, either a non-Christian or a Christian with a weak conscience.

> It is not easy to see how a non-Christian's conscience would enter into the matter, and it is therefore best to suppose that we have to do with a second Christian guest, whose weak conscience, though it permitted him to attend the meal, has led him to make inquiries of his host or in the kitchen, and who, using the most courteous word available, now passes on the fruit of his research to his stronger Christian brother. [Barrett]

Do not eat it, for the sake of the one who informed you = The comment made by this person had just taken the eating of this meat out of the context of a private meal around a dining table and put it into the context of eating meat that had been consecrated to a deity (**hierothuton**). In this new context, a believer should not eat the meat. "If any of the guests apprised them that a particular dish contained meat which had been offered to an idol, out of regard to the conscientious scruples of him who made the intimation, they should abstain." [Hodge]

For conscience sake = This repeats what Paul had said in 1 Cor 8:10-12 where he explained that we should limit our liberty so we do not wound another person's conscience, which is considered to be a sin against that person. As the next verse will tell us, this is out of respect to the conscientious scruples of the person that declared the meat had been offered to idols. Someone else's legalism should not make us legalistic, but we can graciously defer our rights when we are in a specific circumstance with that person. "If someone raised the question, it is obvious that his conscience is having a problem, and out of considerateness and love for him you should forego the exercise of your liberty. In other words, practice your liberty wherever it does not offend or entice to sin." [Boyer]

1 Cor 10:29 I mean not your own conscience, but the other man's; for why is my freedom judged by another's conscience?

Why is my freedom judged by another's conscience? = This may be another direct quote from the Corinthians in the "Christian liberty" party. It is a difficult phrase to understand. One thing we do notice here is that Paul switched from the second person to the first person as a way of instructing them by putting himself in their place. Another thing we notice is that the Greek terms for "the other" (**heteros**) and "another" (**allos**) are different in this phrase. "The other" refers to the specific person who informed them that the meat was idol meat (1 Cor 10:28), but the term "another" could refer to any other person. If another guest knew that the meat was idol meat but the believer did not know it, then the believer should have the freedom to eat it without being condemned by someone else's conscience.

There seem to be three possibilities for the meaning of this phrase:

1. The stronger Christian may be protesting against yielding his rights every time his behavior might wound another person's conscience. "It is attractive to suppose that in these words we hear an interjection made by a strong Christian who objects to being limited by the conscience of others." [Barrett] But this seems contrary to what Paul has been saying to the stronger Christian, that he should yield his rights when another person's conscience may be wounded.

2. Paul may simply be emphasizing the point that he had just made about not eating in cases when it might offend a weaker brother. Another way to say it might be: "Abstain not because your own conscience condemns you, but for the sake of the other man who brought up the fact that the meat was idol meat, in order that he may not be caused to act against his conscience." This option views the phrase as support for eating without asking questions of conscience. If your own conscience is not bothered about eating, and if eating will not offend a weaker brother, then you can eat without fear of judgment.

3. Paul might be giving another reason for what he had just said about a stronger Christian yielding his liberty. He says, "Why should exercising my freedom to eat what I like become a cause of condemnation by a weaker believer who is more scrupulous or legalistic?" This places the emphasis on the term for judgment in this phrase. As one man stated,

   The sense may be thus expressed: I am free; I have liberty to partake of that food if I please; there is no law against it and it is not morally wrong: but if I do after it is pointed out to me as having been sacrificed to idols, my liberty will be misconstrued, misjudged, or condemned by others. The scrupulous believer will censure, judge, or condemn me as one who falls in with the customs of idolaters and will suppose that I cannot have a good conscience. Under these circumstances, why should I act so as to expose myself to this censure and condemnation?" [Barnes] So taken this way, Paul may be saying that it is best for the stronger believer to refrain from eating so as not to expose his liberty to condemnation. This also seems to fit well with the words of the following verse.

We need to realize, though, that the strong Christian is free to partake of anything he is able eat with thanksgiving. If he abstains in certain cases out of regard for the conscience of the other person, that does not mean he has lost his freedom forever. "The Christian is always free to eat any food whatever. Though there may be occasions when he does not take advantage of his liberty, his conscience remains always his own and free and is not called into question by the judgments of others." [Barrett]

1 Cor 10:30 If I partake with thankfulness, why am I slandered concerning that for which I give thanks?

If I partake with thankfulness = This implies that your own conscience is not bothered by eating this meat. It is clearly not a matter of offending yourself, but of offending someone else's conscience.

Why am I slandered = This presents the possibility that the use of one's legitimate Christian liberty could be spoken ill of or slandered by unjust comments. In other words, "Why should my liberty be reproached because of a careless use of it? Is it worth it to incur the risk of being reproached simply for the sake of exercising one's liberty without regard for the conscience of others?"

What about eating at a public feast in the pagan temple?

This was the third case when a believer might come into contact with meat sacrificed to idols, but Paul had actually dealt with this issue first (see 1 Cor 8:10 and 1 Cor 10:14-22). In that case, the believer was to completely avoid a situation where sacrificial meat was served in the context of a religious service focused on idols.

Before we finish this chapter, we should summarize Paul's teaching about how to decide whether activities are acceptable for Christians.

How can a Christian decide whether an activity is acceptable in today's world?

There are some Christians who believe that the life of faith is a matter of black and white. For them, everything falls into one of two categories. A thing is either RIGHT or it is WRONG, and there is no middle ground. There are other Christians who live by a different motto: "That which the Bible does not explicitly prohibit is permitted." To them, everything not specifically identified as a sin in the Bible is allowable under any circumstances.

However, neither of these views is supported by the apostle Paul, and they are not the view presented in the Scriptures. The Christian life would be so much easier if everything were black and white, or if everything not explicitly prohibited were permitted. But in this letter to the Corinthians the apostle Paul presented a significant gray area in which each believer is called upon to make decisions for himself regarding his behavior in specific circumstances. You could almost say that there is such a thing as a biblical situational ethics.

There are some things which are definitely wrong for a Christian under any circumstances, such as participating in immorality (1 Cor 6:18) or idolatry (1 Cor 10:14). There are other activities that are wrong for a Christian, not necessarily because they are inherently sinful but because they could enslave a believer (1 Cor 6:12), or because they are not profitable (1 Cor 6:12; 10:23), or because they do not build up the body of Christ toward maturity in the faith (1 Cor 10:23). Many of these types of activities are never specifically mentioned in the Bible, but it may be wrong for a Christian to be associated with them. Each believer should carefully evaluate his use of the things in this category. Examples of things that could enslave a believer or are unprofitable might include such things as alcoholic drink, drugs, cigarettes, gambling, improper sexual activities, or even an excess desire for power, money, clothes, possessions, food, thrills or entertainment (such as books, television, music, movies, computer games and web sites). It might also include any number of other things that a Christian could be involved in while living in today's world.

From the chart on the next page we see some things that may be acceptable for a Christian in some circumstances or times or places, but these same things may not be acceptable in other circumstances or times or places. Believers need to carefully follow the leading of the Lord through the promptings of the Holy Spirit. We need to be sensitive to the situations we find ourselves in and behave according to what would be most profitable in each circumstance. Sometimes there are no hard-and-fast rules to govern our behavior. This is one of the great challenges of the Christian life.

In commenting on when to apply the principle of yielding one's rights, one man wrote:

> Scripture uses this principle of considerateness for the weaker brother as a secondary principle. It is to be used only if the issue of right or wrong is not involved. If the Bible says a thing is wrong, then this principle has no application whatever. The way it is frequently used by Christians to answer the questions of worldly amusements can hardly be justified unless it has first been determined that the particular worldly amusement under consideration is by scriptural standards not wrong in itself. It is interesting to note that in such applications, the weak are usually the stricter, whereas the strong are more broad. Apparently it is the mature, developed, strong conscience which is less sensitive to these worldly things. Unless one can conceive of increasing worldliness as an indication of greater spirituality, it becomes obvious that the whole application of this principle is a mistake in such cases. [Boyer]

Another man has said: "They accommodated themselves to Jewish or Gentile practices only in matters of indifference. They did not accommodate even in things indifferent, under circumstances which gave to those things a significant religious character. For example, they allowed sacrifices to be eaten, but eating within a temple was forbidden." [Hodge] This whole issue of deciding whether our activities are appropriate certainly emphasizes the fact that all believers should know what the Scriptures say regarding things it explicitly prohibits or allows. In those areas we should always act according to the dictates of the Bible. It is only in things that the Bible does not clearly prohibit that we may have to make a judgment call in specific cases. Believers must clearly know, understand, remember, and obey what the Bible says in all cases. And we must rely on biblical principles to guide us in all other cases.

Everything the Bible specifically prohibits is wrong

Wrong	Immorality	1 Cor 6:18
Wrong	Idolarty	1 Cor 10:14
Wrong	Activities that enslave	1 Cor 6:12
Wrong	Activities that are unprofitable	1 Cor 6:12; 10:23
Wrong	Activities that do not edify	1 Cor 10:23
Wrong	Eating meat sacrificed to idols in a pagan temple	1 Cor 8:10; 10:20
Wrong	Eating idol meat in public when someone identifies it as idol meat	1 Cor 10:28
Okay	Eating idol meat in public if no one identifies it as idol meat	1 Cor 10:27
Okay	Eating idol meat in private in your own home	1 Cor 10:26

The Purpose of Christian Liberty (10:31)

1 Cor 10:31 Whether, then, you eat or drink or whatever you do, do all to the glory of God.

Whether we are eating or drinking or doing any other activity, the purpose that every believer should strive to achieve is the greater glory of God.

> Let self be forgotten. Let your eye be fixed on God. Let the promotion of his glory be your object in all you do. Strive in everything to act in such a way that men may praise that God whom you profess to serve...Philosophers tell us to make the good of others the end; and thus destroy the sentiment of religion by merging it into philanthropy or benevolence. The Bible tells us to make the glory of God the end. This secures the other ends by making them subordinate, while at the same time it exalts the soul by placing before it an infinite personal object. [Hodge]

If every believer kept this purpose clearly in mind at all times, then our activities would surely change. We would do things differently if we understood that everything should contribute to glorifying the One who created and redeemed us.

The Example of the Apostle Paul (10:32-11:1)

The last two verses of this chapter are a single sentence, beginning with a command and ending with a personal example.

1 Cor 10:32 Give no offense either to Jews or to Greeks or to the church of God;

Give no offense (aproskopos) = This word means having nothing to strike against. Put nothing in the path which could cause another person to stumble. Leave a clear road for others to follow, rather than leading others into sin by your bad example.

To Jews or to Greeks or the church of God = This clearly identifies three unique categories of people that have existed since the Day of Pentecost. There are unbelieving Jews as well as unbelieving Gentiles, but the third category consists of believers during the church age.

1 Cor 10:33 just as I also please all men in all things, not seeking my own profit but the profit of the many, so that they may be saved.

Notice here that the subject of the sentence has changed from the second person ("you") to the first person ("I"). Just as Paul did when he ended chapters eight (1 Cor 8:13) and nine (1 Cor 9:26-27), Paul now ends this entire section on a personal note by holding up his own example for them to follow.

This verse reminds us of what Paul had said in 1 Cor 9:19-22. There he also mentioned the three categories of people: Jews, Gentiles, and the Church. He became all things to all men in order to save some. Now Paul connects that to the principle of limiting his own behavior and activities for the benefit of others. "Paul knows that the Christian message is necessarily and intrinsically offensive (1 Cor 1:23). It is more important that Christianity should offend for the right reason and not for the wrong reason; because it is a placarding of Christ crucified, and not because Christians are inconsiderate of the scruples and convictions of their fellows." [Barrett]

1 Cor 11:1 Be imitators of me, just as I also am of Christ.

Be imitators (mimetes) = This is a command in the imperative mood. Just as Paul gave such a command in 1 Cor 4:16, here also he expected them to mimic him to the extent that he was behaving in a Christ-like way.

Abusing Christian Liberty in Church: Inappropriate Behavior for Women

(1 Corinthians 11:2-17)

T he apostle Paul had dealt specifically with several behaviors of the Corinthian believers that involved abusing their Christian liberty. These included engaging in sexual immorality, taking each other to court with lawsuits, and eating idol meat at the pagan feasts. Now in chapter eleven the apostle Paul will deal with two additional issues. In this chapter we see how the Corinthian believers were abusing their Christian liberty even during their church services.

As we have noticed previously, the Corinthian Christians had written to ask Paul several specific questions. As we begin looking at chapter eleven, we should understand that Paul is apparently responding to another of their written questions, but he does not state the question before answering it. Instead, he begins by presenting several facts that he wants them to grasp, and he hopes that they will come to the right conclusion so that the answer to their question will be obvious after their investigation. One man said it this way: "Paul does not at once answer the inquiry and determine what ought to be done; but he invites their attention to a series of remarks on the subject, which will lead them to draw the conclusion which he wished to establish." [Barnes]

The Importance of Holding Firmly to Doctrinal Truths (11:2)

1 Cor 11:2 Now I praise you because you remember me in everything and hold firmly to the traditions, just as I delivered them to you.

Now I praise you (epaineo) = This is the only chapter in this letter in which Paul used this word of commendation, but the other two instances of this word in chapter eleven are in the negative: "I do not praise you" (1 Cor 11:17) and "Shall I praise you? I will not praise you!" (1 Cor 11:22). We have not seen the apostle Paul commend the Corinthian believers so far in this letter. We saw him thank God for the grace and the gifts they had been given (1 Cor 1:4-7), but most of what he has said up to this point has been to exhort or correct them. What is it that Paul is commending them for in this verse?

You remember me in everything = The word "remember" (mimnesko) is related to "imitators" (mimetes) in verse one, and it means to remember, to call to mind, or to remind oneself. Apparently there were some ways in which the Corinthians were imitating the apostle Paul's good example. The phrase "in everything" probably means "in your general practice." As one man put it, they were willing to "regard Paul's authority and seek his direction in matters pertaining to the good order of the church." [Barnes]

Hold firmly (katecho) = Literally this means to hold down; to grip or hold tightly.

To the traditions (paradosis) = The traditions consisted of instructions given by word of mouth or in writing. This refers to the new revelation of the Word of God that was given to them through the teaching ministry of the apostles and prophets.

Just as I delivered them to you = The verb "delivered" (**paradidomi**) is related to the noun "traditions," and it means to deliver verbally or in writing. Paul is saying that there were some teachings they held to just as he had delivered them. "The apostles had delivered to them certain doctrines or rules respecting the good order and the government of the church, and they had in general observed them. For this disposition to regard his authority and to keep what he had commanded, he commends them." [Barnes]

What were these instructions which Paul commends them for holding? They probably related to gathering together on the first day of the week for worship, prayer, and the ministry of the Word of God, because that is the topic of this section. The Corinthian church was at least obeying Paul's instructions to meet together and to celebrate the Lord's Supper, which he will discuss later in this chapter.

The Principle of a Hierarchy of Authority and Responsibility (11:3)

1 Cor 11:3 But I want you to understand that Christ is the head of every man, and the man is the head of a woman, and God is the head of Christ.

But I want you to understand = "But" is the same word translated "now" in verse two. If it is to be understood as a contrast, then it is contrasting with the commendation in the previous verse. In other words, there was also a specific way in which the Corinthians were not holding fast to Paul's teaching. He had something to say beginning in verse three that was not praiseworthy. We could also understand this as something Paul wants to add now to the traditions he had given them previously. Paul wanted the Corinthians, literally, to see something (**eido**); to gain knowledge by examination of evident facts. In the next phrase Paul will begin to present these facts, and at the end of this section he will apply these facts to the specific situation in the Corinthian church.

Head (kephale) = This word represents the physical head or the top of the head. By implication this means that which is prominent or in authority. As we interpret this passage we must determine which meaning is intended in each passage. The parallel uses of this word in Paul's writings include Ephesians 1:22; 5:23; Colossians 1:18; 2:10. These uses show that the word means authority in the context of the relationships between Christ and the church, and between a husband and wife. In the context of a person's physical anatomy, the word obviously means the physical head. What is somewhat confusing in this section is that Paul used both meanings of this word, so we must clearly identify when the word means the physical head vs. the authority of a person. In this verse the word "head" means authority in every instance.

Christ is the head of every man = Christ is in authority over every man, believers and unbelievers alike. Several Scripture passages show that the Lord Jesus Christ has been given authority over every man (Matt 28:18; Phil 2:10-11; Heb 2:8). One of the primary aspects in which Christ is in authority over every man is because He is identified as our Creator (Col 1:16), and Paul will soon use the Creation event as a major part of his argument for the principle of subordination. But in the context of the meetings of the church, we can also see that Christ is in direct authority over every believer (Eph 1:22-23; Col 1:18).

The man is the head of a woman = A man is in authority over a woman in two specific situations within the context of church meetings.

1. If the man is one of the church officers who has authority and responsibility for the spiritual well-being of all the men and women who are present (1 Thess 5:12-13; Heb 13:17; 1 Pet 5:2-3).
2. If the man is the husband of the woman and has authority and responsibility for her well-being in every area (Eph 5:22-28; 1 Pet 3:7).

It seems most likely that this statement refers to the proper relationship of authority within the marriage relationship, although it could also refer to someone who is in spiritual authority over the unmarried women of the church.

God is the head of Christ = The gospel of John gives many clear statements by the Lord Jesus about His relationship to God the Father who sent Him on His mission (see John 4:34; 5:18-19; 5:30; 6:38; 14:28). Jesus is the best example of someone under proper authority, and it may have been put last in this sequence for the purpose of emphasis. It is also possible that Paul put it last to encourage women that they are under authority just like their Lord is under authority.

The guiding principle is that order and subordination pervade the entire universe and are an essential part of its original design by our Creator. Neither the man nor the woman has any ultimate superiority since they are both clearly under the authority of the higher powers. Since this structure of order was divinely established, then both men and women should act in accordance with it. One writer explained that,

> Paul inseparably ties the three aspects of the principle together. As Christ is submissive to the Father and Christians are to be submissive to Christ, women are to be submissive to men. You cannot reject one part without rejecting the others. If Christ had not submitted to the will of God, redemption for mankind would have been impossible, and we would forever be doomed and lost. If individual human beings do not submit to Christ as Savior, they are still doomed and lost, because they reject God's gracious provision. And if women do not submit to men, then the family and society as a whole are disrupted. Whether on a divine or human scale, subordination and authority are indispensable elements in God's order and plan. [MacArthur]

Another point that should be explained is that God did not establish the principle of male authority based on any innate superiority of men. Just because a woman is under proper authority in a particular relationship does not mean that she is in any way inferior to the person to whom she is responsible. One writer said it this way:

> It should be understood clearly that the term head and its corresponding opposite, subjection, have to do with rank, position, and authority; not at all with ability. They denote positions in governmental or administrative organization. They do not in any way reflect inferiority or inequality. Proof of this is seen in the relationships within the Godhead. Christ is every bit as much God as God the Father. He is equal in essence. But, He is second in the Godhead and subordinate to the Father in function (John 4:34; 5:18-19). In another realm, an army captain may not be a better man, either physically or intellectually or morally, than the private. But he is superior in rank and function. So the Christian wife, even though she may be superior to her husband in ability, in personality, even in spirituality, yet she recognizes his headship and gets in rank under him in the divine economy of the home. [Boyer]

The Shame of Violating Customs Supporting the Hierarchy of Authority (11:4-6)

First, for the Man (11:4)

1 Cor 11:4 Every man who has something on his head while praying or prophesying disgraces his head.

Why is the man mentioned first? Possibly because he is mentioned first in the hierarchy of authority above. It seems that men are mentioned throughout this section only for the sake of illustrating this principle. The real issue (as we will see in 1 Cor 11:6) is with the wrong behavior of certain women in the Corinthian church services.

Every man who has something on his head = Literally this says, "down over his head having." It is referring to a man having something that covers his physical head, and possibly hangs down over his face as well. This could describe something like a veil that may be worn by a bride in today's culture. Such a veil was typically worn by decent women in Corinth as a sign of modesty and particularly by married women as a sign of being under the authority and protection of their husband. However, it was not appropriate in that culture for a man to wear such a covering. "It was the Greek custom, and therefore the custom at Corinth, for men in worship to be uncovered." [JFB]

While praying or prophesying = Simply stated, praying is speaking to God on behalf of men. Prophesying is speaking to men on behalf of God.

Disgraces his head = The context here makes it clear that whatever this verse is suggesting, it would have been completely ridiculous in the culture of that day for a man to do it. It seems most consistent to view the word as referring to the man's physical head. To disgrace his head would mean to bring shame upon himself as a person. There are several reasons for this:

– In the preceding clause the word is used of the man's physical head.
– In verse five the unveiled woman is said to dishonor her own head, which indicates the physical head.
– If a man acts inconsistently with his station in life, then he brings more disgrace on himself than on the One who placed him in that position.

Scholars have explained, "Consequently, it was disgraceful in the man to assume the symbol of subordination, and disgraceful in the woman to discard it." [Hodge]

Second, for the Woman (11:5-6)

1 Cor 11:5 **But every woman who has her head uncovered while praying or prophesying disgraces her head, for she is one and the same as the woman whose head is shaved.**

But every woman who has her head uncovered = The Greek word "uncovered" (**akatakalupto**) begins with a negative particle (not) and ends with a compound word **kata** (down) and **kalupto** (to cover). The term **katakalupto** will be used by the apostle Paul in the next several verses to mean a covering on or over the head. History and archeology provide the following facts:

The Greek women rarely appeared in public, but lived in strict seclusion. Unmarried women never left their apartments, except on occasions of festal processions, either as spectators or participants. Even after marriage they were largely confined to the women's rooms. The head-dress of Greek women consisted of nets, hair-bags, or kerchiefs, sometimes covering the whole head. A shawl which enveloped the body was also often thrown over the head, especially at marriages or funerals. This costume the Corinthian women had disused in the Christian assemblies. [VWS]

Another writer says, "It would seem from this that the women removed their veils, and wore their hair disheveled, when they pretended to be under the influence of divine inspiration. This was the case with the pagan priestesses; and in so doing, the Christian women imitated them. On this account, if on no other, Paul declares the impropriety of this conduct." [Barnes] If this were the case, then the issue of women wearing the head covering was very much analogous to the issue of meat sacrificed to idols. If the women were adopting practices carried on in the pagan temple ceremonies, then Paul would tell them to flee from those practices.

While praying or prophesying = This phrase is parallel to what Paul said about the man in verse four. It is not clear whether Paul meant this only as a literary parallel, or if it actually described the practice of some of the women in the

Corinthian church. In either case we should understand that it is quite normal to describe something that was occurring without actually sanctioning it. As one commentator said, "This passage does not necessarily sanction women speaking in public, even though possessing miraculous gifts; but simply records what took place at Corinth, without expressing an opinion on it, reserving the censure of it till 1 Cor 14:34-35." [JFB] Another man writes,

> The New Testament has no restrictions on a woman's witnessing in public to others, even to a man. Nor does it prohibit women from taking non-leadership roles of praying with believers or for unbelievers; and there is no restriction from teaching children and other women (see Titus 2:3-4; 1 Tim 5:16). Women may have the gift of prophecy, as did Philip's four daughters (Acts 21:9), but they are normally not to prophesy in the meetings of the church. [MacArthur]

Later Paul will directly address the issue of women speaking out in the church services at Corinth.

Disgraces her head = In this sentence some of the original Greek manuscripts use the word **heautou** which means "her own" head while other manuscripts use the word **autas** which simply means "her" head. In either case it seems best to understand this as referring to the woman's own physical head. The disgrace falls upon her as a person, rather than upon the one in authority over her.

For she is one and the same as the woman whose head is shaved = Here Paul gives the reason that she disgraces herself. It is because she has identified herself with the category of women in that society whose hair had been cut off. Who was a woman whose head was shaved? Some have identified her with the common prostitute of Corinth.

> The unveiled woman in Corinth was a prostitute. It was the sign of prostitution, and in the most flagrant cases not only was the woman unveiled, she was also shorn or shaven. But these Christian women were saying, All things are lawful to me. We need not wear these veils, nor conform to these things. Paul replied, Yes, that is so, but you are in Corinth, and if you pray or prophesy in Corinth without the veil, you are adopting that which is the ultimate badge of prostitution, and if you appear like that, you are dishonoring your head. Corinthian conditions are clearly in view. [Morgan]

Others point out that the law required the head of an adulteress to be shaved. "The Justinian code prescribed shaving the head for an adulteress whom the husband refused to receive after two years. Paul does not tell Corinthian Christian women to put themselves on a level with courtesans. Clearly Paul uses such strong language because of the effect on a woman's reputation in Corinth by such conduct that proclaimed her a lewd woman. Social custom varied in the world then as now, but there was no alternative in Corinth." [RWP]

Still other scholars emphasize that the head covering was the recognized social symbol of female modesty.

Dress is in a great degree conventional. A costume which is proper in one country would be improper in another. The principle insisted upon in this paragraph is that women should conform in matters of dress to all those customs which the public sentiment of the community in which they live demands. The veil in all eastern countries was, and to a great extend still is, the symbol of modesty and subjection. For a woman, therefore, in Corinth to discard the veil was to renounce her claim to modesty, and to refuse to recognize her subordination to her husband. [Hodge]

In any of these cases, it would have been a disgraceful thing for a Corinthian woman to remain uncovered.

1 Cor 11:6 For if a woman does not cover her head, let her also have her hair cut off; but if it is disgraceful for a woman to have her hair cut off or her head shaved, let her cover her head.

For if a woman does not cover her head = Here Paul is essentially telling these women to act consistently. If they are not going to follow the proper custom of covering their heads in public services, then maybe they should go the whole way and cut their hair short, or to be even more extreme, they should shave their heads.

Let her also have her hair cut off = If a woman is going to set aside her head covering, then why not go the whole way and remove every covering on her head.

If it is disgraceful for a woman to have her hair cut off or her head shaved = This is a first class conditional clause, which is assumed to be true. It could be translated, "Since it is a disgrace." In the culture of that day it was definitely considered shameful for a woman to have her head shaved.

If she wishes to be regarded as a reputable woman, let her conform to the established custom. But if she has no regard to her reputation, let her act as other women of her class. She must conform either to the reputable or disreputable class of her sex, for a departure from the one is conforming to the other. [Hodge]

Let her cover her head = The situation Paul is describing here is similar to the situation with eating meat that had been sacrificed to idols. In that case, there was nothing wrong with the meat, but it would be wrong to eat it in certain circumstances. Here in this case with the woman wearing a covering on her head, there were circumstances where it would be right to wear the covering and situations where the head covering would not be required. The apostle Paul is teaching that in the situation where a woman was attending the public meeting of the church it would be wrong for her to be uncovered.

Reasons for Following Customs Which Support the Hierarchy of Authority (11:7-16)

Wearing some type of head covering was a customary symbol in Corinthian society which indicated that a woman was living under proper authority. Paul will now give several reasons why the Corinthian women should continue to follow the typical practice in their culture and wear this outward symbol that represents the inward truth. The outward symbol may be different from culture to culture, but the principle of authority is not a matter of custom and should not be compromised.

The Argument from the Sequence, Manner, and Purpose of Their Creation (11:7-12)

Sequence: The Man Was Created First in the Image of God (11:7)

1 Cor 11:7 For a man ought not to have his head covered, since he is the image and glory of God; but the woman is the glory of man.

For a man ought not to have his head covered = For a man to cover his head would be a reversal of the customary practice; the man would be acting like a woman. This is a strong phrase that tells men they are obligated NOT to cover their heads.

He is the image and glory of God = The word glory means splendor, brightness, that which stands forth to represent God, or something by which the glory of God is known. "Man is the glory of God as the crown of creation and as endowed with sovereignty like God himself, only on a finite scale." [RWP] Notice that the apostle here is only discussing the original formation of man at the time of Creation. In Genesis 2:7 we see that only the man was originally created from the dust of the ground. And it was the man who was given dominion and authority over the things God had created, since this event occurred before the creation of the woman.

But the woman is the glory of man = In the logical flow of thought, this expresses that the man was created first and was directly fashioned in God's image, while the woman was created later and out of the already existing flesh of man (Gen 2:21-22). "She was made for him; she was made after he was; she was taken from him." [Barnes] Notice that it does not say that the woman is the image and glory of man. The truth is that the woman was created in the image of God, just as much as the man was (Gen 1:26-27). This set of arguments from Creation is based on what we might call seniority. It involves a subordination to man in the order of creation. One commentator of a past generation said it this way: "Therefore as he was first in being, he must be senior to her: this serves to prove all that has been as yet said; as man is the head of the woman, the woman is the glory of man." [Gill] A more recent commentator said, "Woman was made to manifest man's authority and will, as man was made to manifest God's authority and will." [MacArthur]

Manner: The Woman Was Created Out of the Man's Body (11:8)

1 Cor 11:8 For man does not originate from woman, but woman from man;

For man does not originate from woman but woman from man = This is a statement of the facts presented in Genesis 2:21-22. "The woman was made by God mediately through the man, who was, as it were, a veil or medium placed between her and God, and therefore, should wear the veil or head covering in public worship, in acknowledgment of this subordination to man in the order of creation." [JFB]

Purpose: The Woman Was Created to Function as a Helper (11:9)

1 Cor 11:9 for indeed man was not created for the woman's sake, but woman for the man's sake.

Man was not created for the woman's sake = The woman was created later for the purpose of being a helper. "She was not in existence when he was created; and though it is the proper business of man to provide for, take care of, and defend the woman as the weaker vessel, yet these were not the original ends of his creation; he was made for God, for his service and glory." [Gill]

But woman for the man's sake = The woman was made for man, but we must remember that the man was never complete until the woman was there. "The woman was made...not to be a slave, but a help-meet; not to be the minister of his pleasures, but to be his aid and comforter in life; not to be regarded as of inferior nature and rank, but to be his friend, to divide his sorrows, and to multiply and extend his joys; yet still to be in a station subordinate to him. He is to be the head, the ruler, the presider in the family circle; and she was created to aid him in his duties, to comfort him in his afflictions, to partake with him of his pleasures. Her rank is therefore honorable, though it is subordinate." [Barnes] After the Fall in Genesis chapter three, God also confirmed these roles of the man and the woman (Gen 3:16-17).

Conclusion From This Argument and An Additional Reason (11:10)

1 Cor 11:10 Therefore the woman ought to have a symbol of authority on her head, because of the angels.

Therefore = This transition word introduces the conclusion from everything Paul has said so far. Here is the logical result, based on the facts of the Creation, concerning the issue of a woman in the church services. She is to follow the appropriate customs to demonstrate that she is clearly functioning within the sphere of authority provided by her husband and her church leaders.

The woman ought to have a symbol of authority on her head = The word for authority (**exousia**) means the power, strength, ability, or freedom to do something. The woman should clearly be covered and protected by the power or the authority of her husband or her leaders. This indicates that a woman does have power, but it is the power that is hers as a result of living in a proper relationship of authority with her husband or church leaders. We clearly see in this verse that the cultural use of the head covering by women in the Corinthian church services represented the God-ordained principle of a woman's submission to authority. For that reason the woman was obligated to follow this custom which upheld that important principle. "The apostle is saying, Women, you are not belittling yourselves, you are not degrading yourselves when you show proper respect by appearing in public places with your heads covered. You are simply availing yourselves of that which is your protection." [Ironside]

Because of the angels = Paul had mentioned angels in 1 Cor 4:9, saying that angels observe the behavior of men and women. One man explained this by saying,

> Woman best asserts her spiritual equality before God, not by behaving contrary to the common practices, but by recognizing her true position and fulfilling its claims, even as do the angels, who are ministering as well as worshiping spirits (Heb 1:4). She is to fall in obediently with that divine economy of which she forms a part with the angels, and not to break the divine harmony, which especially asserts itself in worship, where the angelic ministers mingle with the earthly worshipers; nor to ignore the example of the holy ones who keep their first estate, and serve in the heavenly sanctuary. [VWS]

The Balancing Truth: The Interdependence of Men and Women Under Christ (11:11-12)

1 Cor 11:11 However, in the Lord, neither is woman independent of man, nor is man independent of woman.

However = This contrasting statement gives an important balancing truth to what has been presented so far regarding the seniority of the man at Creation. "This adversative clause limits the preceding statement. Each sex is incomplete without the other." [RWP] In other words, both genders are necessary and have special value and purpose. "These verses seem to be inserted in order to safeguard his teaching against the false interpretation that woman somehow is inferior. These verses indicate that she is not inferior, but only subordinate." [Boyer]

In the Lord = This was by the design and direction of the Lord. In other words, not only did the Lord place the man in a position of authority, but He also designed the relationship between the man and the woman in such a way that they are intended to function together. The Creator is the one who planned it to work this way. The end of the next verse will also affirm this truth.

Woman independent of man = This may have been the core of the issue Paul was addressing. Christian women were behaving in ways that made them appear independent or out from under the proper hierarchy of authority and protection in the church services at Corinth.

Nor is man independent of woman = This tells us that the man and the woman are interdependent.

> Man's authority over woman is a delegated authority and a derived authority, given by God to be used for His purposes and in His way. Man as a fellow creature has no innate superiority to woman and has no right to use his authority tyrannically or selfishly...The man's proper authority does not make him independent of woman, nor does her proper subordination make her alone dependent. Neither is independent of the other; they are mutually dependent. [MacArthur]

1 Cor 11:12 For as the woman originates from the man, so also the man has his birth through the woman; and all things originate from God.

As the woman originates from the man = This restates the truth presented earlier that in the sequence and manner of the original Creation, the woman came later. Paul's point is that just as this statement is true, so is the next statement true.

The man has his birth through the woman = Even though the woman came second and came out of the man at the original Creation, every man who has come into existence after that initial event has been born of a woman. The preposition means "through" or "by means of" so the woman has a very important function in God's design for the sexes. Ultimately it is not the function of the man or the function of the woman that is of primary importance. The next phrase tells us what is really important for us to remember when considering this issue.

All things originate from God = Everything has its source, purpose, design, and function as a result of the working of God. "This expression seems designed to suppress any spirit of complaint or dissatisfaction with this arrangement. The woman should therefore be contented, and the man should not assume any improper superiority, since the whole arrangement and appointment is of God." [Barnes]

The Argument from Social Propriety in the Culture of That Time (11:13-15)

You Judge: Is It Proper? (11:13)

1 Cor 11:13 Judge for yourselves: is it proper for a woman to pray to God with her head uncovered?

Judge for yourselves = As he did in 1 Cor 10:15, Paul tells the Corinthians to put themselves into the judgment seat and to exercise their own wisdom. They are to use their own sense of propriety for what is right.

Is it proper for a woman to pray to God with her head uncovered? = Paul appeals to their own sense of what is proper in the culture in which they live. From the historical records of that time we get a glimpse of what was normal and proper. One man described it this way: "The Grecian women, except their priestesses, were accustomed to appear in public with a veil. Paul alludes to that established and proper habit, and asks whether it does not accord with their own views of propriety that women in Christian assemblies should also wear the same symbol of modesty." [Barnes] One man puts this question into the form of a normal statement: "His meaning is that it is an improper thing for a woman to appear in a public service with her head uncovered, whether it is joining in the public prayers, or singing of psalms, or in hearing the word expounded." [Gill]

What Does Natural Hair Teach Us About Properly Covering the Head? (11:14-15)

First, for the Man (11:14)

1 Cor 11:14 Does not even nature itself teach you that if a man has long hair, it is a dishonor to him,

Does not even nature itself teach you = The word "nature" (**phusis**) means the nature of things as they exist. "This denotes evidently that sense of propriety which all men have, and which is expressed in any prevailing or universal custom. That which is universal we say s according to nature. It refers to a deep internal sense of what is proper and right." [Barnes] Paul is saying that the cultural practice of women covering their heads as a symbol of subordination reflected the natural order of things in the society of that time.

If a man has long hair, it is a dishonor to him = At the time Paul wrote these words, and even through later history up to our present day, people have recognized that it is considered normal and proper for a woman's hair to be worn longer than the style for men. One commentator put it this way: "It is improper and disgraceful. It is doing that which almost universal custom has said appropriately belongs to the female sex." [Barnes] By dealing with the man first, as he has done throughout this section, Paul introduced the idea that God designed men and women to be distinguishable in appearance, in physiology, as well as in their roles and relationships. "There should be no confusion about male and female identities, because God made the sexes distinct." [MacArthur]

Second, for the Woman (11:15)

1 Cor 11:15 but if a woman has long hair, it is a glory to her? For her hair is given to her for a covering.

But if a woman has long hair, it is a glory to her = In the same way that it is proper for a man to wear his hair shorter, it is proper and brings glory to a woman to wear her hair longer.

Her hair is given to her for a covering (peribolaion) = Previously the term **katakalupto** was used for a covering (1 Cor 11:5, 6, 7, 13), but here Paul used a different word for covering which means something that is thrown around or flung about, as the hair might be tossed by moving the head. The term for "given to her" also indicates something that is given as a permanent gift, rather than a temporary covering such as a shawl or mantle. "It is not in the place of a veil, but analogous to it as a permanent endowment." [RWP] This cannot mean that her hair is the outward sign of authority on her head, because previously Paul had said if a woman would not cover her head then she might as well have her hair cut off, and this implies that the proper covering was something in addition to her natural hair. Paul is using the natural hair as an analogy for whether covering the head is proper for men vs. women. "As woman's hair is given her by nature as her covering, to cut it off like a man, would be improper and unbecoming: therefore, to put away the head covering, too, like a man, would be similarly improper." [JFB]

The Argument from the Common Practice in All Churches (11:16)

1 Cor 11:16 But if one is inclined to be contentious, we have no other practice, nor have the churches of God.

But if one is inclined to be contentious (philoneikos) = This word means fond of strife. In other words, this represents someone who will not be satisfied with the reasons given so far but will argue just for the sake of arguing. "If any man chooses, after all my arguments, to be contentious. If any be contentious and thinks himself right in being so. This is a reproof of the Corinthians' self-sufficiency and disputatiousness (1 Cor 1:20)." [JFB]

We have no other practice, nor have the churches of God = Paul probably refers to himself and the other apostles who were being used by God to write the New Testament at that time. Neither the pronouncements of the apostles nor the practices of the other churches in that area supported what the Corinthians were doing.

> The sense is that it is contrary to custom there for women to appear in public unveiled. This custom, the apostle argues, ought to be allowed to have some influence on the church of Corinth. Even if Paul's reasoning is not sufficient to silence all doubts, the propriety of uniformity in the habits of the churches, the fear of giving offense, should lead you to disapprove the custom of your females appearing in public without their veil. [Barnes]

Did this section of First Corinthians have the desired effect on the church there? It seems that what Paul wrote here did have the desired effect. Evidently the Corinthian believers began to follow Paul's command about women covering their head when in public services in order to affirm the principle of the God-ordained hierarchy of authority. "The testimonies of Tertullian and Chrysostom show that these injunctions of Paul prevailed in the churches. In the sculptures of the catacombs the women have a close-fitting head-dress, while the men have the hair short." [VWS]

The Transition Between This Church Issue and the Next (11:17)

1 Cor 11:17 But in giving this instruction, I do not praise you, because you come together not for the better but for the worse.

But in giving this instruction = The word "this" probably refers to the preceding instruction about the head covering for women, as well as providing a transition to what follows concerning the Lord's Supper.

I do not praise you = The same word is used in 1 Cor 11:2, but this time with the negative (not). In these specific practices, the apostle Paul could not commend them, but needed to rebuke and exhort them to do what was right.

You come together not for the better but for the worse = Coming together refers to their assembling for public worship. These gatherings did not serve to build up the body of Christ, but actually to tear it down.

> Your meetings, and your observance of the ordinances of the gospel, do not promote your edification, your piety, spirituality, and harmony; but tend to division, alienation, and disorder. You should assemble to worship God, and promote harmony, love, and piety; the actual effect of your assembling is just the reverse. [Barnes]

All of the negative things Paul mentions in this letter were part of their regular church services.

Whatever we do in our church services, we should do it for the greater glory of God. One way to affirm God's glory is to follow cultural practices that affirm God-ordained principles, such as God's hierarchy of authority in His created order. In the society and culture that you live in today, what are some of the actions or behaviors that affirm God's principle of the hierarchy of authority?

Abusing Christian Liberty in Church: Misbehavior at the Lord's Supper

(1 Corinthians 11:18-34)

I n the previous section, we saw Paul deal with the misbehavior of some Corinthian women during their church services. He outlined the principle of God's hierarchy of authority, and then described the disgrace of failing to follow appropriate customs that uphold God's hierarchy of authority. In the transition verse between the last section and this one, Paul had said, "In giving this instruction I do not praise you, because you come together not for the better but for the worse" (1 Cor 11:17). The weekly gatherings of the church in Corinth had become times when the local body of Christ was not being built up, but they were in fact being torn down by their own disgraceful practices. In this section the apostle Paul will address another serious problem with their abuse of liberty and unloving behavior. Here he will focus on their celebration of the Lord's Supper.

Specific Problems in their Assemblies (11:18-22)

1 Cor 11:18 For, in the first place, when you come together as a church, I hear that divisions exist among you; and in part I believe it.

In the first place = It is interesting that Paul says, "In the first place" but if we look further down in these paragraphs we never see him say, "In the second place or third place." Evidently Paul is not giving an ordered list of things he wants to discuss. He is using the word first (**protos**) to mean primary. We know that Paul had already spoken about one of the misbehaviors during their church services, that of women going unveiled which was contrary to the cultural practice of that day for women of good character. But now Paul is going to discuss another issue that actually takes precedence or is more severe than the first issue. The issue he is about to address is of primary concern, and as we study his remarks we can understand why. The consequences are actually much more severe for this second issue than they were for the previous one.

When you come together as a church = Here Paul used two Greek words to ensure that we would understand he meant the regular meetings of the local church in Corinth. The word **sunerchomai** means to gather together, and the word **ekklesia** indicates their assembly. In other words, they are gathering together as an assembly of believers on the first day of the week for the purpose of public worship, prayer, and the teaching of the Word. This is the specific occasion that Paul has in mind.

I hear that divisions exist = His first general comment is that he keeps on hearing or is continually hearing (present continuous action) that divisions exist within their assembly. Divisions (**schismata**) are schisms, from **schizo** which means to split, tear, or rend (see Matt 9:16; Mark 2:21). This is the same word that Paul used in 1 Cor

1:10 where he exhorted them to have unity rather than divisions in their assembly. Here Paul is describing another dimension of the divisions within the church. These divisions became especially evident during their gathering together as a church for the Lord's Supper. One writer expressed it this way: "Instead of sharing together in fellowship and worship they spent their time in selfish indulgence, arguing, and disputing...The reasons for their division were carnality, selfishness, and worldliness (1 Cor 3:1). They were walking in the flesh rather than in the Spirit, and following their own wills rather than the Lord's." [MacArthur] The church was supposed to gather together to celebrate their fellowship (**koinonia**) and their unity in the one body of Christ. They were not celebrating their unity, but they were practicing disunity.

In part I believe it = Since Paul had heard this report from reliable people, he could not help but think there was something to it. "I have reason to think that, though the evil may have been exaggerated, yet it is true at least in part." [Barnes]

1 Cor 11:19 For there must also be factions among you, so that those who are approved may become evident among you.

There must also be factions among you = The word factions (**haireseis**) means "an act of choice." It came to mean a chosen way of life; of belonging to a sect or party, not always in a bad sense, but in the sense of schools that were common with the philosophers of that day. This is a different word than he used to describe their divisions, which were splits or tears that characterized the different groups in Corinth. When Paul said, "There must be factions among you" it is almost as if he would expect this kind of taking sides so occur in their situation. And in the next phrase, Paul gives the reason why he expected this.

So that those who are approved may become evident among you = Approved (**dokimos**) means to be proven by testing. Evident (**phaneros**) means to become apparent, manifest, and visible to all. God's purpose in these factions was to make the ones who have been tested and approved to become easily recognizable by everyone. The paradox is that without a dark backdrop, those objects that are light in color will not stand out as clearly. One might say, "The bad exists to make visible the good." It was necessary for there to be factions in order for the ones who were approved to be clearly evident, because the godliness of some would form a stark contrast to the worldliness of the others. "So in all divisions and all splitting into factions, such divisions show who are the restless, ambitious, and dissatisfied spirits; and those who are gentle and peaceful and disposed to pursue the way of truth, and love, and order, without contentions and strifes; see Rom 16:17, 'Mark them which cause divisions, and avoid them.'" [Barnes]

1 Cor 11:20 Therefore when you meet together, it is not to eat the Lord's Supper,

The Lord's Supper = Literally this could be translated, "the supper belonging to the Lord." The word supper (**deipnon**) was the main meal of the day, usually held in the evening. It is possible that this term was used to describe the Christian love feast, which was a sort of church supper that was held before the Lord's Supper or communion service. In following this practice, the church may have loosely patterned this supper after the Passover meal during which Jesus instituted this ordinance. However, it was probably more like the pagan feasts held in the temples of Corinth.

It will be very helpful for us to understand some of the historical background that may have influenced the church supper in the city of Corinth. History tells us that,

> The supper represented the principal meal of the day, like a late dinner. The Eucharist proper was originally celebrated as a private expression of devotion and in connection with a common daily meal, an agape or love-feast. In the apostolic period it was celebrated daily. The social and festive character of the meal grew largely out of the gentile institution of clubs or fraternities, which served as savings banks, mutual-aid societies, insurance offices, and which expressed and fostered the spirit of good fellowship by common festive meals, usually in gardens around an altar of sacrifice. The communion meal of the first and second centuries exhibited this character in being a feast of contribution, to which each brought his own provision. [VWS]

The apostle Paul was saying that when they gathered together as a church, they were claiming to celebrate the Lord's Supper, but really they were imitating the pagan supper clubs that were common in their city. One commentator put it this way: "Though you come together professedly to worship God and to partake of the Lord's Supper, yet this cannot be the real design which you have in view. Your greediness, your intemperance, your partaking of the food separately and not in common, cannot be a celebration of the Lord's Supper." [Barnes] They were making a mockery of the celebration of the solemn Lord's Supper service.

1 Cor 11:21 for in your eating each one takes his own supper first; and one is hungry and another is drunk.

In your eating each one takes his own supper first = Here is Paul's description of the wrong behavior of the Corinthian believers when they met for this group supper. When they arrived for the meal, each person would serve and eat without any consideration for others. The verb translated "take first" (**prolambano**) means to take before others. They had an attitude that we might call first come, first served! As one writer expressed, "It was a mere grab game." [RWP] They were showing no regard for whether there was enough food left for anyone else.

> There is allusion here to what was a custom among the Greeks, that when a festival was celebrated or a feast made, it was common for each person to provide and carry a part of the things necessary for the entertainment. These were usually placed in common, and were partaken of alike by all the company. Thus, Xenophon (Mem. lib. 3:cap. xiv.) says of Socrates that he was much offended with the Athenians for their conduct at their common suppers, where some prepared food for themselves in a sumptuous manner, while others were poorly provided for. Socrates endeavored to shame them out of this indecent custom by offering his own provisions to the en-

tire company. [Barnes]

One is hungry and another is drunk = This was the result of their selfish and unloving behavior. Hungry means "deprived of food" because nothing is left for him at the feast table. The people that came early had plenty to eat and drink, but there was very little left for anyone who came later. Drunken means to become inebriated or intoxicated. At the very least, the drunken man had more than was good for him, while everyone else had less than they needed. This type of disgusting conduct was considered shameful even in the pagan club suppers. These Christians were indulging their own sensual appetites in eating and drinking, and they made this kind of behavior their goal, rather than solemnly celebrating the Lord's Supper itself. Barnes provided an explanation of the pagan background which may have been influencing their behavior:

> There can be no doubt that the apostle meant to say that they ate and drank to excess, and that their professed celebration of the Lord's Supper became a mere revel. It may seem remarkable that such scenes should ever have occurred in a Christian church, or that there could have been such an entire perversion of the nature and design of the Lord's Supper. But we are to remember the following things: These persons had recently been pagans, and were grossly ignorant of the nature of true religion when the gospel was first preached among them. They had been accustomed to such revels in honor of idols under their former modes of worship, and it is the less surprising that they transferred their views to Christianity. When they had once so far misunderstood the nature of Christianity as to suppose the Lord's Supper to be like the feasts which they had formerly celebrated, all the rest followed as a matter of course. The festival would be observed in the same manner as the festivals in honor of idolaters; and similar scenes of gluttony and intemperance would naturally follow. [Barnes]

1 Cor 11:22 What! Do you not have houses in which to eat and drink? Or do you despise the church of God and shame those who have nothing? What shall I say to you? Shall I praise you? In this I will not praise you.

Do you not have houses in which to eat and drink? = If they wanted to have a social banquet, they should do it at home rather than during the public gathering of the church for worshiping the Lord. In this verse the word "drink" is the normal Greek term meaning to take liquid refreshment. But in his previous description of their feasts, Paul had specifically used the term which means intoxicated or drunk. It is fine to take liquid refreshment, but we should not drink to excess even in our own homes. In this statement Paul is saying, "Do you not know that the church of God was not designed to be a place of feasting and revelry. It was grossly improper to make the place of public worship a place for a festival entertainment." [Barnes]

Do you despise the church of God? (kataphroneo) = Literally this means to think down upon; to think little of something; not having the proper respect for something. The kind of partying that the Corinthians were doing was destructive and degrading as part of the regular gathering of the church. "Their conduct was such as if they had held in contempt the whole church of God, by their perverted view of the sacredness and purity of the Lord's supper." [Barnes] Another scholar wrote: "They mocked the very purpose of the occasion, which was to bring harmony and unity among those who belonged to Christ, as they remembered His sacrifice to make them one in Him." [MacArthur] Paul had already described the kind of fellowship (koinonia) and unity that should result from celebrating the Lord's Supper (1 Cor 10:16-17).

And shame those who have nothing? (kataischuno) = Literally this means to shame down; to cause to blush or be embarrassed with dishonor. The ones who have nothing are the "have-nots." They are the ones who are left with nothing to eat at the church gatherings.

What shall I say to you? = This expresses Paul's bewilderment, surprise, and shock. He is almost at a loss for words in expressing his emotions.

Shall I praise you? In this I will not praise you = Here again Paul used the word for praising or commending someone, but again it is in the negative. They did not deserve praise but rebuke. Based on their behavior when they met together, you could certainly not call this a shared supper (koineon deipnon), let alone a Lord's supper (kuriakos deipnon). It was this kind of conduct that eventually led to the complete separation between the love feast and the Lord's Supper in the later church.

The True Meaning of the Lord's Supper (11:23-26)

If the Corinthians were not celebrating the Lord's Supper (1 Cor 11:20) but having a self-indulgent party instead, then they obviously needed to be reminded of the true meaning of that solemn ordinance called the Lord's Supper, the Communion Service, or the Eucharist. That is what the apostle Paul will now do in this next section of chapter eleven. Regarding how the Corinthian Christians were treating the celebration of the Lord's Supper, one man wrote,

> They had mistaken its nature. They supposed it to be a common festival. They had made it the occasion of great disorder. He therefore declares the solemn circumstances in which it was instituted; the particular object which it had in view—the commemoration of the death of the Redeemer—and the purpose which it was designed to serve, which was not that of a festival, but to keep before the church and the world a constant remembrance of the Lord Jesus until he should again return. [Barnes]

Another commentator eloquently expressed it this way: "These verses are like a diamond dropped in a muddy road. One of the most beautiful passages in all of Scripture given in the middle of a strong rebuke of worldly, carnal, selfish, and insensitive attitudes and behavior." [MacArthur]

1 Cor 11:23 For I received from the Lord that which I also delivered to you, that the Lord Jesus in the night in which He was betrayed took bread;

I received from the Lord = The pronoun "I" **(ego)** is placed forward in this phrase for emphasis: "I myself received from the Lord." This is Paul's claim to direct revelation from the Lord Jesus concerning the institution of the Lord's Supper service. The Lord's Supper was not something that Paul created himself, or that some of the apostles developed on their own. This service was something instituted by Christ Himself and delivered to Paul personally through direct revelation. This fact alone should be enough to emphasize the great seriousness and solemnity of the Lord's Supper. It is interesting that Luke's account of the institution of the Lord's Supper (Luke 22:17-20) is almost identical with this one given by Paul. Since Luke was the traveling companion of the apostle Paul, he may have discussed this with Paul, heard Paul teach on this topic, and probably read the letter of First Corinthians before he wrote the Gospel of Luke.

I also delivered to you (paradidomi) = This is the same term that Paul used in 1 Cor 11:2. Paul had founded the church in Corinth and had already taught them about the ordinance of the Lord's Supper. The verb is in the aorist tense, indicating a definite point in time when Paul had taught this doctrine to the Corinthian church.

He was betrayed = The imperfect tense is used here, which means He was being betrayed. In other words, Jesus instituted the Lord's Supper while His betrayal was going on.

> This most beautiful and meaningful of Christian celebrations was instituted on the very night the Lord was betrayed and arrested. In the midst of the world's evil, God establishes His good; in the midst of Satan's wickedness, God plants His holiness. Just as, by contrast, the fleshly factions cause the Lord's approved saints to become evident (1 Cor 11:19), so Jesus' betrayal and arrest cause His gracious sacrifice to become more evident. In the midst of Satan's absolute worst, the condemnation of the Son of God on the cross, God accomplished His absolute best, the sacrifice for the redemption of the world through that cross. [MacArthur]

The apostle Paul described Christ's betrayal as the backdrop for the Lord's Supper in order to show the great seriousness and solemnity of the ceremony. In order to celebrate the Lord's Supper in a proper manner, we must remember the circumstances in which Christ instituted it. One of the circumstances that is most moving is that Christ was betrayed by a friend and follower, and yet in the midst of that evil He went through with His plan to save the world.

1 Cor 11:24 and when He had given thanks, He broke it and said, "This is My body, which is for you; do this in remembrance of Me."

When He had given thanks = This is the Greek word **eucharisteo** from which our word Eucharist is derived. "Eucharist was the technical term for the Lord's Supper as a sacrifice of thanksgiving for all the gifts of God, especially for the greatest gift, which is Jesus Christ." [VWS]

He broke it = We tend to associate the breaking of the bread with the damage it causes to the loaf, and this does indeed represent the damage done to the physical body of Jesus during His crucifixion. But the idea behind the breaking of the bread also involved distributing the pieces equally among all those at the table. This is in direct contrast to the practice of the Corinthian believers, which was every man for himself!

> Christ himself took the bread and broke it, denoting his willingness to lay down his life, to suffer and die in place of his people; and this action of breaking the bread was used in order to be distributed, so that everyone might partake, as all the Israelites did at the Passover, and not as these Corinthians did at their suppers when one was full and another hungry. [Gill]

This is My body, which is for you = The bread was intended by the Lord as a symbol of His own physical body which was broken and damaged, ultimately to the point of death on the cross. "This phrase is to be understood in a figurative sense, that it was a sign of his body, and it being broken into pieces represented his wounds, bruises, sufferings, and death." [Gill] Not one bone of Christ was broken (see Ps 34:20), but His skin and flesh were broken open and wounded with fists, rods, whips, thorns, nails, and a spear.

Do this in remembrance of Me = The preposition "in" means with a view to, which points to the purpose for doing this. The purpose for celebrating this ceremony is to remember the suffering of Christ on our behalf. The word remember (**anamnesis**) means to recall to the mind. It is important for all believers to call to mind what Christ suffered on our behalf. We can each say, "He endured that agony for me! He took the punishment that I deserve!" There are some church groups that believe the service of the Lord's Supper is a reenactment of the actual sacrifice of Christ, so Christ is really re-sacrificed every Sunday, over and over again. It is as if the death of Christ once on the cross was not sufficient to pay for the sins of the world. But this is not so. One writer expressed it this way: "When we partake of the Lord's Supper we do not offer a sacrifice again. We remember His once-for-all sacrifice for us and rededicate ourselves to His obedient service." [MacArthur]

1 Cor 11:25 In the same way He took the cup also after supper, saying, "This cup is the new covenant in My blood; do this, as often as you drink it, in remembrance of Me."

This cup is the new covenant in My blood = The cup stands figuratively for the red liquid which it holds, and this liquid in turn is a symbol for the blood of Christ which was poured out in death for all of mankind. Since this is a symbol within a symbol, it is clear that Christ intended this to be taken figuratively as a representation of His death on the cross for sin.

The new covenant (diatheke) = This term means a disposition or arrangement which a person wishes to be legally valid. Often it represented the last will and testament which a person makes for the distribution of his earthly possessions after his death. Typically this was the meaning of the Greek word **diatheke**. However, in the Greek translation of the Old Testament, the word **diatheke** was used more than three hundred times to translate the Hebrew word **berith** (God's covenant with men). The Greek Old Testament would be used across the world by Gentiles as well as by Jews, and the Gentiles were typically unwilling to think that the eternal and infinite God could enter into a covenant or agreement with mere creatures. Therefore, the translators of the Greek Old Testament chose a word that represented God expressing his will to them in His revelation. This was the term that Paul used here to describe the new agreement or covenant that was in direct contrast to the old covenant made through Moses in the Old Testament Law.

What is the New Covenant?

The New Covenant was first mentioned in the Bible when the prophet Jeremiah predicted the future coming of the New Covenant (Jer 31:31). "Behold, days are coming, declares the LORD, when I will make a new covenant with the house of Israel and with the house of Judah." Here we see that the New Covenant is something God desires to establish with the nation of Israel as a whole, and it will not be established until some time in the future. Jeremiah directly contrasted the New Covenant with the Mosaic covenant, "Which I made with their fathers in the day I took them by the hand to bring them out of the land of Egypt" (Jer 31:32).

One of the unique aspects of the New Covenant is that God will give all of His people a renewed heart and mind, and He will provide forgiveness for all of their sins (Jer 31:33-34). This is a perfect description of what the New Testament calls regeneration which occurs at the time of salvation, and it includes the special ministry of the indwelling Holy Spirit (a ministry which was not available in the Old Testament). We know from the New Testament that many individual Jews did become believers and experienced some of these promised blessings, but that the nation of Israel as a whole has certainly not entered into the New Covenant as it is described in the book of Jeremiah. However, something obviously took place that allowed some of these blessings to be experienced by the Jews who have put their trust in Christ for their salvation. Christ accomplished something important for His people Israel, even though the nation as a whole is not currently participating in it now. Even though the New Covenant is still awaiting enactment with the nation of Israel at Christ's Second Coming (see Rom 11:26-27), Christ certainly set the stage by ratifying the New Covenant through His blood sacrifice on the cross.

What is the relationship of the New Testament Church to the New Covenant promised to Israel?

We also know from the New Testament that many Gentiles experienced the blessings of salvation, but they certainly cannot be said to be fulfilling the New Covenant as it is described in the book of Jeremiah. The New Covenant can be fulfilled only with the intended recipients, which are the people of Israel. When Christ returns in the future to the nation of Israel, He will not need to handle the forgiveness of sin at that time. Because Christ went to the cross and shed His blood for the remission of sin, He has already provided the blood sacrifice that was required to ratify the New Covenant. The testimony of His blood is the guarantee of the New Covenant which will be fulfilled in the future for Israel (Heb 7:22). Christ's ratification of the New Covenant through His blood is the promise that in the future He will enact the New Covenant with Israel at His Second Coming.

The relationship of the New Covenant to the bread and the cup of the Lord's Supper was explained by one commentator this way: "Present day believers have received the temporary tokens of the future enactment of the New Covenant, the bread and the cup. These tokens recall the sacrifice that ratified the covenant until God enacts the covenant itself at the Lord's return." [SRL] In other words, we remember the ratification of the New Covenant that Christ accomplished at His First Coming, until He comes to officially enact the New Covenant with Israel at His Second Coming.

Do this, as often as you drink it, in remembrance of Me = In the original language, "As often as" is the normal way of expressing an activity that is regularly repeated over time. It is intended to be a recurring time of memorial for Christ's work on our behalf.

> Not prescribing any time; and not even specifying the frequency with which it was to be done; but leaving it to themselves to determine how often they would partake of it. The time of the Passover had been fixed by positive statute; the more mild and gentle system of Christianity left it to the followers of the Redeemer themselves to determine how often they would celebrate his death. [Barnes]

In the same way that the broken bread is a symbol for the sufferings of Christ for our redemption, the red liquid in the cup is a symbol of Christ's blood that was shed to pay for our sins.

1 Cor 11:26 For as often as you eat this bread and drink the cup, you proclaim the Lord's death until He comes.

As often as you eat this bread and drink the cup = Notice that not just any bread or cup is being referred to here; it is this bread and this cup. It is no ordinary meal, but it is the bread and cup that are taken in the correct way in celebration of the ordinance instituted by Christ according to His instructions.

There are some church groups which believe that when the bread and wine are blessed, they are actually transformed into the flesh and blood of Jesus. But we can see here in the words which established this ceremony that even after they had been blessed and distributed among the participants, they were still identified as simply bread and wine. One commentator described it this way:

> Here it is expressly called bread, only bread, after the consecration. Before the Savior instituted the ordinance he took bread. It was bread then; it was bread which he blessed and broke, it was bread when it was given to them, and it was bread when Paul says here that they ate. How then can it be pretended that it is anything else

but bread? [Barnes]

You proclaim the Lord's death = The word proclaim (**kataggello**) means to declare, announce, or proclaim publicly. This was intended as a public service which graphically demonstrated all that Jesus Christ accomplished for us. In fact, this was a regular practice of the church throughout the centuries. Even people who were not members of the body of Christ came to understand that this was the message behind this ceremony. One writer said,

> It is a simple memorial or occasion of remembrance, designed to recall in a striking and impressive manner the memory of the Redeemer. The ordinance is rightly observed when it recalls the memory of the Saviour; and when its observance is the means of producing a deep, and lively, and vivid impression on the mind, of his death for sin. [Barnes]

Until He comes = This tells us in no uncertain terms that the Lord Jesus Christ will come again. One writer emphasized that, "The Greek expresses the certainly of His coming." [JFB] This tells us not only that Jesus will return in a glorious Second Coming, but also that the celebration of this church ordinance has a definite ending point. The Lord's Supper is intended as a ceremony for believers to communicate an important message during the church age. Its purpose is to keep alive the memory of Christ's ratification of the New Covenant until the day when He personally arrives to officially enact that covenant with all Israel. When He arrives there will be no need for symbols to represent His body, because He Himself will be present. But our regular participation in this ceremony helps everyone to keep looking forward to that day when He will come again. It is a celebration of what He accomplished for us in the past, while at the same time looking forward to His future return in all His glory.

The Seriousness of Observing The Lord's Supper (11:27-29)

1 Cor 11:27 Therefore whoever eats the bread or drinks the cup of the Lord in an unworthy manner, shall be guilty of the body and the blood of the Lord.

In an unworthy manner = Therefore, as a result of all Paul had just said about the beauty and truth of the Lord's Supper, and in view of all he had said about how the Corinthians' worldliness and selfishness made a mockery of this solemn event, Paul now emphasized the seriousness of celebrating the Lord's Supper in a correct and worthy manner. The word unworthily is an adverb, so it describes the way in which the Corinthians were eating and drinking. In 1 Cor 11:18-22 Paul had already given some specific details of the unworthy manner in which they were taking the Lord's Supper. This is what Paul will also refer to later in 1 Cor 11:29 as "not discerning the Lord's body." One writer gave several specific examples of ways in which people can participate in the Lord's Supper in an unworthy manner:

One can come to His table unworthily in many ways. It is common for people to participate in it ritualistically, without participating with their minds and hearts. They can go through the motions without going through any emotions, and treat it lightly rather than seriously. They can believe it imparts grace or merit, that the ceremony itself, rather than the sacrifice it represents, can save or keep one saved. Many come with a spirit of bitterness or hatred toward another believer, or come with a sin of which they will not repent. [MacArthur]

Shall be guilty of the body and the blood of the Lord = The word "guilty" (**enochos**) means being subject to or liable to something, especially liable to a penalty or a punishment. By approaching the Lord's Supper in the way the Corinthians were doing, they actually incurred punishment from the Lord for failing to give due consideration to this serious occasion. One commentator expressed it this way:

If the Lord's supper be in its very nature a proclamation of the death of Christ, it follows that those who attend upon it as an ordinary meal or in an irreverent manner, or for any other purpose than that for which it was appointed, are guilty of the body and blood of the Lord...To eat or drink unworthily is in general to come to the Lord's table in a careless, irreverent spirit without the intention or desire to commemorate the death of Christ as the sacrifice for our sins...The way in which the Corinthians ate unworthily was that they treated the Lord's table as though it were their own, making no distinction between the Lord's supper and an ordinary meal. [Hodge]

1 Cor 11:28 But a man must examine himself, and in so doing he is to eat of the bread and drink of the cup.

But a man must examine himself = The word examine (**dokimazo**) is related to the word "approved" in 1 Cor 11:19, which means tested and approved. We should hold our actions and attitudes up to the standard of the true meaning of the Lord's Supper which Paul had just presented. We should be certain that we are participating in this ceremony with the right attitude and the right intention, which is to communicate the memory of all Christ accomplished for us on the cross.

And in so doing he is to eat of the bread and drink of the cup = It is only after serious self-examination that a person should participate in the elements of the bread and the cup. One of the earlier commentators listed several reasons why this kind of self-examination should be done before participating in the Lord's Supper:

1. It is well to pause occasionally in life, and take an account of our standing in the sight of God.
2. Because the observance of the Lord's Supper is a solemn act, and there will be fearful results if it is celebrated in an improper manner.
3. Because self-examination imposes seriousness and calmness, and prevents naivete and unconcern, states of mind entirely unfavorable to a proper observance of the Lord's Supper.

4. Because by self-examination one may search out and remove those things that are offensive to God, and the sins which so easily beset us may be brought to mind and forsaken.

5. Because the approach to the table of the Lord is a solemn approach to the Lord himself, a solemn profession of attachment to him, an act of consecration to his service in the presence of angels and of people—and this should be done in a calm, deliberate and sincere manner. Such a manner may be the result of a prayerful and honest self-examination. [Barnes]

1 Cor 11:29 For he who eats and drinks, eats and drinks judgment to himself if he does not judge the body rightly.

Eats and drinks judgment to himself = It is very important that we understand in what sense the word judgment (**krino**) is being used in this verse. First of all, this word does not have a definite article so it is not THE judgment, as in the final and ultimate judgment, but simply a judgment of some kind. In the very next section of this chapter, the apostle Paul will give several examples of the types of judgments he had in mind. One writer put it this way: "**krino** is a temporary judgment, and so is distinguished from **katakrino**, condemnation." [VWS] The judgment Paul is talking about here is equivalent to the consequences of being guilty of the body and the blood of the Lord (1 Cor 11:27), which we saw meant "subject to penalty." This is the way the term judgment is being used in this verse.

If he does not judge the body rightly (diakrino) = This term is a compound form of the word for judgment, and it means "to separate, to discriminate between one thing and another." Here it is being used to describe something like the process of self-examination that Paul discussed in the previous verse (1 Cor 11:28). One scholar expressed it this way: "This passage may therefore mean, not discriminating the Lord's body, that is, making no difference between the bread in the sacrament and ordinary food." [Hodge] Another person said, "One discerns the Lord's body in the sacrament, and therein discriminates the ceremony from all other eating and drinking, precisely what the Corinthians failed to do." [Expositors]

Before we continue with this section of the chapter, it might be helpful to look at the various words Paul used that are related to the term "judgment" (**krino**). Many English translations seem to render these words in confusing ways. Regarding the King James Version one man wrote: "The whole passage in the KJV is marked by a confusion of the renderings of **krino** (to judge) and its compounds." [VWS] Another Greek scholar went so far as to say that, "The alliterative play on **krino** and its compounds is untranslatable" [Expositors]

The diagram at the top of the next page shows how all of these words concerning judgment form a sequence, from left to right, with the nouns serving as bookends for all of the verbs that follow, which have subtle variations in meaning. The chart below the diagram explains the differences in the intended meanings of this sequence of words.

verse 29 | verse 31 | verse 32 | verse 34

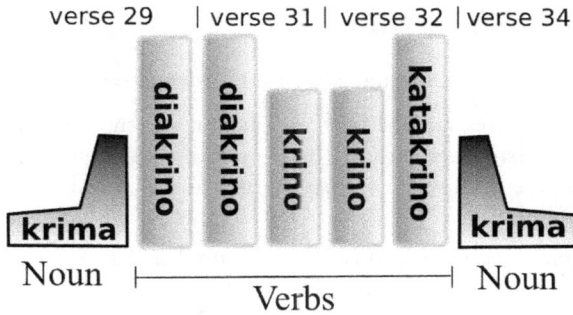

Noun — Verbs — Noun

Verse	Word	Part of Speech	Meaning
29	*krima*	noun	A judgment, decision, or opinion fourmed after considering the facts; a choice made from among the alternatives.
29	*diakrino*	verb	To judge between; to make a distinction; to see or accurately discern a difference between things.
31	*diakrino*	verb	(same word in verse 29)
31	*krino*	verb	To be judged; to undergo examination, scruitiny, or testing regarding what is right and proper, often with the idea of being found worthy of discipline, correction, or punishment.
32	*krino*	verb	(same word in verse 31)
32	katakrino	verb	To reach a final verdict against someone; to sentence someone in condemnation (especially to ultimate condemnation).
34	*krima*	noun	(same word in verse 29)

One writer commented that: "The great difference in Paul's use here of **krino** (judgment) and **katakrino** (condemned) is seen in verse 32, where it is clear that **krino** refers to discipline of the saved and **katakrino** refers to condemnation of the lost." [MacArthur]

Physical Consequences of Improperly Taking The Lord's Supper (11:30-32)

1 Cor 11:30 For this reason many among you are weak and sick, and a number sleep.

For this reason = Because they were not judging rightly, the punishments described in this verse have been inflicted upon them. These judgments represent the Lord's discipline because of the Corinthians' sinful attitudes and actions during the Lord's Supper services.

Many among you are weak and sick, and a number sleep = Many (hikanos) means a sufficient number. Weak (**asthenes**) means feeble or without strength, and sick (**arrhostos**) means suffering from continued ill health. Sleep (**koimao**) is used in a figurative sense for death (see 1 Thess 4:13-15). "God actually put to death a number of believers in Corinth because they continually despised and corrupted the Supper of His Son, just as He had put to death Ananias and Sapphira for lying to the Holy Spirit (Acts 5:1-11)." [MacArthur] These were some of the more extreme punishments that the Corinthians experienced as a result of their wrong attitudes and actions during the celebration of the Lord's Supper, but we should be careful not to form a general principle from this particular case. It seems obvious that the apostle Paul must have had some specific revelation from the Lord about the Corinthian situation. God had told him that some cases of physical affliction were directly related to the sinful behavior among believers in that local church.

1 Cor 11:31 But if we judged ourselves rightly, we would not be judged.

This verse seems to be the inverse statement of 1 Cor 11:29 where in essence Paul said, "If he does not judge rightly, he eats and drinks judgment to himself." Here in this verse Paul says, "If he does judge rightly, he will not be judged."

If we judged ourselves rightly (diakrino) = This means "to carefully discern through examination" as it did in verse twenty-nine.

We would not be judged (krino) = This is the passive form of the verb which is related to the term judgment (**krima**) from verse twenty-nine. The same parallel set of terms for judging and judgment are used in the same way between these two verses. The only difference is in the object of the discernment. One man expressed it this way: "In order to duly judge or discern the Lord's body, we need to duly judge ourselves." [JFB] The problem the Corinthians were having was not with the ceremony, but the problem was with themselves and their wrong attitudes and selfish desires. Another writer explained Paul's meaning this way: "If we would exercise a strict scrutiny over our hearts and feelings and conduct, and come to the Lord's Table with a proper spirit, we should escape the condemnation to which they are exposed who observe it in an improper manner." [Barnes]

1 Cor 11:32 But when we are judged, we are disciplined by the Lord so that we will not be condemned along with the world.

But when we are judged (krino) = This is the term **krino**, just as was used in verse 31 above, and this phrase confirms for us what Paul meant when he used the word **krino** (judging) in the previous verse. This kind of judging is equivalent to the Lord disciplining a believer.

We are disciplined by the Lord (paideuo) = This term literally means "to treat as a child" and its meaning was broadened to "instruction or education, especially through chastisement or disciplinary action." This is the same term that is used in that wonderful passage about the Lord's discipline of believers in Hebrews 12:5-11. "As has already been mentioned, if we come unworthily and are judged by God, it is not for condemnation. It is for the very opposite...Even if the Lord were to strike us dead for profaning His table, it would be to discipline us." [MacArthur]

So that we will not be condemned along with the world (katakrino) = Here Paul used another of the related words for judgment, this time indicating the condemnation of the unsaved. It is somewhat puzzling why Paul included this phrase at the end of this verse, because it might sound like Paul is saying, "Believers need the Lord's discipline so that they will not be condemned as unbelievers." However, we know from other Scripture passages, "There is now no condemnation for those who are in Christ Jesus" (Rom 8:1). So what is Paul saying here?

It seems best to understand that Paul is bringing in another stark contrast in order to drive home his point about the Corinthian believers' wrong attitude toward the Lord's Supper. In verses 31 and 32 Paul used all three of the related terms for judging: **diakrino** (discernment), **krino** (discipline), and **katakrino** (condemnation).

1. Paul picked up the meaning of **diakrino** from verse 29 where he had said they were to discern the Lord's body in the Lord's Supper, and therefore they were to discriminate between this ceremony and everyday feasting.
2. Then he used the term **krino** to indicate the discipline or chastisement of the Lord on those who are His children, but who are misbehaving.
3. Finally, at the end of verse 32 Paul graphically drew attention to the importance of exercising this kind of **diakrino** (discernment) by contrasting it with the term **katakrino**, the final separation of the unrighteous from the righteous.

One commentator explained it this way. "Bringing in 'the world' explains the meaning of **diakrino** here: it expresses a discriminating judgment, by which the Christian rightly appreciates his own status and calling, and realizes his distinctive character, even as the **diakrino** of verse 29 realizes the difference between the Lord's supper (**kuriakon deipnon**) and a common supper (**koineon deipnon**)." [Expositors] In other words, just as a Christian should be able to discern his own unique relationship to God through Jesus Christ as contrasted with the unsaved of the world, in the same way a Christian should also be able to discern the important meaning in the Lord's Supper and distinguish it from sinful indulgence in feasting.

Paul's Instructions for Properly Observing the Lord's Supper (11:33-34)

Paul had explained to them the seriousness and importance of the Lord's Supper celebration, and he had shown them the grave consequences of failing to observe this church ordinance in the proper manner. Finally, Paul will provide some specific instruction for properly celebrating the Lord's Supper. One writer expressed it this way:

> The two great evils connected with the observance of the Lord's Supper at Corinth were, first, that it was not a communion—one took supper before another (1 Cor 11:21); and secondly, that they came to the Lord's table to satisfy their hunger—that is, they made it an ordinary meal. They thus sinned against their brethren (1 Cor 11:22), and they sinned against Christ (1 Cor 11:27). In the conclusion, therefore, of the whole discussion, he exhorts them to correct these evils. [Hodge]

1 Cor 11:33 So then, my brethren, when you come together to eat, wait for one another.

So then, my brethren = Here Paul gives his concluding instructions to them, and he calls them his brethren. Even though he has given them a strong rebuke in this section, he still recognizes and addresses them as his brothers and sisters in Christ. This helps to soften the blow of his rebuke, and it also prepares them to continue listening to the rest of his instructions in the following chapters of the letter.

When you come together to eat, wait for one another = Here is Paul's first instruction: They are to wait for each other. Paul had already told them that if they are hungry they should satisfy their appetite in their own homes (1 Cor 11:22), so here he probably means that when they come together as a church to celebrate the Lord's Supper ceremony they are to wait for each other before beginning.

1 Cor 11:34 If anyone is hungry, let him eat at home, so that you will not come together for judgment. The remaining matters I will arrange when I come.

If anyone is hungry, let him eat at home (peinao) = This is Paul's second instruction: they are to satisfy their appetite at home rather than at church. The term hungry is the same word that Paul had used in 1 Cor 11:21, so here it means that the Corinthians are not to make the church gathering into a time when they focus on satisfying their desire for food and drink. They should take care of those needs in their own homes, rather than expecting to satisfy them at church.

So that you will not come together for judgment (krima) = Here Paul is saying that if the Corinthians will follow these simple instructions, then they can avoid the discipline of the Lord for their wrong actions and attitudes toward the Lord's Supper. This term for judgment (krima) is the same term that Paul used when he began in 1 Cor 11:29. It is placed here like a bookend that brackets this part of the discussion.

The remaining matters I will arrange when I come = Evidently there were several other issues with their practice of celebrating the Lord's Supper, but either they were minor matters that Paul would discuss later, or they were large enough issues that Paul did not think it was proper to discuss them in this letter. The former option is probably the most likely, since Paul has already discussed some very urgent and major issues in this letter so far. According to this verse, Paul was planning to return to them in the future. According to Second Corinthians, Paul did make a brief "painful visit" to Corinth before he wrote that letter (2 Cor 2:1; 12:14; 13:1-3).

We need to be on the alert for fleshly carnal attitudes and behaviors that lead to divisions and selfishness. Rather than serving ourselves, we should focus on serving others and looking out for the interests of others in the church. We also need to make sure we do not allow our gatherings as a local church to become places that look more like the world than like a church where God is worshiped and His Word is honored. If we do stray from Christ and experience the discipline of the Lord, we need to remember that He loves us and that His discipline is given because we do belong to Him. Let us commit to keeping alive the memory of the Lord's death for sin until that wonderful day when He returns again!

The True Source and Purpose of Spiritual Gifts

(1 Corinthians 12:1-11)

In the last chapter of our study, the apostle Paul dealt with problems occurring during the meetings of the local church in Corinth, and in this chapter he begins to address another issue which was causing disruption in the Corinthian church services. This important issue had to do with their use of spiritual gifts, and it will take the apostle Paul three chapters to discuss this problem (1 Cor 12:1-14:40). Evidently, this was one of the issues that was causing the divisions and schisms within the Corinthian church, with some of the very dynamic and charismatic individuals being given greater honor and position within the different factions. There were also some obvious cases of abusing spiritual gifts, and possibly even some counterfeit spiritual gifts that were throwing the church into confusion. "This chapter, therefore, is occupied in stating and illustrating that all spiritual gifts are conferred by the Holy Spirit, and that no one should so value himself on his gift as to despise those who had not been thus endowed; and that no one who had not thus been favored should be dejected or regard himself as dishonored." [Barnes]

Introducing a New Area of Abuses Within the Church (12:1)

1 Cor 12:1 Now concerning spiritual gifts, brethren, I do not want you to be unaware.

One of the tendencies that Christians have in reading 1 Cor 12 is to jump directly to the "good stuff" which discusses the specific spiritual gifts. But as we begin studying this chapter, we must force ourselves not to miss the first three verses upon which Paul builds the rest of this section concerning spiritual gifts. If we skip over the first three verses in order to get into the exciting sections which follow, we will miss many of the truths that he is trying to communicate. 1 Cor 12:1-3 are the foundation on which Paul builds everything that follows. We must restrain our impulse to skim lightly over these first few verses, but instead we should carefully examine Paul's first words here that set the stage for what follows.

Now concerning = This is the same opening phrase that we have seen previously in this letter (1 Cor 7:1, 7:25, 8:1), and it indicates that Paul is giving a response to one of the questions the Corinthians had asked in their original letter to him. Unfortunately, we do not have a copy of their questions, so we must read between the lines to understand what their concern was in this case. "The Corinthian request was probably similar to this: 'We have many richly gifted people in our church, and they all desire to participate in every service. This is particularly true of those possessing the spiritual gift of tongues. Because of this, great confusion reigns whenever we get together. What advice can you give to resolve this problem?'" [Thomas]

In the last section of chapter eleven, we know that the church services in Corinth were characterized by divisions and factions even when celebrating the Lord's Supper. So now Paul is going to deal with one of the key factors that was contributing to those divisions and factions, which involved their abuse of spiritual gifts. We know for certain that they asked Paul for more information regarding how the spiritual gifts or manifestations were being practiced in the local church at Corinth. Because of Paul's lengthy response, we can also assume that the misuse of spiritual gifts was causing quite a bit of trouble and confusion within the Corinthian church.

Spiritual gifts (pneumatikos) = This literally means, belonging to the Spirit. It is very much like the term **kuriakos** from our last section, which was used there to identify the Lord's Supper, or the supper belonging to the Lord. The word gifts is not in the original text, but the entire context shows very clearly that the gifts and enablings of the Holy Spirit are identified as the topic throughout this discussion. "The whole discussion shows that he refers to the various endowments, gifts, or graces that had been bestowed in different degrees on the members of the church, including the distinctions in graces, and in degrees of office and rank, which had been made in the Corinthian church." [Barnes]

I do not want you to be unaware = Again, Paul calls the Corinthians his brothers in Christ, and he tells them he does not want them to remain ignorant of the truths that he is about to explain in the next three chapters of this letter. He wants the Corinthians to gain some specific knowledge and that they come to know certain truths. Literally, he does not want them to not know. By implication the apostle Paul is reassuring them that it is possible to know the truth regarding the spiritual manifestations that were confusing them.

A Reminder of Their Former Pagan Practices (12:2)

1 Cor 12:2 You know that when you were pagans, you were led astray to the mute idols, however you were led.

When you were pagans (ethnos) = This word is a general term for the nations of the world, and it is often used for the Gentiles, in contrast to the Jews. This tells us that the majority of believers in the Corinthian church came out of a Gentile or pagan background, and they would tend to associate any unusual or spectacular manifestations of spiritual gifts in their church with some of their experiences in the pagan temple services.

You were led astray to the mute idols = In 1 Cor 10:19-21 Paul had explained in even more detail that the idols themselves were simply inanimate blocks of wood or stone, but that the power behind them was demonic. As Paul begins the discussion here, we need to remember all that he previously said concerning a Christian's involvement with idolatry and the pagan worship services.

Led astray (apagesthai) = Literally this means carried away. "Led astray" implies being misled or deceived, and this may have been part of the problem in Corinth. One writer stated it this way: "The word which is used conveys the idea of being carried into bondage or being led to punishment, and refers here doubtless to the strong means which had been used by crafty priests in their former state to delude and deceive them. They were under strong delusions and the arts of cunning and unprincipled people." [Barnes]

The phrase "carried away" seems to more accurately describe what those former pagans would have experienced in their religious ceremonies. One scholar said: "It suggests moments of ecstasy experienced in heathen religion when a human being is (or is believed to be) possessed by a supernatural being." [Barrett] Another commentator wrote: "Formerly, they were swayed by a blind, unintelligent impulse which carried them away, and they knew not where. They were controlled by an influence which they could not understand or resist." [Hodge] When Paul called them "mute idols" it was possible that he was contrasting the silent, inanimate statues with the typical noisy yelling and shouting of the pagan worshipers under the influence of demons.

However you were led = Literally this could be translated, "As from time to time you might be led." The imperfect tense gives the idea of having different leadings on different occasions. One commentator put it this way: "The heathen oracles led their votaries at random, without any definite principle." [JFB] There was a great deal of inconsistency and confusion in the pagan temple services, because it was almost as if the people were being led around at random without a discernible pattern or purpose. The important connection we need to understand is that even after these former pagan worshipers became Christians, they still had a tendency to confuse demonic manifestations with those of the Holy Spirit. Here is what we learn from the history of that time period in Corinth:

> Several pagan practices were especially influential in the church at Corinth. Perhaps the most important, and certainly the most obvious, was that of ecstasy, considered to the the highest expression of religious experience. Because it seemed supernatural and because it was dramatic and often bizarre, the practice strongly appealed to the natural man...Ecstasy was held to be a supernatural, sensuous communion with a deity. Through frenzied hypnotic chants and ceremonies worshipers experienced semiconscious euphoric feelings of oneness with the god or goddess. Often the ceremony would be preceded by vigils and fasting, and would even include drunkenness. Contemplation of sacred objects, whirling dances, fragrant incense, chants, and other such physical and psychological stimuli customarily were used to induce ecstasy. [MacArthur]

Another writer said: "The Corinthian Christians had known what it was to be moved by forces outside themselves—demonic forces. Very clear distinctions existed between these forces and powers operative in the gifts. To think that satanic emissaries are incapable of producing counterfeits for any proper function of the Holy

Spirit is a mistake. Great precautions are necessary to keep from confusing these misrepresentations with genuine divine operations." [Thomas]

Distinguishing Between Pagan Manifestations and Spiritual Gifts (12:3)

1 Cor 12:3 Therefore I make known to you that no one speaking by the Spirit of God says, "Jesus is accursed"; and no one can say, "Jesus is Lord," except by the Holy Spirit.

Therefore I make known to you = Therefore, in light of the Corinthians' ignorance about this subject (verse one), and in light of what Paul had just said regarding their former practices as pagan idol worshipers (verse two), he now provides the first bit of knowledge that he wants them to have. He presents a test that can be used to distinguish between demonic activity and the activity of the Holy Spirit, since it seems that there were counterfeit or false gifts which were being manifested in that local church.

One commentator put it this way: "The presence of counterfeit spiritual gifts need be tolerated no longer. A suitable test applied to an utterance makes its source immediately obvious, whether it is the Spirit of God or not." [Thomas] Another writer said: "True spiritual gifts are given by God to strengthen and manifest oneness, harmony, and power. Satan's counterfeit gifts are meant to divide, disrupt, and weaken. God's gifts build up; Satan's counterfeits tear down." [MacArthur] The Corinthian church certainly needed unity and harmony, but it was full of disunity and division partly due to the practice of some so-called gifted people in the church.

Notice that Paul was dealing with speech. Evidently there was a lot of confusion in the Corinthian church about the spectacular behavior of some people who were getting up in the services and exercising their speaking gifts supposedly under the influence of the Holy Spirit. One writer said: "When a person was beside himself with excitement, some accepted this as evidence of the Spirit's presence and activity. A person allowing himself to come under the control of forces outside himself has no guarantee of divine inspiration, for there are inspirations that proceed from other sources as well. A state of ecstasy and outward excitement in the individual speaking should be understood in conjunction with the declaration." [Thomas]

No one speaking by the Spirit of God says, "Jesus is accursed" = As Paul often does, here he first presented the negative test before giving the positive test. We can certainly imagine this kind of statement being made by someone under the influence of demons, since demons are the sworn enemies of Christ. Satan and the demons would like nothing better than to negate or downgrade or demean the work which Jesus accomplished when He came to earth as a man to die for the sins of the world. The enemies of God would do anything to promote the message that Jesus is accursed, and it is possible that some of the pagan worship leaders had actually uttered such statements in Corinth around the time of Paul's ministry there. That seems to be the best way to understand why Paul included this negative statement as a test of authenticity, because it is very difficult to image a circumstance when a born-again Christian in the context of a church service would ever say such a thing about Jesus.

No one can say, "Jesus is Lord," except by the Holy Spirit = On the positive side, it is only possible to believe and to openly confess that "Jesus is Lord" under the influence of the Holy Spirit. The name Jesus points to His human existence during the incarnation when He came as a man to die for the sins of the world. So this statement is very profound. It declares that Jesus is the God-man who now has all authority as the Lord of the universe. It says something about Jesus Himself, that He is truly God in human flesh. But it also says something about the relationship of the one who is speaking to the person of Jesus. It is a statement of personal submission to the authority of the Lord Jesus Christ.

Notice carefully that it is the content of the spoken words that determine their authenticity, rather than the way in which they are spoken. Spectacular behavior, even if it has the appearance of being under the influence of a higher power, is not really important. What really matters is that the content of your statements line up with biblical truth, and that you live in obedience to those truths. One writer put it this way: "Paul follows the lead of the Old Testament (Deut 13:1-3; 18:20-22) in claiming that content, not manner, is the criterion. Inspiration as a religious phenomenon is in itself indifferent, and gains significance only in the context of Christian obedience." [Barrett]

The true test of whether the Spirit is at work is a test of the content of the statements, so it is really a test of correct doctrine. In other words, the only way to verify whether something is spiritual is to see whether it is Scriptural. "Paul would have his readers know that no spiritual gift would result in a statement that was contrary to the truth. The test of doctrinal orthodoxy must constantly apply to spiritual gifts. To be accepted as valid, the spoken manifestation must agree with what has come to be written down in God's Word. The test of verse three is primarily theological in nature and insists upon an accurate view of the person of Jesus Christ. It is only as one maintains the correct view of Him as the God-man that he can confidently identify the activity of the Holy Spirit and spiritual gifts through members of the body of Christ." [Thomas]

The Source of All Spiritual Gifts (12:4-6)

1 Cor 12:4 Now there are varieties of gifts, but the same Spirit.

We have already seen from verse three that any kind of so-called inspiration which is not from God can have no place in the services of the church. But even after an inspired speaker has passed the test of ministering for God, there are some additional questions that believers might have. One man put it this way: "Inspiration that does not come from God has already been excluded by verse three; but inspiration that does come from God is so diverse that its variety can give rise to a further set of problems. Which are the most important spiritual gifts? Can a man who does not have them be counted a Christian at all? Is it not to be expected that a true Christian will manifest all of them?" [Barrett] So in this section, the apostle Paul is going to explain the issue of diversity among the gifts by emphasizing their common and unified source.

There are varieties of gifts = The term "varieties" (**diairesis**) will be used in the following two verses as well, and it indicates the distribution of the gifts as well as the diversity of those gifts. The context in this first section of the chapter seems to point to the idea of a diversity or variety in the different gifts that are mentioned, as contrasted with their single source. Also, the emphasis on the varieties of gifts implies that the Corinthian believers considered only the more spectacular speaking gifts as being important. But Paul clearly shows in this section that the Holy Spirit gave a great variety of gifts, and every spiritual gift is just as important as any other gift.

The term "gifts" (**charismaton**, from the verb **charizomai**) means a gracious favor or benefit bestowed or received without being based on any merit or being deserved by the recipient. This is one of the terms that helps us to understand the meaning of Paul's opening phrase, "Now concerning spirituals" (**pneumatikos**). Those spiritual things are the undeserved gifts that are given by the Holy Spirit.

But the same Spirit = Even though there is a wide variety of gifts, they are all given by the same Holy Spirit. There is a unity behind all of the diversity. God Himself is the one, unified, single source for all of these many gifts, and this verse specifically emphasizes the role of the third person of the Trinity (the Holy Spirit) in the gracious giving of these gifts.

1 Cor 12:5 And there are varieties of ministries, and the same Lord.

There are varieties of ministries (diakonia, from which we get our English word deacon) = In the Corinthian church, spiritual gifts were used as opportunities for comparing, and boasting, and attracting a following. But this verse emphasizes that spiritual gifts should be used as opportunities for humble service to others. The verse also implies that even if several believers were to have the same exact spiritual gift, they may be led to use that gift in many different forms of service or ministry. So there are lots of opportunities for service represented by the diversity of gifts.

And the same Lord = In this phrase, the second person of the Trinity (Jesus Christ) joins the third person (the Holy Spirit) as the source of all the services that are performed through the spiritual gifts in the church.

1 Cor 12:6 There are varieties of effects, but the same God who works all things in all persons.

There are varieties of effects (energema) = This means something that is accomplished through energy. So far we have seen this progression: Spiritual gifts are to be used in service to others, and those ministries are intended to have God-ordained effects or results in the lives of believers. It seems that the Corinthians may have been focusing on the display of their gifts, without as much concern for producing a positive impact in the lives of their fellow Christians. Here the emphasis is on results, something good that will happen in someone's life when a gift is displayed.

But the same God who works (energeo) all things in all = This verb means "to effectively accomplish or produce something." In this verse, the first person of the Trinity (God the Father) joins the Son and the Spirit as the source of all the effects produced through spiritual gifts in the church.

Some people have viewed these verses as outlining three categories of gifts. But it is very clear from the context that the diversity of the gifts is being contrasted with the single source of the gifts in God Himself. One commentator put it this way:

> He is not to be understood as dividing these gifts into three classes, under the heads of gifts, ministrations, and operations...This view of the passage is inconsistent with the constant and equal reference of these gifts to the Holy Spirit; they all come under the head of Spiritual gifts. They are all and equally gifts of the Spirit, modes of serving the Son, and effects due to the efficiency of the Father. [Hodge]

These three verses show that because Christians differ from one another in their natural and spiritual gifts, we should not expect to see a strict uniformity in the way believers serve within the church. Unity is needed, but unity within the church does not mean uniformity of gifts or ministries or effects. And even though there is diversity, there is also the underlying unity which comes from the One who gave all of these various gifts to the members of the church.

The Ultimate Purpose for These Spiritual Gifts (12:7)

1 Cor 12:7 But to each one is given the manifestation of the Spirit for the common good.

But to each one is given (didomi) = This phrase tells us that each and every member of the church has a special spiritual gift that is perfectly appropriate for that individual. Gifts of the Spirit are not reserved only for a few outstanding believers in the church. The opposite is true: according to this verse, every single Christian has at least one spiritual gift.

The manifestation (phanerosis) of the Spirit = This term emphasizes that the results of spiritual gifts are openly displayed for all to see. In this case, these special manifestations of the Holy Spirit are to be expressed and exercised for the benefit of other believers within the church.

For the common good (sumphero) = This term means "to bring together, to confer a benefit, to be profitable or useful for all." Notice that a spiritual gift is never given for the benefit of the individual alone. Spiritual gifts are not merely for private or personal use. Instead they are intended to flow out of the gifted person to touch the lives of others around him or her.

Examples of the Corinthians' Spiritual Gifts (12:8-10)

After emphasizing the great variety of spiritual gifts in these verses, the apostle Paul will now illustrate this variety by giving specific examples from within the church at Corinth. All of the gifts listed here were being used by carnal believers in Corinth for selfish purposes, and some individuals with more spectacular gifts were attracting a following. The church was breaking off into schisms, partly due to the abuse of spiritual gifts.

Regarding this initial listing of spiritual gifts, one man commented, "No doubt all these spiritual gifts were familiar to Corinthian Christians in the first century. Some are imperfectly clear to the modern reader." [Barrett] Even though we may not be able to specifically identify all of these gifts, it is clear that the believers in the church at Corinth knew exactly what Paul was talking about when he referred to each of these spiritual gifts using these specific names for them. What we see here is really a simple list of names or labels, but Paul did not feel the need to give any additional descriptions of these gifts. He did not even define them, let alone explain how they were supposed to function within the church. So from our perspective in history hundreds of years later, we must identify these specific gifts from the terms Paul used to label them, as well as from the structure of the sentences in which he presented them.

1 Cor 12:8 For to one is given the word of wisdom through the Spirit, and to another the word of knowledge according to the same Spirit;

To one is given = The word "one" picks up on Paul's statement in the last verse that to each one is given the manifestation of the Spirit. One individual may have one spiritual gift, while another individual is given a different gift for the benefit of those within the church.

The word of wisdom (sophia) = The apostle Paul had already spent quite a bit of time discussing the difference between God's wisdom and the worldly wisdom of the Greek philosophers (1 Cor 1:18-31). He then went on to give more details about the wisdom of God (1 Cor 2:1-16). Here in chapter twelve, when this verse lists the spiritual gift of wisdom, we should connect it with what Paul said earlier in chapter two and view it as a special manifestation of God's wisdom for the benefit of others within the church. The word of wisdom is the spiritual gift of communicating God's wisdom.

When we studied chapter two we learned that God's wisdom is often veiled in mystery, but that God actively revealed some of His mysteries to specific believers for the benefit of all Christians. In chapter two we saw that God's true wisdom was received by revelation (1 Cor 2:1-11), it was transmitted by inspiration (1 Cor 2:12-13), and it is understood through illumination (1 Cor 2:14-16). From our perspective in history, we now have the completed revelation of inspired Scripture, so the functions of inspiration and revelation are no longer active. But we still need illumination today in order to understand the written Word of God. The spiritual gift of wisdom involves examining the Scriptures in order to perceive God's wisdom, and then it involves communicating God's wisdom to other believers within the church.

To another (allos) = This word means to another of the same kind. Somehow the first two spiritual gifts in this list are connected. They are gifts of a similar kind or type. This would probably be a good place to pause and look at the overall structure of verses eight, nine, and ten. There are two Greek words that can be translated "another." The word **allos** means another of the same kind, while the word **heteros** means another of a different kind. As we look at this passage, we see that three somewhat distinct groups of gifts are being described. With this structure in mind, we can continue to examine the remaining spiritual gifts that are given in this list.

The word of knowledge (gnosis) = The idea of knowledge is also one which the apostle Paul had already spent quite a bit of time dealing with in this letter. In 1 Cor 1:5 he had said that God enriched the Corinthians with knowledge, but in chapter eight Paul described how they were misusing their knowledge by becoming arrogant and even sinning against other Christians by failing to use their knowledge lovingly (1 Cor 8:1-13). The spiritual gift of knowledge seems to represent the kind of knowledge that understands how to apply God's wisdom in specific situations for the common good of others. We might say that the gift of knowledge is the insight required to know when some behavior or activity is right or wrong for a Christian in a particular situation. One man called it "moral wisdom." [Thayer] Viewed in this way, the gift of knowledge is connected to the gift of wisdom because it helps believers to know how to use or apply God's revealed truths in their specific circumstances. We

Structure of this passage

To one is given = Word of wisdom
To another (of the same kind) = Word of knowledge

To another (of a different kind) = Faith
To another (of the same kind) = Gifts of healing
To another (of the same kind) = Effecting of miracles
To another (of the same kind) = Prophecy
To another (of the same kind) = Distinguishing of spirits

To another (of a different kind) = Kinds of tongues
To another (of the same kind) = Interpretation of tongues

could say that knowledge is required for the proper use of wisdom.

Even though the spiritual gift of teaching is not mentioned in this first listing of the gifts, it would seem that a teacher or preacher would need this kind of wisdom and knowledge in order to function within the body of Christ for the benefit of others. One man summarized these gifts this way: "The ability to comprehend spiritual truth is God-given. The gifted person is supernaturally enabled not only to discover truths from the facts of Scripture but to explain and interpret those truths in order to help others understand them." [MacArthur]

According to the same Spirit = Here again the apostle Paul shows that even in the diversity of gifts there is a unity of source. They all come from and are directed by the same Holy Spirit. They are according to His will and as He sees fit.

1 Cor 12:9 to another faith by the same Spirit, and to another gifts of healing by the one Spirit,

To another (heteros) faith (pistis) = The Greek word **heteros** means another of a different kind, so the structure of this passage indicates that here Paul is introducing a new set of gifts that are somewhat different than the previous gifts. The first gift in this list is the gift of faith, which is the ability to trust God based on His Word. We know that basic faith is essential for every believer, so the spiritual gift of faith must be something different than saving faith which is common to all Christians. Since all of the gifts in this short list have to do with speaking or displaying something for the benefit of other believers within the church, it seems best to view the spiritual gift of faith as a special ability to communicate faith to others, to help other people trust in God more fully.

The gift of faith could be exercised by speaking words of encouragement to others, or simply by setting a clear and obvious example for others to follow. One man wrote that this was the kind of faith that "enabled men to become confessors and martyrs, and which is so fully illustrated in Heb 11:33-40." [Hodge] That section of Hebrews does provide outstanding examples of faith which we can all imitate. So the spiritual gift of faith is that special ability that builds the faith of others. Viewed in this way, you can probably think of some believers who have been given this kind of special ability, either directly in your life by their personal influence or indirectly through books and stories which record their display of the spiritual gift of faith.

As the first spiritual gift in this set of similar gifts, faith can be viewed as one of the gifts that draws attention to God or points to God's amazing power and greatness. Therefore, like the other gifts that follow it in this section, the gift of faith operates to encourage believers to trust in God more fully or completely. One writer described the gift of faith in the following words:

> This unusual ability enabled a person to believe God in the face of enormous obstacles. With such a gift the child of God could trust Him to the extent that God intervened and produced a means for overcoming that obstacle. The gift of faith apparently fulfilled the same confirmatory function as did other gifts in its cate-

gory. [Thomas]

To another (allos) gifts of healing (iama) = This term simply means to bring about a return to health, and there are many examples in the New Testament that show the gift of healing being used (Acts 3:6-8; 5:15-16; 8:7; 9:17-18, 33-35; 19:12; 28:8). These examples show that the actual healing usually became a platform for presenting the truths of God's wisdom. The miraculous healing became the divine stamp of approval or authenticity for the message that was proclaimed. This is an important concept. The spiritual gift of healing was never used solely for the purpose of restoring someone's physical health. Paul himself was sick as were many of his companions, but he was not given the ability to heal them. He only exercised the gift of healing through the leading of the Holy Spirit as a means to confirm the power of the gospel, rather than as a way to restore Christians to health.

By the one Spirit = After listing additional examples of very diverse manifestations, here the apostle Paul continued to emphasize that it is the one Holy Spirit who is responsible for them all.

1 Cor 12:10 and to another the effecting of miracles, and to another prophecy, and to another the distinguishing of spirits, to another various kinds of tongues, and to another the interpretation of tongues.

To another (allos) the effecting of miracles (dunamis) = Literally, this means "effects which are powerful or miraculous," and the New Testament records many of these types of supernatural events (Acts 5:5, 10; 9:40; 13:8-11). As was the case with the gift of healing, these events usually became the platform for presenting or confirming the truths of God's wisdom. The miracle provided the divine stamp of approval or authenticity for the message that was being presented. One man has explained the need for this type of gift in the following words:

> The confirmatory effect of the gift of miracles is thus like the effect of the other gifts in this second category: these are a means for validating God's spokesmen and their messages. Such a need existed only so long as the church was without its own authenticated written revelation, a condition that prevailed through the first century AD. Once all had been written that God wanted written, no further place was open for this or any other confirmatory gift. That is not to say that miracles have not occurred since AD 100. They have happened and continue according to God's providence. But the medium of their accomplishment is no longer the spiritual gift of miracles: the need no longer exists to verify specific persons as channels of new revelation, for new revelation ceased with the writing of the last New Testament book. The age of miracles continues, but the age of miracle workers has passed. [Thomas]

To another (allos) prophecy (propheteia) = Here it appears that Paul is emphasizing the more miraculous predictive element in New Testament prophecy (Acts 11:27-28; 21:10-11; 27:21-25; 1 Tim 1:18). This was a special ability given to a believer for accurately predicting future events, and the authentication of the prophet's message occurred when those events actually took place just as they had been described. One writer said this was "Probably not in the wider sense of public teaching by the Spirit but, as its position between miracles and discerning of spirits implies, the inspired disclosure of the future." [JFB]

This miraculous insight into future events became a sign of the authenticity of the message spoken by the prophet during the time before the written Word of God was completed. One commentator remarked:

> God has not continued to bestow the predictive powers that belonged to such first-century Christians as Agabus, the daughters of Philip, and Paul. Written by the apostle John, Revelation gives notice of the termination of prophecy. It specifically states that no prophetic additions are to be tolerated (Rev 22:18). It is quite evident in this prohibition that God incorporated into this one, great, final prophecy, all the predictive elements that would be needed by the church in coming generations, until such time as these find their fulfillment in connection with Christ's second advent...For this reason, the wise approach is to limit prophecy to the period before John concluded the writing of Revelation at the end of the first century AD. [Thomas]

To another (allos) the distinguishing of spirits (diakrisis) = This term is related to the verb **diakrino** which we studied in chapter eleven of this letter (1 Cor 11:29, 31), and it identifies the ability to distinguish or discern whether something is from the Holy Spirit or from some other source. This type of gift would be especially valuable in the Corinthian church so that someone could give an immediate judgment on the things that were being said in that congregation. Later in this letter to the Corinthians, Paul commanded believers with the gift of discernment to judge the ones who were prophesying in that church (1 Cor 14:29). This is the kind of gift that God can use to reveal to the church whether or not a manifestation of the other gifts in this category are coming from Him. One man said it this way:

> The gift of discernment is given to tell if the other gifts are of the Holy Spirit, if they are merely natural imitations, or if they are demonic counterfeits. I believe that God still empowers some of His people to unmask false prophets and carnal hypocrites. He gives them insight to expose imitations and deceptions that most Christians would take as genuine. [MacArthur]

This spiritual gift comes at the end of this second set of gifts because it is a gift that can be used to verify that other gifts in this category are being applied properly. It can provide some of the required checks and balances that are needed for guaranteeing that all the gifts are functioning as intended within the church.

To another (heteros) various kinds of tongues (glossa) = Paul now introduced a third set of spiritual gifts that were somewhat distinct (**heteros**) from the previous set. Notice that the apostle Paul placed the gifts of tongues and the interpretation of tongues at the very end of his list. This would be the opposite order in which the Corinthians themselves would have rated these two gifts. They seemed to place a very high value on them, but Paul listed them last of all.

The spiritual gift of tongues was the ability to speak to people in a language that the speaker had not previously learned. From the other New Testament examples of the use of this gift it is clear that the message spoken in tongues was able to be understood by listeners who knew those languages (Acts 2:7-11; 10:46; 19:6). This means that the tongues are understandable, even though they may seem unintelligible to a person who does not know that particular language. A stranger to that language might think it was an ecstatic utterance. One man put it this way:

> It was not always true that the speaker in tongues could make clear what he had said to those who did not know the tongue (1 Cor 14:13). It was not mere gibberish or jargon like the modern tongues, but a real language that could be understood by one familiar with that tongue as was seen on the great Day of Pentecost when people who spoke different languages were present. In Corinth, where no such variety of people existed, it required an interpreter to explain the tongue to those who knew it not. Hence Paul placed this gift lowest of all. It created wonder, but did little real good. [RWP]

In the city of Corinth the gift of tongues might have been a very useful gift. Here is what history tells us:

> Commercially and geographically, Corinth was a city that merchants and travelers visited. As an evangelistic tool in gaining a hearing for the gospel, as well as a dramatic speaking tool for presenting information to foreign believers, the tongues gift could have ministered to these foreigners to very great advantage. That was the use to which Paul put the gift as he traveled about in his missionary labors (1 Cor 14:18, 22). If one could for a moment ponder the wisdom of God in sovereignly endowing the Corinthian church so richly with this gift, it would seem to have been His intention that the gift be used in metropolitan surroundings exactly like these. [Thomas]

To another (allos) the interpretation of tongues (hermeneia) = Here is the last gift in this third set, and it involves the interpretation of the foreign languages that were spoken by someone with the previous gift. The Greek term used to describe this gift is **hermeneia**, from which we get our English word "hermeneutics" (the art and science of properly interpreting God's Word). There is one question that might arise concerning the gift of interpreting tongues: If a person could speak a foreign language, then why couldn't he also interpret what he said? The simple answer to this question is that he cannot do it because interpretation is not his gift. It seems that one who spoke in tongues was sometimes able to understand what he was saying (1 Cor 14:4), but it is also possible that he was able to correctly speak a message in another language while not being able to understand all that was being said. In that case, the speaker would need someone else to interpret what was said. But even if the speaker did understand his message, it would lend confirmation and authenticity to what was said if a different person interpreted the message.

An additional point is that just because a person had the gift of speaking in tongues, it did not mean that he understood every language. For example, the apostle Paul stated he had this gift in abundance, and yet when he and Barnabas were in Lycaonia, neither of them could understand what the people were saying in their native tongue (Acts 14:11-14). So the gift of tongues did not allow a person to speak or understand every language.

One of the things to notice about these three sets of gifts is that the last gift in each set was apparently given as a check on the use of the other gifts in each set. Clearly, all of these spiritual gifts involve some kind of outward expression, typically speaking to others in order to build them up in their faith. Even spiritual gifts that get their name from some spectacular activity, such as performing healings or miracles, even those gifts became a platform for speaking God's truth to others. The first set of gifts involved delivering information to others in order to help them better understand God's truth. The second set of gifts involved drawing attention to God and helping people to trust more completely in Him. The third set of gifts also involved delivering information, but in a special way and in limited situations that would make it clear that God Himself was behind the message.

So far we have seen nine examples of the spiritual gifts which are distributed by the Holy Spirit to members of the body of Christ. However, think for a moment about what gifts are missing from this list. What we have seen here are examples of spiritual gifts that the Corinthians apparently were abusing in their church services. What about the other gifts necessary for the church, such as the gift of serving, or giving, or administration? It seems that those gifts were not the ones being abused and causing divisions within the church at Corinth, so the apostle Paul does not mention them in this first list. The gifts that became part of this list in 1 Cor 12:8-10 are here for a very specific reason. They were being misused for selfish purposes by carnal Christians seeking attention in the church at Corinth.

The Conclusion Regarding the True Source of Spiritual Gifts (12:11)

Paul's main point in listing all of these gifts was to show that a great variety of gifts all come from the same source. So, in the final verse of this section, the apostle Paul emphasized that the variety of spiritual gifts listed in the previous verses all have their common source in the Holy Spirit.

1 Cor 12:11 But one and the same Spirit works all these things, distributing to each one individually just as He wills.

But one and the same Spirit works all these things (energeo)= This verse is a fitting conclusion to this entire section. Despite the diversity of all these gifts, it is one and the same Holy Spirit who works or energizes all of them. This is the same word that was used in 1 Cor 12:6 where it was said that the same God works (energeo) all things in all. It is God, and specifically God the Holy Spirit, who accomplishes the results of the spiritual gifts that are manifested by believers.

Distributing to each one individually = The word "distributing" is the Greek term **diaireo**, which is the verb form of the word **diairesis** that is translated "varieties" in 1 Cor 12:4-6. In this verse the verb means "dividing into parts and distributing." The Holy Spirit accomplishes this distribution in exactly the right way to exactly the right people. He gives spiritual gifts to each one individually. This reinforces the idea that each individual believer is given at least one spiritual gift that is perfectly matched to that person's personality and character.

Just as He wills (boulomai) = This Greek term emphasizes the deliberate exercise of volition, rather than just a simple desire. The NIV Bible translates this phrase, "He gives them to each one, just as He determines," and this is a good way to express this term. Whether a believer has a certain spiritual gift is completely up to the Holy Spirit, rather than to the believer himself. The implication of this verse was expressed this way by one writer: "Thus it is not for Christians to dictate to the Spirit what gifts they (or others) should have." [Barrett]

The Illustration of the Body of Christ

(1 Corinthians 12:12-31)

In the first part of this chapter the apostle Paul had explained that even though there are a wide variety of spiritual gifts and ministries and effects, all of these diverse things come from the one Holy Spirit, are energized by Him, and are given only as He determines. The Corinthians were focusing on a few of the more spectacular or showy gifts, and they were looking down on believers who did not manifest what they considered to be those "greater" or "better" gifts. In the last section of this chapter, the apostle Paul is going to illustrate the importance of the unity of the members of the church by comparing a healthy church to a properly functioning human body.

Where did this analogy of the body originate? Where had Paul introduced it previously? The first place in this letter that a body was referred to was in 1 Cor 10:16-17 where the apostle Paul was discussing the Lord's Supper. He had said that the red liquid in the cup represented the sacrificial blood which Christ had shed when he paid the penalty for the sins of mankind on the cross, and that the bread represented the broken body of Christ during His death on the cross. Paul then stated that when believers participate in the Lord's Supper they have become sharers in all that the body and blood of Christ accomplished for us. He then went on to say, "We who are many are one body, for we all partake of the one bread" (1 Cor 10:17). At that point in his letter to the Corinthians he was using the Lord's Supper as an example of how it expressed a special relationship of communion with the Lord, and that in just the same way the Corinthians could not participate in the pagan temple feasts without establishing a relationship of communion with demons. That was a very important point, but it seems Paul had more to say about this idea of becoming part of the body of Christ. So in this chapter he proceeded to expand on this illustration and apply it to the relationships between believers who constitute the body of Christ.

1 Cor 12:12 For even as the body is one and yet has many members, and all the members of the body, though they are many, are one body, so also is Christ.

For = This transition word establishes a very close connection with what had just been said about the Holy Spirit being the true source of the spiritual gifts, as well as His distributing and energizing them according to His own will and plan. The church is one, for we were all baptized into one body by the one Holy Spirit.

Even as the body is one and yet has many members = The apostle Paul had been explaining that the diverse manifestations the Corinthians saw in their church were all the result of the working of the one Holy Spirit. Here he is saying that this is similar to the way a human body is a single organism but is composed of many different parts. Even in a single unified body, a diversity of members is required for it to function properly.

And all the members of the body, though they are many, are one body = Here Paul states the same truth in the reverse. Even though there is a diversity of members, they all must work together for the proper functioning of the one body. These phrases give us a summary of this entire section of chapter twelve. They show the flow and movement of thought that Paul is going to follow in this concluding section of the chapter.

So also is Christ = We would almost expect Paul to have said: "For as the body is one, and has many members, so also is the church." After all, that is the organization that Paul wants to apply these truths to ultimately. But instead of identifying the church here, Paul actually opens up an additional set of truths that can also be applied. One writer put it this way: "Paul takes two steps in one. It would not have been wrong to conclude: so also is the church. But the church is the body of Christ. Men are in the body of Christians only as they are in Christ" [Barrett] So, individuals become part of the church only because they first have been placed into Christ.

Paul could not have chosen a more interesting and appropriate illustration to present this idea of diversity and unity in a single organism. The human body is such a marvelous system of very diverse parts that all operate together for the proper functioning of the whole. One commentator expressed it this way: "The human body is by far the most amazing organic creation of God. It is marvelously complex, yet unified. It is a unit; it cannot be subdivided into several bodies. If it is divided, the part that is cut off ceases to function and dies, and the rest of the body loses some of its functions and effectiveness." [MacArthur]

1 Cor 12:13 For by one Spirit we were all baptized into one body, whether Jews or Greeks, whether slaves or free, and we were all made to drink of one Spirit.

For = This provides additional explanation for how these diverse members came to be part of one body, the body of Christ, the church (see 1 Cor 12:27).

By one Spirit we were all baptized into one body = This phrase describes the formation of the one body. Anyone who puts his trust in Jesus Christ becomes a full-fledged member of Christ's body at the moment he is saved. There are no partial Christians or partial members of His body. This miraculous event is accomplished by the one Holy Spirit through a special "baptizing" ministry that has been given to Him for use during the church age.

Whether Jews or Greeks, whether slaves or free = Here Paul explained the meaning of the word "all" in the previous phrase. All means every believer, and believers come from every nationality, every cultural background, every social class, and every economic status. The church as an organism consists of believers from a wide diversity or cross-section of society. "The various national and social groups, and the dissident religious cliques at Corinth, have all entered into the unity of the body of Christ, which they ought to express and not deny, by means of their various gifts." [Barrett]

And we were all made to drink of one Spirit = The previous phrase explained the formation of the body, and now this phrase describes the life principle that fills the one body. Just as there are no partially saved Christians, there are no partially indwelt Christians. At the moment he believes, a person is baptized by the Spirit into full membership in the body of Christ, and the Holy Spirit also comes to live inside the believer. As one man put it, "Like being baptized with the Spirit, being indwelt by the Spirit is virtually synonymous with conversion. When we trust in Christ we are completely immersed into the Spirit and completely indwelt by Him. God has nothing more to put into us. He has put His very self into us, and that cannot be exceeded." [MacArthur] As another commentator expressed it:

> This is the essential point of the analogy between the human body and the church. As the body is one because it is pervaded and animated by one principle of life, so the church is one because it is pervaded by one Spirit. And as all parts of the body which partake of the common life belong to the body, so all those in whom the Spirit of God dwells are members of the church which is the body of Christ. It is by virtue of the indwelling of the Spirit that the church is one. [Hodge]

1 Cor 12:14 For the body is not one member, but many.

This verse is a restatement of the first side of the coin presented in verse twelve, and it puts the emphasis in this section on the fact that diversity is needed within the body.

The Problem of Inferiority (12:15-20)

1 Cor 12:15-16 If the foot says, "Because I am not a hand, I am not a part of the body," it is not for this reason any the less a part of the body. And if the ear says, "Because I am not an eye, I am not a part of the body," it is not for this reason any the less a part of the body.

In this part of the illustration of the body, the foot and the ear are comparing themselves to the hand and the eye, and in their own estimation they view their own gifts as being of less value or of no value at all, in comparison to the gifts of the others. The problem being addressed here is the issue of inferiority. One member is looking down on or devaluing or denying his own gift. But notice that just because one member thinks this and expresses this thought, that does not make it true. It is not what we think that maintains our status as part of the body, it is the one-time action of God the Holy Spirit that makes us part of the body.

Also notice that the truth which was expressed in verse fourteen actually provides the antidote to inferiority. Diversity is required in order for the body to function properly. You may see yourself as a freckle or hangnail on the body of Christ, which you might think to be very insignificant, but the truth is that you are just as necessary to the proper functioning of the body as one of the more showy parts. We may not understand exactly why this is so, but we must believe that this is true because God's Word tells us it is true!

1 Cor 12:17 If the whole body were an eye, where would the hearing be? If the whole were hearing, where would the sense of smell be?

The very existence of the body as a viable organism depends on the union and cooperation of the individual members that carry out different functions. The body could not possibly function if it consisted only of one specific part. A body that had only one part would not even be a body. Paul will return to this idea in verse nineteen.

1 Cor 12:18 But now God has placed the members, each one of them, in the body, just as He desired.

God has placed the members = The verb "placed" (**tithemi**) means to set into a specific location. The truth is that it requires the power and activity of God in order to have a living body. God is at work, and even though we do not realize it, He is the one that causes the body to operate. As one man said, "The eye did not give itself the power of vision, nor the ear its ability to discriminate sounds." [Hodge] God carefully placed, arranged, and connected the members.

Just as He desired (thelo) = This word for the will of God is an even stronger word than the one used previously in 1 Cor 12:11. It involves forethought, intention, and resolve. One writer said, "The will (**boulomai**, v. 11) of the Holy Spirit pictured earlier as a more passive intention is now the will (**thelo**, v. 18) of God the Father pressing this underlying intention into action." [Thomas] With this truth in mind, we can conclude that to think little of your own gift or your place within the body of Christ is to think little of God and His work in placing you exactly where He wanted you. When we express it this way, it is obviously a very serious matter to trust that God has gifted you and placed you so as to have the effect He desired in His body.

1 Cor 12:19 If they were all one member, where would the body be?

Here Paul returns to the idea he expressed in 1 Cor 12:16-17. There he asked, "If the whole body were an eye, where would the hearing be?" But the matter is really more serious than that. If the whole body were an eye, where would the body itself be? A large solitary eyeball would be completely useless because it requires the support of the eye socket within the skull, it requires the connecting nerve fibers to relay its information to the brain, and it even requires the eye lid and tear ducts to provide moisture and protection. The eyeball cannot perform its intended function in isolation. It must have the support of the other members of the body in order to be valuable. And even the eyeball itself is actually composed of smaller parts that were formed to make a single organ.

"If they were all one member, where would the body be?" The answer is that it simply would not be a body. This is Paul's way of expressing the logical contradiction which would result in supposing a body could even exist if it were just one part. A selection of individual body parts all laid out on a table would look more like an autopsy, a dismembered body in which each of the parts is actually dead rather than alive.

> The admonition is: Do not despise your own gift. Diversity is normal and needful to proper functioning of the body. The application of this principle means that the individual gift of each member, no matter how insignificant it may seem, is important to the body. Presumably, the Corinthians were exalting certain of the more spectacular gifts to the point that others felt that they had no gift at all, that they were not of the body. Paul's answer is that it takes many members to make a body. [Boyer]

1 Cor 12:20 But now there are many members, but one body.

This verse marks the second section within this passage, and it is a restatement of the second side of the coin presented in verse twelve. It puts the emphasis on the unity of the parts of the body and the fact that they cannot do without each other.

The Problem of Superiority (12:21-26)

1 Cor 12:21 And the eye cannot say to the hand, "I have no need of you"; or again the head to the feet, "I have no need of you."

Here the eye and the head are comparing themselves to the hand or the feet, and in their own estimation they view their gifts as being of greater value in comparison to the gifts of the others. The problem being addressed here is the issue of superiority. One member is looking down on or devaluing or denying the gifts of others. The truth expressed in verse twenty, that the parts of the body form a unity and cannot do without each other, is actually the antidote to superiority. It seems that a few of the prominent charismatic church members were acting as if they were self-sufficient and did not need other believers who had what they saw as inferior gifts.

1 Cor 12:22 On the contrary, it is much truer that the members of the body which seem to be weaker are necessary;

Seem to be weaker = These are the parts of the body that seem to be more susceptible to being injured, such as the vital soft tissues of the internal organs. The brain, the lungs, and the heart are examples of relatively "weak" organs that need the protection of stronger body parts so they will not be exposed to injury.

Necessary (anangkaios) = This term means something that you cannot do without. If a person's arm or leg is amputated, he can still survive even though the injuries are traumatic. But a person cannot live if his brain, lungs or heart are removed. So, although those internal parts are more delicate they are really more necessary for life.

> Perhaps the idea is—and it is a beautiful thought—that those members of the church which are most retiring and feeble apparently which are concealed from public view, unnoticed and unknown—the humble, the meek, the peaceful, and the

prayerful—are often more necessary to the true welfare of the church than those who are eminent for their talent and learning. And it is so. The church can better spare many a man, even in the ministry, who is learned, and eloquent, and popular, than some obscure and humble Christian, that is to the church what the heart and the lungs are to the life. [Barnes]

1 Cor 12:23 and those members of the body which we deem less honorable, on these we bestow more abundant honor, and our less presentable members become much more presentable,

We deem less honorable (atimos) = Literally this means, "not honored." These are parts of the body which we do not allow to be seen or displayed in public. We keep these body parts well covered.

We bestow (peritithemi) = Literally this means, "to place around." This verb was used to describe wrapping or covering something, such as putting on clothing or enclosing something with a privacy fence. It suggests the possibility of feeling ashamed without proper clothing.

Less presentable members (aschemon) = This term means shameful, indecent, or unpresentable, and so it refers to those parts of the body that are considered private and are covered or clothed. It is not those body parts themselves that are shameful, but it is the act of displaying them that is considered indecent. Therefore we use an external covering to preserve decency and modesty.

1 Cor 12:24 whereas our more presentable members have no need of it. But God has so composed the body, giving more abundant honor to that member which lacked,

More presentable members (euschemon) = This term means "of elegant figure, shapely, graceful, beautiful."

God...gives more abundant honor to members which lack = Here again we see the activity of God working in the body. Previously we saw that God deliberately placed each member exactly where He wanted it, and now we see that God is the one who gives more abundant honor to those members who lacked it. Even though men do not give honor to inferior things, God does bestow honor on things that man sees as inferior.

> The Christian who is aware of his own deficiency and is prone to magnify his unimportance in his own mind can take great comfort in God's equalizing action. It means that neither he nor anyone else is called upon to take a back seat or be looked down upon. Equality of honor reigns within the body of Christ, no matter how great the gradation in functional abilities. It is reassuring to recall once again God's part in putting all on the same plane. Because of this, we have a basis for complete internal harmony. [Thomas]

This is a very encouraging truth, and one which the Corinthians did not understand. They failed to appreciate their members who lacked the spectacular or showy gifts such as prophecy, tongues, and miracles. The members with less noticeable ministries were devalued and neglected in favor of the dramatic members, and they did not understand that God does not behave this way. He honors even the lowly. "The weaker and humbler members of the church should not be despised but treated with special honor. This is how God has treated undeserving mankind as a whole." [Barrett]

1 Cor 12:25 so that there may be no division in the body, but that the members may have the same care for one another.

So that = This expresses the purpose for God's divine arrangements and activity within the body.

That there may be no division in the body = On the negative side, God's intention is to eliminate divisions and schisms in the body. One writer said, "All the parts should be equally necessary, and truly dependent on each other; and no member should be regarded as separated from the others or as needless to the welfare of all." [Barnes]

But that the members may have the same care for one another = This contrast word shows what should happen instead of having divisions in the body. So on the positive side, God's intention is to create mutual care and concern throughout the body.

Same care (merimnao) = This means to care for and look out for someone; to seek to promote the interests of another; to provide for someone. This word expresses the nourishing and cherishing activity that should characterize the members of the body of Christ.

1 Cor 12:26 And if one member suffers, all the members suffer with it; if one member is honored, all the members rejoice with it.

If one member suffers, all suffer = Suffering means to feel pain or suffer evils, troubles, or persecutions with another. Particularly in the context of spiritual gifts in the church, one man said: "If one member of the church appears to be deficient in such gifts, this is no occasion for the rest of the church to despise him. He is not the only sufferer; the whole church suffers through the deficiency. If another member has more than the usual share of inspiration, neither should he boast nor the rest be envious or resentful. All should rejoice together in the gift." [Barrett]

If one member is honored, all rejoice = Literally, if one member receives glory, then all the other members should congratulate or rejoice with him; they should take part in the other member's joy. These phrases bring to mind the famous slogan that expressed the common fellowship of the Musketeers: "One for all, and all for one." That same type of common fellowship should characterize the church. It appears that Paul's metaphor is beginning to break down, since there is no physiological counterpart for body parts giving honor to each other, or showing the emotions of concern and rejoicing for each other. This tells us that Paul is now talking directly to the church.

Directly Applying the Illustration (12:27)

1 Cor 12:27 Now you are Christ's body, and individually members of it.

Now you are Christ's body = Here we learn what the body in this illustration actually represents. It is Christ's body, and in the next verse we see that Christ's body is equivalent to the church, since that is the actual organization to which Paul applies this illustration.

Christ's body = The Greek case ending on the word "Christ" is the genitive of possession. So this is not the body which is Christ, not the body of which Christ consists, but the body that belongs to Christ and over which He has authority.

And individually members of it = This verse repeats the idea of the one body with many members. The one body is Christ's body, and the individual believers are the members.

The Ranking of the Gifts (12:28-31)

1 Cor 12:28 And God has appointed in the church, first apostles, second prophets, third teachers, then miracles, then gifts of healings, helps, administrations, various kinds of tongues.

God has appointed in the church (tithemi) = This is the same term used earlier, and here it continues the thought of setting or placing, but it adds the idea of establishing and ordaining. It is God that has appointed these people to have these gifts for the benefit of the church as a whole.

As we look over this list of gifts it is obvious that Paul is not attempting to provide a complete catalog of all the possible spiritual gifts. He is simply giving the names of some example gifts for the purpose of making his point about the unity of the body. In this second list of gifts, Paul adds some, he repeats others, but also omits some of the previous ones. It is interesting that in the first three gifts Paul refers specifically to the individual people who are characterized by the gift, but later in the list he names the gifts themselves. So instead of "apostleship, prophecy, and teaching" Paul began the list with "apostles, prophets, and teachers" who were specific people that had been given these gifts.

First, apostles = These first two gifts were the main ones in operation at that time for laying the foundation of the church (see Eph 2:20). One of their primary functions was to receive and share the new revelation of God's Word, and God often gave confirmation of His Word through "signs and wonders and miracles" (2 Cor 12:12). The apostles were men specifically chosen by Christ to have a unique ministry in establishing this new entity called the church. Here in this list by referring to the men themselves who had been given the gift of apostleship, Paul is clearly limiting the operation of this gift to the lifetime of those individuals who had the personal qualifications for being apostles. Apostleship was a gift based on personal contact with the Lord Jesus Christ, and it was not a self-perpetuating gift, with the first apostles appointing later apostles to continue throughout the church age. God used the apostles to provide the leadership, inspiration, and direction for getting the church started, and he often used them as channels for His new revelation for the church age. But men who qualified as eyewitnesses of Christ's life and resurrection had passed from the pages of history by AD 100, so the gift of apostleship also passed with them.

Second, prophets = In Paul's earlier list of spiritual gifts, he had classified prophecy with the other sign-oriented gifts being used to confirm that new revelation was indeed from God. Here in this list, the apostle Paul seems to be emphasizing the informational and revelatory aspects of the gift of prophecy, so here it is classified with the gifts that present new information. In a similar way to apostles, the prophets often served as channels of God's new revelation while at other times they were simply used to explain the revelation that had already been given. One writer expressed it this way:

> They always spoke for God but did not always give a newly revealed message from God. Like the apostles, however, their office ceased with the completion of the New Testament, just as the Old Testament prophets disappeared when that testament was completed some 400 years before Christ. The work of interpreting and proclaiming the now-written Word was taken over by evangelists, pastors, and teachers. The offices are listed here in First Corinthians without chronological distinctiveness or reference to duration, because at that time they were all operative. [MacArthur]

Since this spiritual gift helped to lay the foundation for the church, it seems best to limit its operation to the early years of church history. One writer explained that,

> The foundation is the earliest part of a structure to be erected. So it is with the spiritual building that is the church. Certain gifts were necessary in the beginning stages that ceased to be needed later on. So it is that the New Testament assigns the apostles and prophets to the earliest period of church history. Prophecy as a total gift pertained to approximately the first seventy years of church history. This was the period when the Holy Spirit chose to use direct revelation to communicate previously unrevealed truths to the body of Christ. [Thomas]

Another scholar commented, "The fact that any office existed in the apostolic church is no evidence that it was intended to be permanent. In that age there was a plenitude of spiritual manifestations and endowments demanded for the organization and propagation of the church, which are no longer required." [Hodge]

Third, teachers (didaskalos) = This is the common word for a teacher, or one who instructs others. The first three gifts in this list were specifically numbered to indicate their order of importance at that time in church history. The first two gifts were special gifts for communicating God's new revelation being recorded in the New Testament, and they were no longer needed after the first century when the Scriptures were completed. Of these first three gifts, teaching is the only one that is meant to function in the church today. As one man said, "Apostles and prophets, in the strictest sense of the terms, are no longer available to the church as vehicles of ministry to the body. But teachers are. The congregation that gives a prime place to its teachers is steering a wise course in utilizing its personnel to promote growth effectively in the body." [Thomas]

The fourth and fifth gifts are introduced by the word "then," and the final gifts have no introductory word at all. This seems to indicate that the end of this list contains a more miscellaneous grouping that is not necessarily in order of importance, with the exception of the gift of tongues which comes last of all.

Then, miracles = We see here that Paul has shifted his focus from the person possessing a gift, to the gift itself. This is the same gift mentioned in 1 Cor 12:10, and it is listed there as one of the confirmatory gifts. The gift of miracles verified that God was giving His stamp of authenticity to the new revelation that was coming to the early church. "Men specially endowed with this power consistently displayed it along with the preaching of the Word (1 Cor 2:4; 4:20; 2 Cor 6:7; 1 Thess 1:5). In each case, the miracle's effect on the hearers was to create an impression of God's direct involvement in what was being said." [Thomas]

Then, gifts of healings = Again this is the same gift that was mentioned in 1 Cor 12:9, where it was listed as a gift drawing attention to God's involvement in the life of the early church.

Helps (antilepsis) = This is a word that literally means to lay hold of something, but it had the connotation of taking a burden off of someone else and placing it on oneself. In general, this gift functioned to relieve other believers who were struggling under a burden of any kind. In contrast to the speaking gifts for communicating information to the mind, this gift had to do with ministering in the background to the physical needs of other believers. This person was a burden carrier, and even though it was a very valuable gift, it was not considered to be as attractive or desirable. One commentator said,

> The Corinthians apparently were not inclined toward a gift like this because it did not cater to their ambition for public recognition, as did some of the other gifts of verses 8-10 and 29-30. Yet the Scripture placed this gift side-by-side with the more overt manifestations as a reminder that such a behind-the-scenes operation is just as indispensable as the rest. [Thomas]

Administrations (kubernesis) = This word came from the verb that means to steer (**kubernao**). A related word was **kubernatas**, "shipmaster or steersman" (see Acts 27:11; Rev 18:17). So the gift of administration was the ability to direct or steer a straight course for the church, to provide leadership, guidance, and government. These are the kind of people who know how to organize the resources of the church to accomplish its goals in the most efficient and effective way. Though they may not be the captain of the ship, they certainly know how to turn the rudder in order to steer a straight and true course for the church's activities.

Kinds of tongues = This is the same gift what was listed previously in 1 Cor 12:10. It is the ability to communicate to others in their native language, even though the gifted person had not previously learned that language. As we discussed earlier, this gift might have been a very useful gift in the city of Corinth, but it was one of the main gifts that were being misused by the showy Corinthian believers.

1 Cor 12:29-30 All are not apostles, are they? All are not prophets, are they? All are not teachers, are they? All are not workers of miracles, are they? All do not have gifts of healings, do they? All do not speak with tongues, do they? All do not interpret, do they?

The Greek word "not" is used to introduce each of these questions, and this indicates that a strong negative answer is expected. So, the answer to each of these questions is, "No." The thought expressed in these questions is equivalent to the thought expressed in the illustration of the body in verse nineteen: "If they were all one member, where would the body be?" Just as it would be ridiculous to think that you could have a body made up of just one part, it also would be ridiculous to think that you could have a church containing just one kind of spiritual gift. All of the gifts are equally important because they are all necessary in some way to the proper functioning of the entire body. This also tells us that no one individual can possess all of the gifts. God has designed the body so that various members each have parts of what is needed. There is no single individual that can do everything required by the body.

Paul's main point in listing these gifts was to emphasize again the amazing "variety of ministries" (1 Cor 12:5). "God does not intend for everyone to have the same gift, and He does not intend for everyone to have gifts that are out front and noticed. He distributes the gifts according to His sovereign purpose, 'just as He wills' (1 Cor 12:11). The responsibility of believers is to accept the ministries they are given with gratitude and to use them with faithfulness." [MacArthur]

1 Cor 12:31 But earnestly desire the greater gifts. And I show you a still more excellent way.

But earnestly desire (zeloo) = This word means to burn with passion. This refers to a very strong emotional desire for something.

The greater gifts (megas) = Literally, these were the mega-gifts. What we need to do is determine whether the passion and mega-gifts Paul refers to here were to be taken in a positive or a negative sense. Because of the construction of the Greek sentence, it could have either of two possible meanings. The Greek indicative and imperative forms of this verb are identical, so usually the context must determine whether the author intends it to be taken as a command or a simple statement.

1. As a command, it would be translated: "Earnestly desire the greater gifts." This is how most of the modern translations have rendered this sentence. In this case, Paul is commanding the Corinthians to have a passionate desire for the greater or more valuable gifts in the list he has just given. However,

since possessing a specific gift is totally out of the believer's control, but instead is completely up to the Holy Spirit, Paul cannot be commanding them to desire having the greater gifts for themselves. This would be up to God, not up to the believer, no matter how much he passionately desired it. So with this translation, "desire" would be exchanged for something more like "esteem"—that they were to highly value the more useful gifts at the top of Paul's last listing. This would be a true statement and an important thing for all of us to do, but it is not exactly what the verb **zeloo** typically means.

2. As a statement, it could be translated: "You are eagerly coveting the showier gifts." This translation seems to be a better fit for the context of this passage. The Corinthians were indeed coveting the showier gifts, the ones they believed were the greater gifts. It would be silly for Paul to command them to do something bad that they were already doing. In the previous verses Paul had actually commanded them to do the opposite, to stop putting such a high value on the showier gifts, and to remember that God is the one who determines who gets what gift. Translating the sentence this way also gives us a true statement, as well as a needed rebuke for the bad behavior of the Corinthians.

I show you a still more excellent way = Literally, "I will show you a way beyond ways." It is as if Paul were telling them that, instead of seeking after spectacular manifestations which were beyond their grasp, there is a better way of behaving that is available to all believers, no matter what gift they have been given. Despite all that has been said about the spiritual gifts, Paul is about to describe for them a way of living, a habitual rule of life, that should be followed by every Christian. No matter what gifts the Holy Spirit has given to a believer, that individual should use his gifts in a loving way. This is what Paul will explain in the following chapter.

Love as a Way of Life

(1 Corinthians 13:1-13)

At the end of chapter twelve the apostle Paul had hinted that there was a way of life that was more valuable than any of the gifts, and which was available to every believer. Now in chapter thirteen Paul is going to explain this superior way of life, which he simply calls "love." Paul had already introduced the idea of the superiority of love in chapter eight when he said, "Knowledge makes arrogant, but love edifies" (1 Cor 8:1). When we studied that passage we saw that love for others is the best guide for setting limits on our Christian liberty. Limiting our freedom in Christ for the sake of others has always been the most loving thing to do. Here the apostle Paul will elaborate on this concept by proving that the greatest spiritual gifts are worthless unless they are used with Christian love.

The Concept of Christian Love

The word "love" is the Greek term **agape**, which is used nine times in this chapter. It is obviously the subject of this entire chapter, and it is identified in the very first verse as what Paul had called "the most excellent way" at the end of chapter twelve. He is talking about **agape** love as a way of life that should characterize the Christian.

People across the world today are very confused about the meaning of love. In most cases, what they call love could be better described as uncontrollable feelings of affection or lust. But this is really the exact opposite of what love is, as the term is used here by the apostle Paul. The noun **agape** and the verb **agapao** are used in the New Testament to describe the kind of love expressed by God the Father toward His Son, the Lord Jesus (John 17:26). It was also used to describe the love of God toward sinful mankind (John 3:16; Rom 5:8). Scripture also commands believers to practice this type of love toward each other (John 13:34), as well as toward all other people (1 Th 3:12; 1 Cor 16:14; 2 Pet 1:7). One of the most amazing truths is that this word for love is used to express the very nature of God Himself (1 John 4:8).

This is the kind of love that can only be known from the actions that flow from it. God's **agape** love is seen in the sacrificial gift of His Son (1 John 4:9-10). This kind of love is obviously not just a mere internal feeling of affection, and it is not the kind of love which is a natural response to something within the one being loved. If this kind of love is something that can be commanded, then it is definitely not a feeling, but it involves an act of willing obedience to God. It is a deliberate choice, it is a decision, and it is self-sacrificing in nature rather than based on anything lovable in the recipient of this love. It is God's kind of love which can only be expressed by mankind if it has first been "shed abroad in our hearts" (Rom 5:5).

Christian love has God for its primary object, and expresses itself first of all in implicit obedience to His commandments, (John 14:15, John 14:21, John 14:23; John 15:10; 1 John 2:5; 1 John 5:3; 2 John 1:6). Christian love, whether exercised toward the brethren, or toward men generally, is not an impulse from the feelings, it does not always run with the natural inclinations, nor does it spend itself only upon those for whom some affinity is discovered. Love seeks the welfare of all (Rom 15:2) and works no ill to any (Rom 13:8-10); love seeks opportunity to do good to 'all men, and especially toward them that are of the household of the faith,' Gal 6:10. [Vine]

Great Spiritual Gifts are Useless without Love (13:1-3)

1 Cor 13:1 If I speak with the tongues of men and of angels, but do not have love, I have become a noisy gong or a clanging cymbal.

If = The first three verses of this chapter consist of a series of conditional clauses which are called Greek third class conditionals. They present cases that are proposed for the sake of argument whose likelihood is very remote. It is a hypothetical condition, something which is not intended to be true or false, but is used for the sake of argument. It is not a requirement that some believer actually possess these gifts in this extreme measure. In fact Paul paints a picture for us of a totally unrealistic situation, of a super-human Christian who is supposed to possess each gift in the most extreme possible degree. That, of course, would be an earthly impossibility.

I = Again we see the apostle Paul using himself as the example for the sake of argument. At the end of chapter twelve he had said, "And I am going to show you a still more excellent way." It seems that Paul literally meant what he said. He is going to use himself as the hypothetical case in all of the comparisons he will make in chapter thirteen.

Speak with the tongues of men and of angels = It is interesting that Paul chose to begin this beautiful chapter by mentioning the spiritual gift of tongues. This was the gift that the Corinthians thought was the greatest gift, but Paul had consistently mentioned it last in his previous lists of spiritual gifts. Here the apostle Paul puts the gift of tongues first, but he is using it as the first in a series of negative examples. So we might say that tongues is the greatest example of their worst behavior!

In this verse Paul actually specified two different kinds of tongues that might be proposed for the sake of argument. The tongues of men are obviously the kind of tongues that we have been talking about when we discussed this spiritual gift previously. These are known languages spoken by men in various parts of the world. The tongues of angels are introduced here purely for the sake of argument or for the sake of exaggeration. Paul is proposing the most extreme case of being able to speak in different languages, those known to men as well as those that might possibly exist only in the realm of angels. One writer has said,

The language of angels here seems to be used to denote the highest power of using language, or of the most elevated faculty of eloquence and speech. It is evidently derived from the idea that the angels are superior in all respects to human beings; that they must have endowments in advance of all which man can have. It may possibly have reference to the idea that they must have some mode of communicating their ideas one to another, and that this dialect or mode must be far superior to that which is employed by man. [Barnes]

It is obvious that Paul is proposing the most extreme or hypothetical case of being gifted in the use of languages, and he is doing this for the sake of comparison between the spiritual gift and the loving use of that gift.

But do not have love = With this contrast word, Paul sets up a stark contrast between having the maximum amount of a spiritual gift vs. actually using that gift in Christian love. This is a chapter about the highest form of love, but it is introduced by way of negative contrast. Love is the essential ingredient in Christian behavior, and here is a picture of what the greatest possible spiritual gifts are like when love is missing. "Paul is not saying that love is better than gifts. Rather he is showing that love is the only way to make gifts effectual. The contrast is between gifts with love and gifts without love." [Boyer]

I have become a noisy gong or a clanging cymbal = Noisy gong is a translation of two Greek terms that mean sheets of metal which produce noises when they are struck. "The word here does not mean a brass instrument, but a piece of unwrought metal, which emitted a sound on being struck." [VWS] Clanging cymbal is a translation of two different Greek words which mean a pair of metal cups that are struck together to give off an echoing noise. "The cymbal consisted of two half-globes of metal, which were struck together." [VWS] Both of these examples represent what we might call noise-makers, but they are not musical instruments that are capable of producing a melody. "The comparison is between the unmeaning clash of metal and actual music." [VWS] What the Corinthians thought was such a beautiful-sounding gift was nothing more than irritating noise if it was not manifested for the right motives and in the right spirit.

1 Cor 13:2 If I have the gift of prophecy, and know all mysteries and all knowledge; and if I have all faith, so as to remove mountains, but do not have love, I am nothing.

If I have the gift of prophecy = The next gift that Paul mentions is the gift of prophecy, and he used the same word that was listed in 1 Cor 12:10 (**propheteia**). This was the special ability to accurately predict future events for the purpose of confirming the truths that God was communicating through the apostles and prophets of the early church. It was a special speaking gift that was used to present truth, as well as to confirm the authenticity of that truth. Paul is saying that, even as great as this gift is, it would be completely worthless without love.

And know all mysteries and all knowledge = This set of gifts seems to correspond to the word of wisdom and the word of knowledge from Paul's earlier list (1 Cor 12:8). He describes them here as the ability to perceive mysteries and knowledge which were truths that were previously unrevealed, but that God now desired to communicate to believers during the church age (Rom 16:25-26). It was through the use of gifts such as these that the New Testament was communicated and recorded for future generations. Here again Paul is giving a very extreme case. He is saying, "Suppose I were able to know every single mystery and understand every possible truth in the universe!" This is quite an exaggeration for the purpose of illustration. It is really impossible for any human being to meet this criterion. We are all finite and limited in our ability to understand God's truth. But, even if a person could have the highest possible level of knowledge, it would be utterly useless without love.

And if I have all faith = Here Paul listed the gift of faith, just as he listed it when he began his second group of gifts in 1 Cor 12:9, the gifts that were primarily intended to draw attention to the greatness of God and His direct involvement in what was being communicated by His servants. Faith was at the head of that list, not only because the gifted person had the special ability to trust God for amazing things, but because the gifted person could point others to God and help them to trust Him more fully. Notice the word "all" that describes faith, which is included to take the illustration to an extreme that is humanly impossible. But, Paul said, for the sake of argument, assume that someone did have this perfect kind of faith. It would also be of no value at all without love.

So as to remove mountains = This is the kind of faith that resulted in miracles, and the moving of mountains represented this kind of miracle. This was typical language for expressing complete trust in God's power. Jesus also used this metaphor when He said, "Truly I say to you, if you have faith the size of a mustard seed, you will say to this mountain, Move from here to there, and it will move; and nothing will be impossible to you" (Matt 17:20). Even the ability to work the greatest miracles such as this one, would be totally meaningless without love. Notice that the gifts Paul has mentioned so far are ones that he discussed in the first part of chapter twelve. They were the specific gifts which were being abused in the Corinthian church.

But do not have love, I am nothing = As with the gift of tongues presented in the first verse, all of these marvelous spiritual gifts listed here amount to nothing if they are not motivated by and used with love. The term translated "nothing" in this verse means nil, non-existent, a complete zero. What seemed so important to the Corinthians really amounted to nothing.

1 Cor 13:3 And if I give all my possessions to feed the poor, and if I surrender my body to be burned, but do not have love, it profits me nothing.

And if I give all my possessions to feed the poor = The verb in this phrase is an interesting one in the original language. It is the Greek word **psomiso**, which means to divide something into portions and dole out the parts in order to nourish other people. It was often used for feeding small bits of food to young infants. The words "giving" and "feeding" the poor are not in the original text, but this verb definitely contains the idea of distributing one's property in small portions for the support of others. So if a person were to take all of his property and distribute it to help others, that would be an extreme example of the way the spiritual gifts of giving and helps could be expressed.

> To make the case as strong as possible, Paul says that if all that a man had were dealt out in this way, in small portions so as to benefit as many as possible, and yet were not attended with true love toward God and toward man, it would be all false, hollow, hypocritical, and really of no value. [Barnes]

And if I surrender my body to be burned = In the previous phrase Paul talked about everything that a person owns, but that did not include the person's physical body. Here, however, Paul says that if a person were to go to the extreme of giving up his own body, it would not count for anything without the motivation of self-sacrificing love. A person could go to the extreme of laying down his life in the most painful way possible, but without love it would not accomplish anything.

> Many of the ancient prophets were called to suffer martyrdom, though there is no evidence that any of them were burned to death (Dan 3:19-26; compare Heb 11:34). Though Christians were persecuted early on, there is no evidence that they were burned as martyrs as early as this Epistle was written. Nero is the first one who is believed to have committed this horrible act; and during the persecution which he incited, Christians were covered with pitch and set on fire to illuminate his gardens. It is possible that some Christians had been put to death in this manner when Paul wrote this Epistle; but it is more probable that he refers to this as the most awful kind of death, rather than as anything which had really happened. Subsequently, however, as we know, this was often done, and thousands of Christians have been martyred in the flames. [Barnes]

But do not have love, it profits me nothing = Even the extreme case of yielding all you possess, including your physical existence, if it is done without God's kind of unselfish love, there is absolutely no profit or benefit in it. In these first three verses, the apostle Paul has demonstrated the superiority of love by contrasting it with the greatest manifestation of the spiritual gifts. Even the most noble things done through the spiritual gifts are absolutely worthless if they are not accomplished in the spirit of self-sacrificing love. It is interesting to notice that love is never called a spiritual gift. In Gal 5:22 love is listed as the primary fruit of the Holy Spirit, and Christians are expected to live according to the way of love.

The Characteristics of Love (13:4-7)

In this section of the chapter, Paul is going to focus on both the positive and negative aspects of how love behaves and what love can accomplish. Because no additional description is provided, we must resort to word studies in order to learn about what Paul means in this section.

1 Cor 13:4 Love is patient, love is kind and is not jealous; love does not brag and is not arrogant,

Love = When Paul uses the word love, he is letting that word stand for the person who is motivated by God's kind of love. It would not be wrong to substitute your own name in each of these examples for the word love, because if you and I were motivated by this kind of love then our lives and actions would be characterized by each of the things described in this section of the chapter. Many of these aspects of love given in this section were in direct contrast to how the Corinthians were behaving.

Love is patient (macrothumeo) = This term means to be long-suffering, slow to anger, slow to punish. "It is that quality of self-restraint in the face of provocation which does not hastily retaliate." [Vine] This shows how a loving person should behave when he is on the receiving end of offenses.

Love is kind (chresteuomai) = It means to demonstrate grace and good nature; to act benevolently. This next quality shows us how a loving person should behave when he is on the giving end of the relationship. "A man who truly loves another will be kind to him, desirous of doing him good; will be gentle, not severe and harsh; will be courteous because he desires his happiness, and would not pain his feelings." [Barnes]

Is not jealous (zeloo) = This word means to passionately covet for oneself the things which another person possesses; to burn with envy against another person. We might call this quality "selfish passion." This kind of attitude is sometimes produced by a deep sense of personal inferiority, and the apostle Paul had addressed the issue of inferiority in chapter twelve. But the attitude produced by God's kind of love is one of contentment and joy. One man expressed it this way:

> Love does not envy others the happiness which they enjoy; it delights in their welfare; and as their happiness is increased by their endowments, their rank, their reputation, their wealth, their health, their domestic comforts, their learning, etc, those who are influenced by love rejoice in all this. To envy is to feel uneasiness or discontent at the sight of superior happiness or reputation enjoyed by another; to complain at another's prosperity; and to fret on account of his real or imagined superiority. [Barnes]

Love does not brag (perpereuomai) = This term means to boast about one's own greatness; to display oneself prominently. This kind of attitude is often produced by a sense of one's own superiority over others, and Paul had dealt with the issue of superiority in chapter twelve. Boasting expresses itself through feelings of contempt or disregard for others, but God's kind of love has just the opposite effect.

Is not arrogant (phusioo) = This word means to be inflated, puffed up with pride, haughty. This is the same term that was used previously in this letter (1 Cor 4:6, 18, 19; 5:2; 8:1), and from these references we know that this was a serious problem in the Corinthian church. In the previous phrase ("Love does not brag") Paul was describing the expression of an attitude of superiority, but here in this phrase Paul is describing the inward attitude that produces those kinds of expressions. "A man may be very proud and vain, and yet not express it in the form of boasting. That state is indicated by this word. If he gives expression to this feeling, and boasts of his endowments, that is indicated by the previous word. Love would prevent the feeling, as well as the expression of it." [Barnes]

The believers in Corinth were acting in ways that could be described as the opposite of the traits exhibited by Christian love. One writer put it this way:

> There were contentions and strifes among them; there were of course suspicions, and jealousies, and unkind judging, the imputation of improper motives, and selfishness; there were envy, and pride, and boasting, all of which were inconsistent with love; and Paul therefore evidently designed to correct these evils, and to produce a different state of things by showing them what would be produced by the exercise of love. [Barnes]

1 Cor 13:5 does not act unbecomingly; it does not seek its own, is not provoked, does not take into account a wrong suffered,

Does not act unbecomingly (aschemoneo) = This term means to act in an inappropriate or unseemly manner. This is the verb form of the same word Paul had used in 1 Cor 12:23 to describe the less presentable members of the body which we keep covered from view. Here this verb means that we are to treat others with the appropriate deference that is due to them, no matter what their position in life. And we are to behave in ways that will not offend another person's sense of decency and propriety. One writer said that love, "would lead a man to avoid profane and indecent language, improper allusions, double meanings and innuendos, coarse and vulgar expressions, because such things offend the heart of purity and decency. There is much that is indecent and unseemly in society that could be corrected by Christian love." [Barnes]

It does not seek its own (zeteo) = The word means to seek one's own interests as the primary concern. Paul used this same term when he made a similar statement in 1 Cor 10:24, "Let no one seek his own, but the good of his neighbor." There Paul explicitly stated what a man was to seek, rather than seeking after his own interests. "The expression used here is comparative, and denotes that this is not the main, the chief, the only thing which one who is under the influence of love will seek. True love of others will prompt us to seek their welfare with self-denial, personal sacrifice and toil. There is not a particle of selfishness in true love." [Barnes]

Is not provoked (paroxuno) = This term means not to be easily irritated, or goaded into anger and indignation. "The meaning of the phrase in the Greek is that a man who is under the influence of love or religion is not prone to violent anger or exasperation; it is not his character to be hasty, excited, or passionate. He is calm, serious, patient. He looks soberly at things; and though he may be injured, yet he governs his passions, restrains his temper, subdues his feelings." [Barnes]

Does not take into account a wrong suffered (logizomai) = This word means to keep a record of offenses. The term was actually an accounting or bookkeeping term, so it has the idea of keeping a detailed history or inventory of wrongs. Not to keep such a record means that we will have short memories of wrongs that were committed against us. This is impossible to accomplish without practicing true forgiveness.

1 Cor 13:6 does not rejoice in unrighteousness, but rejoices with the truth;

Does not rejoice in unrighteousness (chairo) = This word means to be glad or to take pleasure in injustice or what is wrong.

But rejoices with the truth (chairo) = This means to be glad or take pleasure in what is true and right.

> It does not rejoice in the vices but in the virtues of others. It is pleased, it rejoices when they do well. It is pleased when those who differ from us conduct themselves in any manner in such a way as to please God, and to advance their own reputation and happiness. [Barnes]

1 Cor 13:7 bears all things, believes all things, hopes all things, endures all things.

Bears all things (stego) = This Greek verb is related to the noun **stege** (roof), so the verb means to cover or protect as a roof would protect what it covers. "It keeps out resentment as the ship keeps out the water, or the roof the rain." [VWS]

> It means, that in regard to the errors and faults of others, there is a willingness to conceal or to bear with them patiently. All universal expressions of this kind demand to be limited. The meaning must be, 'as far as it can consistently or lawfully be done.' There are offenses which it is not proper or right for a man to conceal, or to allow to pass unnoticed. Such are those where the laws of the land are violated, and a man is called on to testify, etc. But the phrase here refers to private matters; and indicates a disposition not to make public or to avenge the faults committed by others. [Barnes]

Believes all things (pisteuo) = This word means to place one's trust in the fact that God is in control of all things. "It believes all that is not palpably false, all that it can with a good conscience believe to the credit of another." [VWS]

> The whole scope of the argument here requires us to understand this of the conduct of others. It cannot mean, that the man who is under the influence of love is a man of universal credulity; that he is as prone to believe a falsehood as the truth. But it must mean, that in regard to the conduct of others, there is a disposition to put the best construction on it; to believe that they may be actuated by good motives, and that they intend no injury. [Barnes]

Hopes all things (elpizo) = This means to have a confident positive expectation or anticipation of good. The implication is also that the person is trusting completely in God. This means that the person does not despair or wallow in negative expectation. "This must also refer to the conduct of others...This hope will extend to all things—to words and actions and plans; to public and to private contact. Love will do this, because it delights in the virtue and happiness of others, and will not credit anything to the contrary unless compelled to do so." [Barnes]

Endures all things (hupomeno) = Literally this means to remain under; to bear up under suffering or external circumstances that are unpleasant. "It endures without divulging to the world personal distress. So the charitable man contains himself in silence from giving vent to what selfishness would prompt under personal hardship." [VWS]

1 Cor 13:8a Love never fails

Love never fails (pipto) = Literally this word means that love never falls away; it always holds its place. Love is of permanent, lasting value throughout time and eternity. Love is an essential aspect of the character of God Himself, and it will continue to endure.

The Permanence of Love Contrasted with the Temporary Spiritual Gifts (13:8-13)

1 Cor 13:8b But if there are gifts of prophecy, they will be done away; if there are tongues, they will cease; if there is knowledge, it will be done away.

But = This contrast word sets up love on one side with prophecy, tongues, and knowledge on the other side. Here we see some important truths about the transitory nature of this group of spiritual gifts, but we must not lose sight of the main point Paul is emphasizing about the permanence of the lifestyle of Christian love.

Sixteen Descriptions of the Way of Love

What Love Does	What Love Avoids
Is patient	Is not jealous
Is kind	Does not brag
Rejoices with the truth	Is not arrogant
Bears all things	Does not act unbecomingly
Believes all things	Does not seek its own interests
Hopes all things	Is not provoked
Endures all things	Does not hold a grudge
Never fails	Does not rejoice in unrighteousness

The Gifts for Revelation and Confirmation Will Pass Away (13:8b)

Here Paul selected three gifts representing the three groupings of special confirmatory gifts that were listed in 1 Cor 12:8-10. By choosing these three gifts, he is focusing attention on their use in bringing the new revelation that was coming to the early church at the time he was writing to the Corinthians. "These were important gifts in the early church, and Paul and his readers rightly recognized them as such. No matter how significant their contribution at that time, however, the Holy Spirit predicted through Paul that some day their work was to end." [Thomas]

If there are gifts of prophecy, they will be done away (katargeo) = This word means to render inactive or inoperative; to cause something to have no further efficiency or power; to put an end to, do away with, annul, abolish. Both times this verb is used in this verse it is in the passive voice, and this indicates that the action is accomplished by something outside of the thing itself.

If there are tongues, they will cease (pauo) = This is a different verb than the one used of the gift of prophecy, and it means to cease, end, or stop. This time the verb is in the middle voice which indicates a reflexive or self-causing action. The action is somehow accomplished by the thing itself. Here Paul is saying that the spiritual gift of tongues will automatically stop or cease all by itself. By using a different verb and a different voice for that verb, Paul is showing that the spiritual gift of tongues will end in a somewhat different way than the gifts of prophecy and knowledge. Prophecy and knowledge will come to an end, but the gift of tongues will have ceased by itself probably at an even earlier time.

If there is knowledge, it will be done away (katargeo) = Here we see the same fact stated about the spiritual gift of knowledge as was given concerning the spiritual gift of prophecy. Paul's main point in this verse is that the special spiritual gifts for bringing new revelation to the early church will stop or end. These special spiritual gifts were not permanent, but they were intended by God to be temporary endowments for the benefit of the church.

It might be helpful to look at a brief history of biblical revelation. The following time line shows how God has chosen to reveal Himself to people at various times throughout history.

From left to right, this diagram pictures six historical periods of biblical revelation.

1. Face-to-face revelation in the Garden of Eden before the Fall.
2. Revelation through intermediaries during the period of the Old Testament, using the prophets of that time. Revelation from the prophets was recorded and collected as the writings we now know as the Old Testament.
3. A very long period of silence between the Old Testament and the New Testament.
4. Revelation through intermediaries again during the period of the New Testament, using the apostles and prophets of that time. This was the period of

Timeline of Biblical Revelation

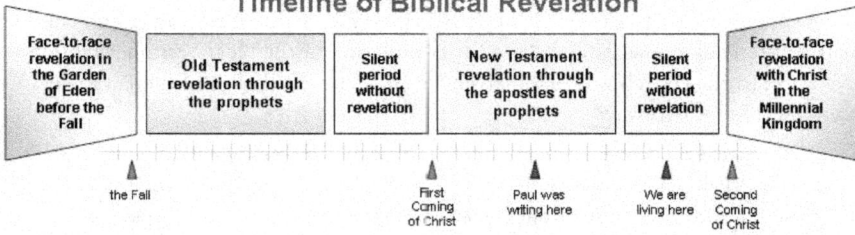

Face-to-face revelation in the Garden of Eden before the Fall	Old Testament revelation through the prophets	Silent period without revelation	New Testament revelation through the apostles and prophets	Silent period without revelation	Face-to-face revelation with Christ in the Millennial Kingdom

the Fall   First Coming of Christ   Paul was writing here   We are living here   Second Coming of Christ

time in which Paul was living, and during which he functioned as one of the channels of New Testament revelation. Revelation from this time period was recorded and collected as the writings we now know as the New Testament.

5. A very long period of silence between the New Testament and the time of Christ's return.

6. Face-to-face revelation in the Millennial kingdom when Christ will be present on earth and there will no longer be any need for intermediaries to deliver revelation.

This is how one Bible scholar expressed the situation.

Paul knew of an earlier period when God spoke directly to His prophets. That period had come to an end with the prophets Haggai, Zechariah, and Malachi, and was followed by four hundred silent years. He also knew that the close of the Old Testament canon coincided with the cessation of Old Testament prophecy. He was conscious that he was now in the midst of a new period during which God was speaking directly to His apostles and prophets, resulting in inspired utterances, part of which were taking their place alongside the Old Testament canon as inspired Scripture. One possibility he foresaw was that this period of prophecy could come to its conclusion before the second advent of Christ just as Old Testament prophecy had come to its conclusion four hundred years before the First Advent. It would come to a close with the completion of a new canon of an unknown number of writings that would result from New Testament prophecy. [Thomas]

This Group of Gifts Provides Partial or Incomplete Value (13:9)

1 Cor 13:9 For we know in part and we prophesy in part;

For we know in part (meros) = Here Paul is going to provide additional explanation for what he had just said in verse eight about the temporary nature of these three spiritual gifts. The Greek word **meros** refers to the parts that when put together will constitute the whole or entire thing. Here Paul is saying that the knowledge provided through the spiritual gift of knowledge in the early church consisted of pieces which will eventually make up the whole body of knowledge that God wants the church to have.

We prophesy in part = Paul says the same thing about the important revelations being given through the use of the spiritual gift of prophecy in the early church. At the time Paul was writing, before the completion of the New Testament, God's revelation to the church was being given "in part," here a little and there a little. One man described it this way:

> The apostle Paul describes the early period of partial, piecemeal revelation in these words. A believer endowed with the gift of prophecy stood up in the meeting in AD 57 and by direct revelation from the Spirit taught on the rapture or the judgment seat of Christ or the marriage of the Lamb or the New Jerusalem. But all this teaching was bit by bit and fragmentary. Another with the gift of knowledge would stand to his feet and discourse on the church, the body of Christ, or the gifts of the Spirit, or the believer's position in Christ. [Unger]

This is what it may have been like in the church gatherings, with God's revelation coming to the church a little at a time in partial form.

> As rich as they were through receiving direct communications from God, the apostles and prophets could lay claim only to part of all that could be known. What they understood, and incidentally what Christians today understand on the basis of their writings in the New Testament, is only a faint image of what will come following the Lord Jesus' return. In comparison with the full light yet to come, the gifts of knowledge and prophecy were mere glimpses. [Thomas]

Why is Tongues not mentioned in this list? It is probably because tongues will have dropped away separately at a previous time. "It is worth noting that only knowledge and prophecy carry over from v. 8 to vv. 9-10 since they reflect, in a way distinct from tongues, inscripturated revelation and as such they become the center of the argument being developed in vv. 9-10." [McDougall]

These gifts will be superceded at a time coming soon (13:10)

1 Cor 13:10 but when the perfect comes, the partial will be done away.

But when the perfect (telion) comes = The Greek word **telion** means perfect, complete, or mature. The question is what is being referred to by "the perfect?" Bible scholars have considered many different possibilities, the most important of which are listed below:

– The completion of the canon of the New Testament.
– The second coming of Christ.
– The perfect existence of believers during the eternal state.

Based on Paul's use of this word in his other writings as well as in the immediate context of this letter, it seems that the best choice for its meaning here is "mature." In contrast with the "partial" it does not refer to perfection in quality but to completeness in quantity. Paul is referring to a time in the future when a point of maturity would come in the life of the church, and at that point in time the spiritual gifts for providing new revelation would be rendered inactive by God. This point in time would correspond to that point in Old Testament history which began the four hundred silent years between the testaments. It was at that point in time when all of the specific revelation God desired people to have would finally have been delivered and recorded.

The partial will be done away (katargeo) = In the second half of verse eight we saw that it was the gifts of prophecy and knowledge what will be "done away," and the passive form of this same verb was used there. So here we can conclude that "the partial" is referring to the partial or sporadic revelation that was being given in the history of the early church through the use of those two spiritual gifts.

We need to carefully follow Paul's progression of thought in these verses. In this verse, Paul is not talking about the ultimate revelation when believers will see Christ face to face. Here he is talking about the partial or piecemeal content from the revelatory gifts that were available to the church at the time he was writing. He was making the point that this partial, sporadic, and unsystematized revelation given among the churches would be available in the near future at that point of maturity when the complete body of revelation would be recorded in the New Testament. One writer expressed it this way: "What this verse clearly communicates is that there would be a time at the maturation of the church when the revelatory process would cease to exist and the revelatory gifts brought to an end." [McDougall]

The Illustration of Growth Toward Maturity (13:11)

1 Cor 13:11 When I was a child, I used to speak like a child, think like a child, reason like a child; when I became a man, I did away with childish things.

So that we will not miss the point Paul had just made in verse ten, he goes on in verse eleven to illustrate this time of maturity in the church age by comparing the time in which he was living, when revelation was still being given through these special spiritual gifts, to the period of childhood in human development. When Paul was writing to the Corinthians, we might say that the church was in its childhood. But at the point when all of this new revelation would be completed and made available to the church in the New Testament, that time is compared to the time of official manhood.

From Paul's Jewish background, official manhood would happen at the age of thirteen when a boy was declared to be a man. This did not mean that there would be no further growth or development, but it simply pointed to a time when official adulthood would come, after which the church would continue to grow and develop in maturity as a result of the on-going ministry of the completed Word of God in the lives of believers We must remember that Paul is introducing the illustrations in verses eleven and twelve to support the point he had already made in verses nine and ten. So here, childhood corresponds to "the partial" of verse ten. That was the time during which Paul was living when the spiritual gifts of tongues, knowledge, and prophecy were operating.

It is interesting that those three spiritual gifts roughly correspond to the activities of childhood that Paul mentions here: speaking, thinking, and reasoning. Speaking (**laleo**) means uttering sounds using the voice. Thinking (**phroneo**) includes the aspects of feeling and desiring along with the use of the mind, while reasoning (**logizomai**) is more often used for purely intellectual or knowledge-related activities. The idea in Paul's illustration here is that there would come a time of maturity when a person's speaking, thinking, and reasoning would change into the speaking, thinking, and reasoning of an adult who then would have complete control of his fully developed faculties. In a similar way as with human development, the church would also experience a time of "coming to maturity" by having the entire body of revelation that God desired it to have during the church age.

The Ultimate Face-to-face Revelation (13:12)

1 Cor 13:12 For now we see in a mirror dimly, but then face to face; now I know in part, but then I will know fully just as I also have been fully known.

In this verse it seems that Paul's illustration is being taken to an entirely new level. What he has said up to this point about attaining the fullness of God's revelation for the church age has made him think of that even more glorious future time when we will have no further need of revelation through intermediaries, but instead we will once again have face-to-face personal interaction with God Himself. One writer expressed it this way:

> He began by referring to three revelatory gifts, prophecy, knowledge, and tongues in v. 8, as he discusses revelation being given at the time of the writing. He then narrows this to two revelatory gifts, prophecy and knowledge, in vv. 9-11 as he discusses a fuller revelation, specifically inscripturated revelation. He then narrows further to one gift, knowledge, and that in a secondary manner, in v. 12 as he moves to the ultimate revelation of Christ Himself...To him, that the process of revelation was taking place (v. 8) and that there would be a time when the revelatory process would come to an end (vv. 9-11) was a conceptual truth, but he saw that even such revelation, no matter how great, could not begin to compare with the final and full revelation when seeing Christ face to face (v. 12). [McDougall]

For now we see in a mirror dimly, but then face to face = By way of analogy, Paul is saying that our present knowledge of God is like looking at a poor reflection in a mirror. Even at the time when the New Testament writings were complete, they still only express the things of God in words which are sometimes difficult to understand. In speaking of this situation, one commentator wrote:

> We do not see the things themselves, but those things as set forth in symbols and words which imperfectly express them...The clearest revelation of the things of God in words is as an enigma when compared to sight...The word of God is a mirror wherein even now we behold the glory of the Lord, but what is that to seeing him face to face! [Hodge]

Now I know in part, but then I will know fully just as I also have been fully known = Here we see that another of the three spiritual gifts has dropped away, and we are left only with knowledge. As Paul said earlier, his knowledge of God was partial, and even after the completion of the New Testament writings, our knowledge of God is still incomplete. Our limited knowledge of God now through the writings of intermediaries, however, is nothing compared to our first-hand experience and understanding of Him at the time when we will see the Lord face to face. As one Bible scholar said: "The general drift of this verse is clear; it brings out the inadequacy of man's present knowledge in contrast with the knowledge of God that man will have in the future." [Barrett]

The Abiding Nature of Love (13:13)

1 Cor 13:13 But now faith, hope, love, abide these three; but the greatest of these is love.

But now = Paul might also have written, "Now, since these things are so." Since the spiritual gifts for revelation were to pass away, what are we left with? Paul's answer here at the end of this chapter is that faith, hope and love abide or remain.

Faith, hope, love, abide these three = "These three" form a contrast with "those three" (tongues, prophecy, and knowledge). Even after some of the special enablings of the Holy Spirit are gone, there are Christian virtues that will continue throughout the church age.

The greatest of these is love = Finally we see that the greatest of all these great Christian virtues is the lifestyle of Christian love. Love will outlast all the other virtues. One man said it this way: "Faith and hope are encompassed by love, which believes all things and hopes all things (v. 7). Because faith and hope will have no place in heaven, where everything true will be known and everything good will be possessed, they are not equal to love." [MacArthur]

Can each of us read the list of the characteristics of love and honestly substitute our own name for the word love? Could each of us in good conscience say these words? "I am patient, I am kind and I am not jealous; I do not brag and I am not arrogant, I do not act unbecomingly; I do not seek my own interests, I am not easily provoked, I do not take into account a wrong suffered, I do not rejoice in unrighteousness, but I rejoice with the truth; I bear all things, believe all things, hope all things, endure all things."

Rules for Using Spiritual Gifts in the Church

(1 Corinthians 14:1-40)

As we begin this chapter, it might be helpful to briefly review what Paul has said up to this point. You will remember that in chapter eleven Paul dealt with problems during the communion service in meetings of the local church, and then in chapter twelve he began addressing another issue which was also disrupting their church services. This important issue had to do with the use of spiritual gifts, and Paul devotes three chapters to discussing this problem. So as we come to chapter fourteen, we must remember that this is the conclusion of Paul's discussion on the misbehavior of the Corinthians in their church services.

The Rule for Determining the Value of a Spiritual Gift (14:1-5)

In this section, Paul turned his attention directly to the misuse or abuse of speaking in tongues. He proves the inferiority of tongues by comparing it with the gift of prophecy, and he lays down the criteria for determining which spiritual gifts are greater than others (see 1 Cor 12:31).

Transition from Love to Using Spiritual Gifts (14:1)

1 Cor 14:1 Pursue love, yet desire earnestly spiritual gifts, but especially that you may prophesy.

Pursue love (dioko) = This verb means to run swiftly in order to catch a person or thing. It was used to describe someone who swiftly runs in a race to reach the finish line. This fits well with Paul's earlier description of the life of Christian love being like a path or a road that must be followed (see 1 Cor 12:31). We are to live a life filled with God's kind of love, especially when we are exercising the spiritual gifts that God has given to us for the benefit of others within the church.

Yet desire earnestly spiritual gifts (zeloo) = This is the same word that Paul used in 1 Cor 12:31 when he said that the Corinthians were "earnestly desiring" the greater gifts. Here he is connecting what he said in chapter twelve with the idea of pursuing a life of Christian love from chapter thirteen. Paul begins this next section by saying, "Tenaciously follow the way of Christian love while you fervently desire to exercise your spiritual gifts."

But especially that you may prophesy = Here Paul singles out the gift of prophecy as being of greater value in some way. We know that he had already listed several of the spiritual gifts in order of importance (1 Cor 12:28). There he ranked them as follows: 1) apostle; 2) prophet; 3) teacher; 4) miracles and healings; 5) helps, administrations, and tongues. It seems as though Paul is referring back to that list here as he deals with the misuse and abuse of the gift that the Corinthians were giving top priority. Essentially they were turning Paul's order of importance upside-down. They had tongues on top instead of on the bottom, while Paul was telling them that God ranks apostleship and prophecy at the top and tongues on the bottom.

There was something wrong with the tongues that were manifested at Corinth (14:2)

1 Cor 14:2 For one who speaks in a tongue does not speak to men but to God; for no one understands, but in his spirit he speaks mysteries.

Here Paul is saying that there was something wrong with what the Corinthians were calling tongues. The purpose of the spiritual gifts was to benefit other people within the church, and to serve others by contributing to the common good of all (see 1 Cor 12:7). But the Corinthians had a misguided view of the spiritual gifts, and they were feeling either superior or inferior based on an incorrect evaluation of the gifts' importance. They valued the showier speaking gifts, especially those that drew attention to themselves because of their spectacular and mysterious manifestations.

As we discussed previously (1 Cor 12:2-3), there may even have been counterfeit spiritual gifts that mimicked what was going on in the pagan love feasts, where the participants would whip themselves into a frenzy and loudly shout out gibberish in highly emotional outbursts. As one man said, "Devotees of a god would drink and dance themselves into frenzies until they went into semi-consciousness or even unconsciousness—an experience they considered to be the highest form of communion with the divine...In the church at Corinth much of the tongues-speaking had taken on the form and flavor of those pagan ecstasies." [MacArthur]

For one who speaks in a tongue does not speak to men but to God =
The idea here is that someone who was speaking in the kind of tongues the Corinthians were practicing could only be understood by God Himself. There is an English expression that is sometimes used when you have no clue what is going on. In that situation some people might say, "God only knows!" It seems that is what Paul is saying here in relation to the type of utterances that were being manifested in the Corinthian church services. It would take a god to understand them! In fact that might be a better way to understand this sentence. One commentator wrote: "I believe a better translation, however, is 'to a god.' The Greek has no definite article, and such anarthrous constructions usually are translated with an indefinite article. The translation here of 'a god' is supported by the fact that the Bible records no instances of believers speaking to God in anything but normal, intelligible language." [MacArthur] This would also fit well with the idea that the Corinthians were imitating the pagan temple services, with their frenzied, ecstatic shouting of gibberish.

For no one understands = Here is the real issue with the kind of tongues that the Corinthians were practicing. They were unintelligible. No one could understand what was being said.

But in his spirit he speaks mysteries = The Corinthian tongues speakers were acting as if their words contained secret truths that others were not allowed to share. In behaving this way, their only concern was for the attention they would get for speaking mysteries in the spirit. They did not care whether those so-called mysteries were understandable by themselves or by anyone else. "The satisfaction many of the believers experienced in their abuse of tongues was self-satisfaction, which came from pride-induced emotion, not from spiritual edification. It was an illegitimate self-building, often building up nothing more than spiritual pride." [MacArthur]

Regarding this unintelligible manifestation of speaking in tongues, one writer said, "The necessary implication is that it could not have been miraculous, in the sense that it was the direct working of God which enabled them to speak in tongues, else God was misusing His gift. If they could speak in tongues only as God gave them to speak, then when many of them caused confusion by speaking all at one time it was really God causing the confusion by performing many miracles of speaking at one time." [Boyer] Obviously, God could not be the author of this kind of manifestation. It would violate His whole purpose for giving such a gift in the first place. This kind of manifestation could certainly not be from the Holy Spirit. The true manifestation of the gift of tongues was described in this way: "If speaking in tongues was the ability to speak a foreign language not previously learned, then it was a miraculous power which could be performed only when God enabled, and could not be performed by more than one at a time unless God did it. It is simply impossible to conceive of the misuse of a totally miraculous gift." [Boyer] So the conclusion we reach is that something was terribly wrong with the kind of tongues that the Corinthians were manifesting in their church services. Whatever those tongues were, they manifested themselves in behavior that could be used and controlled by the individual for unworthy and improper purposes.

The rule for determining the value of a spiritual gift (14:3)

1 Cor 14:3 But one who prophesies speaks to men for edification and exhortation and consolation.

But one who prophesies speaks to men = This sentence begins with a contrast. In contrast to someone who speaks unintelligible gibberish, one who speaks in prophecy can be understood by others so that they can clearly understand and learn what God wants them to know.

Edification (oikadome)= This word means building up; the act of one who promotes another's growth in Christian wisdom and holiness.

Exhortation (paraklesis) = This term means to call near for the purpose of helping; to exhort, admonish, or implore.

Consolation (paramuthia) = This word means to speak or relate a story, whether for the purpose of persuading, or of arousing to action, or of calming and consoling. From these three terms we get the well-rounded picture of what it means to speak to others in the church for their common good. Whatever is said, it must have the effect of stimulating believers to Christian growth and godly behavior. The benefit of other people in the church is always the goal of this kind of speaking.

The failure of tongues to measure up to this rule (14:4)

1 Cor 14:4 One who speaks in a tongue edifies himself; but one who prophesies edifies the church.

One who speaks in a tongue edifies himself = The tongues speaker might be excited by the things he is saying, and he might be aware that he is displaying a spectacular manifestation, but there is nothing in what he says that is having a positive impact on other people around him in the church. His spectacular display only serves the purpose of drawing attention to himself. He himself is the only one who is being built up by focusing all eyes on himself. This kind of manifestation is completely selfish and self-centered in its orientation. So the type of tongues that the Corinthians practiced had no edifying value at all for the church as a whole.

But one who prophesies edifies the church = In contrast to what was said about tongues, the one who prophesies provides a direct edifying benefit to others around him in the church. What he says serves to build others up, encourage them, help them, and support them in their growth toward Christian maturity.

The superiority of the gift of prophecy (14:5)

1 Cor 14:5 Now I wish that you all spoke in tongues, but even more that you would prophesy; and greater is one who prophesies than one who speaks in tongues, unless he interprets, so that the church may receive edifying.

Now I wish that you all spoke in tongues = Here Paul was stating something impossible for the sake of emphasis. He already wrote that not all believers could have the gift of tongues (1 Cor 12:30). As one scholar said, "Paul was simply making it clear that he did not despise the genuine gift of tongues, the true manifestation which is of God. If the Holy Spirit chose to endow every one of you with the gift of tongues, he was saying, that would be fine with me." [MacArthur]

But even more (mallon) that you would prophesy = The Greek word **mallon** means even more in a greater degree. Even if all of them could speak in other languages, Paul desired even more that they would all prophesy.

> Even more, however, Paul wished that all of the Corinthian believers would prophesy. He knew that that also was impossible, for the same reason that their all having the gift of tongues was impossible. His point was that, if they insisted on clamoring after the same gift, it would be much better if they clamored after prophecy. Not only was prophecy superior to tongues in edifying the church, but it was a longer-lasting gift, one Paul knew would continue to be used by the Lord long after tongues had ceased. [MacArthur]

Greater is one who prophesies than one who speaks in tongues = It is as if Paul is saying that if a tongues speaker is spiritually gifted, then the prophet is mega-gifted.

248

Unless he interprets, so that the church may receive edifying = The only exception or qualification to this rule is that there may be some benefit to the church if the tongues message is translated into an understandable language so that believers may get some edification from it. This is a Greek third class conditional clause, and the word "interpret" is a Greek compound word from **dia** (through) and **hermeneuo** (to explain). It means that there may be a case when the message can be translated and thoroughly explained so that everyone in the meeting would be able to understand it.

So, to summarize, in this section Paul has clearly stated the superiority of the gift of prophecy over the gift of languages, and he has laid down the rule for determining the value of a spiritual gift. Any spiritual gift is truly valuable if it is used in love for the edification of others.

The Superiority of Prophecy over Tongues in Church Services (14:6-19)

In this section, Paul is going to elaborate on the idea that prophecy is far superior to the gift of languages.

Personalizing the rule for valuing spiritual gifts (14:6)

1 Cor 14:6 But now, brethren, if I come to you speaking in tongues, what will I profit you unless I speak to you either by way of revelation or of knowledge or of prophecy or of teaching?

But now, brethren, if I come to you speaking in tongues what will I profit you = Again writing in the first person, Paul used himself as an illustration of a person who was exercising a spiritual gift, and he personalized the effect of that ministry by asking what profit or benefit they themselves would have received if he had exercised a speaking gift but used a language that they could not understand.

Unless I speak to you either by way of = The following list is placed in contrast to the kind of speaking in tongues that the Corinthians were practicing. Their tongues were unintelligible, but the things in the following list were clearly understandable ways of speaking.

Revelation (apokalupsis) = the reception of truth from God.

Knowledge (gnosis) = the practical application of God's truth.

Prophecy (propheteia) = the communication of truths that were previously unknown.

Teaching (didache) = the communication of doctrine or practical instructions.

An illustration from woodwind and stringed instruments (14:7)

1 Cor 14:7 Yet even lifeless things, either flute or harp, in producing a sound, if they do not produce a distinction in the tones, how will it be known what is played on the flute or on the harp?

Yet even lifeless things, either flute or harp, in producing a sound =
People have used musical instruments for creative expression, even though they produce no words. The sounds that are made by these instruments are intended to be pleasing and enjoyable, and this can happen only when the notes are clearly distinguishable and arranged in special sequences and combinations. A random, confused set of noises cannot be called music in any sense of the word.

If they do not produce a distinction in the tones, how will it be known what is played on the flute or on the harp = You may have heard the noises that someone makes when they are first learning to play a musical instrument. It can be sheer agony listening to someone practice the violin or the saxophone, for example. But once the person has mastered the basics of the instrument and is able to play actual pieces of music, then it is a pleasure to listen to the sounds that are made.

An illustration from brass instruments (14:8)

1 Cor 14:8 For if the bugle produces an indistinct sound, who will prepare himself for battle?

Here is a case in which the distinction of the sounds is intended to have a specific meaning. The bugle was used as a signaling device in battle, and there were special meanings or messages that were communicated by the various tunes. "The trumpet may sound the battle call, but if that call is not understood, who will heed it? So the speaker with tongues may announce the most important truths, he may unfold mysteries, or pour forth praises as from a harp of gold, but what does it profit those who do not understand him?" [Hodge]

The application of these illustrations to human language (14:9)

1 Cor 14:9 So also you, unless you utter by the tongue speech that is clear, how will it be known what is spoken? For you will be speaking into the air.

So also you, unless you utter by the tongue speech that is clear (eusemos) =
This word means clear, distinct, and easy to understand.

> It is plain from what follows, as well as from the drift of the whole discourse, that the simple point of the analogy is that as we cannot know what is piped or harped, or be benefited by it unless we can discriminate the sounds emitted, so we cannot be benefited by listening to one who speaks a language which we do not understand. It is not the nature of the gift but the folly of the use made of it which is the point which the apostle has in view. [Hodge]

How will it be known what is spoken? For you will be speaking into the air =
This is a proverbial saying that means their efforts are having absolutely no effect. "The difficulty is not in the language used, but in the ignorance of the hearer." [Hodge]

There is no such thing as a meaningless language (14:10)

1 Cor 14:10 There are, perhaps, a great many kinds of languages in the world, and no kind is without meaning.

This is a very important verse for understanding what the gift of tongues or languages really was.

There are, perhaps, a great many kinds of languages in the world = The simple meaning of this phrase is that there are many languages in the world. In fact, there are so many languages that no one man could possibly know all of them.

No kind is without meaning = The main point of this verse is expressed in this phrase. Stated positively Paul's point is that every language has meaning. Language is intended to clearly communicate thoughts and ideas between human beings who have a common understanding of that language. There is no language that was ever intended NOT to communicate meaning between people. This truth rules out the idea that there are valid languages which use only meaningless gibberish. That type of language does not exist. It would violate the very definition of a language. This verse also implies that the kind of tongues being practiced by the Corinthians was a violation of this principle. They were pouring out meaningless gibberish, rather than speaking in a human language which would have meaning to a listener who knew that language.

Lack of common understanding divides people (14:11)

1 Cor 14:11 If then I do not know the meaning of the language, I will be to the one who speaks a barbarian, and the one who speaks will be a barbarian to me.

If then I do not know the meaning of the language = Notice how Paul keeps returning to the idea of communicating understandable meanings to other people. Here again he used the first person, holding himself up as an example of what he was talking about.

I will be to the one who speaks a barbarian, and the one who speaks will be a barbarian to me = This is the practical effect of people's inability to understand each other. "The Egyptians called anyone barbarous who did not speak their tongue. The Greeks followed suit for all ignorant of Greek language and culture. They divided mankind into Hellenes and Barbarians." [RWP] The point here is that a lack of common understanding becomes a barrier that divides people, rather than uniting and educating them. One commentator summarized what Paul was saying this way:

> Therefore, that is, because the sounds uttered are significant, because the man does not make a mere senseless noise but speaks a real language, therefore, if I do not know the meaning of the language, I stand in the relation of a foreigner to him and he to me...If a man utters incoherent, inarticulate sounds which no man living could understand, that would not make him a foreigner. It might prove him to be deranged, but not a foreigner. [Hodge]

Applying this truth about human language to speaking gifts (14:12)

1 Cor 14:12 So also you, since you are zealous of spiritual gifts, seek to abound for the edification of the church.

So also you, since you are zealous of spiritual gifts = This connects back to what Paul had said in 1 Cor 12:31 and 14:1 about their desire for spiritual gifts.

Seek to abound for the edification of the church = Here Paul reminds them of the true purpose of spiritual gifts which are to be used in service for the benefit of others.

The requirement for interpretation of the gift of tongues (14:13-19)

1 Cor 14:13 Therefore let one who speaks in a tongue pray that he may interpret.

Therefore = As a result of what Paul had just said, he now gives the rules or requirements for using the gift of tongues in a church service. The tongues speaker must ask God for the ability to clearly explain the truths he is communicating. It is a requirement that every message must be clearly understandable to those who hear it.

1 Cor 14:14 For if I pray in a tongue, my spirit prays, but my mind is unfruitful.

For if I pray in a tongue = Here Paul gives the reason why the tongues speaker should pray for the gift of interpretation. Once again he used himself as the subject for the purpose of illustration. "The reference to prayer here, and to singing in 1 Cor 14:15, is designed to illustrate that public worship should be conducted in a language that would be intelligible to the people. However well meant it might be, or however the heart might be engaged in it, yet unless it was intelligible and the understanding could join in it, it would be vain and profitless." [Barnes]

My spirit prays, but my mind is unfruitful = The word "mind" (nous) is a general term for all the activities of perceiving, understanding, judging, determining, and feeling. To be unfruitful means to be barren or unproductive. Paul is saying, "My mind does not receive or produce any benefit, either to myself or to others who are listening." This is a very interesting description of the tongues that were being practiced in the Corinthian church. Since there was no understanding, there was no benefit from them.

1 Cor 14:15 What is the outcome then? I will pray with the spirit and I will pray with the mind also; I will sing with the spirit and I will sing with the mind also.

I will pray with the spirit and I will pray (proseuchomai) with the mind also = This word is the most frequent word for prayer and is only used of prayer to God. It could include the broader idea of worship as well.

I will sing with the spirit and I will sing (psallo) with the mind also = This word means to sing psalms or to celebrate the praises of God in music. So here we see that the activities of worship (prayer and singing) must involve an intelligent exercise of the mind. As one commentator put it, "Paul prefers singing that reaches the intellect as well as stirs the emotions. Solos that people do not understand lose their value in church worship." [RWP] If you want to commune with God, you must make certain that your mind is engaged.

1 Cor 14:16 Otherwise if you bless in the spirit only, how will the one who fills the place of the ungifted say the "Amen" at your giving of thanks, since he does not know what you are saying?

How will the one who fills the place of the ungifted say the "Amen" at your giving of thanks = Here we see that Paul clearly has the public gatherings of the church in view. He is saying that if you speak, pray, sing, or worship in a language that no one understands, how will they be able to agree with your message of praise to God? AMEN is the traditional expression of agreement with something that was said.

He does not know what you are saying = Here is the crux of the problem. Everything that is said in the public gatherings of the church must be understandable. If other believers do not know what you are saying, then that utterance has no place in the public gatherings of the church.

1 Cor 14:17 For you are giving thanks well enough, but the other person is not edified.

You are giving thanks well enough = Paul affirms that the spiritual gift of tongues is a legitimate gift and that it can be used in appropriate ways. Giving thanks **(eucharisteo)** means to express gratitude, especially to God, and Paul is saying that it might be possible to praise and thank God in languages the person had not studied. The tongues speaker may indeed be uttering a message of thanks, BUT...

But the other person is not edified = The problem is that those who are hearing this message cannot understand it and so they are not built up in their faith. Here edification is stated as the primary purpose of the gifts that are to be used in the church services. By implication, if believers are not edified, then that gift is not appropriate for use in church.

1 Cor 14:18 I thank God, I speak in tongues more than you all;

This proves that Paul was not devaluing or despising the legitimate spiritual gift of tongues. He was grateful to God that he had been gifted in this way and could legitimately use that gift to fulfill its primary purpose. HOWEVER...

1 Cor 14:19 however, in the church I desire to speak five words with my mind so that I may instruct others also, rather than ten thousand words in a tongue.

In the church = Here again we see that Paul is focusing on the use of these gifts in the services of the church. He is saying that the church services are not the place even for the appropriate use of the gift of languages.

I desire to speak five words with my mind so that I may instruct others also, rather than ten thousand words in a tongue = Five understandable words are worth more than ten thousand unintelligible words. Literally in the Greek text this clause reads: "In an assembly I want five words with the mind of me to speak, for the purpose that others I may instruct." This provides a clear purpose statement for the public gatherings of believers. The goal that must be accomplished in church services is the instruction or edification of believers.

In this section we saw the apostle Paul prove the superiority of prophecy over tongues for use in the services of the church. Prophecy was a spiritual gift which functioned to communicate God's truths to believers in ways they could understand and apply to their lives. Since tongues did nothing of the kind, it actually failed to qualify as a valuable spiritual gift for use in the church.

The Superiority of Prophecy over Tongues even for Unbelievers (14:20-25)

In this section Paul will describe the legitimate purpose for the gift of tongues, but he will show that even in that capacity tongues are inferior to prophecy.

1 Cor 14:20 Brethren, do not be children in your thinking; yet in evil be infants, but in your thinking be mature.

Brethren, do not be children in your thinking = In 1 Cor 3:1 Paul said he could not speak to the Corinthians as spiritual men, but as men of flesh, as mere infants in Christ. Here Paul is pointing out that they continued to have a childish attraction for things that were amusing or spectacular. "This church which prided itself on its wisdom and intellectual enlightenment, was in the matter of tongues, showing a childish fascination for a gift which appealed to their love for personal display, rather than their love for the benefit of the church." [Boyer]

Yet in evil be infants, but in your thinking be mature = Almost as an afterthought here, Paul thinks of one area in which it is okay to be mere infants, and that is in regard to their understanding of and participation in evil. But in all other areas, they are to continue to add to their knowledge.

1 Cor 14:21 In the Law it is written, "BY MEN OF STRANGE TONGUES AND BY THE LIPS OF STRANGERS I WILL SPEAK TO THIS PEOPLE, AND EVEN SO THEY WILL NOT LISTEN TO ME," says the Lord.

Here Paul focuses on the type of tongues that the Corinthians were manifesting in their church services. He gives a quote that is loosely translated from Isaiah 28:11-12 which points to an event in the history of his people Israel. In this quote it is as if God were saying, "Israel refused to listen to me even though I spoke to them in their own language, so now I will speak to them in a strange foreign language, namely, the language of the enemy I will send against them in judgment. But even then they will still not listen to Me!" One thing we can see from this Old Testament quote is that the tongues described there were actual foreign languages. They were not simply gibberish, but they were real human languages that had meaning to those who spoke them.

From this example in the history of Israel, we clearly see that it is not a positive thing to have someone speak to you in a language that you cannot understand. One writer explained Paul's use of this passage by saying, "The point of the quotation is that speech in strange tongues was a chastisement for the unbelief of God's ancient people, by which they were made to hear His voice speaking in the harsh commands of the foreign invader. So in the Corinthian church, the intelligible revelation of God has not been properly received." [VWS] Taken this way, Paul may be saying that the power of speaking foreign languages does not necessarily guarantee obedience to God's Word. "The Corinthians tend to shut their ears to prophecy because they gain more satisfaction from listening to tongues than from hearing their faults exposed and their duties pointed out in plain rational language." [Barrett]

1 Cor 14:22 So then tongues are for a sign, not to those who believe but to unbelievers; but prophecy is for a sign, not to unbelievers but to those who believe.

So then tongues are for a sign, not to those who believe but to unbelievers = This presents the logical conclusion from all that Paul has said about tongues so far. The truth was that tongues were to serve as a sign, specifically to unbelievers rather than to believers. It was unbelievers that might benefit from some type of miraculous sign which drew attention to the fact that God Himself was involved in this message.

> Those who had already converted to Christianity were not the target of these signs, for they needed no proof of the message's divine source. They were already convinced of the veracity of the message. Yet, the Corinthians insisted on giving major attention to one particular sign gift in their public meetings. That was wrong; it was immaturity on their part (cf. v. 20). The mature mind realized the proper place for tongues was among unbelievers to play a confirmatory part in their conversion experience. [Thomas]

But prophecy is for a sign, not to unbelievers but to those who believe = By way of contrast, the spiritual gift of prophecy is not primarily for unbelievers but for believers, and Paul has already said that prophecy is to be used for the edification of believers in the services of the church.

1 Cor 14:23 Therefore if the whole church assembles together and all speak in tongues, and ungifted men or unbelievers enter, will they not say that you are mad?

This is a Greek third class conditional clause which assumes that the statement is only somewhat possible. When the church assembles together it is remotely possible that an unbeliever might enter the service. One of the truths that we should not miss in this verse is that the assembly of the church is to be focused on edifying believers. It is not to be focused on attracting unbelievers into the services for the purpose of evangelizing them and winning them to Christ. In other words, the presence of unbelievers in a church service is incidental. In the unlikely event that an unbeliever were to attend a church service, here is how they would respond to the type of tongues that the Corinthians were manifesting.

Will they not say that you are mad? = This is exactly what happened on the day that the very first use of the spiritual gift of tongues was manifested (see Acts 2:13). The initial response of those who did not understand the foreign languages was to say that the disciples were talking like drunken or insane men. But the tongues were effective in grabbing the attention of the multitude, especially of those whose language was being spoken by the disciples. And immediately after the tongues speaking event, the apostle Peter stood up and addressed the crowd with a clear gospel presentation. The authenticating event of speaking in tongues was followed by the clear communication of the gospel. The effect of prophecy in the life of an unbeliever is the next topic that Paul deals with in the following two verses.

1 Cor 14:24-25 But if all prophesy, and an unbeliever or an ungifted man enters, he is convicted by all, he is called to account by all; the secrets of his heart are disclosed; and so he will fall on his face and worship God, declaring that God is certainly among you.

But if all prophesy, and an unbeliever or an ungifted man enters = Paul is taking the same unlikely case of an unbeliever entering the church services, but this time instead of hearing the confusing noise of many different languages, suppose he were to hear someone speaking understandable and piercing words from God. What would be the result then?

He is convicted by all (elengcho) = This word means to bring to light; to bring conviction, generally with a suggestion of shame in the person convicted. It is quite possible in this case that the unbeliever would be convicted of his sins, and would repent and turn to God for salvation.

He is called to account by all (anakrino) = This term means to examine or probe, such as occurred during cross-examination in a courtroom. "The word implies inquiry rather than sentence. Each inspired speaker shall utter words which shall reveal the hearer to himself." [VWS]

The secrets of his heart are disclosed (phaneros) = This means brought to light or made apparent for all to see. He sees his own inner character brought out into the open. As one man said, "This describes the proper and common effect of truth, when it is applied by a man's own conscience." [Barnes]

He will fall on his face and worship God, declaring that God is certainly among you = The word worship (**proskuneo**) means to do homage or declare one's obedience to something. Paul is saying that even if an unbeliever were to come into the services of the church, the gift of prophecy could have this kind of positive effect on his life, even to the point of turning an unbeliever into a believer. So in this section we can see the relative effectiveness of the gifts of tongues and prophecy in the life of an unbeliever who might happen to be in the services of the church.

Instructions for Regulating the Gifts in the Church (14:26-40)

A description of the current situation in Corinth (14:26)

1 Cor 14:26 What is the outcome then, brethren? When you assemble, each one has a psalm, has a teaching, has a revelation, has a tongue, has an interpretation. Let all things be done for edification.

What is the outcome then, brethren? = Literally this says, "How is it, then?" We could state it this way: "What is the condition of things among you?" or "How are you conducting yourselves, then?"

When you assemble, each one = Notice here what Paul does not say. He does not say, "When a properly functioning church gathers together, each one has a psalm, has a teaching, has a revelation, has a tongue, has an interpretation." Instead he says, "When you Corinthians assemble for your church services, each one has a psalm, has a teaching, has a revelation, has a tongue, has an interpretation." This verse is really a description of the main problem in the Corinthian church. When they gathered together, it seemed as if every individual would clamor for a speaking part in the service.

Many Christians take this passage as an example of the typical life of the early church, and they often assume that this example is normative for the church today. In other words, they believe this verse contains a statement of how church meetings should be conducted today. But this passage is not prescriptive as much as it is descriptive. This really is a description by the apostle Paul of the incorrect conduct of the church meetings in Corinth, and he is about to put strict regulations in place to fix the problems he describes in this verse. So churches today should not try to emulate the practices of the Corinthian church. Church meetings today should be centered around the teaching of the Word of God, the completed text of the Bible, which was not yet available to the Corinthians. We need to remember that the Bible was still being written at the time Paul was addressing the Corinthians, and the special spiritual gifts were still operating which authenticated the new revelation being given at that time. Now, however, those gifts are not required and new revelation is not required. We now have the completed text of the Word of God available to us, and today the church must focus on explaining and teaching and applying the Scriptures to the lives of believers today.

Psalm (psalmos) = This was a song of praise to God, and was probably an impromptu composition in which someone was prompted to sing or chant words of praise to God.

Teaching (didache) = This word identifies a teaching or instruction; the presentation of a doctrine or truth about God or about the Christian life.

Revelation (apokalupsis) = This term means a disclosure of truth, especially a truth that had been previously unknown.

Tongue (glossa) = This word identifies the spiritual gift of tongues that has been in view throughout this section of Paul's letter. It was a message presented in a foreign language that may not have been previously known to the speaker, and typically it accompanied and confirmed the authenticity of a truth that was being presented in a known language.

Interpretation (hermeneia) = This word meant the interpretation or explanation of something that had already been presented to people, but for which more explanation was needed so they could have a clear understanding.

The problem in the church at Corinth was that, whether they had a psalm, a teaching, a revelation, a tongue, or an interpretation, each of the members wanted to participate at the same time, including both the men and the women. As one man said, "They were not interested in serving, or learning, or edifying, but only in self-expression and self-display. Everyone vied for attention and preeminence." [MacArthur] Another commentator put it this way:

> On any given occasion these Christians arrived for worship with a predetermination to have a speaking part on the program for the day. It may have been something prepared in advance, as in the case of a teaching or something improvised on the spur of the moment, such as a tongue. Whether it was something given through an advance working of the Spirit or a product of His simultaneous working, each spokesman appeared with the eager purpose of exercising his own gift. The inevitable consequence was a display of competition and rivalry in the church meeting...The picture emerging in the present verse is one of selfishness and self-assertion. In such an atmosphere the inherent value of any spiritual gift disappeared. [Thomas]

One of the additional issues with this type of church meeting is that both the men and the women would equally participate in these outbursts. It seems that in the Corinthian church there was a tendency to give men and women equal status when taking the lead in these types of manifestations. One writer said, "At Corinth there was a disposition to put men and women on an equal footing in public speaking and church leadership." [Expositors] In some of the following verses the apostle Paul is going to address the issue of male and female roles for directing the services of the church (1 Cor 14:34-35).

Let all things be done for edification (oikodome) = Here is the guiding principle for everything that is done in the meetings of the local church. Every activity must be done with the goal of edifying the believers who are present at the service. To edify means to build up or to promote another person's growth in Christian wisdom, knowledge, contentment, and holiness. As we saw earlier in chapter fourteen, this can only be accomplished if believers' minds are engaged along with their spirits. Believers need to be able to hear and clearly understand what is being said, and they need to process or think about the message with the ultimate goal of applying that message to their own lives. This becomes almost impossible in an environment where every person is speaking or chattering or singing all at the same time.

Regulating the Use of Tongues (14:27-28)

1 Cor 14:27 If anyone speaks in a tongue, it should be by two or at the most three, and each in turn, and one must interpret;

In the next two verses Paul begins by giving rules or restrictions for the use of the spiritual gift of tongues, which was one of the gifts that the Corinthians were especially fond of using.

If anyone speaks in a tongue, it should be by two or at the most three = First Paul puts limits on the number of tongues speakers that may participate in a church service. Paul is not requiring that anyone must speak in tongues at their meetings, but he is saying that if any of the members do speak in a tongue the church should only allow one or two to speak, and the most that could be allowed to speak in a tongue would be three people.

Each in turn = Next Paul puts a limit on how the two or three tongues speakers may present their message. They must give their message in sequence, each waiting for the previous speaker to finish before he can begin. There was never a time when two or more people were allowed to address the congregation at the same time. One writer said,

> One of the strongest indictments of the modern charismatic movement is the common practice of many persons speaking, praying, and singing at the same time, with no one paying attention to what others are doing or saying. It is everyone for himself, just as it was in Corinth, and it is in clear violation of Paul's command that each speak in turn. [MacArthur]

And one must interpret = Finally Paul limits the tongues speakers regarding the interpretation of their message. Before a tongues speaker can open his mouth, he must be certain that there is someone else present in the meeting who has agreed to give the proper interpretation of the tongues message. This would require quite a bit of planning and coordination before the tongues speaker is even allowed to begin. The presence of the interpreter would ensure that everyone could clearly understand the message that was being presented, because without clear mental understanding there could be no edification in the life of each believer. It was only with proper interpretation that tongues could have a possibility of providing edification.

1 Cor 14:28 but if there is no interpreter, he must keep silent in the church; and let him speak to himself and to God.

But if there is no interpreter, he must keep silent in the church = Here Paul presents the case where no interpreter could be found for the tongues messages. If that were the situation, then the tongues speaker must keep silent during the church meeting. He was not allowed to exercise his gift, because there could be no possibility of edification. As we saw in 1 Cor 12:8-10 in Paul's list of the speaking gifts, the gift of interpretation was the controlling gift for the gift of tongues. Here Paul clearly states that if an interpreter is not present, the gift of tongues cannot be used.

This verse proves that a person with the gift of tongues was able to remain in complete control of himself at all times. As one writer expressed it, "His tongues gift did not compel him to speak on every occasion. It was within the realm of human choice to refrain from utilizing this gift or any other gift, particularly so if considerations of love and edification required non-participation." [Thomas]

Let him speak to himself and to God = If no interpreter can be found, the tongues speaker should commune silently with God. "This required the tongues speaker to meditate quietly on what his own mind could grasp of the tongues message that he might otherwise have given publicly, thereby deriving for himself whatever edifying benefit he could. 'Speaking to oneself and to God' was a proverbial expression for meditation. The guideline calls upon the tongues speaker to engage in such a contemplative activity rather than speak up in the absence of an interpreter, which would have no benefit for anyone else in the audience." [Thomas] These regulations on the use of the gift of tongues would ensure that if a tongue were spoken it would have the best chance of edifying those who were present in the church meeting.

Regulating the Use of Prophecy (14:29-33)

1 Cor 14:29 Let two or three prophets speak, and let the others pass judgment.

Let two or three prophets speak = Here Paul puts the same numerical limits on the gift of prophecy as with the gift of tongues. Only two or three prophets were allowed to speak during any meeting of the local church. So far Paul had only spoken in praise of the gift of prophecy, but here he shows that, just like any other gift, prophecy also must be regulated and kept under control in order to ensure that people were edified.

Let the others pass judgment (diakrino) = This is the verb form of the same term that Paul used in describing the second set of speaking gifts in 1 Cor 12:8-10. There we saw that the last gift in each set was given as a way to verify that the other gifts in each set were being used correctly, and the gift of distinguishing spirits was the controlling gift for the spiritual gift of prophecy. Not only believers with the gift of discernment, but all believers attending the services of the church have a duty to carefully examine what is being said and to determine if it is the truth. One commentator explained it this way:

> It was possible that those who claimed to be prophets might err, and it was the duty of all to examine whether that which was uttered was in accordance with truth. And if this was a duty then, it is a duty now; if it was proper even when the teachers claimed to be under divine inspiration, it is much more the duty of the people now. No minister of religion has a right to demand that all that he speaks shall be regarded as truth. No minister who has just views of his office, and a proper acquaintance with the truth and confidence in it, would desire to prohibit the people from the most full and free examination of all that he utters. [Barnes]

1 Cor 14:30 But if a revelation is made to another who is seated, the first one must keep silent.

But if a revelation is made to another who is seated = This gives the case where a second teacher was also given something to say in the assembly. In this case, here is what should be done.

The first one must keep silent = Once the first speaker had concluded his message, he was to remain silent while the second person was allowed to speak. This does not mean that the first speaker was to be abruptly cut off in mid-sentence. As one writer said, "It does not follow, however, that he was to be rudely interrupted. He might close his discourse deliberately, or perhaps by an intimation from the person to whom the revelation was made." [Barnes] But sometimes it was the most loving thing to do for a prophet to stop speaking and let another person have his turn. Here as with the gift of tongues, not even the prophets were allowed to talk all at the same time. Everyone who exercised a speaking gift in the church services was to do it one at a time so that every message could be understood, evaluated, and applied.

1 Cor 14:31 For you can all prophesy one by one, so that all may learn and all may be exhorted;

For you can all prophesy one by one = Within the limits of two or three prophets that were allowed to speak in any one church gathering, they were all permitted to exercise their gift one by one. They would all be given an opportunity to share God's message, but not in a way which might cause disorder and chaos.

So that all may learn and all may be exhorted = This is a purpose clause, and it gives the reason why all must speak in turn. It is so that everyone who is present may learn and be exhorted or edified.

1 Cor 14:32 and the spirits of prophets are subject to prophets;

This is a very important verse regarding the gift of prophecy, and it applies to all of the Spirit-prompted speaking gifts that Paul has listed so far. These gifts were not irrational or uncontrollable compulsions, like fits or convulsions that overwhelm and take control of a person. The spiritual gifts are given by the Holy Spirit, but they are under the control of the human recipient. Each gifted person is able to exercise self-control even over the supernatural gifts bestowed by the Spirit. One commentator expressed it this way:

> This verse gives confirmation to the supposition that the extraordinary endowments of the Holy Spirit were subjected to substantially the same laws as a man's natural endowments. They were conferred by the Holy Spirit; but they were conferred on free agents and did not interfere with their free agency. And as a man, though of the most splendid talents and commanding eloquence, has control over his own mind and is not compelled to speak, so it was with those who are here called prophets. [Barnes]

Evidently, this was not what was happening in the Corinthian church services. As was previously mentioned, they were probably imitating the pagan temple services more than behaving as Paul described in this verse. "In the pagan world, the priests and priestesses supposed or pretended that they were under an influence which was uncontrollable, which took away their powers of self-command, and which made them the mere organs or unconscious instruments of the gods. The Scripture account of inspiration is, however, a very different thing." [Barnes]

1 Cor 14:33 for God is not a God of confusion but of peace, as in all the churches of the saints.

For God is not a God of confusion but of peace = This verse gives the reason why the spirits of the prophets are subject to the prophets. It is because those spiritual inspirations come from God, and God Himself is not the author of confusion. "He is the God of peace; and his religion will tend to promote order. It is calm, peaceful, and thoughtful. It is not boisterous and disorderly." [Barnes]

As in all the churches of the saints = This phrase does not seem to belong with what has just been said as much as it belongs with what follows. In the original text of the New Testament the Greek words were listed sequentially without paragraph or punctuation marks. Verse thirty-three already has an appropriate conclusion, and the addition of this phrase at the end does not enhance it. But if we connect this phrase with the following verse, then it is parallel to what Paul already expressed in 1 Cor 11:16 where the customary practices of all the churches were authoritative when it comes to the behavior of the women in church services. In that previous section, the apostle Paul seemed to indicate that women might receive and exercise the spiritual gift of prophecy (1 Cor 11:5), so here in this next section Paul will specifically deal with the issue of women exercising their speaking gifts within the public service of the church.

Regulating the Outspoken Women in the Church Services (14:34-35)

1 Cor 14:34 The women are to keep silent in the churches; for they are not permitted to speak, but are to subject themselves, just as the Law also says.

The women are to keep silent in the churches = First, notice the definite article before "women." This identifies a specific group of women. If this were not the case and Paul wanted to refer to all women in general, then the definite article would not be required.

For they are not permitted to speak (laleo) = The verb "to speak" is a very general term in Greek, and it is used over 300 times in the New Testament. It can have a variety of implications depending upon the context in which it is used. It can mean "to make a sound, to talk, to question, to argue, to chatter, to protest." Some commentators have assumed that in this verse "to speak" means that women are not permitted to make a sound or talk in any way. But if we look at the context in First Corinthians we see that of the 34 times this term is used, 28 times Paul used this word to indicate someone who was speaking "by the Spirit," and specifically someone who was speaking a prophecy (2 times) or speaking in tongues (22 times). In the immediate context, we see that this Greek word is used almost exclusively to indicate speaking in tongues. One writer said it this way: "The context here suggests strongly that this prohibition applies specifically and only to speaking in tongues." [Boyer] So from the context we can be certain the apostle Paul means that women are not permitted to exercise speaking gifts which take on the character of leadership in the services of the church.

But are to subject themselves, just as the Law also says = The main contrast in this sentence is between the exercise of a speaking gift vs. being under proper authority within the church service. What Paul is communicating here has to do with specific gifted women who were speaking out authoritatively in the meetings of the Corinthian church. They were putting themselves in the role of spiritual authorities based on the perceived importance of their speaking gifts, which may or may not have even been genuine. As one commentator said, "Paul is thinking of church teaching and authoritative direction as a role unfit for women." [Expositors]

What Paul is saying here corresponds to what he had said previously in chapter eleven of this letter to the Corinthians. There is a God-ordained hierarchy of authority that is built into God's created order, and it is pictured by Paul as a chain of authority and subordination beginning with God the Father and extending down to Christ, Man, and Woman. As we noted in chapter eleven, Paul specifically stated, "The man is the head of a woman." We saw that a man is in authority over a woman in two specific situations within the context of church meetings.

1. If the man is one of the church officers who has authority and responsibility for the spiritual well-being of all the men and women that are present (1 Thess 5:12-13; Heb 13:17; 1 Pet 5:2-3); or
2. If the man is the husband of the woman and has authority and responsibility for her well-being in every area (Eph 5:22-28; 1 Pet 3:7).

One commentator described the situation in Corinth this way:

Undoubtedly there were arguments in those meetings, and women were taking a very definite part in those arguments, questioning, protesting, trying to show their ability and their freedom, and doing it in an improper way, and creating confusion where there should have been peace and quietness...Evidently there were women in Corinth given to careless and contentious talk, and that is what Paul was prohibiting. [Morgan]

But even beyond that, the apostle Paul was regulating the leadership of the local church gatherings. Another writer said that Paul, "had discussed speaking in foreign languages and prophecy; and the evident sense is that in regard to these things they were to keep silence or were not to engage in them. These things constituted the business of the public teaching; and in this the female part of the congregation were to be silent. They were not to teach the people, nor were they to interrupt those who were speaking. It is probable that, on pretense of being inspired, the women had assumed the office of public teachers." [Barnes]

We need to understand that Paul is not denying women the appropriate use of their legitimate spiritual gifts. He is simply regulating the way that the services of the local church are to be directed. One writer said, "He is not denying women the use of their speaking gifts (cf. Acts 21:9), but he is saying they should use them in circumstances other than meetings of the whole local assembly...For a speaker to address an audience was tantamount to his or her assuming authority over those who listened." [Thomas] That type of leadership role was contrary to God's plan for the direction of the local church (see 1 Tim 2:11-12).

1 Cor 14:35 If they desire to learn anything, let them ask their own husbands at home; for it is improper for a woman to speak in church.

Some of the Corinthian women might try to avoid the rule in the previous verse by simply asking questions in the public church services. Here Paul says that the women are not even to do that, and this rule may have been necessary because even the act of asking a question can be a means of directing a conversation. This verse closes that loophole for the more forward or ambitious women in the Corinthian church. One commentator explained that, "This restriction presupposes that occasionally a simple question or the manner in which it is phrased may sow seeds of dissension and undercut the speaker's authority. To avoid this danger, she should limit such questioning to the privacy of the home." [Thomas]

If they desire to learn anything = The desire to learn is not what is being regulated in this verse. A woman's desire to learn should be encouraged and fostered, just as should a man's desire to learn. But women are free to learn without having to exercise speaking gifts in the public worship service of the church.

Let them ask their own husbands at home = The home is a setting where every family member is able to interact freely and discuss any issues that arise in the public service of the church. This also implies that one of the duties of every husband is to help answer questions and to be willing to discuss biblical issues as they relate to the lives of his family members. The husband does not need to know everything or be an expert on everything, but he must be willing to ask and learn and discuss. Some people may wonder how these verses apply to the unmarried women of the church. The words used for man and woman are general terms that can mean husband and wife or simply adult men and women. The unmarried women or widows can ask the other men in their lives, such as fathers, brothers, or the elders of the church in a more informal setting.

For it is improper for a woman to speak in church = Here Paul is simply restating what he had previously said, that in the public services of the church the leadership roles for the edification of the congregation belonged to the mature Christian men of the church. That does not mean, however, that women have no outlet for their speaking gifts. One commentator has said, "The assembly is made up of males and females, of old and young, and there it is improper for the women to take part in conducting the exercises. But this cannot be interpreted as meaning that it is improper for females to speak or to pray in meetings of their own sex, assembled for prayer or for benevolence; nor that it is improper for a female to speak or to pray in a small group setting outside of the formal church service." [Barnes]

Before we leave this section we should remember that Paul is not denying women the use of their legitimate speaking gifts. He is simply saying that the proper place is not during the public services of the local church. One man put it this way:

> The requirements for female Christians in verse 34 are stringent. Many a woman in her zeal to contribute to the work of the Lord has sensed a strong compulsion to speak up in a Christian worship service where she felt she could make a definite contribution. Many sisters in Christ have been and are well-taught biblically and are quite capable of communicating their learning to those around them. It is doubtless their responsibility to do this very thing, but in the proper setting. A service where the whole church meets is not that proper setting, according to 1 Cor 14:35. In the wisdom of God, that is not orderly procedure. The order of creation (Gen 1-2) and consequences of the Fall (Gen 3) establish a divine mandate for conduct in the Christian assembly: only the male members are to engage in leading the service. In the interests of love and becoming conduct (1 Cor 13:5), women are to refrain from speaking. [Thomas]

Ensuring that the Corinthians have the right attitude about his instruction (14:36-38)

1 Cor 14:36 Was it from you that the word of God first went forth? Or has it come to you only?

This thought seems connected to 1 Cor 14:33, "As in all the churches of the saints," or even farther back to 1 Cor 11:13. "But if one is inclined to be contentious, we have no other practice, nor have the churches of God." The Corinthians were acting as if they were the first or the only church that mattered, but Paul is pointing out that there are other more mature churches from which Corinth should take its pattern. One writer paraphrased Paul's comments this way:

> Is the church at Corinth the mother church? Was it first established or has it been alone in sending forth the Word of God? You have adopted customs which are unusual. You have permitted women to speak in a manner unknown to other churches. You have admitted irregularity and confusion unknown in all the others. You have allowed many to speak at the same time, and have tolerated confusion and disorder. Have you any right thus to differ from others? Have you any authority, as it were, to dictate to them, to allow these disorders? Should you not rather be conformed to them, and observe the rules of the churches which are older than yours? [Barnes]

1 Cor 14:37 If anyone thinks he is a prophet or spiritual, let him recognize that the things which I write to you are the Lord's commandment.

If anyone thinks he is a prophet or spiritual = If a person regards himself as a prophet who is being led by God's Spirit and who understands God's truth, then he should have no trouble recognizing a true message when he sees one.

Let him recognize that the things which I write to you are the Lord's commandment = A truly spiritual person will be able to see that what Paul writes is truly from the Lord. Here Paul is asserting the authority of God behind his words. He is claiming divine inspiration for the commands he is giving.

1 Cor 14:38 But if anyone does not recognize this, he is not recognized.

If someone claims to be a spiritual person but cannot recognize the truth of what Paul is saying, then he really is not a spiritual person at all, and he should not be acknowledged as a spiritual person.

Summary concerning the use of Prophecy and Tongues (14:39-40)

1 Cor 14:39 Therefore, my brethren, desire earnestly to prophesy, and do not forbid to speak in tongues.

Desire earnestly to prophesy = As Paul brings this section to a close he restates what he had said in 1 Cor 14:1. In essence he is saying that it is good for a man to speak under the influence of the Holy Spirit, but it should always be done in such a way as to edify the church.

Do not forbid to speak in tongues = This implies that Paul's instruction up to this point might lead them to forbid speaking in tongues altogether. But Paul is saying here that the legitimate gift of speaking in tongues does have a place. However, that gift was intended to convince unbelievers of the authenticity of the gospel, and it was not to be used in the services of the local church unless an interpretation could be given which would edify those who were listening.

1 Cor 14:40 But all things must be done properly and in an orderly manner.

This is the primary guideline for the conduct of the services of the local church. Everything should be done in a way that promotes decency and propriety, as well as in an orderly, controlled, and structured manner. One commentator summarized the teaching of this section in the following words:

> Although there were officers in every church, appointed to conduct the services and
> especially to teach, yet as the extraordinary gifts of the Spirit were not confined to
> them or to any particular class, any member present who experienced the working
> of the Spirit in any of its extraordinary manifestations, was authorized to use and
> exercise his gift. Under such circumstances confusion could hardly fail to ensue.
> That such disorder did prevail in the public assemblies in Corinth is clear enough
> from this chapter. To correct this evil is the apostle's design in this whole passage. It
> was only so long as the gifts of tongues, of prophecy, of miracles, and others of a like
> kind continued in the church that the state of things here described prevailed. Since

those gifts have ceased, no one has the right to rise in the church under the impulse of his own mind to take part in its services. The general rule which the apostle lays down, applicable to all gifts alike, is that everything should be done unto edifying. [Hodge]

The Doctrine of the Resurrection

(1 Corinthians 15:1-58)

As we begin this new chapter of First Corinthians, we must remember that the apostle Paul has been dealing with many problems, errors, and issues within the Corinthian church. This new chapter occurs in the same flow of thought, and Paul has a new error or problem in mind as he begins. In several of the preceding chapters we have seen a special phrase which Paul used to introduce new topics of discussion: "Now concerning" (1 Cor 7:1; 7:25; 8:1; 12:1). Here in chapter fifteen all we have is the word "Now," and the transition is rather abrupt between the last topic of spiritual gifts and the new topic concerning the resurrection. As one writer put it, "This doctrinally important chapter on the resurrection is thrust before us by Paul without explaining why." [Boyer] But, as we have seen, it is not unusual for Paul to begin a new topic in a somewhat abrupt fashion. For example, the topic of sexual immorality in chapter five is introduced simply by saying: "It is actually reported that there is immorality among you." Also the topic of lawsuits between believers in chapter six is introduced by a question: "Does any one of you, when he has a case against his neighbor, dare to go to law before the unrighteous and not before the saints?"

However, here in chapter fifteen Paul opens his discussion of the resurrection of the dead by presenting the exact message he typically used when sharing the gospel, and this does not seem to have a clear connection with the Corinthians' problem or error regarding the resurrection. What we need to do as we begin this chapter is to look ahead at the statement in the second half of 1 Cor 15:12 where Paul explicitly pointed out the Corinthians' error. Then we can put the first part of this chapter in context with the overall flow of the argument Paul used when dealing with their doctrinal error. There Paul clearly explained that some of the Corinthians were teaching that there is no resurrection of the dead. They were denying the doctrine of the resurrection, and this whole chapter is devoted to correcting that error.

Greek Philosophy and the Resurrection

In some ways it is not surprising that the Corinthians would deny the doctrine of the resurrection, because to the Greek way of thinking it would have been almost inconceivable that a person's earthly body would come back to life after death. Greek philosophers such as Plato taught that the body was an evil prison in which the soul was trapped, and that only the soul itself was immortal. One commentator explained the situation in these words:

> There were three views held by the Corinthian teachers and philosophers: Epicureanism, Stoicism, and Platonism. These were three distinct schools of philosophy, and they all held certain views on this subject of resurrection. The position of the Epicurean was that of materialism. He denied any existence at all beyond death. The position of the Stoic was that at death the soul was merged with Deity, and so

there was a loss of personality. Third, there was Platonism which insisted upon the immortality of the soul, but absolutely denied the idea of bodily resurrection. [Morgan]

We know that when the apostle Paul met with the philosophers on Mars Hill in Athens (Acts 17:18-34), he spoke of Christ's resurrection from the dead and most of the philosophers mocked him. The doctrine of the resurrection of the body was completely nonsensical to them. because it was so contrary to what they believed about the existence of the soul. We need to understand what Paul was proclaiming when he taught about the resurrection. The word translated resurrection is the Greek term **anastasis** which literally means to stand up again. The doctrine of the resurrection has to do with the physical body. Its focus is not really on the immortality of the soul or whether there will be some kind of existence after the grave. Resurrection means that a person will quite literally "stand up again" after he dies, and that he will come back to life bodily.

The chapter we are studying now is one of the most extensive teachings about resurrection in all of the Bible, so it is a very important chapter for understanding this important doctrine. This chapter is also the earliest New Testament teaching about the resurrection, because it was written several years before any of the four gospel accounts and before the completion of the Book of Acts. This helps us to understand that the doctrine of the resurrection was one of the most foundational teachings of the church from the very beginning of Christianity. When we have this background information about the situation in the church at Corinth, it becomes easier to understand Paul's flow of thought in chapter fifteen. Since some of the Corinthians were denying the resurrection, Paul begins his argument for this important doctrine by focusing on Christ's resurrection and its importance to the gospel message.

Is there a resurrection of the dead? (15:1-34)

Proofs that Christ rose from the dead (15:1-11)

Scripture and the Gospel message claim that Christ was resurrected (15:1-4)

1 Cor 15:1 Now I make known to you, brethren, the gospel which I preached to you, which also you received, in which also you stand,

Now I make known to you, brethren = This opening phrase is similar to the one used by Paul in 1 Cor 12:1 when he was teaching the true nature of spiritual gifts. Here Paul is teaching the true nature of the resurrection. The Greek verb **gnorizo** means to declare, to certify, or to present knowledge so that it will be clearly recognized. Paul also begins by calling the Corinthians his brothers and sisters in Christ. This puts the discussion into the context of a family matter which should be understood by all of God's children.

The gospel which I preached to you, which also you received, in which also you stand = Paul is going to set the stage for correcting their error on the resurrection by going back to the very foundation of their faith. Here he clearly restated the message of the gospel which he originally preached to them and which they originally believed at that time. This is the message which they recognized as being true. You might say they staked their very lives on this message when they originally heard it. As one writer expressed Paul's words, "I would remind you, that however that truth may now be denied by you, it was once received by you, and you professed to believe in the fact that Christ rose from the dead." [Barnes] All of this is what Paul is reminding them of in this first verse of the chapter.

1 Cor 15:2 by which also you are saved, if you hold fast the word which I preached to you, unless you believed in vain.

By which also you are saved = This is a very important phrase, because it declares that a believer's salvation itself depends upon acknowledging the truths which Paul will state in the next few verses, including the truth of the resurrection.

If you hold fast the word which I preached to you = This is a Greek first class conditional clause, which is assumed to be true. The word or message that Paul originally preached to them was a true message, and if anyone does hold tightly or places his trust in those truths then he is exercising saving faith. God is the one who does the saving work, so the only condition for salvation on the human side of the equation is that a person put his complete trust in what God has done for him.

Unless you believed in vain = The phrase "Unless you believed in vain" is set in opposition to the previous phrase "If you hold fast the word." Paul is saying the same thing, first positively and now in the negative. This phrase is also a Greek first class conditional clause, which is assumed to be true. It simply states the opposite side of the issue. If a person places his trust in something that is not true, then he is not saved. The Greek word translated "vain" (eike) means without cause or without effect. If you believe in something that does not have the power to effect your salvation, then you are not saved. Paul is implying here that people who deny the truth of the resurrection are believing only half the gospel, and that is not effective for their salvation. Jesus Christ was not simply a good human being who died in someone else's place. Jesus Christ is the God-Man who died to take the infinite punishment that all human beings deserve, and He proved that He is God through His resurrection on the third day. Paul will make a statement in a later verse that unless you believe the whole gospel message, including the resurrection, then your faith is in vain (1 Cor 15:14).

1 Cor 15:3 For I delivered to you as of first importance what I also received, that Christ died for our sins according to the Scriptures,

For I delivered to you as of first importance what I also received = Paul was a faithful servant of Christ, and since he had received these truths directly from Jesus (Gal 1:12), he faithfully delivered them to others. Paul did not create this message; he only served as the messenger from Jesus to deliver it. But he is claiming divine authority for the truths he is declaring. The following truths are of primary importance and they form the foundation for the gospel message and for our salvation. The true gospel message consists of two important facts, each of which is proven, verified, or certified by the statements that follow:

That Christ died for our sins = The simple subject and verb are "Christ died." The verb is in the aorist tense which indicates a definite event which occurred at a past point in time. The last words in this phrase tell us why Christ died. The preposition "for" can mean concerning, on behalf of, or in order to deal with. "This passage is full proof that Christ did not die merely as a martyr, but that his death was to make atonement for sin. He died as an atoning sacrifice or as a vicarious offering." [Barnes] From this short phrase it is clear that Christ died in order to deal with our sins, but exactly how the death of Christ dealt with our sins is not discussed here. That is why Paul included the next phrase in this verse.

According to the Scriptures = The Scriptures are the important key to explaining and interpreting the death of Christ for our sins. There are many other places in the Bible that help us to understand more fully what the death of Christ accomplished in dealing with our sins.

1 Cor 15:4 and that He was buried, and that He was raised on the third day according to the Scriptures,

And that He was buried = The verb here is also in the aorist tense, telling us that this event happened at a single point in time during human history. The burial of Christ is what certified that He did indeed die, and that He paid the ultimate price for the sins of the whole world. Christ's burial was a fact of history which was witnessed by His friends as well as his enemies (see Matt 27:62-68). One commentator has said, "It was the necessary stage between death and resurrection, and it confirmed the reality of both. If he was buried, he must have been really dead; if he was buried, the resurrection must have been the reanimation of a corpse." [Barrett]

And that He was raised on the third day = Here is the second great truth of the gospel message. Not only did Christ die for our sins, but He also rose from the dead in His resurrection body. The verb translated "was raised" is not in the aorist tense like the previous verbs, but it is in the perfect tense which indicates that an event happened in the past which has consequences that carry forward up to the present time. Not only did Christ rise from the dead, but His resurrection remains in force and is His present condition even today. As one writer said, "Paul wishes to emphasize the permanence of the resurrection of Jesus. He is still risen." [RWP]

According to the Scriptures = As with the first great gospel truth, the Scriptures are the important key for explaining and interpreting the resurrection of Christ. There are many other places in the Bible that explain in more detail that Christ is the God-Man, which was a requirement for accomplishing an infinite atonement for the sins of all human beings throughout history. "Over and over again, either directly or indirectly, literally or in figures of speech, the Old Testament foretold Jesus' death, burial, and resurrection. No Jew who believed and understood the Scriptures, referring to what we now call the Old Testament, should have been surprised that the Messiah was ordained to die, be buried, and then resurrected." [MacArthur]

The testimony of eyewitnesses proves that Christ was resurrected (15:5-11)

1 Cor 15:5a and that He appeared to Cephas,

Christ's post-resurrection appearances where what certified or proved His resurrection from the dead. As with His burial, His resurrection was also a historical fact that was witnessed by many people, as Paul will continue describing in the following verses. The Bible does not give the specific time or place where Jesus appeared to Peter, but we can assume that it was sometime after He appeared to Mary and before He appeared to the men on the Emmaus Road (Luke 24:34).

1 Co 15:5b then to the twelve.

We need to remember that after the death and burial of Christ, the disciples were a defeated, discouraged, and frightened group. It was only when they saw Jesus alive in His resurrection body that they were transformed into the bold, excited, powerful group of witnesses who went on to change the world. Luke 24:35 and John 20:19 record that Jesus appeared to the eleven remaining disciples as they gathered in a house on the evening of the resurrection. Even before they replaced Judas, they were still referred to as "the twelve" because that designation had come to mean the small inner circle chosen by Jesus.

1 Cor 15:6 After that He appeared to more than five hundred brethren at one time, most of whom remain until now, but some have fallen asleep;

After that He appeared to more than five hundred brethren at one time = The Bible does not provide any specific details about Jesus' appearance to this group, but it must have been an event that was well known in the early church. One hint for the location of this appearance was given by Jesus Himself when he spoke to the women at the tomb: "Then Jesus said to them, 'Do not be afraid; go and take word to My brethren to leave for Galilee, and there they will see Me.'" (Matt 28:10)

Most of whom remain until now, but some have fallen asleep = Paul was writing this letter more than two decades after that event had occurred, and yet most of the large group who saw Jesus were still alive to testify to the facts.

1 Cor 15:7 then He appeared to James, then to all the apostles;

There were two disciples named James (Mark 3:17-18), but it seems likely that Paul is referring to the most prominent church leader named James who was the half-brother of Jesus. He was the key leader of the Jerusalem church (Acts 15:13-21), as well as the author of the Bible book of James. The Bible does not record the exact time when the private meeting took place between Jesus and James. In Acts 1:3 we are told that during the forty day period between His resurrection and His ascension, Jesus appeared to all the apostles on several occasions. An example of one of these events is recorded in John 21:1-14.

1 Cor 15:8 and last of all, as to one untimely born, He appeared to me also.

Jesus' appearance to Paul was not only after Christ's resurrection but also after His ascension. Paul described this unusual appearance using the analogy of a child who is born well after his due date. "Paul saw Him, who certainly did not expect to see Him, who certainly was amazed beyond measure when he did see Him; and not only was the vision unexpected and amazing, it was absolutely revolutionary. The man's whole life was changed by the vision of the risen Lord. It is interesting to remember that after he had been to Damascus, he went into Arabia and was there two years, probably three. What was he doing? He was under the shadow of Mount Sinai, from whence the law had come, reconsidering it all in the light of the resurrection of Christ." [Morgan] For more information about Jesus' appearance to Paul, see chapters 9, 22, and 26 in the Book of Acts.

1 Cor 15:9 For I am the least of the apostles, and not fit to be called an apostle, because I persecuted the church of God.

For I am the least of the apostles, and not fit to be called an apostle = Paul could not forget that he was the least likely person to be given this office by Christ, based on his personal background. He was an enemy and persecutor of the church, and he knew he did not deserve to be chosen as an apostle.

1 Cor 15:10 But by the grace of God I am what I am, and His grace toward me did not prove vain; but I labored even more than all of them, yet not I, but the grace of God with me.

But by the grace of God I am what I am = The background Paul shared in the previous verse made it humanly impossible for him to qualify as an apostle. It was completely by God's grace, so Paul says, "I am what I am by God's grace alone!"

And His grace toward me did not prove vain, but I labored even more than all of them = Paul did labor even more than the other apostles. He became completely dedicated to the work of the ministry that God gave him to do, and much of the New Testament is a witness to the accomplishments of the apostle Paul.

Yet not I, but the grace of God with me = By saying what he just said, however, Paul was not boasting of his own spirituality or personal abilities. The credit for all of his accomplishments can only be given to the grace of God working in him to do everything he did. "The same grace responsible for his calling was responsible for his faithfulness." [MacArthur]

1 Cor 15:11 Whether then it was I or they, so we preach and so you believed.

This verse summarizes the common testimony of all the witnesses Paul had just listed. Whether it was Peter, or the twelve, or the 500, or James, or Paul, they all preached a consistent message based on the common experience of seeing the resurrected Lord Jesus Christ.

The logical consequences of denying Christ's resurrection (15:12-34)

The statement of the problem in Corinth which prompted this chapter

1 Cor 15:12 Now if Christ is preached, that He has been raised from the dead, how do some among you say that there is no resurrection of the dead?

Now if Christ is preached, that He has been raised from the dead = Here Paul is recapping the gospel message that he preached among the Corinthians, and which he summarized in the first four verses of this chapter. The resurrection of Christ was a central part of the gospel message.

How do some among you say that there is no resurrection of the dead? = Here we see that some of the Corinthians were denying that there was a resurrection of the dead. They were following the teachings of the Greek philosophers rather than the truth of the inspired message presented to them by Paul and others. This shows that it was a common error even in the early church to allow the ungodly culture or society to determine truth, rather than letting the inspired Word of God be our standard of truth. We must constantly be on our guard, and we must prayerfully weigh the messages of our society against the truths of God's Word. The apostle Paul is now going to give a series of logical conclusions that would result if a person accepted the tenet that there is no such thing as the resurrection of the dead.

Conclusion #1: If there is no resurrection, that would mean not even Christ was raised

1 Cor 15:13 But if there is no resurrection of the dead, not even Christ has been raised;

If there is no such thing as the resurrection of the dead, then Christ Himself would not have been able to rise from the dead. "He was dead and was buried. He had lain in the grave three days. His human soul had left the body. His frame had become cold and stiff. The blood had ceased to circulate, and the lungs to heave. In his case there was the same difficulty in raising him up to life that there is in any other; and if it is held to be impossible and absurd that the dead should rise, then it must follow that Christ has not been raised." [Barnes] However, in the previous section Paul just finished proving that Christ did rise from the dead. So to state the case positively, if Christ was resurrected then the Corinthians should see that resurrection is possible.

Conclusion #2: If Christ was not raised, then Gospel preaching and conversion are in vain

1 Cor 15:14 and if Christ has not been raised, then our preaching is vain, your faith also is vain.

Earlier in this section Paul made it very clear that the heart of the gospel message was the resurrection of Christ. So if there were no resurrection then the "good news" of the gospel would actually be "bad news" and there would be nothing worth preaching or believing. "The substance of their preaching was that Christ was raised up, and all their preaching was based on that. If that were not true, then the whole system was false!" [Barnes]

Conclusion #3: The apostles would be deliberate liars and wicked deceivers

1 Cor 15:15 Moreover we are even found to be false witnesses of God, because we testified against God that He raised Christ, whom He did not raise, if in fact the dead are not raised.

Paul had given a detailed list of people who were eye-witnesses of the resurrected Lord, but if there is no resurrection then all of those people are false witnesses. If there is no resurrection of the dead, then God did not raise Christ from the dead, and to proclaim that fact would mean contradicting God Himself. "To deny the resurrection is to call the apostles and every other leader of the New Testament church not simply mistaken but willfully mistaken, that is, liars. There is no possibility, as many liberals claim, that such a mistake could have been innocent or naive. Those witnesses could not have been honest men who unwittingly gave bad advice, but were liars who would have had to conspire together in order for their lies to have been so consistent." [MacArthur]

Conclusion #4: The Corinthians' own faith would be vain; they are still unredeemed sinners

1 Cor 15:16-17 For if the dead are not raised, not even Christ has been raised; and if Christ has not been raised, your faith is worthless; you are still in your sins.

Here Paul repeated his first and second logical conclusions (see verse thirteen), but he added the terrifying idea that people who put their trust in such an obviously false system would have no advantage over unbelievers. "If Jesus remained dead, then when we die we too will remain dead and damned...If Christ was not raised, His death was in vain, our faith in Him is in vain, and our sins are still counted against us." [MacArthur] That is the main point of this verse, that there is no actual redemption and forgiveness of sin if Christ has not been raised.

Conclusion #5: All their dead Christian friends must be regarded as forever lost

1 Cor 15:18 Then those also who have fallen asleep in Christ have perished.

Here Paul shares that any believer the Corinthians know who had already died would be completely and eternally lost. The term perished means "to put out of the way entirely; to utterly and permanently ruin; to give over to eternal misery in hell." As one scholar states, "Obviously the same consequence would apply to every saint who has died since Paul wrote. Paul himself, the other apostles, Augustine, Calvin, Luther, Wesley, and every other believer of every other age would spend eternity in torment, without God and without hope." [MacArthur]

Conclusion #6: Christians would be in a more miserable condition than unbelievers

1 Cor 15:19 If we have hoped in Christ in this life only, we are of all men most to be pitied.

Without the resurrection Christianity would be pointless, and anyone who believes in it should be pitied. Without the resurrection, there would be no gospel, no salvation message to believe, no forgiveness of sins, and no hope of a meaningful life either now or after death. "To have hoped in Christ in this life only would be to teach, preach, suffer, sacrifice, and work entirely for nothing...The Christian life would be a mockery, a charade, a tragic joke." [MacArthur]

Theological arguments for the doctrine of the resurrection (15:20-28)

Here Paul is going to give several theological arguments for the resurrection. Many people even today who reject the doctrine of the resurrection do not realize that this impacts other areas of their system of theology. One commentator expressed it this way: "To teach that there is no resurrection is to teach that there is no atonement and no pardon. Errorists seldom see the consequences of the false doctrines which they embrace. Many allow themselves to entertain doubts as to this very doctrine of the resurrection of the body, who would be shocked at the thought of rejecting the doctrine of atonement. Yet Paul teaches that the denial of the one involves the denial of the other." [Hodge]

A clear affirmation of Christ's resurrection (15:20)

1 Cor 15:20 But now Christ has been raised from the dead, the first fruits of those who are asleep.

First Paul gives a clear affirmation of the fact of Christ's resurrection. He simply says, "But now Christ has been raised from the dead." This simple truth contradicts the false teaching that some people in the Corinthian church were believing. Paul described Christ as the "first fruits" and this referred to the Jewish practice of sacrificing the first part of their harvest to God.

Before Israelites harvested their crops they were to bring a representative sample, called the first fruits, to the priests as an offering to the Lord (Lev 23:10). The full harvest could not be made until the first fruits were offered...The significance of the first fruits, however, not only was that they preceded the harvest but that they were a first installment of the harvest. The fact that Christ was the first fruits therefore indicates that something else, namely the harvest of the rest of the crop, is to follow. In other words, Christ's resurrection could not have been in isolation from ours. His resurrection requires our resurrection. [MacArthur]

So here in this verse Paul is affirming not only that Christ did rise from the dead, but that we as believers in Him will also be raised.

The origin of sin and death from Adam's sin (15:21)

1 Cor 15:21 For since by a man came death, by a man also came the resurrection of the dead.

This verse makes it clear that Adam was the physical father of everyone in the human race, and that sin and death entered the human race through his sin in the garden of Eden.

> Just as Adam was the progenitor of everyone who dies, so Christ is the progenitor of everyone who will be raised to life. In each case, one man doing one act caused the consequences of that act to be applied to every other person identified with him. Those who are identified with Adam—every person who has been born—is subject to death because of Adam's sinful act. Likewise, those who are identified with Christ—every person who has been born again in Him—is subject to resurrection to eternal life because of Christ's righteous act. [MacArthur]

The transmission of the sin nature to all who are in Adam, and the imparting of eternal life to all who are in Christ (15:22)

1 Cor 15:22 For as in Adam all die, so also in Christ all will be made alive.

To be "in Adam" means simply to be a human being born as a descendant of Adam. Because of Adam's sin each one of his descendants comes into the world spiritually dead and will suffer the consequence of physical death. However, to be "in Christ" simply means to be trusting in Christ for one's salvation. Because of Christ's substitutionary death on our behalf, every person who puts his faith in Christ will be given spiritual life, and even if he dies physically he will be resurrected bodily to enjoy eternal life with God. As one writer summarized it, "Union with Adam is the cause of death; union with Christ is the cause of life." [Hodge]

The order of the resurrection events (15:23-28)

1 Cor 15:23 But each in his own order: Christ the first fruits, after that those who are Christ's at His coming,

Here Paul will expand on the idea that Christ was the first fruits or the first to be raised, but that every other believer will also be raised at His coming. Using Paul's analogy, Christ was the first fruits, but "those who are in Christ" will follow afterward just as the full harvest followed that first offering. God has a predetermined order of events involving the resurrection of the dead, and the resurrection of different groups of believers will happen in several stages.

1. The resurrection of Christ
2. At Christ's return for church age saints, He will come down as far as the clouds and believers who are already dead will rise first to meet Him in the air (1 Thess 4:16)
3. After that event then believers who are still alive will rise to meet Him in the air (1 Thess 4:17)

It is probably the rapture that Paul had in mind in this verse when he described "His coming." However, at the end of the Tribulation period Christ will also resurrect every person who has come to faith in Him but had died or been killed for his faith during that horrible time (Rev 20:4). In addition to this there will be a resurrection of everyone who was a believer during the period of the Old Testament, from the Garden of Eden until the beginning of the church age (see Dan 12:2).

1 Cor 15:24 then comes the end, when He hands over the kingdom to the God and Father, when He has abolished all rule and all authority and power.

Paul went on in this section to explain some of the other events that will occur during the end of human history on this planet, including the Millennial Kingdom during which Christ will reign over all the earth. It is during this thousand-year period when the Lord Jesus Christ will centralize all rule and authority and power under His absolute sovereign control. The Old Testament contains many descriptions of life during this time period.

– Christ's government will be one of absolute authority (Ps 2; Rev 19:15), but it will also be characterized by complete righteousness and peace (Ps 72; Isa 11).
– Israel will be restored to the promised land (Jer 30-31; Ezek 39; Amos 9), but Gentiles will also have abundant blessings (Isa 2:2-4, 19:24-25, 49:6, 60:1-3, 62:2, 66:18-19; Jer 3:17, 16:19).
– The earth will be full of the knowledge of the Lord (Isa 11:9), and the millennial temple will be a center of worship (Ezek 40-46).
– There will be tremendous social and economic development on a world-wide basis, and many of the effects of the curse on the productivity of the earth will be rolled back (Isa 35:1-2).
– At the end of this time, Christ will deliver the kingdom to God the Father (see 1 Cor 15:28).

1 Cor 15:25-26 For He must reign until He has put all His enemies under His feet. The last enemy that will be abolished is death.

Here Paul described the course of events during the Millennial Kingdom, where Christ will ultimately put down the final rebellion inspired by Satan after his release (Rev 20:7-9). This language is very similar to Psalm 2:6-9 and 110:1. The last enemy (death) will not be completely abolished until after the Great White Throne judgment (Rev 20:11-13), and then death itself will be thrown into the lake of fire

(Rev 20:14).

> 1 Cor 15:27 For HE HAS PUT ALL THINGS IN SUBJECTION UNDER HIS FEET. But when He says, "All things are put in subjection," it is evident that He is excepted who put all things in subjection to Him.

Paul seems to have in mind the words of Psalm 8:6, which in the original context refer to the dominion of mankind over the earth as originally given by God in Gen 1:26-28. Since the Fall in the Garden of Eden there has never been a time when mankind maintained benevolent dominion over all of creation, but this will finally be fulfilled by the Lord Jesus Christ during His Millennial Kingdom reign. In the last part of this verse Paul has in view some of his opponents at Corinth who might try to use logic against him. You may have heard someone say, "ALL means ALL, and that's all ALL means!" They claim that the word "all" must always be used in a universal sense, but that is not true. The word "all" is always limited by its context. That is what Paul is teaching here in this verse. It is as if he says, "When I state that God has put all things in subjection to Christ, of course that does not mean that God Himself is in subjection to Christ." In this context he means everything except God Himself.

> 1 Cor 15:28 When all things are subjected to Him, then the Son Himself also will be subjected to the One who subjected all things to Him, so that God may be all in all.

Finally Paul concludes this description of the final days of human history by telling what will happen at the end of the Millennial Kingdom. After Christ has completed all the work He was given regarding human salvation and government in the plan of God, then Christ will be in a position to give His final account to God of his work. This verse provides a brief and rare glimpse into the relationships within the godhead itself. The Eternal Son of God is fully God and completely equal with God the Father in His divine status. However, during Christ's earthly ministry at both His first and second comings, there is a sense in which He is fulfilling a subordinate function by carrying out the will of God the Father. One scholar states that, "In light of Paul's major argument in this chapter, it is obvious that his point here is that, if there were no resurrection, there would be no subjects for God's eternal kingdom; and there would be no Lord to rule." [MacArthur]

Conclusion #7: If there is no resurrection, then baptism for such a resurrection would be absurd

Now Paul continues his list of logical conclusions that must be true if there were no resurrection from the dead.

> 1 Cor 15:29 Otherwise, what will those do who are baptized for the dead? If the dead are not raised at all, why then are they baptized for them?

Otherwise = In this verse Paul continues giving arguments for the truth of the resurrection of the dead. The word "otherwise" would not make much sense in this sentence unless we insert Paul's premise for the argument. It is as if he is saying, "There really is such a thing as the resurrection of the dead, otherwise what will those do who are baptized for the dead? The dead certainly ARE raised, otherwise baptism for the dead would be absurd!" Here, the word "otherwise" marks the beginning of Paul's next set of arguments for the resurrection of the dead.

Verse twenty-nine falls into the category of what might be called a "Bible difficulty." It is one of the verses in Scripture that is very difficult to interpret properly. For this verse there are literally dozens of recorded interpretations, most of which are completely outlandish. Some of these strange interpretations have been used to create heretical doctrines or unorthodox practices. There are some recorded interpretations that could be legitimate, but with a difficult verse like this it is actually easier to explain what it does not mean than to be dogmatic about its correct intended meaning.

In order to handle a difficult passage like this, we must apply the principle that "Scripture interprets Scripture." In other words, we must base our understanding on the fact that the entire Bible is God's inspired, inerrant, and authoritative revelation to us. We must compare the difficult passage with other passages that relate to the same subject, and we must work from the assumption that Scripture cannot contradict itself. We must admit that while some passages are difficult, the majority of the Bible is clearly understandable. We should never base a theological doctrine on an unclear or ambiguous passage.

When problems of interpretation arise or a passage seems unclear, we should never assume that the Bible contains a mistake. It is not the Bible that is wrong, but it is our own finite, limited, and fallen minds that are the problem. We must give the Bible the benefit of the doubt, and work from the assumption that we are only required to find a plausible interpretation that is not in conflict with the clear teaching of the rest of Scripture. Also, we are not required to prove beyond a shadow of a doubt that our plausible interpretation is the only true and correct one. With difficult Bible passages we must leave our doubts in God's hands, knowing that when we see Him face-to-face these difficulties will all be resolved.

What this verse does NOT mean

We know from comparing this difficult passage with the other clear teachings of Scripture that this passage is not teaching vicarious baptism for the salvation of the dead. The Bible teaches that people can only be saved while they are alive and can consciously understand and respond to the gospel message. It never teaches that a person can be saved after death. The Bible teaches that salvation is an individual event or experience of placing one's personal faith and trust in Christ alone for one's eternal destiny. It never teaches that a person's faith can save anyone but himself. Those who have already died cannot be helped toward salvation in any way, and certainly not by another person's being baptized on their behalf. All opportunities for salvation end when a person dies (Hebrews 9:27).

We also know from the clear teaching of Scripture that baptism is not necessary for salvation but is only the outward, public declaration of a salvation that had already been achieved at the time one placed his faith and trust in Christ alone. This verse cannot be teaching the doctrine of baptismal regeneration, that one is saved by being baptized or that baptism is somehow required for salvation. If a person cannot even save himself by being baptized, then he certainly cannot save someone else by being baptized on his behalf. If one person's faith cannot save another person, then one person's baptism certainly cannot save another person.

Those who are baptized = The concept of baptism refers primarily to the public declaration of a believer's intimate association with the Lord Jesus Christ after entering into a salvation relationship by placing his personal faith in Christ and all that He accomplished on our behalf. In First Corinthians chapter one Paul used the word baptism six times with this meaning. To be baptized means to give public testimony to the fact that you are a Christian, that you have placed your personal faith in Christ for your salvation and are completely identified with Him.

The dead = This phrase is used thirteen times in First Corinthians, and all of those cases are in chapter fifteen where the context concerns the resurrection of the dead or the dead being raised. Apart from that, the phrase "the dead" does not occur in this book. This tells us that when Paul used the phrase here in verse twenty-nine he was still speaking of the resurrection of the dead.

Baptized FOR the resurrection of the dead = The preposition "for" (**huper**) can mean above, about, beyond, on behalf of, because of, or in reference to. Although the English word "for" is a legitimate translation of this Greek preposition, it seems clear from the context that Paul means because of or in reference to. In other words Paul may be saying, "If there were no resurrection of the dead, it would be absurd to become a Christian with a hope of being resurrected to eternal life." As one commentator put it, "Unless the dead arose, it would be vain to be baptized with the belief that Christ rose and on the ground of the hope that they would rise." [Barnes]

If the dead are not raised at all, why then are they baptized for them? = This phrase adds another shade of meaning to the previous phrase. Here the implication is that a powerful motive for becoming a Christian is the testimony of other believers who have already died and gone to be with the Lord.

> Paul may have simply been saying that people were being saved (baptism being the sign) because of the exemplary lives and witness of faithful believers who had died. Whether this is the right interpretation of this verse we cannot be certain, but we can be certain that people often come to salvation because of the testimony of those whom they desire to emulate...In 1 Corinthians 15:29 Paul may be affirming the truth that Christians who face death with joy and hope are a powerful testimony. The prospect of eternal life, of resurrection life, of reunion with loved ones, is a strong motive for people to listen to and accept the gospel. Resurrection is one of

the greatest assurances that God gives to those who trust in His Son. For those who believe in Jesus Christ, the grave is not the end. Not only that, but one day our glorified bodies will rejoin our spirits, and we will live as whole, completed human beings throughout all of eternity with all who have loved and worshiped God. [MacArthur]

In the first verse of this new section, then, Paul may be saying that the truth of the resurrection of the dead is a powerful motive or incentive for putting one's faith in Christ and being baptized. By denying the truth of the resurrection of the dead, the Corinthians were taking away this wonderful motive for salvation.

Conclusion #8: Ministry activity and suffering for one's faith would be meaningless (15:30-32a)

1 Cor 15:30 Why are we also in danger every hour?

The apostle Paul and his companions were prime examples of servants of the Lord who were being persecuted for proclaiming the gospel message. If there is no resurrection of the dead, why should they put themselves in harm's way for something that is not true? "They had no other object in encountering these dangers than to make known the truths connected with that glorious future state; and if there were no such future state, it would be wise for them to avoid these dangers." [Barnes]

1 Cor 15:31 I affirm, brethren, by the boasting in you which I have in Christ Jesus our Lord, I die daily.

When Paul says, "I affirm" he is using a term that meant taking a formal oath. So here Paul is affirming the truth of his previous statement that he and his companions were constantly in danger. In fact Paul expressed the intensity of this danger by saying that he was in peril for his very life on a daily basis. It is as if Paul is saying, "I am constantly in danger of my life, and my sufferings each day are equal to the pains of death." [Barnes]

1 Cor 15:32a If from human motives I fought with wild beasts at Ephesus, what does it profit me?

In this verse Paul goes on to say that putting himself in harm's way out of purely human motives would certainly not gain anything. It would be silly to face the perils that Paul faced in Ephesus if he were doing it for something that was not true. Paul mentions his troubles in Ephesus at this point because those horrible persecutions must have been widely known to the entire church of Paul's day. One scholar said, "Paul's Epistles and Acts (especially chapter Acts 19) throw light on Paul's argument. He was never out of danger from Damascus to the last visit to Rome. There are perils in Ephesus of which we do not know (Cor 1:8)." [RWP] So Paul and his ministry team are a perfect example of what it meant to suffer for one's faith while proclaiming the gospel, and that doing so would be silly if such efforts were not based on the truth of the resurrection.

Conclusion #9: Denying the resurrection results in a hedonistic philosophy of life (15:32b)

1 Cor 15:32b If the dead are not raised, LET US EAT AND DRINK, FOR TOMORROW WE DIE.

Here Paul presents the opposite side to his argument by saying, "If there is no resurrection of the dead, then live purely for pleasure today because you may die and cease to exist tomorrow." These words might appear in special lettering in your Bible because they are a excerpt from comments made by the Jews during the siege of Jerusalem by the army of the Assyrians (Isaiah 22:13). Instead of weeping and fasting, which were more appropriate to their situation, many of the Jews focused on getting one last night of pleasure before the attack which they expected would lead to their deaths. This unbiblical attitude was not unique to the Jews of Isaiah's day, but it was also the motto of the Epicurean philosophers of Paul's day. Near Paul's home town of Tarsus there was a statue of the city founder with an inscription which read: "Eat, drink, enjoy thyself. The rest is nothing." So by using this quote, Paul is giving the philosophy of the people who deny the resurrection.

Paul rebukes this worldly attitude and the Corinthians' infiltration by their culture (15:33-34)

1 Cor 15:33 Do not be deceived: "Bad company corrupts good morals."

Now Paul gives a very serious rebuke to the Corinthians for their worldly and unbiblical attitude. Since he is very familiar with the philosophical culture of his day, it seems Paul cannot resist using their own words against them. In addition to being a true statement, this verse was also a common proverb of the day. It first appeared in the plays of the Greek poet Menander around 280 BC. It is as if Paul is saying, "Even you Corinthians who are steeped in the worldly philosophy of the day should know that what you are doing is wrong."

1 Cor 15:34 Become sober-minded as you ought, and stop sinning; for some have no knowledge of God. I speak this to your shame.

In this verse Paul gives the Corinthians two commands: be sober-minded and stop sinning! When Paul says "Become sober-minded" he used a word that means to wake up from a drunken stupor. This word picture is comparing their worldly mindset to the thinking of someone under the influence of alcohol, and Paul tells them to rouse themselves and come back to reality and to the truth! When Paul says, "Stop sinning" he does not hesitate to call their behavior what it really is: SIN. In other words, it is a sin to deny the truth of the resurrection of the dead, and that sin will lead to all of the consequences that Paul outlined in the previous verses. Finally Paul gave the last shameful conclusion about the behavior of those who denied the resurrection of the dead: They have no knowledge of God. The grammar of this verse tells us that these people were continually and habitually living in a state of ignorance about the truths of God, as well as ignorance of the power of God in being able to raise the dead to life again. As one commentator put it: "This is stronger than simply to have ignorance. These people have it and constantly keep a tight hold on it." [VWS]

What will the resurrection body be like? (15:35-57)

The Objection of Paul's Opponents (15:35)

1 Cor 15:35 But someone will say, "How are the dead raised? And with what kind of body do they come?"

The word translated "but" at the beginning of this verse is a very strong contrast word. Paul had just finished proving the truth of the resurrection of the dead, but in direct contrast to those who believe these truths, there were still some people who wanted to show the foolishness of the truth. Their main objection to the resurrection of the dead was expressed in a two-part question:

1. How are the dead raised? In other words, "How could the dead possibly be raised?" How can the particles of a dead and decayed body be restored to life? We might rephrase this question as a statement: There is no way to reassemble a dead person's body out of the randomly scattered and disorganized particles that have long since returned to the dust of the earth. Even after Paul had already proved that the resurrection of the dead is possible, he knew some of his opponents would still say that the dead cannot be raised. They would argue that it is impossible to gather and assemble the decomposed particles of a dead person's body, and their reason for continuing to say this was based on their misconception of what the resurrection body would be like.
2. With what kind of body do they come? This second question implies that the only conceivable body a person could have would be the same one the person always had. If we rephrase this question as a statement they might be saying: "The body cannot be reconstituted!" They were stating that there is no other kind of body a person could have other than the one that has now died and is impossible to reconstruct.

In both of these questions, we see that they are not the questions of someone who is genuinely seeking to understand the truth. They are questions posed by Paul's opponents among the false teachers in Corinth. In that sense they are very much like the question about the resurrection that was asked of Jesus by the Sadducees, who also denied the resurrection of the dead (Matt 22:23-32).

Understanding the true nature of the resurrection body (15:36-41)

The main assumption of Paul's opponents was that resurrection meant reconstructing the former body which the person had during this lifetime. Throughout the rest of this chapter Paul will show that this is a false assumption, and in this section he will use several illustrations to help us understand what the actual resurrection body will be like.

An illustration from the life cycle of plants (15:36-38)

1 Cor 15:36 You fool! That which you sow does not come to life unless it dies;

You fool = Paul's first two words in this verse tell us what he thinks of his opponents as well as of their objection to the doctrine of the resurrection. He calls them and their argument foolish. This also helps us to understand that the questions in verse thirty-five were not sincere questions, but were manipulative trick questions posed by foolish opponents of God's truth.

In this illustration from the life cycle of plants, Paul used an analogy to say that the present body must die and decay. Like a seed that has been sown, you will never see that seed again. Its original form is gone forever. His point is that the old body decays and will never be reconstituted. As one commentator said, "Resurrection is not reconstruction. Nowhere does the Bible teach that at the resurrection, God will put together the pieces and return to us our former bodies. There is continuity (it is our body) but there is not equality (it is not the same body)." [Wiersbe]

The word "dies" (**apothnesko**) comes from the root word to die, with an added preposition which intensifies the meaning. It is a strong word that describes the physical death of an organism. This tells us that the new body cannot appear until the old body has completely died off, never to return again. Regarding this verse one man has written,

> It was the senselessness of the objection that roused the apostle's indignation. Fool! says Paul. The body cannot live again unless it dies. A seed cannot live unless it dies!...How then can the disorganization of the body in the grave be an objection to the doctrine of the resurrection?...To doubt the fact of the resurrection because we cannot understand the process is, as the apostle says, a proof of folly. [Hodge]

1 Cor 15:37 and that which you sow, you do not sow the body which is to be, but a bare grain, perhaps of wheat or of something else.

Paul starts this verse by saying, "and that which you sow," as if to say, "Think for a moment about what is sown. Focus for a moment on the seed itself." The sown seed does not come back in its original form. It does not reappear as exactly the same thing you placed into the soil. You sow a single seed, but what comes up is an entire plant. The plant is related to the seed, but it is completely different in form. When you sow a seed you do not expect it to come up again as a seed. Paul's point here is that the same is true of the resurrection body. When a person's body dies and is placed into the grave, we should not expect it to be resurrected in exactly the same form that it had before. When Paul says, "you do not sow the body which is to be," he is saying that the present body is not the future body. The body laid in the grave is not the one which will be resurrected. One commentator stated Paul's point this way: "Nature itself therefore teaches that there is no basis for the objection that the future body must be identical to the present." [Hodge]

1 Cor 15:38 But God gives it a body just as He wished, and to each of the seeds a body of its own.

The previous verse discussed the planting of a simple seed, and it mentioned the example of a grain of wheat. Paul could have mentioned many other types of seeds with a wide variety of forms, and this brings up the amazing creativity of God as the designer of life in His created universe. God Himself is ultimately responsible for the variety of life forms, and He gave each type of plant the specific form that He desired to give it. In this verse Paul's point is that since God the Designer created an amazing variety of seeds, we must also credit Him with the amazing differences in the plants which arise from those simple seeds. If this is true for simple plant life, how much more is it true for human life and the design of the resurrection body that He will provide after death? As one commentator stated, "The point of this is, if God thus gives to all the products of the earth each its own form, why may he not determine the form in which the body is to appear at the resurrection?" [Hodge] Paul is emphasizing that the Creator God is capable of giving people resurrection bodies that are very different from their earthly bodies, while yet maintaining the identity and continuity of their individual personalities in the process.

An illustration from the types of physical forms and bodies (15:39)

1 Cor 15:39 All flesh is not the same flesh, but there is one flesh of men, and another flesh of beasts, and another flesh of birds, and another of fish.

Here it is as if Paul is saying, "Look around at the other forms of life God has created!" God is quite capable of giving different creatures many different forms, even throughout their own earthly life cycles. If we see this is true during the earthly life cycle of God's creatures, surely it is not too difficult to believe that God can do similar things after death too! One purely natural example of this is the difference in form between a caterpillar and a butterfly. It is almost inconceivable what a difference in form this one creature can take during its short lifetime. Our best example of this is seen in the differences between Christ's earthly body and His resurrection body. As one man wrote,

> When Jesus was raised from the dead His glorified body was radically different from the one which had died. What came out of the grave was different from what was placed in the grave. It was no longer limited by time, space, and material substance. During His appearances, Jesus went from one place to another without traveling in any physical way. He appeared and disappeared at will, and entered rooms without opening the door (Luke 24:15, 31, 36; John 20:19). In His earthly body He had done none of those things...After Jesus was raised, no one recognized Him unless He revealed Himself to them. But once revealed, He was recognizable. The disciples knew His face, and they recognized His wounded side and His pierced hands. In a similar way, our resurrected bodies as believers will have a continuity with the

bodies we have now. Our bodies will die and they will change form, but they will still be our bodies. Surely it is not too hard to believe that the God who has worked this process daily through the centuries in His creatures, can do it with men. [MacArthur]

An illustration from the differences between heavenly and earthly bodies (15:40)

1 Cor 15:40 There are also heavenly bodies and earthly bodies, but the glory of the heavenly is one, and the glory of the earthly is another.

Here Paul extends his analogy beyond the realm of planet Earth by comparing the glory of the earthly bodies he just mentioned with the glory of the heavenly bodies, the objects in the night sky. God has given each created thing its own qualities and abilities to glorify Him, and they are vastly different.

An illustration from the differences among heavenly bodies themselves (15:41)

1 Cor 15:41 There is one glory of the sun, and another glory of the moon, and another glory of the stars; for star differs from star in glory.

Paul here states that even among the heavenly bodies themselves there are amazing differences in their forms, capabilities, and capacity for glorifying their Creator. One man said it this way: "Resurrection bodies will differ from earthly bodies just as radically as heavenly bodies differ from earthly. And resurrection bodies will be as individual and unique as are all the other forms of God's creation...God has infinite creative capacity, including the capacity to make infinite variety. Why would anyone think it is hard for Him to resurrect human bodies, no matter what the form might be?" [MacArthur]

Characteristics of the resurrection body (15:42-49)

By way of analogy, using comparisons between things we are aware of in our present universe, Paul has shown us that the resurrection body will be far superior to the earthly body. But all analogies to things in our present world will eventually break down. So in the next section Paul will use several contrasting pairs of words to explain the true superiority of the resurrection body.

Imperishable

1 Cor 15:42 So also is the resurrection of the dead. It is sown a perishable body, it is raised an imperishable body;

The earthly body that goes into the grave is perishable; however, the resurrection body is imperishable.

Perishable = The Greek word is **phthora** which means "subject to decay or corruption." Another connotation is "subject to moral decay, or ultimate misery in hell." This is a perfect word to describe the condition of fallen people living in a fallen world. When applied to our earthly bodies, this term points to the ultimate fate of every living creature. Just like the seed, at death our bodies are sown for decay.

Imperishable = This is the Greek word **aphtharsia** which means incorruptibility, purity, or genuineness; it is sometimes used to mean "unending existence or perpetuity." This word seems perfect for describing the type of body one would require to live an eternal existence without sin or blemish of any kind. As one man wrote: "Its parts will be no more subject to corruption; it will not be supported by corruptible things; it will be immortal, and never die, and it will be clear of all its moral corruption; it will no more be a vile body, but fashioned like to the holy and glorious body of Christ." [JFB]

Glorious

1 Cor 15:43a it is sown in dishonor, it is raised in glory;

Dishonor = This is the Greek word **atimia** which can be translated dishonor, disgrace, indignity, shameful, vile, or lowly. Again, this seems a perfect term for describing the condition of the earthly body at the time it is placed into the grave.

Glory = The Greek word used here is **doxa** which can mean splendor, brightness, excellence, honor, or blessedness. As one commentator expressed it, the resurrection body shall be raised "in honor; in beauty; honored by God by the removal of the curse, and in a form and manner that shall be glorious. It shall be adapted to a world of glory; and everything which here rendered it vile, valueless, cumbersome, offensive, or degraded, shall be there removed." [Barnes]

Powerful

1 Co 15:43b it is sown in weakness, it is raised in power;

Weakness = The Greek word **asthenia** is used here, and it means frail, feeble, liable to sickness and infirmity. It sometimes conveys the idea of lack of ability to restrain corrupt desires, and the inability to do great things that glorify God. It is certainly true that a person's earthly body is very frail and subject to death from what might look like very small injuries or inconsequential traumas. Life is indeed fragile.

Power = This is the Greek word **dunamis** which means inherent strength or ability that resides in something by virtue of its nature. It is sometimes used in the context of power for doing mighty works that bring glory to God. As one man wrote:

> It is raised by the power of God, and with great power in itself; being able to subsist without food, and of moving itself from place to place with great agility; and capable of the highest services before God without weariness; nor will it be ever more liable to weakness or death; death shall have no more power over it; nor shall it be encompassed or attended with any infirmity whatever. [Gill]

Spiritual

1 Cor 15:44 it is sown a natural body, it is raised a spiritual body. If there is a natural body, there is also a spiritual body.

Natural = The Greek word here is **psuchikos** which describes something that is governed by the soul. One commentator wrote: "The expression natural body signifies an organism animated by a soul, that immaterial part of man which is more nearly allied to the flesh, and which characterizes the man as a mortal creature." [VWS]

Spiritual = The Greek word here is **pneumatikos** which means governed by the spirit. One Bible scholar has described this as a "body in which a divine spirit supersedes the soul, so that the resurrection body is the fitting organ for the Spirit's indwelling and work, and so is properly characterized as a spiritual body." [VWS]

Notice this verse does not say that in the resurrection everyone will become a disembodied spirit. That is not a biblical teaching. The verse specifically states that each believer will be given a spirit-governed body. As one man says, "The body which we now have is one suited to life on the level of the soul. But the resurrection body will be one suited to life lived on the level of the spirit. Spiritual does not mean immaterial, as opposed to material. He does not say it will be a spirit; he says it will be a spiritual body." [Boyer]

When Paul says, "If there is a natural body, there is also a spiritual body," he is answering the objection of someone who might see a contradiction in the phrase "spiritual body." Someone might say, "Is it a body or is it a spirit? You cannot have both at the same time." But Paul used a Greek first class conditional clause, which is assumed to be true, to prove that since our bodies now are adapted to life on the level of the soul, then our future resurrection bodies will be adapted to life on the level of the spirit. As one writer expressed it: "This is a vindication of the apparently contradictory expression, spiritual body...Just as certainly as we have a body adapted to our lower nature, we shall have one adapted to our higher nature. If the one exists, so does the other." [Hodge]

Like the body of Christ (15:45-49)

1 Cor 15:45 So also it is written, "The first MAN, Adam, BECAME A LIVING SOUL." The last Adam became a life-giving spirit.

This section is clearly connected with the previous verse, since both the natural (**psuche**) and the spiritual (**pneuma**) are mentioned. In this verse the contrast is between the soul-centered body of Adam and the spirit-centered body of Christ. Paul begins by quoting the last part of Genesis 2:7 from the Septuagint, the Greek translation of the Hebrew Old Testament: "man (**adam**) became a living soul (**psuche**)." Here Paul appeals to the Scriptures for his authority in saying that the body of Adam was focused on life at the level of the earthly soul.

Then Paul introduced the second half of his comparison by referring to Christ as the last Adam. We need to understand in what sense Adam was the first while Christ was the last. Adam was certainly the first created human being, as Genesis clearly stated. But as the first human being, Adam was also responsible for the destiny of the human race following his sin in the Garden of Eden. In that sense, Adam was the originator and the responsible leader or head of the human race in its sinful condition. By contrast, Christ has become the last man who could be considered the originator, leader, or responsible head of the human race by blazing the trail into eternal resurrection life. One commentator wrote:

> Christ is called the last Adam, meaning that there shall be no other after him who shall affect the destiny of man in the same way, or who shall stand at the head of the race in a manner similar to what had been done by him and the first father of the human family. They sustain special relations to the race; and in this respect they were the first and the last. [Barnes]

Paul states here that Christ became a life-giving spirit to all those who put their faith and trust in what He accomplished for mankind by dying on the cross. Christ has the power to impart life to those who are related to Him. The term spirit is used as a direct contrast to the term soul (**psuche**) that described Adam. As Adam's body was a natural, soul-centered body, so is Christ's body a spirit-centered one. There are several aspects of the contrast between Adam's earthly body and Christ's resurrection body that Paul will continue to describe in the following verses.

1. The sequence of existence

1 Cor 15:46 However, the spiritual is not first, but the natural; then the spiritual.

This verse describes the order or sequence of existence for mankind. The natural is first, followed by the spiritual. As one writer put it, "This order was necessary, and it is observed everywhere. It is seen in the grain that dies in the ground, and in the resurrection of man." [Barnes] Every human being starts life in a physical body. Even in the case of the Lord Jesus Christ, He began his incarnate life in a physical body, and after His death that physical body was buried in the ground. However, at His resurrection He was given an eternal spiritual body. The natural comes first, followed by the spiritual.

2. The realm of existence

1 Cor 15:47 The first man is from the earth, earthy; the second man is from heaven.

The first man (Adam) was literally made from the dust of the earth (Genesis 2:7). The natural body that he was originally given was well suited for his existence on planet Earth. The second man (Christ) was given a resurrection body that is well suited for an eternal existence in heaven. As one man said of Christ, "He lived on earth in a natural body, but He came from heaven. Adam was tied to the earth; Christ was tied to heaven." [MacArthur] Whatever the resurrection body is like, it will be well-suited to our existence in the heavenly realm.

3. The certainty of this happening

1 Cor 15:48 As is the earthy, so also are those who are earthy; and as is the heavenly, so also are those who are heavenly.

These last two verses of the section state the absolute certainty that these things are true and that they will happen just as they have been described. In this life we are all very familiar with the earthly existence that is the plight of mankind. Here in verse forty-eight Paul is saying that the heavenly existence he has described is just as certain as the earthly one we are experiencing. In this verse, Adam is the earthy one and his descendants are those who are earthy. Therefore, Christ is the heavenly one, and those who have trusted in Christ are those who are heavenly. One commentator said, "Because of our natural descent from Adam we are a part of those who are earthly. But because of our inheritance in Jesus Christ, we also have become heavenly. One day our natural bodies from Adam will be changed into our heavenly bodies from Christ." [MacArthur]

1 Cor 15:49 Just as we have borne the image of the earthy, we will also bear the image of the heavenly.

In this verse Paul used the truth that we all have earthly bodies in this life as a guarantee of the certainty of life in a resurrection body in eternity future. Just as we are now experiencing the "image of the earthy," we will certainly bear the image of the heavenly in the future. One Bible scholar wrote:

> The apostle is countering the objection to the doctrine of the resurrection founded on the assumption that our bodies hereafter are to be of the same kind as those which we have here. This is not so. They are to be like the body of Christ. As we have borne the image of Adam as to his body, we shall bear the image of Christ as to his body. [Hodge]

What will happen to living believers' bodies when the Lord returns? (15:50-57)

1 Cor 15:50 Now I say this, brethren, that flesh and blood cannot inherit the kingdom of God; nor does the perishable inherit the imperishable.

Here Paul summarizes much of what he has said so far about the natural body, and why it is unsuitable for our future existence in eternity. He says that a natural body which consists merely of flesh and blood would never survive in the eternal realm. He has already told us that the natural body is perishable, but what is needed for an eternal existence is a body that is imperishable. Therefore, our earthly bodies must be exchanged for ones that are imperishable, glorious, powerful, spiritual, and like Christ's. One man has said: "The mortal cannot be immortal; the perishable imperishable. Incorruption cannot be an attribute of corruption. Our bodies, therefore, if they are to be immortal and imperishable must be changed." [Hodge]

Summary of the Characteristics of the Resurrection Body

Description or Characteristic	Earthly Body	Resurrection Body
Ability to sustain life over time.	**Perishable:** Subject to deterioration and finally death and decay.	**Imperishable:** Incapable of deterioration; the 2nd Law of Thermodynamics will no longer affect it.
Potential for glorifying God.	**Dishonor:** Characterized by disgrace, shame, and indignity.	**Glory:** Characterized by excellence, honor, splendor, brightness, and blessedness.
Physical ability to carry out one's intended purpose.	**Weakness:** Fragile, feeble, liable to sickness and infirmity, lack of ability to restrain fleshly desires.	**Power:** Inherent strength or ability; capable of the highest service before God without weariness.
Intended sphere of existence.	**Natural:** Limited to life in a fallen, earthly realm.	**Spiritual:** Suited to life in an eternal and heavenly realm.
Basic orientation, tendency, or focus.	**Adam-like:** Tending downward toward sinfulness and deterioration.	**Christ-like:** Tending upward toward righteousness and holiness.

1 Cor 15:51 Behold, I tell you a mystery; we will not all sleep, but we will all be changed,

As we have seen previously, a mystery is something that cannot be known apart from direct revelation from God. In the historical progress of biblical revelation, a mystery is something that was not previously revealed but which is now being made known to all future generations as God is revealing it through the apostle Paul in this letter to the Corinthian church.

Through Paul, God had previously revealed to the Thessalonians that believers who have already fallen asleep in Christ would not miss the resurrection of church-age saints (1 Thess 4:13-18). In that passage Paul had said that the dead in Christ would rise first, followed by those who are alive at the time of His coming. But in that Thessalonian passage Paul gave no details about the condition of the bodies of believers who would be taken up to be with the Lord. The mystery Paul reveals here in 1 Cor 15:51 is that, "We will not all sleep, but we will all be changed." Previously Paul had told the Thessalonians that not all would sleep, that not all would die before the coming of the Lord, so that cannot be the additional mystery he is now revealing. The new revelation here is that all will be changed. He is saying that believers who remain alive until the coming of the Lord will not have to die in order to receive their resurrection bodies. Whether believers are alive or dead, at the resurrection of the church their bodies will be changed from perishable to imperishable, from natural to spiritual, with all of the characteristics Paul has described throughout this section of the chapter. One Bible scholar expressed it this way:

> Paul had said that flesh and blood cannot inherit the kingdom of God. All, therefore, who enter that kingdom, whether they die before the second advent or survive to the coming of Christ, must be changed. And that is the fact which Paul says had been revealed to him...Those who would be alive when He came, could not be left in their corruptible bodies. Both would be changed, and thus prepared for the heavenly state. [Hodge]

1 Cor 15:52 in a moment, in the twinkling of an eye, at the last trumpet; for the trumpet will sound, and the dead will be raised imperishable, and we will be changed.

As Paul continues in this verse, he tells us how and when this change will happen. The change will be instantaneous; in a moment (**atomos**). This is the same Greek word from which our English word "atom" is derived, and it literally means "uncut or indivisible." This change will happen within the smallest possible unit of time. In the ancient world, the smallest perceptible unit of time was the time it took for a person to blink his eye. From this we can see that resurrection is not an evolutionary process which requires a significant amount of time.

The exact historical moment for this change will be "at the last trumpet." Paul provides help in determining when this trumpet will sound, and why it can be considered the last of its kind. He has identified this event as one at which both living and dead believers will be changed and will rise together. There is only one event in Scripture which corresponds to these circumstances, and that is the resurrection of the church prior to the Great Tribulation (1 Thess 4:13-18). There is no other time in biblical history when both living and dead believers will be called upward together. So this trumpet is the last trumpet of the church age, and it signifies the closing of that remarkable and important period of biblical history.

The key point of the mystery Paul is revealing in this verse is that we will all be changed. The Greek term "changed" (**allasso**) means to make something different in kind, to exchange, to transform. At the resurrection of the church, both living and dead believers will be given their resurrection bodies. As Christ was the first-fruits, so these believers at the end of the church age will be the next of many more who will eventually follow after Him in His resurrection.

1 Cor 15:53 For this perishable must put on the imperishable, and this mortal must put on immortality.

Now Paul tells us why this change must happen. Here Paul expressed the necessity and certainty of the resurrection by using the word "must" (**dei**). This important Greek term denotes something that is absolutely necessary. Why will this change happen? Because it must happen based on all that Paul has said about the plan and work of God Himself. Unless the perishable body is exchanged for an imperishable one, there is no hope of existence into the future. Unless the mortal body is transformed into an immortal one, any hope of eternal life would be impossible. It is because of this impossibility that this change must happen.

1 Cor 15:54-55 But when this perishable will have put on the imperishable, and this mortal will have put on immortality, then will come about the saying that is written, "DEATH IS SWALLOWED UP in victory. "O DEATH, WHERE IS YOUR VICTORY? O DEATH, WHERE IS YOUR STING?"

The final verses in this section emphasize what will happen at the time when these events take place. It focuses on one of the most important consequences of that resurrection day. The saying Paul provides will become true forever for those who receive their resurrection body. In this saying, Paul is not quoting directly from Scripture but paraphrasing the first part of Isaiah 25:8 and Hosea 13:14. "He will swallow up death for all time" and "O Death, where are your thorns? O Sheol, where is your sting?" One of the amazing things that believers have to look forward to is their ultimate victory over death, which occurs only because of all Christ has accomplished on our behalf. Every person who has ever lived has agonized under the fear of death, and for those living in their mortal bodies death is indeed something that is greatly to be feared. But for those who know of the certainty of their resurrection, the sting of death can be greatly lessened because we know Christ has gained the ultimate victory for us. In the resurrection body, a believer will never need to fear death again!

1 Cor 15:56-57 The sting of death is sin, and the power of sin is the law; but thanks be to God, who gives us the victory through our Lord Jesus Christ.

Here Paul explains why death is so fearful. Death carries a wicked sting, but the agony that death holds was actually given to it by the sin, disobedience, and corruption of man. The institution of death itself was only as a consequence of man's sin. And the law, the standards and expectations of God, are what reveal or show man's sin to be what it is. One commentator has this to say about the relationship between the law, sin, and death:

> The very idea of sin is lack of conformity on the part of moral creatures to the law of God...If you take away law, men may act unreasonably or in a way injurious to themselves or others, but they cannot sin...If there were no sin, there would be no death. Death is by sin. [Hodge]

We should note that Paul is going to expand on this thought in his later epistle to the Romans, where he will develop the theological relationships between these things. At the end of this section in First Corinthians, Paul breaks out into glorious praise and thanksgiving to God who is the one providing everything for our victory over sin and death through the Lord Jesus Christ. One writer summarized this very eloquently:

> That which we could not do for ourselves God has done for us through our Lord Jesus Christ. We cannot live sinlessly and thereby fulfill the law, nor can we remove sin once we have committed it, or remove its consequence, which is death. But on our behalf Jesus Christ lived a sinless life, fulfilling the law; removed our sin by Himself paying the penalty for it, satisfying God with a perfect sacrifice; and conquered death by being raised from the dead. All of that great victory He accomplished for us and gives to us. He took our curse and our condemnation and gives us victory in their place. [MacArthur]

Concluding exhortation based on the truth about resurrection (15:58)

1 Cor 15:58 Therefore, my beloved brethren, be steadfast, immovable, always abounding in the work of the Lord, knowing that your toil is not in vain in the Lord.

Therefore = This transition word means "In light of all that has been said about the resurrection of the dead." Here Paul tells believers how the knowledge of this theological truth should impact their behavior. As is true everywhere in Scripture, sound doctrine should always result in good deeds. Theology is never given simply for the sake of increasing our knowledge. Theology never stands alone, but always provides the foundation for more confident work in the service of the Lord.

There are two exhortations in this verse:

1. **Be steadfast/immovable** = These two Greek words mean almost the same thing. The first has the idea of being firmly planted or settled, while the second means to remain persistently in the place where you have been rooted. Paul is telling them that they are to anchor themselves firmly to a foundation of sound doctrine, and let nothing pull them away from the truths of God's Word. The false teachers in Corinth were trying to gain followers from within the church, and Paul is essentially saying to them, "Stay put with the sound theology you have been taught, and do not stray toward false teaching, no matter how enticing or popular it seems."

2. **Always abound in the work of the Lord** = In this second exhortation the main action word could be translated "super-abound." It means to abundantly overflow with excellence. And to this Paul adds: "always, at all times, or forever." This forms a very powerful expression which causes us to ask: "In what activities are we to always overflow with excellence?" Paul answers by saying we are to continually overflow with excellence in the work of the

Lord. Our efforts should be focused on doing the things that further God's work and His plan in this world.

We can confidently spend ourselves on the Lord's work for the reason Paul provides at the end of this verse. We can know and trust in the fact that our toil, pain, or sacrifice in the work of the Lord will not be vain, empty, or without effect. If we really want to spend ourselves on something that has a guaranteed rate of high return, then we should spend ourselves on the Lord's work.

Paul's Closing Words

(1 Corinthians 16:1-24)

I n this final section of Paul's letter to the Corinthians he begins by giving instructions about the relief effort to support the churches in Jerusalem. Paul will have more to say about this relief effort when he writes his second letter to the Corinthians in the near future (2 Cor 8-9). We know from other New Testament references that the churches in Judea were suffering economically, and Paul had previously delivered funds to Jerusalem (Acts 11:27-30). One commentator described the situation like this:

> Poverty was one of the social evils prevalent in the world of that day. There were many others: slavery, materialism, immorality, disease, violence, drugs, discrimination, and more. Paul's gospel was not a social gospel in the modern sense of that term, but it was aware of and concerned for these problems...The example of the early church's concern for the poor in Jerusalem shows the basic gospel method: They cared and they shared. [Boyer]

Guidelines for Christian Giving (16:1-4)

1 Cor 16:1 Now concerning the collection for the saints, as I directed the churches of Galatia, so do you also.

Now concerning the collection for the saints = The opening words of this chapter tell us that Paul is again responding to one of the questions asked by the Corinthians (see 1 Cor 7:1, 25; 8:1; 12:1). Evidently Paul had already mentioned the charity project or relief fund for the Christians in Judea, and the Corinthians wanted to know more about Paul's plans for this effort.

As I directed the churches of Galatia, so do you also = Although the exact time is not mentioned, Paul had already discussed this collection with the other churches in the area. The churches of the Galatian region were south and east of the churches in Asia Minor where Paul was ministering at the time he wrote this letter. We also know from Paul's first letter to the Galatian churches that the leaders of the mother church in Jerusalem encouraged him to "remember the poor" (Gal 2:10), and this relief effort was an example of Paul's willingness to do exactly that.

1 Cor 16:2 On the first day of every week each one of you is to put aside and save, as he may prosper, so that no collections be made when I come.

On the first day of every week = This verse describes the procedure for church giving, and it explains when the funds were to be set aside. We see here that it should be done on a regular basis. The first day of the week was the day that the church gathered together, and Paul encouraged them to use the beginning of the new week as a reminder to put aside some amount of money from what had been earned during the previous week.

Each one of you = This shows who was supposed to participate in giving to the needs of others. Each one indicates that every individual with some type of income was able to participate in the process.

Put aside and save = Here Paul tells them where the funds were to be accumulated. They were to put aside part of their income privately, literally "by themselves," or in their own homes. They were being asked to create a savings plan so the accumulated funds could be used eventually to help others in need. Paul left it up to the individual Christian whether to bring the funds to the church meeting, because we do not see Paul commanding them to put their money into the collection plate every week.

As he may prosper = Finally, Paul tells them how much money they were to set aside. The giving was to be proportionate to their income, so that any individual, no matter how small his income, could participate in the project. The money saved was to be proportional to how much was made. They were to accumulate the money little by little on a regular basis so that when the time was right, they could contribute as much as was required for meeting the needs of others.

Many believers today view the pattern of the Old Testament tithe as a requirement for giving ten percent of their income to the church, but the New Testament epistles never mandate that amount for church giving. For the nation of Israel in the Old Testament, the tithe was used to support the tribe of Levi which maintained the tabernacle and temple services, and we see that the required amount for giving far exceeded ten percent. After a detailed study, one commentator described the Old Testament practices this way:

> The amount paid annually to the theocracy of Israel was approximately 23 percent, and it essentially was a tax used for the operation of Israel's government. It never involved freewill, spontaneous giving to the Lord. The condemnation of Malachi 3:8-10 is for failure to pay the required taxes to support the priests who ran the nation...Required giving was taxation... A Christian is required to give taxes to support the government under which we live (Rom 13:6), just as the Israelites were to give tithes to support the divinely ordained system under which they lived (Matt 17:24-27; 22:15-21). [MacArthur]

By contrast, New Testament church giving is to be a free will offering out of gratefulness for what the Lord has done for us. The New Testament does not specify any amount or percentage that is required of believers. Today we are each to contribute willingly and gratefully in order to meet the needs of others out of compassion and common caring. In his second letter to the Corinthians, Paul will have much more to say about New Testament giving for today.

So that no collections be made when I come = If the Corinthians would follow the procedure that Paul outlined here, then the result would be that when the time came for actually sending the funds to the needy Christians in Judea, they could avoid scurrying around trying to gather money on the spur of the moment. Also, as one commentator put it, "The amount would be greater through systematic weekly saving than through collections made once for all on his arrival." [VWS]

1 Cor 16:3 When I arrive, whomever you may approve, I will send them with letters to carry your gift to Jerusalem;

Paul now turns to the subject of how the final collection should be handled and delivered. It is important that church funds are handled carefully, using a good system of accountability. Notice that Paul was not going to receive and deliver the funds himself. The Corinthians were to choose men that they trusted to handle and carry the money. Paul also says that letters of recommendation or letters of authority would be given to the men chosen to carry the money. This would give the entire process an official sanction. The men would be acting as representatives for the whole church and would be exercising a special stewardship or fiduciary responsibility. One writer said,

> Where the handling of money is involved Christians should take every precaution
> to secure trustworthy and honest men and to use business-like methods of proce-
> dure. Paul did not want to allow any occasion for scandal by handling the matter
> himself." [Boyer]

At the end of this verse we also see the final destination for these relief funds. They were intended to relieve the poverty of the Christians in the churches at Jerusalem.

1 Cor 16:4 and if it is fitting for me to go also, they will go with me.

With the phrase "if it is fitting" Paul implies that he may or may not be required to go with the funds. This is a Greek third class conditional clause, indicating only that there is a possibility it could be fulfilled. Paul leaves the matter undecided, but it is possible that he would travel with the relief funds. As one commentator put it, "If it be judged desirable and best. If my presence can further the object; or will satisfy you better; or will be deemed necessary to guide and aid those who may be sent, I will be willing to go also." [Barnes]

Paul's Travel Plans (16:5-9)

1 Cor 16:5-6 But I will come to you after I go through Macedonia, for I am going through Macedonia; and perhaps I will stay with you, or even spend the winter, so that you may send me on my way wherever I may go.

Here Paul gives an indication of his travel plans. He had decided not to travel to Corinth immediately, since he wanted to wait until he had visited the churches of Macedonia. Notice that Paul intends to "go through" the region of Macedonia. He does not plan to stay there like he plans to do with the Corinthians. He even hopes that he can spend the winter months in Corinth. He wants to have an extended time with them, to devote greater time and attention to their needs. This letter has been his way of helping them with their difficulties even though he is managing the situation remotely, but he knows this is no substitute for being there in person to deal with the issues in the Corinthian church. In the last phrase of this verse, Paul seems to be somewhat uncertain of his plans after his stay in Corinth. But wherever the Lord leads him, he is hoping that the Corinthians will assist him in fulfilling that purpose.

1 Cor 16:7 For I do not wish to see you now just in passing; for I hope to remain with you for some time, if the Lord permits.

Here Paul makes sure they understand he does not intend to simply pass through Corinth, but he definitely wants to remain with them for as long a time as the Lord will allow.

1 Cor 16:8 But I will remain in Ephesus until Pentecost;

It is clear from this verse that Paul was writing from Ephesus and that this letter to the Corinthians was written in the spring sometime before Pentecost. According to his previous statements, he was intending to pass through the Macedonian churches during the summer of that year, so that he could spend the fall and winter in Corinth.

1 Cor 16:9 for a wide door for effective service has opened to me, and there are many adversaries.

Here Paul tells the Corinthians why he is remaining in Ephesus, and it has to do with both positive and negative factors. On the positive side, Paul had recently seen some type of great (**megas**) opportunity for fruitful ministry there. The word for "effective service" (**energes**) is a Greek term that could be translated simply as "activity," but it also implies the effective outpouring of energy. Something was happening in Ephesus that led Paul to believe there was a rich harvest to be worked. On the negative side, Paul saw that there was quite a bit of opposition to his ministry in Ephesus and he took this as a validation of his efforts. Sometimes you only know how much good you are doing for the Lord when you see how powerfully God's enemies are trying to oppose it. Paul already alluded to these struggles when he mentioned that he "fought with wild beasts at Ephesus" (1 Cor 15:32). One commentator has said, "Ministers should not be discouraged because there is opposition to the gospel. It is one ground of encouragement. It is an indication of the presence of God in awakening the conscience. And it is far more favorable as a season to do good than a dead calm, and when there is universal stagnation and unconcern." [Barnes]

Timothy's Travel Plans (16:10–11)

1 Cor 16:10 Now if Timothy comes, see that he is with you without cause to be afraid, for he is doing the Lord's work, as I also am.

Now Paul mentions Timothy's travel plans, because it is likely that the Corinthians will see Timothy before they see Paul. Remember that Timothy and Erastus had been sent into Macedonia before Paul wrote this letter to Corinth (Acts 19:22), and they were planning to travel to Corinth after their work in Macedonia was complete. Paul wants to be sure that Timothy is not mistreated by the factions in Corinth. He does not want them to give Timothy any cause to be afraid, and evidently Paul had a good reason for thinking there might be trouble for Timothy (1 Cor 4:17-19). So here, he commands them not to give Timothy any grief as he fulfills his ministry obligations among them.

1 Cor 16:11 So let no one despise him. But send him on his way in peace, so that he may come to me; for I expect him with the brethren.

Apparently some of the Corinthians had demonstrated an arrogance which resulted in spiteful behavior toward Paul and his representatives. One British commentator described the situation in typically understated terms when he said, "The Corinthian church could, when it chose, make itself a very unpleasant and threatening society." [Barrett] Here Paul commands them to send Timothy on his way in peace. Paul says that he is waiting for Timothy and his traveling companions, and he expects him to arrive without any trouble from the Corinthians.

Apollos' Travel Plans (16:12)

1 Cor 16:12 But concerning Apollos our brother, I encouraged him greatly to come to you with the brethren; and it was not at all his desire to come now, but he will come when he has opportunity.

Paul now discussed the travel plans of Apollos. This verse begins with the phrase "Now concerning" and it implies that the letter from the Corinthians had asked that Apollos be sent to them. Evidently Apollos was in Ephesus with Paul when he was writing to Corinth, and Paul had encouraged Apollos to return to Corinth. But for some reason Apollos would not return immediately. Some commentators think Apollos left Corinth in disgust over the dissension there, some of which involved their admiration of his speaking gifts. The phrase "it was not at all his desire" implied that Apollos refused to return, but notice that the word "his" is not in the original text. We could also translate this, "It was not the Lord's will for him to come now." Whatever the reason, it is clear that the time was not right for either Paul or Apollos to return to Corinth. Both of them would eventually go back to Corinth, but they were following the Lord's timetable rather than their own. This passage tells us that just because there is an immediate need, that does not mean we are to immediately attend to it. As someone once said, "The need does not always constitute the call." Timing is important, and the Lord's timing is everything.

Commands Summarizing the teaching of this letter (16:13-14)

1 Cor 16:13 Be on the alert, stand firm in the faith, act like men, be strong.

Literally Paul says, "Stay awake." Evidently their tendency was to be spiritually asleep. One writer said, "They were to watch or be vigilant against all the evils of which he had admonished them, the evils of dissension, of erroneous doctrines, of disorder, of false teachers, etc." [Barnes] Next Paul says, "Stand still" or "Stand firmly in place." Figuratively they were on the verge of tottering wildly about and falling down. Paul commands them to remain firmly rooted in the faith. This is Paul's way of telling them to hold firmly to the doctrinal truths of the faith. They are to take their stand on the doctrines of the Bible, and not to fall prey to the unstable ideas that were being presented to them by the false teachers and philosophers of their culture. Next Paul commands them to act like mature men. They are to increase in wisdom and strength in their walk of faith.

1 Cor 16:14 Let all that you do be done in love.

Finally, Paul reminded them of the important truth that Christian love should guide all that is said and done. We should read all of chapter thirteen back into this one short sentence. Those truths are so important that here Paul simply commands them to follow the way of Christian love.

Commending Stephanas, Fortunatus, and Achaicus (16:15-18)

1 Cor 16:15 Now I urge you, brethren (you know the household of Stephanas, that they were the first fruits of Achaia, and that they have devoted themselves for ministry to the saints),

Before Paul closed his letter to the Corinthians, he wanted to be sure he commended the leadership of Stephanas and his companions. He emphasized the important role that Stephanas had taken in the Corinthian church. Not only were Stephanas and his household Paul's first converts in the province of Achaia, but they immediately took on a leadership role in the church there. Based on a literal reading of the text, one man described the situation this way:

> They were not appointed by Paul; they were not appointed by the church; in a spirit not of self-assertion but of service and humility they appointed themselves. In other words, they were appointed directly by God, who pointed out to them the opportunity of service and (we may suppose) equipped them to fulfill it. It is now for the church to recognize this ministry, as Paul does. [Barrett]

1 Cor 16:16 that you also be in subjection to such men and to everyone who helps in the work and labors.

In light of his previous comments about Stephanas, here is what Paul wants the Corinthians to do. He wants them to submit to leaders such as these. "When natural leaders such as Stephanas arise, they should be recognized, and the recognition should take a practical form." [Barrett] Instead of having factions and rifts within the church, believers are to solidly stand behind leaders who are teaching the truths of the Word of God. Stephanas and his household were not the only ones in the Corinthian church whose leadership should be valued and respected. The Corinthians were to demonstrate a similar attitude toward all of the people who are truly contributing to the ministry of the church.

1 Cor 16:17-18 I rejoice over the coming of Stephanas and Fortunatus and Achaicus, because they have supplied what was lacking on your part. For they have refreshed my spirit and yours. Therefore acknowledge such men.

The news of Corinth which was brought by Stephanas, Fortunatus, and Achaicus made Paul extremely joyful. Their coming had filled an empty spot in his experience of them. The letter and the fellowship they supplied must have been extremely important to Paul as he was laboring in a distant region. He described their influence as being a refreshing of his spirit, just as they had refreshed the Corinthians' spirits while they ministered in that church. Paul ends his commendations for them by repeating his command that the Corinthian church was to acknowledge such men. This meant to recognize them in a somewhat official manner, to set a mark of recognition upon them, to know them well and follow their example.

Greetings from believers in Asia Minor (16:19-21)

1 Cor 16:19 The churches of Asia greet you. Aquila and Prisca greet you heartily in the Lord, with the church that is in their house.

Paul was ministering in Ephesus at the time he was writing to Corinth, and we know that his influence from Ephesus had an impact on that entire region (Acts 19:10). From this verse we see that many churches were established in that region as a result of Paul's ministry there. The Corinthians' friends Aquila and Priscilla had previously traveled to Ephesus to help Paul in his work there, and they sent their personal greetings to Corinth as well. One of the church gatherings in Ephesus was meeting in their home.

1 Cor 16:20 All the brethren greet you. Greet one another with a holy kiss.

This tells us that all the believers with whom Paul was ministering in Ephesus were very concerned about the church in Corinth. All of them had an intense interest in what was going on in one of their sister churches in the province across the sea. Paul then told the Corinthians to greet each other with a holy kiss. This was a customary greeting showing love and respect to the other person, with men greeting men and women greeting women in this way. It was probably similar to the greeting custom still maintained in may European countries today.

1 Cor 16:21 The greeting is in my own hand—Paul.

Literally this says, "With the hand of me, Paul." Even though Paul dictated his letters to a recording secretary, he took the pen and signed his name at the end of the letter. This was his common custom (2 Thess 3:17).

Final Exhortations (16:22-24)

1 Cor 16:22 If anyone does not love the Lord, he is to be accursed. Maranatha.

Paul ended the letter with a very solemn truth: "If anyone does not love the Lord, he is to be accursed." A person cannot truly love the Lord without understanding who He is and trusting only in what He has done in order to have eternal life with Him. Anyone who does not love the Lord in this sense will truly be cut off or accursed for all eternity. And the final word (**Maranatha** = "the Lord comes") would be like saying, "The Lord will make this happen soon."

1 Cor 16:23 The grace of the Lord Jesus be with you.

As was Paul's custom in all his letters, he closed with the strongest desire for God's grace to powerfully work in their lives. Grace is usually defined as the unmerited favor of God in our lives, but someone once operationalized the definition of grace by saying that it is the God-given desire and power to do what the Lord wants us to do. In this sense, grace is an active force in the life of every believer.

1 Cor 16:24 My love be with you all in Christ Jesus. Amen.

Paul's final words to those misbehaving Corinthians was that he loved them deeply. Even though he had said some very strong things and rebuked them severely at times, all that was said was given out of his deep love for them. It was Paul's love "in Christ Jesus" which was expressed to all those who also loved the Lord. What an amazing motive for an amazing letter!